THE STATE
OF DEMOCRACY
IN AMERICA

T0346398

THE STATE OF DEMOCRACY IN AMERICA

WILLIAM CROTTY, EDITOR

GEORGETOWN UNIVERSITY PRESS
WASHINGTON, D.C.

Georgetown University Press, Washington, D.C.
© 2001 by Georgetown University Press. All rights reserved.
Printed in the United States of America

10 9 8 7 6 5 4 3 2 1   2001

This volume is printed on acid-free offset book paper.

Library of Congress Cataloging-in-Publication Data

The state of democracy in America edited by William Crotty.
        p. cm. — (Essential texts in America)
    Includes bibliographical references and index.
    ISBN 0-87840-861-4 (pbk. : alk. paper)
        1. Democracy—United States.   2. Political participation—United
States.   3. United States—Politics and government—1993–2001.
    4. United States—Politics and government—2001–   .   I. Crotty,
William J. II. Series.

JK1726.S73 2001
320.973′09′049—dc21   2001023263

Contents

CONTENTS

List of Figures

List of Tables

Preface

John F. Kennedy once said that "the United States has to move very fast to even stand still." There is a good deal of truth in this. At present the nation is moving into a new age of globalized economics and interdependent political institutions, many evolving, others yet to be devised. The social changes in progress will be substantial, in the view of some a redesign of the social community as we know it.

At the same time, social problems exist and questions arise as to who will benefit from the new economic and social ordering, who will be left out, and what can be done to alleviate the transition and address the problems we already know to exist and those that are sure to develop. Maintaining a form of equitable sharing in the rewards to come and a vital and responsive democratic system in the face of concentrations of economic power and uncharted transnational institutions will provide one of the more formidable challenges for the nation in the new century.

The essays in this volume explore some of these concerns. The focus is on the quality of political representation, the adequacies of basic agencies of mass mobilization, and the policy areas of significance in progressing toward a more equitable, open, and accountable politics in the new era already underway.

Each essay is by an authority in the field with significant previous contributions to developing an understanding of the issues and concerns in the area being examined. A number of the chapters were originally given as papers in a national conference on "American Democracy Entering the Twentieth Century" sponsored by the Center for the Study of Comparative Democracy at Northeastern University. Others were commissioned to explore areas important for a broader understanding of the state of political society in the United States as it began the twenty-first century.

As editor, I would like to thank the staff of Georgetown University Press for their work in developing this publication; and at Northeastern University, President Emeritus John A. Curry, President Richard M. Freeland; former

Provost Michael A. Baer, now senior vice President for Programs and Analysis at the American Council on Higher Education; former Dean Robert P. Lowndes of the College of Arts and Sciences; Dean James R. Stellar and Associate Dean Kay P. Onan of the College of Arts and Sciences; Professor Christopher J. Bosso, chair of the Department of Political Science, and Professor Suzanne P. Ogden, the previous chair; Professors Eileen L. McDonagh, Robert E. Gilbert, David A. Rochefort, and John H. Portz, all of whom participated in the conference; Janet-Louise Joseph, who helped in a number of ways with the conference and the book; Barbara McIntosh-Chin, Marie Arnberg, James Rossi, Robert Curtin, and Pamela Potoma, and from Northwestern University, Melissa Kurtz Miller. Each contributed to the development of this volume. To each, my thanks!

1

Politics and Policy for a New Century

MICHAEL S. DUKAKIS

I am by nature an inveterate optimist. In fact, you cannot be in politics and be a pessimist. If you do not believe that good people, working together, can make a difference in the lives of their fellow citizens, then politics is not the business for you.

On the other hand, I am not a cockeyed optimist. I have been in and around politics for over four decades, and I know that effective political leadership is not for the fainthearted. It requires commitment, tenacity, and the ability to savor victory and sustain, and recover from, defeat. Nevertheless, I believe that we have a right to be genuinely optimistic about the future of the United States and the world as we enter a new millennium.

The Cold War is over, and for those of us whose entire adult lifetime has been spent in a world obsessed with the seemingly endless struggle between East and West, communism and capitalism, Moscow and Washington, it is hard to exaggerate just how dramatic that change has been. We lived for nearly forty years in a world where almost everything was interpreted through the prism of the Cold War. The Soviet Union went broke in the process. We almost did. Trillions were spent by both sides on weapons of mass destruction. Virtually every regional conflict, rightly or wrongly, was viewed as being part of the ideological struggle.

Today, regional conflict has diminished dramatically. Admittedly, regional tensions will continue to be a part of the world we live in. But if anyone had suggested fifteen years ago that Nelson Mandela would be president of South Africa; or that Israel and the Palestinians would be engaged in ongoing negotiations, however frustrating, for a peaceful solution in the Middle East; or that Gerry Adams and Tony Blair would have met at 10 Downing Street, we would have been incredulous. In fact, this is the most peaceful era I have ever lived in.

All of these things and more are taking place in a world where the international community is attempting for the first time in the history of mankind to set standards for the conduct of nations and enforce them. That will not be easy. We are at a point in world history not unlike the years when a new America was trying to govern itself under the Articles of Confederation in the immediate postrevolutionary era. There will be defeats and setbacks along the way. But no one who lived through a time when the United States and the Soviet Union each had approximately fifteen thousand nuclear missiles pointed at each other could possibly argue that the prospects for world peace and stability are not infinitely better than they were just a few years ago.

Here at home, it would be foolish to suggest that race is no longer a factor in American life. But I remember growing up in the 1950s when the barbershops of Swarthmore, Pennsylvania, were racially segregated; when an African American required a pass from his or her employer to be on the streets of Miami Beach after sundown; and when Washington, D.C., the capital of the "free world," was as segregated as Johannesburg, South Africa.

Furthermore, do not let anyone tell you that the public schools in America back in the 1940s and 50s were just Jim-dandy and that they have been going to hell in a handbasket ever since. The high school dropout rate in the 1950s in this country was over 50 percent and over 70 percent for minority youngsters. It is true that a high school dropout forty or fifty years ago might still have been able to get a factory job and make a decent wage. But public schools in this country have improved dramatically over the past half century, and test scores for black and Latino kids are rising steadily, something we tend to forget in our concern for those youngsters of whatever background who don't seem to be making it in a world where a high school diploma and at least two years of postsecondary education are almost a prerequisite for a decent job.

Those of us who believe strongly that all Americans, and especially working Americans and their families, should be guaranteed basic health security were deeply disappointed at the failure of President Clinton's efforts to ensure that the United States would finally join all of the other advanced industrialized nations in insuring all of its citizens. On the other hand, the fact that a conservative Republican Congress has approved legislation during the past few years limiting the right of health insurers to deny coverage and dramatically expanding health insurance for America's children is a clear sign that we are making progress on the health front, even though it may have to be accomplished in chunks rather than in one coherent and comprehensive effort.

Thanks to Social Security and Medicare, poverty among the elderly in America has been virtually eliminated. Our commitment to environmental quality is far stronger than it was just a few decades ago. The status of women, the disabled, and the other disadvantaged groups has improved markedly. And while I personally continue to be deeply troubled by our failure to deal effectively with the problem of chronic and severe mental illness, we have certainly come a long way from the days when mental institutions in this country were a national embarrassment.

In short, never in my lifetime have the prospects for doing good things, building a more peaceful world, and coming to grips with the real challenges that face us been better. What we must now do is determine what those challenges are and how we go about solving them.

On the international front, there are at least five critical areas in which we must be actively and deeply involved: the threat of nuclear proliferation; continued, though declining, international terrorism; ongoing regional conflict; the degradation of the international environment; and human and worker rights. None of them is easy. All will require the United States to work closely with our friends and allies in the international community, whenever and wherever possible through existing international institutions, and especially the United Nations, which, with all its weaknesses, continues to be the best forum in which to resolve differences and develop common policies.

Here at home, I believe we face four fundamental challenges. First, the issue of race, which continues to bedevil American life and which, while we have made huge gains since *Brown v. Board of Education*, continues to confront people of color with obstacles that are almost never placed in the way of their white brethren. Second, the quality and integrity of our political system, which, despite the well-intended reforms of the post-Watergate era, is once again awash in special interest money and an increasingly cynical public. Third, the large and growing disparity between the rich and poor and, just as important, the fact that virtually all of the income gains of the past twenty years have gone to the wealthiest 20 percent of the population and almost none to the bottom 60 percent. In fact, the United States now has the dubious distinction of having the greatest gap between the rich and poor of any of the advanced industrialized nations. Our minimum wage falls far short of the poverty line. Forty-four million Americans do not have a dime of health insurance, 17 million more than when Jimmy Carter was president. Middle-class families are going broke trying to send their kids to college, and younger Americans don't believe that Social Security and Medicare will be there for them when they reach retirement age. Fourth, the steady decline in citizen involvement and voter participation; huge amounts of special interest money that are pouring into the system through the soft money loophole; new technologies like polling, television, and direct mail that have spawned a whole new generation of political consultants; politicians spending too much time with the fat cats and not enough time in backyards and living rooms recruiting supporters from the people who ought to count in this country; and, as an inevitable consequence of all this, the growing unwillingness of ordinary citizens to get deeply and actively involved in public life.

What is even more troubling, however, is the virtual disappearance of genuine, partisan grassroots politics in America. Nobody has written more perceptively or accurately about this phenomenon than Marshall Ganz, one of the best political organizers in the state of California and more recently, a fellow at the Institute of Politics at the John F. Kennedy School of Government at Harvard University.

"Campaigns and elections," he writes, "are the lifeblood of American democracy and the principal means by which citizens form and express political opinions. Any less than full and equal electoral participation puts democracy at risk. Today electoral participation is neither full nor equal, and it is getting worse."[1]

No longer, he argues, is running for office an organizational activity; it is now an entrepreneurial endeavor in which traditional forms of campaigning have given way to consultants who are paid by commission. The more advertising and contracts they place with subconsultants, the more they make.[2]

Both of our major political parties have walked away from the old grassroots model in which local and precinct organizations reached out to all potential voters, recruited party workers, and gave young people and newly arrived immigrants an avenue into the political process. Instead, highly paid consultants segment the market, seek to depress the turnout of those they don't want to see at the polls, and use television and direct mail to target segments of the electorate. Ganz points to a recent California assembly race where married Catholic voters got the family values letter and single Jewish women under the age of forty got the pro-choice letter.[3]

In short, the recipe these days goes something like this: target supporters only; never go after "unlikelies"; devote the maximum time and concentration of resources to a minimum universe; don't spend any time or money on voter registration because new voters aren't likely to vote in great numbers; even where you decide to do a serious preelection and election day campaign, contract with one of the so-called "instant organizations" that bring in paid telephone canvassers, using prepared scripts, who are paid on a per-head basis and have no personal connection with the district; and the day after the election shift to raising money to pay off your debt, begin putting money away for the next campaign, and start the whole depressing process all over again.[4]

For most Americans these days, there is absolutely no personal connection with the political process. Nobody calls unless it is a paid caller with a canned message. Nobody rings your doorbell. Nobody asks what you think are the most important issues that public officials should address.

In fact, particularly at the national and statewide level, the political process for most Americans has become a movie. We sit in our living rooms watching thirty-second attack commercials between warring candidates, and then, with luck, barely half of us troop down to the polls to vote for the most important political office in the world. In Oregon, even that is too much of a burden to impose on the voter. In that state, people can now mail their ballots the way they mail in their electric bill. They don't even have to walk to the polls and mark their ballots in what I believe is one of the most important symbolic aspects of American citizenship.

All of this means that while the major political parties are not totally dead at the grassroots, rigor mortis is in danger of setting in. Only the labor unions and the conservative Protestant churches seem to understand that the more traditional forms of political organizing can yield real dividends on election day.

Not surprisingly, the demise of serious grassroots campaigning has been accompanied by a steady decline in turnout, especially at the lower end of the socioeconomic spectrum; fewer and fewer ties to party; less and less understanding of the issues; and an alienation from the political process that is both understandable and tragic if one believes in the importance of democratic activism.

Why the parties have virtually abandoned grassroots activity is a mystery to me. There is good research that demonstrates conclusively that grassroots organizing can make a significant difference in turnout and results. The Christian Coalition's activity in the 1994 congressional campaign made a decisive difference in that year's Republican victory after decades of defeat. Paul Wellstone of Minnesota, the number one target of the Republican National Committee in the 1996 senatorial campaign, beat a tough and heavily financed opponent with ease by focusing his efforts on grassroots organizing and recruiting.

In California in 1996, 1 million more Latinos voted than had ever voted before. The results were dramatic. Congressman Robert Dornan was ousted from Congress by a young Latino businesswoman; Latinos won a record number of seats in the California legislature; and the new Speaker of the California Assembly was a legislator from Fresno named Cruz Bustamante.[5]

In short, the abandonment of the grassroots by both the Republican and Democratic parties is not only having a profound effect on voter attitudes and participation—it is dumb politics. It is a particularly dumb strategy for my party. We can't possibly match the Republicans in the raising of campaign money. But I believe we have an opportunity to change the politics of this country for a generation if we can build—or rebuild—a powerful coalition of working Americans and their families who have been getting the short end of the stick for the past twenty years, and millions of newly naturalized and enfranchised immigrants who took one look at the Republican Congress in 1995 and its anti-immigrant legislation and decided that the new congressional majority did not like people like us. And if more proof is needed about the effectiveness of grassroots activity, we need to look no further than November of 1998, when the Democratic get-out-the-vote campaign not only confounded the pollsters; it led to an unprecedented pick-up of five Democratic House seats and the resignation of Newt Gingrich.

In short, what is needed to transform American politics and restore citizen participation and citizen trust is nothing less than the reconstruction of the two major political parties into genuine grassroots organizations that get back to the precincts, ring doorbells, enlist their fellow citizens in the political process, and breathe some fresh air into the current consultant-run, TV-dominated election-year circus that passes for American politics.

The parties, despite their weaknesses, are still the best institutions to pull together computerized lists of voters; run serious registration drives; develop permanent, ongoing precinct organizations; and conduct the kinds of campaigns that encourage serious party membership. Campaign finance reform that eliminates soft money and forces candidates and parties back to the grassroots for their money and their organizations will certainly help. But unless the parties understand how important all this is not only to the revival of a genuine, citizen-based politics in this country but to their own success, we will continue to wallow in what Ganz calls "a political cacophony in which one coalition of dissonant and powerful interests seeks to defeat another—a grim prospect for the future of American democracy."[6]

In short, Abraham Lincoln's advice to the Whigs of Illinois is as relevant today as it was when he first gave it: "organize the whole state, so that every Whig can be brought to the polls . . . divide the country into small districts and appoint in each a sub-committee . . . make a perfect list of voters and ascertain with certainty for whom they will vote . . . and on election day see that every Whig is brought to the polls."[7] The Whigs are no longer with us, in part because they ignored Lincoln's advice. But in this, as in so many other ways, he was a wise and perceptive political leader.

There is much to do and much to accomplish as we enter a new century. It is not like 1900, or even 1950; and for young people particularly, it is a wonderful time to become deeply and actively involved in public life and public service. But the fundamentals, as any good football coach will tell you, are still what wins football games—blocking and tackling still make a difference.

That does not mean that a football coach who wants to win ignores the new technologies any more than a politician or a campaign manager can ignore survey research, television, or the new media. He has his coaches watching the game high above the field and communicating directly and instantaneously with him. He uses film of previous games extensively and well. He applies the latest lessons in good nutrition and strength training as effectively as he can.

But he does not do what the major political parties have done in this country—walk away from the fundamentals that win ball games. If he does, he will not be doing much winning or coaching.

Notes

1. Marshall Ganz, "Voters in the Crosshairs," *American Prospect*, no. 16 (1994): 100.
2. Ibid., 102–3.
3. Ibid., 106.
4. Ibid., 104–8.
5. Bustamante was elected lieutenant governor of California in November of 1998.
6. Ganz, "Voters in the Crosshairs," 108.
7. Ibid., 100.

2

Introduction: Perspectives on an Evolving Democratic Experiment in a New Century (and Millennium)

WILLIAM CROTTY

A Present Built on a Past

> [T]his is what America is about. It is the uncrossed desert and the un-climbed ridge. It is the star that is not reached and the harvest that's sleeping in the ground. (Lyndon B. Johnson January 20, 1965)

Lyndon B. Johnson was accused of many things as president, but eloquence was not one of them. Yet his words at his 1965 inauguration did much to capture a sense of what many believe America to be about: optimism in the future and faith in a favored nation gifted by God and nature to fulfill the democratic dream.

The sentiments are familiar, voiced by political leaders and proponents of the American Dream; found in one form or another in every state of the union and major political address; and generally accepted and believed by the nation's citizens. Prosperity, equality, opportunity, vision, peace—all achievable and all characteristics of a nation blessed like no other and destined to lead the world.

Such objectives may not only be part of the American psyche, but many believe they can be achieved. Such a vision could come close to being realized in the new century and the new millennium. Optimism reigns. Further, there are signs that it may be justified. Compare the United States with where it and the world were a few short generations ago.

America is the preeminent world leader as we enter the twenty-first century, its only superpower, and a country without natural enemies. The Berlin Wall has fallen, and Communism and with it the fight for world supremacy are relics of the past. The world's single, dominant ideology is democracy, whether practiced or not in all nations. Led by a confident, economically and militarily unchallenged United States, globalization of trade, commerce, finance, and technology is the order of the day; the assumptions of a free-market economic system are part of the newly dominant ideology; and a more economically and politically independent world is well on its way to being the defining reality of the new age. It is a world order in which, through force of values, quality of performance, and abundance of resources, the United States has emerged as the global leader.

It is a position of power and a world few could have imagined a few decades ago. A brief overview of major developments since the end of World War II serves to reemphasize the fortunate state of the contemporary period. In the early postwar period, for the veterans and their families reentering a peacetime economy, needing housing, education, and jobs, it was a matter of adjusting to the demands of a new life and a new world. For the country, it was the fight for survival in the face of a totalitarian threat from the U.S.S.R. leading over time to rearmament, the Cold War, a hot war (Korea), and, internally, McCarthyism. A determinedly inward-looking, conventional, and seemingly uneventful fifties gave way to the widespread challenge to authority of the sixties: the Civil Rights Revolution, Black Power, the rise of feminism as a social force, and the assassination of President Kennedy, the marking point for an age of cynicism, upheaval, and violence that was to follow. Most divisively, there were the Vietnam War and the domestic reactions to America's involvement in Southeast Asia in what many felt was a colonial war and others saw as a stand against Communism. Demonstrations, sit-ins, protests on the campus and in the streets, the assassinations of the Reverend Martin Luther King, Jr. and Robert Kennedy, and the upheaval of the Chicago Democratic Convention of 1968 came to mark a period of social turbulence like no other in modern history. The criminal actions of a president (Richard Nixon) and his near impeachment followed, a drama that further divided the nation and one unthinkable in a more innocent earlier age. The energy and unrest released by the fury of the sixties and early seventies contributed to a reconstructing of forms of democratic representation during the decades that followed, most notably in presidential nominating procedures, campaign finance, and internally within the Congress.

An international oil crisis and the taking of hostages in Iran during the late seventies led to the Reagan years, the attacks on social programming, a largely successful effort to redistribute wealth upwards, historic budget deficits, the Contra War in Central America, a special counsel investigation, and again talk of impeachment. Reagan's successor and presumptive heir, George Bush, and his "kinder, gentler nation" became known primarily for the seemingly overwhelming success of its Persian Gulf War directed against Saddam Hussein and Iraq. The Bush presidency was followed in turn by the Clinton era, the economic restructuring that followed, its greatest achievements, and the interminable scandals and accusations of ethical violations, personal and professional misconduct, congressional investigations, court actions and controversial special counsel investigations, and, ultimately, the impeachment and Senate trial of a president. All of this was punctuated by an unexpected Republican victory in the 1994 off-year elections and the party's takeover of both houses of the Congress. These successes led to efforts to enact the "Contract with America," a traditionally conservative economic and social package of programs that provided the party's agenda (although most proposals never made it out of the Congress) for the balance of the nineties and into the early years of the twenty-first century.

In all, it has been an eventful and unpredictable ride, as these sketches suggest. In retrospect and overall, however taxing the challenges along the way have proved, the culmination of all of this has been the prosperity and peace the nation currently enjoys. There is also the promise of better things yet to come. It is a period of international cooperation, well-being, social stability, and broad optimism with few if any antecedents in contemporary history.

No one, and especially social scientists, can predict future developments with any degree of authority. Still the material changes—if nothing else—evidenced in broad strokes over recent decades tell an impressive, if somewhat complicated and uneven, story. The general outlines of the developments, however, are clear enough.

A Historical Overview of National Change

The developments of the last half-century are, without exaggeration, extraordinary. Taking the post-World War II period of the late forties/early fifties to the turn of the new century, a few statistics illustrate the broad trends. These are divided in the following sections into social, economic, and governmental (see Tables 2.1 through 2.3).

Social Setting

America as a society is larger (the population has increased by over 100 million), better educated, more prosperous, and more racially and ethnically integrated and culturally diverse, more socially responsible (based on the amount of funds invested in social programs) and healthier (judged by the same standards) than it was a half century ago (Table 2.1). Family income is up, although remaining significantly greater for whites than for blacks and Hispanics; percentage-wise (although not in absolute numbers) fewer fall below the poverty line (although one-fifth of the minorities continue to do so); three out of four whites have completed high school (up from less than 15 percent in 1947) as have over one-half of blacks and Hispanics; a quarter of the white and 10 to 15 percent of the minority population have college degrees (up by a factor of 4 or 5); and social spending has dramatically increased. Less encouraging, crime rates have also risen, as has the number of people imprisoned (presently just below 1.2 million as against 166,000 in 1950).

THE STATE OF DEMOCRACY IN AMERICA

TABLE 2.1
Selected Social Indicators (by year)

I. Population Size (in millions)

1950	1990	2000 (est)
150,697,361	248,709,873	285,000,000

II. Family Income (median income; constant 1997 dollars)

	1950	1997	Change (%)
TOTAL	20,332	44,568	119
WHITE	21,104	46,754	122
BLACK	11,449	28,602	150
HISPANIC	8,193 (1972)	28,142	243

III. Education (over 25 years old; in percentage)
    A. Completed Four Years of High School

	1947	1980	1998
WHITE			
Males	33.2	71.0	83.6
Females	36.7	70.1	83.8
BLACK			
Males	12.7	51.1	75.2
Females	14.5	51.3	76.7
HISPANIC			
Males	—	46.4	55.7
Females	—	44.1	55.3

    B. Completed Four Years of College

	1947	1980	1998
WHITE			
Males	6.6	22.1	27.3
Females	4.9	14.0	22.8
BLACK			
Males	2.4	7.7	13.9
Females	2.6	8.1	15.4
HISPANIC			
Males	—	9.7	11.1
Females	—	6.2	10.9

IV. Persons Below Poverty Line (percentage)

	1959	1973	1997
TOTAL	22.4	11.1	13.3
WHITE	18.1	8.4	11.0
BLACK	55.1	31.4	26.5
HISPANIC	—	21.9	27.1

TABLE 2.1 *(Continued)*
Selected Social Indicators (by year)

V. Social Welfare Expenditures (billions)

  A. Federal, State, and Local Governments

	1950	*1994*	*Change (%)*
FEDERAL GOVERNMENT	10.5	852.6	8,020
(% Federal Outlays)	26.2	58.3	32.1
STATE/LOCAL GOVERNMENT	13.0	582.0	4,376
(% State/Local Outlays)	59.2	—	—
TOTAL	23.5	1,434.6	6,005
% of GDP	8.5	21.0	12.5

  B. Social Welfare Expenditures of Federal Government, Selected Areas (millions)

	1950	*1994*	*Change (%)*
SOCIAL INSURANCE	2,103	557,389	26,404
PUBLIC AID	1,103	162,675	14,648
HEALTH/MEDICAL	604	34,770	5,657
VETERANS' PROGRAM	6,386	37,262	483
EDUCATION	157	24,084	15,240
HOUSING	15	24,724	164,727
TOTAL	10,541	852,622	7,989
(Expenditures for all Social Welfare Programs)			

VI. Crime

  A. Crime Rates (per 100,000 population)

	1960	*1997*	*Change (%)*
VIOLENT	161	611	280
PROPERTY	1,729	4,312	149
TOTAL	1,887	4,923	161

  B. Federal and State Prisoners

	1960	*1997*	*Change (%)*
NUMBER	166,173	1,197,590	621
RATE	109	445	308

Source: Adapted from the data in Harold W. Stanley and Richard G. Niemi, *Vital Statistics on American Politics 1999–2000* (Washington, DC: CQ Press, 2000), and the sources cited therein.

Economic Development

Economic restructuring may be the hallmark of an age that some economists have compared to the beginnings of the Industrial Revolution. These forces are presently underway. Tracing economic indicators over recent decades, the advances that have already taken place are impressive (Table 2.2). Starting with the Gross National Product (GNP) and the Gross Domestic Product (GDP), the increases are roughly from $1.6 trillion to $7.2 trillion, evidence of a wealthier and economically more powerful nation. It is also a more expensive

TABLE 2.2
Selected Economic Indicators (by year)

I. Gross National Product (GNP)/Gross Domestic Product (GDP) (constant 1992 dollars; in billions)

	1950	1997	Change (%)
GNP	1,619.1	7,266.2	349
GDP	1611.3	7,269.8	351

II. Consumer Price Index

   A. Combined Measures

	1950	1997	Change (%)
COMMODITIES	29.0	141.9	389
SERVICES	16.9	184.2	990
TOTAL (all items)	24.1	163.0	576

   B. Selected Areas

	1950	1997	Change (%)
MEDICAL CARE	15.1	242.1	1503
FOOD	24.1	163.0	576
SHELTER	22.1 (1955)	182.1	724
CLOTHING	40.3	133.0	230

III. Participation in Labor Force, by Gender and Race (percentage)

	1950	1998	Change (%)
TOTAL	59.2	67.1	7.9
GENDER			
Males	86.4	74.9	−11.5
Females	33.9	59.8	25.9
RACE			
White	58.7 (1955)	67.3	8.6
Minority	64.2 (1955)	66.0	1.8

IV. Unemployment, by Gender and Race (20 years old or older; percentage)

	1950	1998	Change (%)
TOTAL	5.3	4.5	−0.8
GENDER			
Males	5.1	4.4	−0.7
Females	5.7	4.6	
RACE			
White	4.9	3.9	−1.1
Black	9.0	7.8	−1.2

V. Labor Union Membership (thousands)

	1950	1998	Change (%)
MEMBERSHIP	14,294.2	16,211.0	13
% OF LABOR FORCE	23.0	11.8	−49

TABLE 2.2 *(Continued)*
Selected Economic Indicators (by year)

VI. Federal Budget, National Defense, and Nondefense Spending (constant 1992 dollars; billions)

	1950	2000 (est)	Change (%)
NATIONAL DEFENSE	113.5	233.5	106
NONDEFENSE	187.4	1,257.1	571
TOTAL	301.0	1,490.5	395

VII. Federal Expenditures in Selected Nondefense Areas by Year (billions of dollars)

	1920	1999 (est)	Change (%)
HUMAN RESOURCES TOTAL	75.3	1,087.4	1,344
HEALTH	5.9	143.1	2,325
MEDICARE	6.2	205.0	3,206
SOCIAL SECURITY	30.3	392.6	1,196
VETERANS' BENEFITS	8.7	77.8	794
EDUCATION/ TRAINING	8.6	60.1	599
INCOME SECURITY	15.7	243.1	1,448

VIII. The National Debt (millions of dollars)
A. Total

	1950	2000(est)	Change (%)
PUBLIC DEBT	219,023	3,571,830	1,530.8
% GDP	80.1	39.2	−40.9

B. Interest on Debt (billions)

	1920	1999 (est)	Change (%)
NET INTEREST	14.4	227.2	1,477.8
% TOTAL FEDERAL OUTLAYS	7.4	7.6	0.2

IX. Foreign Investments in United States (millions of dollars)

	1950	1995
	3,391	560,088

X. United States Investment in Other Countries (millions of dollars)

	1950	1995
	11,788	860,723

XI. Balance of Trade (millions of dollars)

	1950	1998
VALUE OF GOODS	1,122	247,985
TOTAL VALUE OF GOODS, SERVICES, MONEY EXCHANGES	1,840	168,587

Source: Adapted from the data in Harold W. Stanley and Richard G. Niemi, *Vital Statistics on American Politics 1999–2000* (Washington, DC: CQ Press, 2000), and the sources cited therein.

country in which to live, the Consumer Price Index rising on average by a factor of 6 or more, with even more substantial increases in the costs associated with health care and housing. Female participation in the labor force is up by almost 75 percent and unemployment is lower, although still running just under 8 percent for blacks. The national debt, while increasing, constitutes a substantially lower proportion of the GDR than it did in the fifties. In addition, the debt declined significantly during the Clinton presidency and is projected to continue to do so. The political debate in the early twenty-first century centers on how to use the budgetary surpluses, the first since an escalation of the Vietnam War began in earnest, and the amounts of surplus to be devoted to further reducing the nation's indebtedness, tax relief, social spending, and/or military preparedness. All of this constitutes a fundamental turnaround and a welcome change for the nation and provides stark contrast, given the historic levels of debt run up in the 1980s. A debate over a politics of prosperity is a new experience for adults who came of age in recent generations. On the international front, peace reigns, foreign trade has expanded markedly, and foreign investment in the United States has also increased substantially.

Less successfully, the balance of trade deficits continued to mount and remain a problem for which no one seems to have a politically acceptable solution. For the working class, labor union membership has declined as a proportion of the labor force to less than half of what it was in 1950, a product of labor's own leadership failings and strategies and of changes in the country's economic directions favoring white-collar, informational services and entrepreneurial pursuits.

Overall, as these data show, the economy and the economic condition of most individuals are better than they have been at any point in contemporary history. The country also appears poised to continue to take advantage of the economic restructuring in progress and the globalization of markets, finance, and trade. This is the Clinton administration's principal legacy and, if properly managed, its gift to future generations.

Governmental Size and Services

Clearly, the federal government has continued to expand, reinforcing its role as the principal political agent in American life. Several indicators make the point (Table 2.3): civilian employment in the federal government is up from 2 to 2.8 million; the *Federal Register*, which can serve as a shorthand index of federal activity, has increased from 9,500 to 72,000 pages; the number of civil and criminal cases initiated in U.S. district courts climbed from 80,000 to 310,000 by 1998; and federal grants-in-aid to states and localities rose from $2.3 billion in 1950 to an estimated $283.5 billion by the year 2000, a threefold rise in both federal budget and GDP share. Finally and possibly most significantly in this context, the federal budget estimated for 2000 (and the years immediately thereafter) increased roughly by a factor of 35 (17 for national defense spending, 43 for nondefense spending), with 84 percent of current budgeting going for nondefense programs (up from 67 percent in 1950)

TABLE 2.3
Government Indicators

I. Employment (civilian)

	1950	1998	Change (%)
FEDERAL GOVERNMENT	1,960,708	2,798,992	42.8
	1952	1997	Change (%)
STATE/LOCAL	116,807,000	87,504,000	−25.1

II. Federal Register

	1950	1998	Change (%)
NUMBER OF PAGES	9,562	72,356	656.7

III. Cases Filed in U.S. District Courts (civil and criminal)

	1950	1998	Change (%)
	44,454	256,787	477.6

IV. Federal Grants-in-Aid to States and Localities

	1950	2000 (est)	Change (%)
TOTAL (billions of dollars)	2.3	283.5	12,226
% OF FEDERAL OUTLAYS	5.3	16.1	10.8
% GDP	0.8	3.1	2.3

V. Military

A. Defense Spending

	1950	2000 (est)	Change (%)
% FEDERAL OUTLAYS	32.2	15.5	−16.7
% GDP	5.0	3.0	1

B. Active Duty Forces (thousands)

	1965	1998	Change (%)
TOTAL	2,656	1,395	−47.5
FEMALES (%)	1.2	14.0	12.8
BLACKS (%)	9.5	20.0	10.5

Source: Adapted from the data in Harold W. Stanley and Richard G. Niemi, *Vital Statistics on American Politics 1999–2000* (Washington, DC: CQ Press, 2000), and the sources cited therein.

(Stanley and Niemi 2000). Since 1970 alone, the increase in federal expenditures for targeted programs—health, Social Security, and Medicare—has risen enough to have become contentious, with calls for cost containment and a possible redesigning of the programs in question or in their financing (Crotty 1995). In addition, the interest on the debt has attracted notice, and continuing to down-pay it with part of the budgetary surplus is an option that has political support. On another level, state and local government expenditures have also risen dramatically, from a total of $30 million in 1952 to $1.3 billion by the mid-1990s.

Overall, however, the nation is in the best economic condition it has been in during the postwar decades and, going further back in time, since the New Deal and the Great Depression. As an indicator of the present era's good fortune, budgetary surpluses have continued to exceed projections. As noted earlier, this is a new and welcome experience for the country.

Evolving since the 1930s, the federal government (in particular) and its programs have been a dominating force in American life, directing the country's energies, establishing its priorities, and mobilizing its resources. They have survived the reengineering and downsizing movements of the last few decades (from Carter to Clinton to George W. Bush) and the efforts to reduce or minimize government social spending (the Reagan presidency) or restrain its expenditures with more traditional conservative fiscal policies (the "Contract with America"). The prospects are that government's influence on American life and policy not only will be maintained but will increase in an era of globalized economic and political interdependency. A likely scenario is that there will be less energy devoted to reducing the government's influence and more put into guaranteeing a reasonable level of political representation and accountability in the conduct of public and international affairs.

An Adequate Level of National Defense

Finally, and reflecting the economic and social trends already examined, military spending, while it has increased in absolute dollars, has fallen to 3 percent of the GDP. For the decade 1985–1995 alone, it decreased by $76 billion, from 6.1 percent to 3.8 percent of the GDP and by one-third in per capita assessments (Table 2.3) (Stanley and Niemi 2000). In relation to social trends in the military, the proportion of blacks has doubled and that of women is elevenfold greater (while still constituting only 14 percent of all forces) from the early and mid-sixties to the late nineties.

One additional point in this regard: modest increases in national defense budget outlays over the next few years, to improve the living standards of military personnel and/or update technology in order to respond to emergencies in a world offering different challenges, are also budgetary possibilities. The need for global international cooperation in meeting less conventional challenges, many in the form of small-scale ethnic uprisings, and in pursuing peace initiatives, will test the military's capabilities and its more traditional conception of its role. The consequences may be to spur further reevaluations of the nature of America's commitment to its national security. It is worth noting that there have been no less than seventy military missions abroad between the early 1950s and the late nineties, some substantial (Korea, the Persian Gulf War), others less conventional (Kosovo, Haiti).

The nation as it enters a new century, then, is not that of the 1950s. In many respects (if not most) bears little resemblance to an age receding quickly into the historical mist. Fundamental, prolonged change has taken place at all levels of the society and in its politics and policy objectives. Another period of broadly based transitions, along with their inherent uncertainties, appears to be in its initial phases.

The overall picture is one of expansion of a governmental presence, the services and programs it provides, and the impact it has on individual lives. The economic indicators point to an individually and collectively wealthier citizenry. The need for a large military presence with its accompanying ideology of the national security state has lessened, if not fundamentally disappeared. The nation has demonstrated that it has the resources and economic muscle, as well as the vision, to position itself appropriately to profit from the new age of information technology and a globalized economy interdependency.

Although there is much to be satisfied with, in retrospect, and present conditions are decidedly favorable, there are issues of concern that need to be addressed. Those brought about by the social transformations underway are only beginning to be discussed. Still, we do know some of the costs occasioned by the dislocations progress brings and, as a consequence, the types of social problems needing attention.

Issues of Concern in a New Social Order

The questions of greatest significance are likely to be who profits the most from the new social and economic order, who gets included and who does not, whose interests get represented, and whose do not. The political debate on these points has already been engaged and it holds every promise of being both prolonged and contentious. Many of the fundamental concerns are not new. The potential solutions—or, at present, the political will to recognize the concerns as legitimate social issues deserving of reevaluation—are not completely evident.

Among the first of the social analysts to point out the consequences of the economic restructuring underway was Kevin Phillips. His influential "inflammatory" (in his own words) focused primarily on the shifts in wealth during the Reagan years. The administration's polices at the time ("supply-side economics") promoted a redistribution of wealth upwards, a reversal of the New Deal's objectives and ones that had dominated American politics for a half century. Ideologically committed, persuasive, and politically skilled in mobilizing broad public support, the Reagan presidency managed to take a process slow to take root during the seventies and give it the momentum in the eighties that was to take on a life of its own.

According to Phillips: "The liberal style that prevailed from 1932 to 1968 had left a legacy of angry conservatives indignant over two generations of downward income redistribution. A reorientation in the opposite direction was all but inevitable in the 1980s . . . " (1990, XIX).

He continues:

> We are talking about a major transformation. Not only did the concentration of wealth quietly intensify, but the sums involved took a mega-leap.

> The definition of who's rich changed as radically during the Reagan era as it did during the prior great nouveau riche periods whose excesses preceded the great populist upheavals of the Bryan era and the New Deal. (1990, XXIII)

Phillips adds the caution (probably unnecessary today) that "powerful currents of global change are operating quite beyond our power to offset them" (1990, XXIII).

The ramifications of the economic changes introduced would last well beyond the Reagan years and helped set the stages for the accentuation of the problems to follow. Others were to focus on similar concerns. Political scientist Margaret Weir:

> The cumulation of dissatisfactions, doubts, and gaps in the current public-private system of social provision has brought us to a turning point . . . it is one that our political system is ill equipped to manage in a way that brings both expertise and broad political engagement to bear on decision-making. The shrill partisan debate that characterized social policymaking in the first [and it could be added second] Clinton administration[s] and the mobilization of Washington-based interests to defend their turf only reinforced public disengagement from government. This kind of politics will make it very difficult to reform social policies in ways that promote security and opportunity for people across the income spectrum. [Instead] this political process is likely to exacerbate already widening inequalities and place heavier burdens on those striving to manage family and work lives under new social and economic conditions (1998, 525).

Frances Fox Piven and Richard A. Cloward in arguing against "the breaking of the social compact" and the impact of the emerging economies on the working class attack the assumptions underlying globalization and the feeling that little of consequence can be done:

> The key fact of our historical moment is said to be economic globalization, together with the domestic restructuring of the "Fordist" industrial era regime of mass production and mass consumption. These transformations are said to entail shattering consequences for the economic well-being of the working class, and especially for the power of the working class and, . . . the power of democratic publics more generally. . . . The implication is that the global economy is in command; in effect, markets no longer permit politics, at least not a politics which sustains the industrial era social compact . . . the explanation itself has become a political force, helping to create the institutional realities it purportedly merely describes. In fact, globalization is as much political strategy as economic imperative. (1997, 5)

They are more than likely correct. If globalization can be seen as a political option, it can be controlled—certainly channeled within broad limits—and the social problems associated with it given priority. To give them a presence in the nation's agenda requires both a national discussion of the issues involved and the potential solutions available as well as a broad mobilization of political forces demanding they receive attention. To date, neither has been evident.

Sociologist Beth A. Rubin posits two potential outcomes from all of this, one favorable, the other not. First, the more pessimistic outcome:

> [T]he economy continues to globalize, with powerful high-tech corporations accumulating more and more, further freeing them from any political or economic limits. . . . Without responsibility to any place or people, and more or less without regulation, these corporations continue to pollute the environment. International inequality becomes extreme, with a small group of countries doing well but most of the world growing increasingly impoverished (1997, 182).

The optimistic (and more than likely overly optimistic) view is that:

> Educating and retraining displaced workers . . . would create a work force of experienced and empowered workers who could use that experience to further develop production facilities. Those with the entrepreneurial spirit could have greater freedom to devise new businesses and services. A growing, creative small-business sector, aided by easier access to colleges and universities, could free up much of the stymied creativity that has historically fueled economic growth. On a global level, the economic, personnel, and technological resources of advanced nations might allow coordination among them for coherent, compassionate, and collaborative intervention in those countries that want economic and political assistance. . . . [G]lobal corporations would put thousands of people to work and continue to profit by putting their energies into creating new products and markets, exploring and colonizing both the ocean and space (1996, 184–85).

Rubin herself indicates this latter scenario may seem unlikely. The positive outlook appears more visionary than reality-based, too idealized and too demanding of human nature. Yet the early twentieth century could never have anticipated the technology, communications, scientific, and health advances that were to take place in the decades to follow or the social changes that accompanied them. The real point, however, is the extent to which advances and changes in the social and economic order can be harnessed to serve human needs and to better lives collectively and individually on a reasonably equitable basis. These social objectives, more than the technological ones that are sure to come, appear decidedly more difficult to address in any meaningful manner.

A number of problems are clearly identifiable at present and are of such a magnitude that an easy resolution is not in sight. Further problems, unanticipated now, inevitably will arise, impacting the social system and making new demands on the political order. The real struggle will be to evolve political institutions capable of dealing with these problems and able to function in a democratic and representative manner in an increasingly interdependent world economic and political community. It is destined to be the major challenge facing the nation in the twenty-first century.

Addressing Democratic Concerns

The essays that follow are intended to be selective and problem-oriented. They are not meant to identify or assess every problem that might exist or might occur in the foreseeable future. The approach is selective, with the focus on the political—the nature of representation and the dynamics of change in areas considered crucial to the operations of a democratic system. These include assessments of the performance of contemporary democratic institutions and the conditions that support them, from indications of satisfaction with the functioning of the current system to levels of political involvement, the mobilization of interests, and the operation of policymaking agencies. Issues fundamental to the quality of the democratic experience are of concern, from racial tolerance to policy developments of economic and budgetary consequence.

Each chapter is by an acknowledged expert in the area with extensive experience in dealing with the issues raised. Each should contribute to our understanding and our appreciation of the complexity of change and some of the pressures it generates within a nation as it, and we, enter new and uncertain stages in the evolution of the democratic experiment in the United States.

A brief introduction to the chapters follows:

Chapter 1, "Politics and Policy for a New Century," by Michael S. Dukakis, sets the context. The Cold War that dominated American, and world, politics and thinking since the end of World War II is over. It is a new era. As Dukakis says in comparing efforts at effective world governance and multination cooperation to early American struggles to fuel a constitutional framework for the colonies: "the international community is attempting for the first time in the history of mankind to set standards for the conduct of nations and enforce them." It is heady stuff, bound to be frustrating, but full of promise and, more than that, a necessity in the contemporary world.

Domestically, the United States has done well, as the present chapter indicates Dukakis reviews these changes in broad perspective while lamenting the low levels of political participation and "the virtual disappearance of genuine, partisan grassroots politics in America," a condition that M. Margaret Conway fully documents in chapter 3, "Political Mobilization in America." The changing political landscape, the reasons for it, and the consequences experienced are developed in depth by Conway.

Beyond civic involvement as a challenge to the vitality and representativeness of the American system (a point Conway addresses), Dukakis identifies three other areas of concern: racial problems and their continuing effect in discriminating against some groups and dividing, one way or another, us all; "the quality and integrity of our political system," including the corrupting influence of special interest money; and the growing economic disparity in this country between the better-off and the less well-off: "[T]he United States now has the dubious distinction of having the greatest gap between the rich and poor of any of the advanced industrialized nations."

We approach each of these concerns in turn, although not necessarily in the order presented. The quality of electoral performance and the decreasing participation of Americans in determining their own political future has been already commented on. Conway lends further support to Dukakis's emphasis on the need for organization and the efficacy of personal contact to achieve political success. Of the five measures examined, only two—being contacted by a party or a religious group—led to increased participation. The organization of interests is critical to achieving political goals.

The composition of the electorate is changing (the eligible black and Hispanic populations are increasing faster than the white population). Significant improvement in turnout is clearly possible and, normatively speaking, is highly desirable. Conway writes that "political mobilization efforts matter. Targeted get-out-the-vote campaigns can have a significant impact both on who votes and on electoral outcomes. . . . [M]ultiple opportunities exist for effective mobilization drives. . . . [T]hese campaigns are most effective when substantial resources are employed to communicate the consequences of the electoral outcome for a group's issue interests." The outcome of the 2000 presidential election makes this point forcefully.

Three chapters deal with representative institutions, two approach the party system from differing perspectives, and one focuses on the Congress. In chapter 4, "Public Support for the Party System in the United States," Diana Owen, Jack Dennis, and Casey A. Klofstad address the question of whether the parties are failing. The authors explore the nature of support for the party system, through data gathered in a specially designed nationwide survey. It is an area that they have explored in earlier works. They extend their prior contributions toward understanding a complex and socially imbedded set of attitudes by analyzing different types of potential support—diffuse, broad, indiscriminate, and unrelated to performance, specific, based on measures of party achievement, and party assumptions as incubators of social and institutional reform.

Antiparty sentiments have increased in recent decades, yet, as the authors find, the dissatisfaction, though focused on the parties, may well be a more generalized disillusionment with how the democratic system more broadly conceived is operating. Those who are ideological or who see governing institutions in general operating successfully are positively inclined to evaluate the parties. Political independents rank parties low and in turn, united with those more broadly dissatisfied with governing institutions, tend to form third parties.

Owen, Dennis, and Klofstad advance the study of approval/disapproval of the party system through an examination broader than its predecessors, and one that employs more refined measures of political attitudes. They indicate that as the party system weakens, "a more complex representative process has evolved—one in which the role of the parties . . . may be increasingly constricted." If so, the party system and more broadly, representative political institutions may be undergoing changes in legitimation and acceptance that will lead to reformulation of their role in society.

William Crotty in chapter 5, "Party Relevance over Time," examines a related problem—in this case public perceptions of the importance of parties and the feelings (positive/negative) directed at them. The assumption in both studies is that political parties are the key agencies in linking the citizenry to representative political institutions, in influencing the direction of public policy, and in holding the nation's elected leadership accountable for its actions.

The measures in this study are more indirect: the salience measure is used as an indicator of how significant respondents in the National Elections Studies believe parties to be as indicated by the total of their references to parties, good and bad, made in election years over a period of four decades. The feelings, or affect, measure is the reduction of negative evaluations from positive ones and is both more volatile and less supportive than the salience indicators.

The overall conclusion is that is that the public does see parties as important and they respond to them in this context. At the same time, they are more critical (with specific exceptions) and less forgiving in relation to the emotional associations they make with the parties. The changes in these measures vary considerably by election year, in response to the presidential candidates running and in relation to the context in which the election takes place. Also, and unlike those interviewed in the Owen, Dennis, and Klofstad study, respondents are more constrained in how they evaluate the parties. In the data used in this study, they were required to react in the context of the specific parties contesting a given election. The strength of this approach is that it provides a measure of the continuing perceptions of immediate, election-specific relevance in a variety of national campaigns.

Similar questions as to the quality of democratic choice are explored by Donald R. Matthews in chapter 6, "Does Congress Represent the American People?" in a sharply focused structural analysis of representation within both houses of Congress. Matthews asks a basic question: "How well does the U.S. Congress represent the American people?" As he notes, confidence in the Congress has declined in recent decades. At the same time, the amount of attention devoted to congressional research has increased voluminously. Yet the research does not directly answer, and often does not actually consider, the quality of congressional representation. It does look at institutional structures, policy formulation and output, legislative behavior, outside influences (groups, PACs) on the process, the dynamics of congressional elections, congressional oversight of administrative agencies, congressional-presidential relations, budgetary procedures and their consequences, rules of behavior, the careers of individual senators or representatives, roll call voting, and a host of other issues.

Matthews posits that members of Congress respond to constituents in three areas—policy, service, and symbolic representation. He chooses to focus on the collective behavior of Congress (most studies analyze the individual-level behavior as it relates to policy). This approach, in turn, draws attention to the political and constitutional context in which the institution operates. In relation to the Senate, "one of the most strangely apportioned democratic legislatures in the world," and calling upon the work of Donald McCrone, who modeled Senate representation in relation to strict population guidelines, he finds a number of groups overrepresented—those from large urban areas, blacks, Hispanics, true foreign-born, and Jewish populations. Those states penalized the most in representation include the converse of those with the largest concentration of these groups. These would include the states most likely to have voted for Ronald Reagan (and later George W. Bush) and those with the lowest abortion rates, a measure of policy preferences and attitudes.

In relation to the House of Representatives, with its single-member plurality elections in a weak party system, minorities, Chicanos, and women suffer from underrepresentation; the Democratic Party in general gains bonus seats; and the service dimension of representation is considerably more pronounced and more important than it would be in a multimember, proportional parliamentary voting system.

The overall consequence is a significant partisan and policy bias that affects the quality and fairness of representation. The tendencies in the two houses of Congress may cancel each other to a degree, but they also build in more conflict over policy formation than may be necessary or desirable.

The social problems associated with race and the continuing struggle to promote greater equality and multicultural understanding are addressed in two significant undertakings. Both represent broad assessments of the social and cultural factors underlying discrimination in the United States. The first is by George E. Marcus in chapter 7, "The Enduring Dilemma of Political Tolerance in American Political History." The second, by Edward G. Carmines and Paul M. Sniderman (chapter 8, "The Future of Racial Politics: Beyond Fatalism"), is a more experimental analysis designed to test the limits of public acceptance for policies directed toward achieving racial equity.

Each of the authors has dealt extensively with the problem before in a number of influential works. Marcus in a balanced and nuanced review traces the concern with protecting the political rights of all citizens in American society. It has been a noble if uneven venture. He argues that we can better prepare future generations of children for the tests ahead. We can also speak out decisively and act when critical problems arise. Marcus concludes:

> [P]olitical and social intolerance will be recurring problems for a liberal society such as ours. We need not despair, for there is much we can do. We can remind ourselves, especially in moments of crisis, that political tolerance serves all of us. . . . [W]e can take on the important responsibility to take up public action in support of political tolerance.

It is both a sound and realistic assessment. Racial concerns have preoccupied Americans since the nation's founding, as Marcus shows. They are not about to disappear in the twenty-first century. Yet there is much we as a society can do to diffuse racial politics and increase social tolerance in the years to come.

Carmines and Sniderman approach the problem from a different perspective. They point out that there are "gaping cleavages" in society over racial issues and programs—affirmative action in particular—that have been prominent in politics for decades. Attempting to channel support into more fruitful directions, they assess various means for framing the approach. The essence of their findings has a clear relevance for policymakers. They write that identifying the beneficiaries of a racial policy in racial terms may be costly, not primarily because it is racial, but more fundamentally because it is particularistic. . . . [W]hether a policy is targeted in racial terms or not, it can be argued for on grounds that go beyond race. This distinction between how a policy is targeted—and whether that is racial or not—and how it is justified—and whether *that* is racial or not—is, we think, crucial.

The analysis is creative. The resolution to the problem advocated could result in a more responsive and, at the same time, less conflictual national approach to ameliorating the social divisions that continue to provide one of the society's least defensible and, historically, most profound challenges.

Three interrelated chapters deal with the economic dimensions of representation in terms of the impact of a free-market, globalized economy on the quality of life of Americans. In chapter 9, "The Limits of the Market: New Examinations of an Old Problem," Betty Glad makes a strong case for the need to control the economic forces that affect us all. Recent decades have been witness to profound changes: a broader social acceptance of the benefits of deregulated, or essentially unregulated, markets; free trade; a decreased government oversight of a variety of economic activities; and the proposed privatization of everything from trash collection and drinking water to schools, prisons, and Social Security. These constitute a reversal of protections initiated during the New Deal, and Glad argues that they expose the United States unduly to the uncertainties of the world economic order. One result of the fundamental redirection of policy objectives has been a renewal of the historic debate over the nature of the market and its relationship to the government.

Glad reviews the evolution of Social Darwinism and its assumptions, many of which underlie the free-market philosophies of Milton Friedman and the Chicago School, among the most influential advocates of the neoliberal approach. For Friedman and others, the *only* proper functions of government are public order and national defense. They place their emphasis and, beyond that, their trust on the opportunities implicit in an open economic order.

The assumptions as to the relative value of a free market in spurring economic advances or in contributing to social progress are questionable. One consequence is clear, however: the increasing disparity in income and social benefits among different socioeconomic classes. An increasing polarization of wealth is the result. Neoliberal assumptions that the most deserving benefit the most, that a free-market discipline for troubled economies maximizes productivity, and that a natural equilibrium in global and national trading systems exists need revisiting. To date in the emerging global order, the United States, with its vast resources of wealth, has acted as a court of last resort in stabilizing the international economic policy. Whether it can continue to do so indefinitely is debatable.

The social costs of an unregulated market are great. As Glad concludes, we have a fair idea of what not to do. "What is needed . . . at this point is some serious rethinking about how the American people can regain some control over the operation of the economy that has so much impact on their lives." This point of view nicely summarizes assumptions underlying a number of the analyses in this volume.

In chapter 10, "Crossroads Blues: Business Representation, Public Policy, and Economic Growth for the Twenty-First Century," Cathie Jo Martin argues that capitalism in the United States is at a crossroads in deciding what policies to pursue in order to sustain economic growth and inspire future prosperity. She argues for a government-directed investment in human resources, a course of action considered by free-market economists to be detrimental to an efficient market. It is a position she shares with Glad. Martin looks at the impact of business on the formulation of public policy and argues that the business community is divided; that it encounters formidable difficulties in identifying, much less agreeing on, long-term collective outreach strategies; and that large and small businesses differ in their objectives and their perception of the need to commit to developing worker skills and increased social services. The battle, then, between the "high-performance-workplace" advocates and laissez-faire governmental minimalists has resulted in an increased fragmentation of corporate objectives. At present they appear "less capable than ever of finding common ground." The divisions within the nation's political leadership have accentuated the fragmentation in interest representation contributing to a form of "least-common-denominator politics." Such conflicts have made policy resolutions (including, for example, health care reform) difficult, if not impossible, to achieve. While the large corporate interests struggle with their sense of political identity, small business wields considerable power. Its impact on public policy is often not fully appreciated. It has managed to unite in opposing governmental social policies that it perceives to be an impediment to bottom-line profits. The demonstration of its political clout in defeating a series of social initiatives, including mandated family and medical leave, has been impressive.

A two-tiered approach to economic policy (large corporations versus small business) is transforming the regulatory state. It may well have consequences for high-end markets in terms of the policy preferences extended small domestic concerns over international ones. In turn, the increasing deficit in human resources investment not only makes it harder for firms to compete in high-skilled markets but also accelerates the polarization of views between rich and poor, which in turn could contribute to increased social tension.

The greater equalization of wealth and social benefits, as Martin argues, and the ability to compete globally suffer from centrist policies designed to minimize the government's role in the economy. On this point, as on a number of others, both Glad and Martin are in agreement.

Thomas Ferguson in chapter 11, "Blowing Smoke: Impeachment, the Clinton Presidency, and the Political Economy," pulls all of this together within the turmoil and contradictions of the 1990s and the Clinton presidency and, most specifically, the president's impeachment. It is a formidable undertaking and one that skillfully adds perspective and depth to the interplay of economics and politics in contemporary America.

Ferguson's perspective he labels an "investment theory" of politics, with its dominating focus being money.

> [T]his approach emphasizes that the critical factor in shaping public policy is normally the process of bloc formation among major investors. . . . [A] political party's real market is defined by major investors, who generally have good and clear reasons for investing to control the state. In analyzing political outcomes, accordingly, the place to begin is with a systematic study of blocs of large investors. In most cases in the modern era—and certainly during the Clinton presidency—this requires a careful assessment of the regime's macroeconomic policies, since these usually relate very closely to the hopes and fears of both friends and foes of the ruling political coalition. One also pays careful attention . . . to the subsidized "politics of ideas" and domestic social conflicts, particularly as these are affected by a changing world economy.

It is an enormous task and results in an original and unparalleled assessment.

The data for the analysis came from the Federal Election Commission files and cover the balance of the nineties, from the election of 1992 through to the closing years of the twentieth century. Employing it, Ferguson shows how center-right business interests attempted to reorient the Democratic Party's policy objectives, succeeding with Bill Clinton's victory in the presidential race. The administration's early battles over taxes, regulation, and Big Tobacco sent hundreds of millions of dollars into the Republican Party's treasury for the 1994 off-year election. Policy, money, and politics were ultimately related in this election, as they are in every election. Pharmaceuticals, insurers, chemicals, and transportation firms, along with those interested in scuttling environmental restrictions, led the support for Newt Gingrich and the "Republican Revolution" that followed.

Post-1994, Clinton's resuscitation began with the ability to "court" defense and oil interests. "The White House also vigorously promoted expansion of American exports abroad, in many instances apparently linking its support to contributions to the DNC [Democratic National Committee]." Opponents would allege it was a pattern that became all too common during the Clinton years. It is a pattern also that, within the limits of the data, Ferguson traces out, linking policies advocated and legislation submitted to the Congress, and its fortunes, to financial support extended to the administration or to its opponents. The most dramatic act in the presidential-congressional battles came in the battles over the budget and the shutdown of the federal government in a series of fights that ultimately hurt the GOP.

Critiquing the corporate distribution of funds in the 1996 election and the administration's response to the international economic crisis of 1998, Ferguson writes:

> We now have more than enough evidence to answer the question posed at the beginnning of the chapter. . . . The American political system is not essentially driven by votes. Public opinion has only a weak and inconstant influence on policy. The political system is largely investor-driven, and runs on enormous quantities of money—more than $4 billion since Clinton took office in narrowly construed and (more or less) publicly recorded

electoral expenses along with at least something like ten to thirty times that in lobbying and broader public relations costs. . . .

Ever since America's great "Right Turn" in the mid-seventies, most of American business and the super-rich have espoused increasingly radical versions of "laissez-faire" economics—save, of course, when oil fields are in play, trade needs to be subsidized, or a transnational bailouts become imperative. With an intensity moderated only by extremes in the business cycle, demands for tax "relief," freedom from regulation, cuts in social welfare expenditures, labor cost reductions, and tighter control of increasingly decentralized production systems dominate their consciousness and thus public consciousness. Epitomized in the buzz word "globalization," this "neoliberal" political ideology has had essentially no rival in the Anglo-Saxon countries since 1989.

Ferguson brings economics, politics, and policy to bear in a broad-ranging and extensively developed analysis of the political events, from elections to impeachment, of the 1990s. He foresees free-market economics and globalized competition as setting the context for political representation into the foreseeable future. The Republicans, he argues, are total captives of laissez-faire ideology, and the Democrats, as conservative as they try to be in efforts to increase their corporate sponsorship, will remain unattractive to the right and "unacceptably liberal to Republicans and most of the American business community." The result is that

the real tension that shapes America today is the enormous and growing gap between elites and the population. In a changing world economy, their aspirations now diverge more dramatically than ever. As a consequence, the United States is facing many more years of conflict. . . .

It is not a happy prediction, given the battles of the 1990s, yet one with consequences for political representation in this country that show few signs of moderating.

The final chapter, by Roger W. Cobb and Joseph F. Coughlin, projects policy questions into the twenty-first century. Proceeding from the assumption that "politics involves a battle over who is going to control the political agenda," the authors explore the role of what they refer to as issue "initiators/expanders," who desire to bring attention to their needs, and "containers," who oppose them and want to narrow the scope of conflict and maintain things the way they are.

Cobb and Coughlin explore the strategies and limitations of each set of adversaries. The advantage is to the containers. Initiators "are faced with a daunting task. They must show that their issue can be ranked high on some misery scale that requires action." The key is the manner in which the issues are framed: "naming" them in a publicly acceptable and attractive way; "blaming," the act of fixing responsibility for the problem on some group or action; and "claiming," the demands to be made on the government for a change in policies of benefit to the group.

Exploring these perspectives, Cobb and Coughlin look at the elderly, one of the most rapidly growing segments of the population (a projected one in five by 2010). As a group, they will be making a series of escalating demands in the political system. One area of contention will relate to driving. If anything, as people age they become more dependent on their automobiles. At the same time their physical skills decline; the elderly are second only to young people as the most dangerous group on the road.

The initiators identify the public to be impacted and responded to as those injured in accidents with, or having family members killed by, elderly drivers; transportation and medical people aware of the potential problems; and, sporadically, the media. The containers include groups representative of the older drivers, such as the politically powerful AARP.

The battle then becomes one of framing the areas of concern in the most dramatic and persuasive manner possible. The issue has not been embraced by state or federal governments, and few projected responses to limiting elderly driving have been explored. These could include retesting aging drivers and restricting licenses, an approach that would require a substantial financial investment, for example, increasing the number of road inspectors; cosmetic resolutions, such as requiring larger letters on highway signs, the resolution government prefers when pressed to do something; technologically "smart cars" that do the actual driving, a development well into the future and of questionable impact; and a greater investment in public transportation. All solutions cost money, some substantially more than others. To date, it appears the containers have done the most effective job in using cultural symbols, misinformation, and sheer political power to keep the issue off the political stage.

The nation's policy agenda is limited, with many problems competing for government attention. A number of these will include addressing the concerns of an aging population, with the framing of the issues having more to do with the types of problems that receive the greatest public response.

Conclusion

Clearly, the United States is undergoing a process of fundamental change with consequences that should at least parallel and will more than likely outstrip the changes that have taken place over the last half of the twentieth century. If the early twenty-first century bears an increasingly vague relationship to the mid-twentieth century—a prehistory era for many today—imagine (if possible) what the next fifty years will bring and how society will respond to the new forces being set loose. At present, the most we can say is that transformative change is well underway.

Where this will all lead is uncertain, but it is reasonable to believe that the reshaping of American society is underway. It has a considerable way to go before reaching its full momentum. The impact of the social and economic transformations has resulted in problems that the selections in this volume help identify, and many have little in common with those of the United States of a few generations ago. Yet the American democratic experience has both survived and prospered over the last two centuries despite a series of challenges equal to or more demanding than those faced in the contemporary period. With a degree of care and a sensitivity to its underlying assumptions, it should continue along much the same path in the foreseeable future.

There is, however, little reason to believe that no matter how enlightened the country's leadership and whatever the social changes to come, the problems addressed in this volume will disappear. The quality of American political life and the representativeness of its governing institutions; race and the tensions it has introduced into American society since the earliest days of the Republic; the restructuring of the nation's and the world's economy; and the further accentuation of inequalities in wealth and life opportunities associated with the move toward a more technologically sophisticated, information-driven, laissez-faire, and globalized system all are likely to remain dominant concerns well into the twenty-first century. As indicated in selection after selection, we as a nation are in the early stages of dealing with the political and social changes now in progress. In this context, the warnings put forth in chapter 1 by Michael S. Dukakis and in relation to political mobilization by M. Margaret Conway bear careful thought. Dukakis argues for the need for a more vital and participatory public life, and Conway identifies the "real electorate," those who participate and wield political power. The effective electorate is about one-half of the eligible electorate. This is the targeted electorate as defined by the candidates and their campaigns, the voters policymakers attempt to reach, and those whose concerns they address. To the extent that public accountability for actions in office and political representation exists, it is in relation to these subgroups within the population. These voters represent the outer bounds of political action. Those who participate in elections predict everything else—who wins, what policies are enacted, what groups and whose interests are given attention, and, correspondingly, which are (beyond occasional rhetorical calls for action) ignored. This real electorate effectively determines the public universe, where government energies are directed, who pays for what, and who benefits the most. The rest of the population must depend on a prayer or the goodwill of others. To be realistic, the likelihood is that their interests will be effectively ignored and that they, as they have in the past, will passively accept their lot. It is not the most pleasant of projections.

How governing institutions respond to transformative economic and social change, how all of this settles into political patterns that reinforce or strain existing agencies of political representation, and the adaptation processes just beginning to be experienced are the fundamental concerns that will serve to determine the continuing quality of American political life.

References

Crotty, William, ed. 1995. *Post-Cold War Policy*. Vol. 2. Chicago: Nelson-Hall Publishers.

Phillips, Kevin. 1990. *The Politics of Rich and Poor: Wealth and the American Electorate in the Reagan Aftermath*. New York: Harper Perennial.

Piven, Frances Fox, and Cloward, Richard A. 1997. *The Breaking of the American Social Compact*. New York: The New Press.

Rubin, Beth A. 1996. *Shifts in the Social Contract: Understanding Change in American Society*. Thousand Oaks, CA, London, and New Delhi: Pine Forge Press.

Stanley, Harold W., and Niemi, Richard G. 2000. *Vital Statistics on American Politics 1999–2000*. Washington, DC: Congressional Quarterly Inc.

Weir, Margaret, ed. 1998. *The Social Divide: Political Parties and the Future of Activist Government*. Washington, DC and New York: Brookings Institution Press.

3

Political Mobilization in America

M. MARGARET CONWAY

The Puzzle of Political Participation

Political participation in the form of voting turnout has declined precipitously since the 1960s, falling from 69 percent of the voting age population in 1964 to 54 percent in 1996 (Table 3.1). Turnout in midterm elections declined from 55 percent in 1966 to 45 percent in 1994, and in 1998 continued at low levels in most states (Table 3.2). No compensating increases have occurred in other forms of electoral participation.[1]

One perspective on electoral behavior discounts the impact of campaigns on vote choice and voter turnout, with strength of party identification, presidential popularity, the condition of the economy, and retrospective evaluations of other policies seen as determining vote choice and contributing significantly to voter turnout.[2] Certainly many citizens either continue a standing decision of how to vote or make up their minds early in the campaign. However, campaigns can make a difference, in part through the information they convey to citizens through convention events, candidate debates, other campaign events, and coverage of those in the news media.[3] A second way that campaigns can make a difference is through influencing who votes. In part that is done through providing the information that individuals consider in assessing the choices presented to them in the election. But campaigns also influence electoral outcomes through the deliberate mobilization of targeted sets of voters.[4] That is the focus of this chapter.

Campaigns have several goals in selecting targets for their efforts. One is to persuade the undecided or those weakly committed to an opposing candidate to vote for the campaign's candidate. Of course, where a candidate is elector-

TABLE 3.1
Reported Voter Turnout in Presidential Elections,
1964 to 1996

Year	Reported Voting (%)
1964	69.3
1968	67.8
1972	63.0
1976	59.2
1980	59.2
1984	59.9
1988	57.4
1992	61.3
1996	54.2

Source: U.S. Department of Commerce, Bureau of the Census, "Voting and Registration in the Election of November 1996," *Current Population Reports*, P20-504, July 1998.

ally secure, as is frequently the case with an incumbent, that goal may receive less emphasis. A second goal is to reinforce an already existing base of supporters. The third is to motivate turnout by those who would support the candidate if they voted. The weights given to these goals of conversion, reinforcement, and activation vary both with the nature of the contest and the time frame of the campaign.

This chapter focuses on efforts at political mobilization in the 1996 and 1998 elections. First, examples of mobilization efforts by the political parties, candidate organizations, PACs, labor unions, and other groups are discussed. Then, the effects of mobilization efforts at the individual level are examined.

TABLE 3.2
Reported Voter Turnout in Midterm Elections,
1966 to 1998

Year	Reported Voting (%)
1966	55.4
1970	54.6
1974	44.7
1978	45.9
1982	48.5
1986	56.0
1990	45.0
1994	45.0
1998	41.9

Sources: http://www.census.gov/population/socdemo/voting/history/htable01.txt; U.S. Bureau of the Census, "Voting and Registratioin in the Election of November, 1998," *Current Population Reports*, Series P20-523RV, Figure 1.

Third, the potential implications of changes in voter registration laws for political mobilization are considered. Finally, changes in the composition of the eligible electorate and the implications of those changes for political mobilization efforts are discussed.

33

Explaining Patterns of Participation

Several explanations exist for patterns of voter turnout and other types of political participation. One focuses on the effects on political participation of individuals' resources for participation and of changes in social status, such as increasing levels of educational attainment, changing income levels, and altered occupational patterns. These may interact with changes in political attitudes, beliefs, and values to alter patterns of participation.[5] Generational differences in attitudes, resources, political engagement, and life experiences are also associated with differences in patterns of participation.[6]

Some research highlights the importance of political mobilization efforts in stimulating turnout, finding that the effects of mobilization remain after controlling for a number of sociodemographic and attitudinal variables.[7] Another focus of research is the effects of the electoral structure and administration and the legal requirements for voting on electoral turnout.[8]

Combining these variables into alternative models, research finds significant effects for a number of different types of variables. *Voice and Equality* by Verba, Schlozman, and Brady presents the most prominent recent example of this approach. They suggest that citizens fail to participate because they can't (as a consequence of a lack of necessary resources—time, civic skills, and money), or because they don't want to (insufficient levels of political engagement), or because nobody asked them (isolation from the social networks through which political mobilization occurs).

Political Mobilization

In many areas of the country in the nineteenth and early twentieth centuries personal contacts by local political party organizations' precinct leaders were effective in mobilizing the electorate. However, the local party's ability to perform that role has declined substantially in many areas. Nonetheless, carefully targeted voter mobilization efforts occur, carried out by political parties, candidate organizations, or other groups, such as labor unions, PACs, and religious or other issue-based groups.

Targeting can focus on several different characteristics of potential voters. One major target for mobilization efforts is those who are registered in the party and have a record of voting in a selected set of prior elections. In addition, individuals are targeted because they have group memberships and other characteristics—issue concerns or policy preferences—that suggest a high probability of supporting a particular party or candidate if those individuals go to the polls. Issue enthusiasts identified as supporting particular issue positions would be targeted to receive messages relating to that issue. Members of an ethnic or racial group whose members are highly supportive of a particular party or concerned with a specific issue are also prime targets for mobilization efforts. Mobilization activities may use direct mail, automated phone calls, and/or personal phone calls to contact a targeted subset of the eligible electorate. The technology of modern communications permits this to be done efficiently by candidate organizations or their consultants or by any level of party organization that possesses the necessary resources.

Personalized mobilizing contact often occurs through membership groups. These include contacts through religious organizations (the church, synagogue, or mosque), workplace-related contacts from unions, coworkers, or employers, and contacts with members of other nonpolitical social or civic organizations. The elections in 1996 and 1998 provide a number of examples of both party and nonparty efforts at targeted voter mobilization drives aimed at winning elections in particular states or congressional districts.

A political party's carefully targeted, well-executed mobilization drive can effectively increase voter registration and turnout. The Democratic Party's efforts in Georgia in 1998 illustrate the effectiveness of a targeted get-out-the-vote campaign by a political party. Every identified African-American household in Georgia received at least two mailings and three phone calls urging support for the Democratic Party's candidates. Two of the phone calls were automated messages from Representative Cynthia McKinney and President Bill Clinton, while the third was a personal call from a party worker. In addition to the stimulus provided by these direct contacts, the party advertised extensively on black-oriented radio.[9] These efforts contributed to the Democratic Party's success in the 1998 election; the party retained control of both houses of the state legislature and elected a Democratic governor and lieutenant governor.

Turnout by the opposition candidate's supporters can also be stimulated by a campaign organization's errors in strategy and tactics. For example, in 1998 the Georgia Republican Party made issues of affirmative action and the way the city of Atlanta was governed. Mitch Skandalakis, the Republican candidate for lieutenant governor of Georgia, offended many members of the electorate by referring to the African American mayor of Atlanta as an "incompetent boob" and the African-American chairwoman of the mass transit authority as a "welfare queen." This contributed to the higher-than-usual rates of voting participation among African Americans, who comprised 28 percent of Georgia's voters in 1998, compared with 19 percent in 1994. The attacks also offended many whites, who perceived them to be race baiting.[10]

A number of other political actors sought to mobilize groups within the electorate in 1998. One very active group was Emily's List, a political action committee that supports pro-choice Democratic women candidates for statewide offices and for the United States Congress and, in elections prior to congressional redistricting, pro-choice Democratic women candidates for state legislative office. In 1998, Emily's List coordinated mobilization efforts with the Democratic Party's and candidates' campaigns in twenty-four states. Those efforts targeted 3.4 million women voters in selected states and congressional districts. This "Women Vote!" campaign carried out by Emily's List focused on senior citizens, African Americans, Latinas, professional women, and women without college degrees. Using direct mailings designed to appeal specifically to each targeted group, Emily's List claimed substantial success for its efforts.[11]

In its postelection assessments of electoral outcomes, Emily's List credited much of the Democrats' success in the 1998 congressional elections to increased turnout by Latina and African-American voters. The PAC's estimates indicate that Latino voters increased from 3 percent of the national electorate in 1994 to 5 percent in 1998, with 63 percent voting Democratic. In the key state of California, Latinos constituted 14 percent of the electorate and cast 72 percent of their votes for Emily's List-endorsed candidate Democratic Senator Barbara Boxer.[12] African Americans increased their share of the electorate from 6 percent in 1994 to 10 percent in 1998. Postelection estimates indicate that 42 percent of those eligible (59 percent of those registered) voted in California in the 1998 elections. In comparison, in the rest of the nation an estimated 36 percent of the voting age population voted.[13]

But credit for turnout and vote choice patterns in California must also be given to a number of targeted voter registration and voter mobilization drives conducted by other groups. While some groups sponsoring registration and mobilization drives supported particular parties or candidates, others focused on ballot initiatives. For example, supporters of California's Proposition 5, which related to Indian gambling casino rights, targeted 1.2 million Latinos with a past history of voting turnout.[14] Partial credit for increased Latino participation in California must also be given to negative reactions to several statewide initiatives on the ballot in previous years. Those include Proposition 187 (targeting illegal immigrants), Proposition 209 (ending affirmative action as state policy), and Proposition 227 (ending bilingual education in public schools). These helped stimulate increased Latino voter registration and turnout in 1998. The attack on affirmative action also fueled increased turnout among African-Americans.

An ethnic group's mobilization can be stimulated by having candidates from that group on the ballot. Political observers credit this as another cause of increased Latino turnout in California. In 1998 Latino voters helped elect the first Hispanic statewide official since the 1870s (Lt. Governor Cruz Bustamente) in addition to several members of the U.S. House of Representatives, ten additional members of the California Assembly (seven new members of the lower chamber and three in the state senate), and the first Latino mayor of a major city (Ron Gonzales of San Jose). The estimated Latino share of the total California vote in 1998 (14 percent) contributed significantly to winning margins for the Democrats' statewide victories. For example, exit polls indicate that Latinos cast 76 percent of their votes for the winning Democratic candidate for U.S. Senate (Barbara Boxer), 81 percent for the winning Democratic candidate for governor (Gray Davis), and 84 percent for the Democratic candidate for Lieutenant Governor (Cruz Bustamente).[15]

Other carefully targeted and executed mobilization drives also resulted in increased turnout and had a significant impact on electoral outcomes in 1998.

For example, a South Carolina poll conducted by the *Charleston Post and Courier* in June 1998, indicated that 26 percent of South Carolina's African-American voters would support Republican Governor David Beasley for reelection. Beasley had opposed removing the Confederate battle flag from the statehouse and was perceived by black elites as insensitive to the concerns of South Carolina's African Americans. The poll's results stimulated African-American leaders throughout the state to persuade black citizens to register and to vote for the Democratic Party's gubernatorial candidate, Jim Hodges. A major policy change advocated by Hodges was the creation of a state lottery with the proceeds to be dedicated to additional funding for public education in South Carolina. Although controversial, this proposal was perceived by many as promising significant support for a policy of much-needed improved educational funding. Using grassroots meetings, the African-American leaders worked to solidify support for Hodges. In what was regarded by many as an upset, Hodges defeated Beasley, winning 53 percent of the vote.[16] Also playing a role in Governor Beasley's defeat in his reelection bid were the Democratic Party's targeted voter mobilization efforts. The party spent $2 million in the South Carolina get-out-the-vote efforts.[17] These and other mobilization efforts in the state were successful, with African Americans contributing 25 percent of the total turnout in 1998.

In contrast, Republicans were less successful in mobilizing their base in 1998. As a share of the national electorate, conservative voters declined from 37 percent in 1994 to 31 percent in 1998, and religious conservatives declined from 17 percent to 13 percent of the active electorate. Furthermore, a Christian Coalition-sponsored exit poll found that 31 percent of Christian conservatives reported voting for Democratic congressional candidates.[18]

Another electoral contest in which targeted electoral mobilization efforts played a major role in determining an electoral outcome in 1998 was the reelection bid of Maryland's Democratic Governor Parris J. Glendening. The elected county executives (both Democrats) of two of the five largest local jurisdictions in the state (Prince George's County and Baltimore City) were accused of providing only minimal help to Glendening's campaign. In contrast, other Democratic Party leaders in Prince George's County and in Montgomery County led the mobilization effort in their counties. County Executive Douglas Duncan helped mobilized labor union members, civic associations, and environmental activists in Montgomery County, a populous suburb of Washington. In neighboring Prince George's County, Representative Albert Wynn (4th Congressional District, D-MD) played a major role in stimulating leaders of community organizations to mobilize local groups and especially African-American voters. That mobilization effort helped activate the African-American communities in Prince Georges' County, while a similar effort led by nonparty groups mobilized African-American voters in Baltimore City. These efforts were also fueled by the Glendening campaign's portrayal of Republican gubernatorial candidate Ellen Sauerbrey as insensitive to minority interests. Her vote as a member of the Maryland state legislature against a civil rights bill received heavy emphasis in Glendening's campaign. These efforts were successful, increasing the African-American share of Maryland's turnout from 12 percent in 1994 to 19 percent in 1998.

In 1998 labor unions also increased their efforts to mobilize their members. While in 1996 labor's strategy emphasized television ad campaigns, in 1998 the unions reverted to more traditional mobilization methods, handing out campaign flyers at factory gates, using phone banks to contact union members, and even walking precincts in highly unionized areas. "Our focus was on one-to-one contact with union members and family members . . . reaching back to our roots to make this the year of the worksite and the doorstep and the telephone," stated AFL-CIO President John Sweeney.[19] An estimated 46 percent of union members voted, compared with 36 percent of the voting age population. According to exit polls conducted by Voter News Service, 70 percent of union voters cast their ballots for Democratic candidates, with union members constituting about one-quarter of the electorate in 1998. The union effort at voter mobilization is credited with contributing significantly to the success of Democratic candidates in several states, including California, Kansas, Iowa, Nevada, North Carolina, and Washington. Unions also assisted in mobilizing minority voters in areas such as parts of the South where union membership is low.

Individual-Level Analysis of the Effectiveness of Political Mobilization Efforts

To this point the evidence presented for the effectiveness of voter mobilization campaigns is based on evidence provided by campaign activities and aggregate data. The effectiveness of political mobilization drives can also be assessed using individual-level data from surveys. The American National Election Studies surveys conducted after the 1996 and 1998 elections enable assessment at the individual level of the effects of mobilization efforts.

In both 1996 and 1998, those interviewed by the American National Election studies were asked if they had been contacted either by anyone from one of the political parties[20] or by someone other than a representative of the two major parties.[21] They were also asked if they had been urged to vote in a particular way by any groups concerned with moral or religious issues or by the clergy or other church leaders at their place of worship, and if information about candidates, parties, or political issues had been made available in their place of worship.[22] To what extent did citizens report such contacts? Did those contacts reach individuals who had not voted in the previous election? How effective were those efforts at political mobilization?

Substantial differences exist in the extent of perceived contacting by different types of mobilizers. In 1996, 29 percent, and in 1998, 28 percent were contacted by political party operatives, while only 11 percent in 1996 and 10 percent in 1998 reported being contacted by any other group (Table 3.3). Contacts by party campaign operatives and by others do stimulate increased levels of turnout. Individuals reporting political party contacts had turnout rates 20 percent higher in 1996 and almost 30 percent higher in 1998 than those not contacted by the parties' campaigns. Persons who reported contacts by other

TABLE 3.3
Voter Turnout and Contacting by Party and Other Political Organizations, 1996 and 1998

	1996		1998	
	Yes (%)	No (%)	Yes (%)	No (%)
Contacted by political party about the campaign	29	71	28	72
Voted	91	71	73	44
	$X^2 = 68.004$, p<0.001, $tau_b = 0.212$		$X^2 = 86.193$, p<0.001, $tau_b = 0.260$	
Contacted by others about supporting particular candidates	11	89	10	90
Voted	88	76	72	50
	$X^2 = 12.324$, p<0.001, $tau_b = 0.113$		$X^2 = 22.302$, p<0.001, $tau_b = 0.132$	

Sources: 1996 and 1998 American National Election Studies.

groups voted at a 12 percent higher rate in 1996 and at a 22 percent higher rate in 1998 than did those who did not experience such contacts.

Certainly groups other than political parties or candidate organizations sought to mobilize their supporters to vote for the candidates and issues preferred by the group's leaders (see Table 3.4). One example in 1996 was the effort made by representatives of religious and moral issue groups. Twelve percent of those surveyed in 1996 reported they were contacted by a religious or moral issue group, compared with 9 percent in 1998.[23] Voting turnout was 17 percent higher in 1996 and 23 percent higher in 1998 among those contacted by a religious or moral issue group than among those who were not. In contrast, being urged to vote by a member of the clergy produced only a 7 percent higher rate of turnout in 1996 but a 17 percent higher voting participation level in 1998. Of those who attend religious services, 11 percent reported that information about a party, candidate, or issue was available at their place of worship in 1996, and they had a 15 percent higher turnout rate than individuals who did not have access to political information at that source. In 1998, 12 percent reported such information was available, and turnout was 14 percent greater among that group than among those who did not have such information available at their place of worship.

Efficient campaigns seek to maximize voter turnout among those who will be most supportive of their candidates. One method is to contact individuals who have a history of turning out to vote in primary or general elections. For example, in 1996, 89 percent of those who reported being contacted by groups other than congressional or political party campaigns reported that they had voted in the 1992 general election. Similarly, 90 percent of those contacted by party or candidate campaigns in 1996 indicated that they had voted in 1992. In 1998, 85 percent of those contacted by party or candidate organizations and 84 percent

TABLE 3.4.
Voter Turnout and Political Mobilization Activities, Moral or Religious Groups, 1996 and 1998

	1996		1998a	
	Yes (%)	No (%)	Yes (%)	No (%)
Contacted by moral or religious group	12	88	9	91
Voted	92	75	73	50
	$X^2 = 30.894$, p>0.001, $tau_b = 0.142$		$X^2 = 21.683$, p<0.001, $tau_b = 0.130$	
Clergy or church leaders at your place of worship encouraged voting for a particular candidate	4	96	4	96
Voted	84	77	70	53
	$X^2 = 2.032$, NS		$X^2 = 5.328$, p = 0.015, $tau_b = 0.071$	
Information about candidates, parties, or political issues made available in your place of worship before the election	11	89	12	88
Voted	90	75	67	53
	$X^2 = 19.388$, p<0.01, $tau_b = 0.113$		$X^2 = 10.592$, p<0.001, $tau_b = 0.100$	

Source: 1996 and 1998 American National Election Studies.

contacted by other organizations reported that they had voted in 1996. The differences suggest that in 1998 mobilizing agents were making a greater effort to reach beyond habitual voters in their efforts to stimulate voting turnout.

One explanation for patterns of political participation is that those who are more socially rooted in a community are more likely to participate in politics. Thus, those who have lived longer in a community and longer in a particular residence would be expected to be more involved in the community. That involvement would include higher rates of turnout in elections, and indeed in both 1996 and 1998, those who had lived in the community for five years or more were slightly more likely to vote. Those who had lived in their current residence for five years or longer were also more likely to vote than those who had lived in their residence for less than five years.

Another indicator of community involvement is participation in groups within the community. Our measure of community involvement is the number of different types of community groups in which the individual is a member. In 1996, those who were members of more different types of community groups were more likely to participate.[24]

Although in simple bivariate comparisons some of the measures of political mobilization are significant, what happens when they are included in analyses with a number of variables known to be related to voting turnout? Do they remain significant? Tables 3.5 and 3.6 report the results of logistic regression equations in which the five measures of political mobilization are included along with a number of other predictor variables. These tables report, from a much larger number of variables,[25] the coefficients for those variables that are significant in either 1996 or 1998 as well as the five political mobilization measures.[26] Indicators of resources incorporated into the analyses are age (a measure of life experiences), income, and education. The measure of political engagement consists of a survey item that assesses whether the respondent cared about who wins the election. To control for the political mobilization efforts of labor unions, the analysis contains a measure of whether anyone in the household is a member of a labor union. Because voting tends to be habitual for many of those who vote, also included in the equations is reported voting turnout in the prior presidential election. Those with stronger ties to the political parties expected to be more likely to vote. Therefore, three categoric variables were created from the strength of party identification. The base against which they are compared is strong party identifiers—hence the negative sign for the coefficients reported.

In Table 3.5, which reports the results of the logistic regression for 1996, age, education, caring about who wins the presidential election, voting in the prior presidential election (1992), and the categories of strength of party identification are all significant, while income and being in a household with a union member are not. The crucial question of interest is, are the measures of political mobilization significant? Of the five measures of mobilization, only two—being contacted by a party organization and by a religious or moral group—have a significant impact on turnout.

Were the same patterns present in 1998? Table 3.6 shows that age, education, income, caring about who wins the House elections, the categories of the strength of party identification, membership in a union household, and reported voter turnout in 1996 are significant in accounting for voting turnout in 1998. As in 1996, two of the five mobilization measures are significant, and again those are being contacted by representatives of a political party and being contacted by a religious or moral group.

That being a member of a union household is significant in 1998 but not in 1996 may reflect the change in union mobilization tactics in 1998. While in 1996 labor unions relied more on the use of the mass media, such as television ads, to deliver mobilization messages, in 1998 the unions switched to much greater reliance on personal contacts with union members and union households.

Changing Legal Requirements for Registration and Voting

The goal of increasing turnout resulted in major changes in voter registration and election administration processes during the 1990s. These were accomplished in part through the passage and implementation of the National Voter Registration Act of 1993 (frequently referred to as the "motor voter" law) to make voter registration easier. How effective has this law been in increasing voter registration and, more important, in increasing voter turnout? Another

TABLE 3.5
Logistic Regression Voter Turnout in the 1996 Presidential Election

	B	Standard error	Wald	Significance	R	Exp (B)
Age	0.0165	0.0055	8.8224	0.0030	0.0681	1.0166
Education	0.2478	0.0657	14.2073	0.0002	0.0912	1.2812
Income	0.0274	0.0155	3.1507	0.0759	0.0280	1.0278
Union household	-.0401	0.0593	0.4583	0.4984	0.0000	0.9607
Care who wins	-0.9276	0.1927	23.1795	0.0000	-0.1201	0.3955
Strength of party identification[a]			24.719	0.0000	0.1131	
Independent	-1.6857	0.3417	24.3349	0.0000	-0.1233	0.1853
Leaning to one party	-0.7099	0.2602	7.4436	0.0064	-0.0609	0.4917
Weak party identifier	-0.7408	0.2399	9.5333	0.0020	-0.0716	0.4767
Voted in 1992	2.4648	0.1913	165.9844	0.0000	0.3341	11.7608
Contacted by party or candidate	0.5389	0.2300	5.4904	0.0191	0.0487	1.7141
Contacted by other group	0.2123	0.3468	0.3747	0.5404	0.0000	1.2365
Contacted by moral or religious group	1.5758	0.3787	17.3178	0.0000	0.1021	4.8346
Candidate choice urged by clergy	-0.8890	0.4844	3.3682	0.0665	-0.0305	0.4111
Voter information available at place of worship	0.5158	0.3436	2.2542	0.1333	0.0132	1.6751
Constant	-3.2960	0.5920	30.9925	0.0000		

[a]The base category to which these are being compared is strong party identifier.

$-2 \times$ Log Likelihood = 905.952; Goodness of Fit = 1217.200; Percentage Classified Correctly = 86.61; Cox and Snell R^2 = 0.337; Nagelkerke R^2 = 0.513; N of Cases = 1369.

TABLE 3.6
Logistic Regression Voter Turnout in 1998 Midterm Election

	B	Standard error	Wald	Significance	R	Exp (B)
Age	0.0316	0.0053	35.9923	0.0000	0.1570	1.0321
Education	0.1755	0.0595	8.7108	0.0032	0.0698	1.1919
Income	0.0272	0.0131	4.3173	0.0377	0.0410	1.0275
Union household	0.5623	0.2264	6.1662	0.0130	0.0550	1.7547
Care who wins	0.9312	0.1691	30.3259	0.0000	0.1433	2.5376
Strength of party identification[a]			24.0188	0.0000	0.1143	
Independent	−0.9466	0.3128	9.1580	0.0025	−0.0720	0.3881
Leaning to one party	−1.0468	0.2351	19.8334	0.0000	−0.1137	0.3510
Weak party identifier	−0.8251	0.2116	15.1988	0.0001	−0.0978	0.4382
Voted in 1996	1.9866	0.2139	86.2683	0.0000	0.2472	7.2907
Contacted by party or candidate	0.5316	0.1961	7.3494	0.0067	0.0623	1.7017
Contacted by other group	0.4768	0.2948	2.6146	0.1059	0.0211	1.6109
Contacted by moral or religious group	0.9156	0.3284	7.7718	0.0053	0.0647	2.4982
Candidate choice urged by clergy	−0.0328	0.4610	0.0051	0.9433	0.0000	0.9677
Voter information available at place of worship	0.4993	0.2875	3.0164	0.0824	0.0271	1.6476
Constant	−4.0317	0.4206	91.8792	0.0000		

[a]The base category to which these are being compared is strong party identifier.

− 2 × Log Likelihood = 903.659; Goodness of Fit = 1035.996; Percentage Classified Correctly = 78.70; Cox and Snell R^2 = 0.378; Nagelkerke R^2 = 0.506; N of Cases = 1,000.

step in the attempt to increase turnout has been to make absentee voting easier. What have been the consequences of these efforts to reduce the costs and increase the convenience of registering and voting?

One estimate is that an increase of 1 million registered voters per year can be attributed to the existence of the more accessible voter registration procedures in the states. By 1998, an estimated 5 million additional voters had registered through "motor voter" procedures.[27] However, turnout did not increase in most states. One expert on voting participation estimated that it increased in eleven states and decreased in thirty-seven. Where contests or issues were important to the electorate, participation increased.[28] The increased levels of voter registration create an environment where effective political mobilization could have a significant impact on electoral outcomes.

Several studies compare turnout in states where easier registration procedures were available before the passage of the National Voter Registration Act of 1993 with turnout in states that did not have such accessible registration processes. The studies generally conclude that turnout is higher in those states with easier ballot access laws.[29] Parties' political mobilization efforts are also more successful in states where liberal absentee voter eligibility exists. The parties' efforts through sending out absentee ballot applications significantly increases turnout in states with more liberal laws. Rates of absentee voting were 10 percent higher in those states, with total turnout 2 percent higher.[30]

The Changing Composition of the American Electorate

The changing composition of the American electorate presents substantial opportunities for political mobilization. One element of this change is the shift in racial and ethnic composition. Between 1990 and 1998, the voting age black population increased by 13.7 percent, voting age Hispanics increased by 34.2 percent, while the voting age white population increased by 6.3 percent.[31]

Changes in eligibility for citizenship enacted in the Immigration Reform and Control Act of 1986 significantly increased the proportion of noncitizen Latino and Asian American residents who became citizens during the 1990s. The 1986 law permitted individuals who had entered the United States illegally to seek legal alien status if they could prove residence in the United States since before January 1, 1982. Those persons became eligible for citizenship in 1993. The 1986 law created sanctions against employers who knowingly hire illegal aliens. A 1996 law ended the eligibility of permanent resident aliens for most federal social welfare programs. Certainly these provisions of immigration laws provided a powerful incentive for both illegal immigrants and resident aliens to become citizens.[32] One of the consequences was a surge in new citizens in several states, and new citizens tend to have higher levels of turnout.[33] This in part also accounts for higher turnout among Latino voters in California and other states with increased levels of citizenship among Latinos. For example, Hispanic voter registration in California increased from 600,000 in 1994 to 2 million in 1998.[34]

Significant shifts also occurred in the age composition of the electorate. Since 1996, the greatest increase has occurred in the 45-to-64 age group, which grew by 7 percent. However, the largest age group in the electorate remains the 25- to 44-year-olds, who in 1998 constituted 41 percent of the voting age population.[35] These two generations are less likely to have a strong party identification. Together with the under-25 age group, they are, therefore, less likely to be motivated to vote by a commitment to a party and its candidates, and they represent a challenge to political mobilization activities by political parties, candidate organizations, and other mobilizing agents. However, given the low rates of turnout nationally among both younger voters and Hispanic voters, significant opportunities for effective political mobilization drives to increase turnout remain.

Conclusions

Both the examination of mobilization activities in specific electoral contests and analysis of individual-level turnout patterns in 1996 and 1998 provide strong support for the conclusion that political mobilization efforts matter. Targeted get-out-the-vote campaigns can have a significant impact on both who votes and electoral outcomes. Given the low levels of turnout in the United States, multiple opportunities exist for effective political mobilization drives. The evidence from 1996 and 1998 suggests that these campaigns are most effective when substantial resources are employed to communicate the consequences of the electoral outcome for a group's issue interests.

Notes

1. M. Margaret Conway, *Political Participation in the United States*, 3d ed. (Washington, DC: CQ Press, 2000), Table 1–2.
2. See the review of that research in Thomas M. Holbrook, *Do Campaigns Matter?* (Thousand Oaks, CA: Sage, 1996), pp. 5–12.
3. Holbrook, op. cit., pp. 12–17.
4. Steven J. Rosenstone and John Mark Hansen, *Mobilization, Participation, and Democracy in America* (New York: Macmillan, 1993). For a discussion of differences in perceived campaign effects between scholars and political practitioner, see Marni Ezra and Candice J. Nelson, "Do Campaigns Matter?" in James A. Thurber and Candice J. Nelson (eds.), *Campaigns and Elections American Style* (Boulder, CO: Westview Press, 1995).
5. Ruy Teixeira, *The Disappearing American Voter* (Washington: Brookings Institution, 1992); Raymond Wolfinger and Stephen J. Rosenstone, *Who Votes?* (New Haven, CT: Yale University Press, 1980).
6. Warren E. Miller and J. Merrill Shanks. *The New American Voter* (Cambridge, MA: Harvard University Press, 1996); Linda L.M. Bennett and Stephen E. Bennett, "Changing Views about Gender Equality in Politics: Gradual Change and Lingering Doubts," in Lois Duke Whitaker (ed.), *Women in Politics Outsiders or Insiders?* 3d ed. (Upper Saddle River, NJ: Prentice Hall, 1999); Diana Owen, "Mixed Signals: Generation X's Attitudes toward the Political System," in Stephen C.

Craig and Stephen E. Bennett (eds.), *After the Boom: The Politics of Generation X* (Lanham, MD: Rowman and Littlefield, 1997).

7. Rosenstone and Hansen, op. cit.; Sidney Verba, Kay Lehman Schlozman, and Henry E. Brady. *Voice and Equality* (Cambridge, MA: Harvard University Press, 1995).

8. Wolfinger and Rosenstone, op. cit.; Verba, Schlozman, and Brady, op. cit.; Benjamin Heighton, "Easy Registration and Voter Turnout," *Journal of Politics* 59 (May 1997): 565–66; Frances Fox Piven and Richard A. Cloward, "Northern Bourbons: A preliminary report on the National Voter Registration Act," *PS: Political Science and Politics* 29 (March 1996): 39–42.

9. Tom Baxter, "Turnout by Black Voters Key to Victory," *Atlanta Constitution*, 5 Nov. 1998, 1A.

10. Ibid.

11. "Turnout Patterns Boost Democrats," *Notes from Emily*, Emily's List, Washington, DC, December 1998, p. 6.

12. Terry Neal and Richard Morin, "For Voters It's Back to the Middle," *Washington Post*, 5 Nov. 1998, final edition, A33.

13. "Turnout Patterns Boost Democrats," *Notes from Emily*, op. cit.

14. "Latino Voters Make the Difference in Historic California Election: The 'Sleeping Giant' Has Awoken—California Latino Voters Provide Essential Margin of Victory in Governor's Race, Prop.5," *PR Newswire*, 4 Nov. 1998.

15. Maria Puente, "Hispanics Prove Pivotal," *USA Today*, 4 Nov. 1998, p. 4A; Carl Marinucci, Tyra Lucile Mead, and *Chronicle* staff writers, "Year of the Latino," *San Francisco Chronicle*, 5 Nov. 1998, A24.

16. Sen. Robert Ford, "Blacks Deserve Recognition for Winning Election for Hodges," *Charleston Post and Courier*, 20 Nov. 1998, A23.

17. Nationally, the Democratic Party spent $30 million in 1998 in targeted political mobilization campaigns.

18. "Turnout Patterns Boost Democrats," *Notes from Emily*, Emily's List, Washington, DC, December 1998, p. 6; Richard Benedetto, "Turncoats in Key Groups Lead Democratic Rebound White Males Part of Switch from 1994," *USA Today*, 5 Nov. 1998, final edition, 4A.

19. Quoted in Alissa Rubin, "This Time, Unions Mobilize the Troops," *Los Angeles Times*, 7 Nov. 1998, home edition, A22.

20. 1996, Variable 961162; 1998, Variable 980349.

21. 1996, Variable 961164; 1998, Variable 980351.

22. 1996, Variables 961175, 961177, and 961176; 1998, Variables 980355, 980356, and 980357.

23. One concern is that individuals would include contacting by moral or religious groups in their responses to the item asking if they had been contacted by a group other than a political party. However, in 1996 only 20 percent and in 1998 only 12 percent of the respondents reported being contacted both by nonparty groups and by moral or religious groups. The weighted n's from the cross tabulations are as follows:

    1996: Contacted by other groups = 166.
          Contacted by moral or religious groups = 199.

    1998: Contacted by other groups = 128.
          Contacted by moral or religious groups = 117.

24. Five measures of community group involvement are included in the survey instrument. Each item was asked about twenty-two different types of groups. The number of responses was then summarized for each type of item. Those summary measures were highly correlated. Therefore, only one measure, the number of different

types of community groups in which the survey respondents were members, is used in this analysis. Equivalent measures of group involvement are not available in the 1998 American National Election Studies data set.

25. Other variables included in the initial logistic regression equations but dropped from the reduced equations because of their lack of significance were age squared, political efficacy, marital status, length of residence in the community, length of residence in the current domicile, home ownership, race, and sex.

26. Logistic regression estimates the probability of an event's occurring, in this case the probability of voting in an election. The estimated coefficients for each variable are under column heading B. For large samples, the test of whether or not a coefficient is zero can be based on the Wald statistic. The significance column reports the statistical significance of the Wald coefficient. The test used here is that the Wald statistic has a probability of .05 or less. Several statistics can be used to evaluate the goodness of fit of the model. These include the percentage of respondents whose behavior (voting or not voting) is predicted correctly, the $-12 \times \log$ likelihood value (the smaller the better the fit of the model), the goodness of fit statistic, and the two pseudo R squared coefficient.

27. B. Drummond Ayres, Jr. "Law to Ease Voter Registration Has Added 5 Million to the Rolls; But Ultimate Success Hinges on Actual Turnout," *New York Times*, 3 Sept. 1995, 1.

28. These estimates by Curtis Gans of the Center for the Study of the American Electorate were reported by CNN at http://CNN.com/AllPolitics/stories/1998/11/05/turnout.ap/.

29. See James D. King, "Political Culture, Registration Laws, and Voter Turnout among the American States," *Publius* 24 (fall 1994): 115–28; J. Eric Oliver, "The Effects of Eligibility Restrictions and Party Activity on Absentee Voting and Overall Turnout," *American Journal of Political Science* 40 (May 1996): 498–513; Staci Rhine, "An Analysis of the Impact of Registration Factors on Turnout in 1992," *Political Behavior* 18 (June 1996): 171–85; Raymond Wolfinger and Stephen Rosenstone, *Who Votes?* (New Haven, CT: Yale University Press, 1980); Jonathan Nagler, "The Effects of Registration Laws and Education on U.S. Voter Turnout," *American Political Science Review* 845 (December 1991): 1393–1405.

30. See Oliver, op. cit.

31. U.S. Bureau of the Census. "Projections of the Voting-Age Population for States: November 1998," *Current Population Reports*, Series P25-1132, April 1998, Table A, p. 2.

32. For a discussion of immigration and naturalization laws, see Louis DeSipio and Rodolfo O. de la Garza, *Making Americans, Remaking America* (Boulder, CO: Westview Press, 1998).

33. Lorreta E. Bass and Lynn M. Casper, "Are There Differences in Registration and Voting Behavior between Naturalized and Native Born Americans?" Population Division Working Paper No. 28, Feb. 1999, U.S. Bureau of the Census; Pei-te Lien, *The Political Participation of Asian-Americans* (New York: Garland Press, 1997).

34. Miguel Perez, "Courting Latinos," *Bergen (County, N.J.) Record*, 6 Nov. 1998, L11.

35. See U.S. Bureau of the Census, "Projections of the Voting Age Population for States: November 1998," *Current Population Reports*, Series P25-1132, Figure 1.

4

Public Support for the Party System in the United States

DIANA OWEN, JACK DENNIS, AND CASEY A. KLOFSTAD

Introduction

Democratic regimes as we define them today are complex objects. Each, somewhat uniquely, takes its own path through a rich variety of potential principles, themes, procedures, institutions, and practices that may, only in the main, reinforce each other. As Robert Dahl and other major theorists remind us, these themes and principles of democracy have emerged through a long evolutionary process, in which the possible contradictions among them, such as between liberty and equality, direct and indirect democracy, or majority rule and minority rights, often remain as both theoretical and practical issues (Dahl 2000; also see Sartori 1987). Thus today, we often envision a host of variants upon the basic themes of democracy—libertarian, or classically liberal democracy versus more egalitarian forms such as social democracy; plebiscitary, populist or direct democracy versus republican, indirect or representative democracy; or pluralist versus elitist democracy.

The theme of representative democracy attempts to bring together a variety of these potentially competing emphases of democratic thought and practice. Madison, Mill, Dahl, and others have argued that some form of indirect, or republican, democracy is likely to be the main solution to the problem of keeping a democracy workable and thus in business over the long haul in complex, large-scale societies. What somehow must be maximized in the making, working, and maintaining of democracies, in the face of changing conditions, is the capacity of the general public to take control of their government, and thus of major decisions that affect their lives, while at the same time allocating most of the day-to-day conduct of government to their freely chosen and recallable representatives.

The balance that gets struck in the United States is thus between getting most citizens involved effectively in choices of leadership and policy and still giving enough freedom of action to those so chosen that they are able to be effective. Somewhere along the representation continuum from "mandate to independence" (Pitkin 1978), between "delegate versus trustee roles" (Wahlke et al.1962), between radical and aristocratic versions of republicanism (Dahl 1986), or between "agency" and "division of labor" models of representative government (King 1997; also see Rosenthal 1997), a practical and widely acceptable equilibrium has to be found if democracy is to remain legitimate.

When we think about the problem of establishing and maintaining a workable vision of representative democracy in the United States, we have a lot of experience to draw upon, not all of which is positive. We have tried to infuse some representative spirit and control into many parts of our political system, including the judiciary and the civilian and military bureaucracies where the system emphasis is more upon executive and legislative officers, and upon less formal aspects of the political system, such as the political parties, the interest groups, and the mass media.

Since the early part of the nineteenth century, political parties have been the centerpiece institution on the side of the less constitutionally established aspects of democratic representation. The parties perform a variety of essential representative functions (Sorauf 1976). Perhaps the most central function is the meaningful linkage of average citizens to those who make public policy within the formal institutions of government. Burnham (1970) has argued, for example, that the parties are the only effective devices that are able to generate countervailing collective power on behalf of the many individually powerless against the few who are individually or organizationally powerful. Some students of the American parties, such as Schattschneider, have indeed argued that democracy is impossible without competing parties. Schattschneider forcefully observed that "modern democracy is unthinkable save in terms of parties," and "the condition of the parties is the best possible evidence of the nature of any regime" (1942; quoted in White and Mileur 1992, p. 167).

Our Inquiry

Our empirical task in the present inquiry follows from these broader theoretical considerations. Though democracy may remain strong in the United States, there is a real question about the trends that apply to representative democracy, particularly if its central institutions include legislative bodies, party organizations, and interest groups. All of the latter have come under significant public and elite criticism in recent years and may have begun to suffer a loss of legitimacy.

Our focus here is more specifically upon the changing condition of the political parties, at least at one level. We may assume, as have a number of students of democracy and of political parties (but not all—see Epstein 1967; and King 1969), such as Ranney and Kendall (1956), that the parties are crucial and central to the task of linking citizens, especially voters, to government, and thus providing them with effective representation by structuring meaningful alternatives of leadership and policy. Around these central linkage roles radiate several other important functions of the parties: recruitment, socialization, selection, and electioneering support of candidates; articulation, aggregation, and preprocessing of citizens' political demands (Easton 1965; Beck 1997); and providing greater coherence, responsibility, responsiveness, and programmatic direction among officeholders and groups operating under the same partisan framework. In short, parties provide an essential structuring principle that helps everyone—masses, activists, and elites—make common sense of a political process that without them might otherwise degenerate into collective, or at least highly cleaved, chaos. If American parties fail in some fundamental sense, we must ask whether American representative democracy more generally is likely to be threatened.

Are the Parties Failing?

What we need to recognize at the outset of our empirical inquiry is that institutions, such as the parties, because of their long-standing status and complex set of interwoven connections into the fabric of government, will necessarily command important resources to bolster their persistence. It is likely that by the end of the twentieth century the two-major-party system may exhibit areas of strength and resilience in certain respects, yet be subject to decline, or even failure, in others. For example, in terms of a robust organizational life and the ability to provide services for lower-level party candidates, both the Democratic and Republican national party organizations have been on the upswing over the past few decades. With an expanded capacity to extract financial contributions from individuals, PACs, and others, such as in the increased flow of party-directed "soft money," the party organizations in some respects seem to be as healthy as they have been at any time since the 1960s, and perhaps even since the "Party Period" (McCormick 1986; Chambers and Burnham 1967; Hofstadter 1955) that preceded the rise of antiparty Progressivism earlier in the twentieth century.

At another level, in terms of the "party in government," there are few signs that partisanship as a principle of organization, agenda-setting, debate, and policy choices has subsided. The "partisan aspects" of government, especially in the executive and legislative branches, suggest that the parties are alive and well. The Clinton impeachment process, for example, strongly reinforces the impression that partisanship within the central policymaking branches of American national government has not subsided. From the standpoint of the average person, partisanship of the present era among elites has become only more highly divisive and intransigent rather than more representative or effective in government. The trend in legislative bodies has been toward more strictly party-line voting, and thus toward clearer rather than less distinct lines of difference between the two major parties.

The question that arises, when we step beyond the partisan behavior of activists and legislative elites to what is often termed "parties in the electorate"

(Sorauf 1976), is whether such robustness of party in activist and elite politics is equally evident to the average citizen. We know already from very extensive and continuing time-series evidence, such as that provided by the American National Election Studies (NES), that political party identification, relative to the two major parties, gradually weakened from the 1960s to the 1990s. With this decline in party identification have come both greater overt independence and more volatile voting patterns. These effects seem to be part of a long-term, not yet reversed, secular trend. How can it be that at the same time the two major parties are exhibiting renewed organizational strength and policy commitment, partisan identification has not recovered? This appears also to be the case with popular images of each of the two major parties. Are there some discoverable reasons why the average person is less caught up in the "life of the parties" today than was formerly the case? Indeed, are we able to dig beneath these more surface-level attitudes toward the two major parties, to see what deeper cultural factors might serve as the underpinnings for such increasing partisan alienation?

We suspect that a shift in the political culture that pertains to the party system has been underway for some time, operating at several levels. This shift, which seems to apply in a variety of postindustrial societies, is complex and not yet fully understood. Traditional formal institutions of representation, such as legislatures, and less formally constituted institutions, such as parties, apparently have become the main objects of declining popular support and legitimacy. "When parties fail" (Lawson and Merkl 1988), the average person is likely to turn to alternative means of getting her or his public policy demands represented. These kinds of broad shifts of experience and sentiment may go well beyond the restricted phenomenon of "realignment" between the two existing major parties, and proceed apace despite the efforts of party leaders to enhance the professionalization, staffing, financing, facilities, or services of the major party organizations. The drift toward delegitimation may nonetheless be strongly in evidence in "the party in the electorate" (Beck and Sorauf 1976).

The Present Study

The reasons behind the apparent long-term decay of public approval of the role and status of the parties are not as yet fully known. We face a major problem in accounting for the major dimensions, causes, and possible consequences of this phenomenon for representative democracy. The objective of the present essay is to examine the nature of support or lack of support for the parties at several levels. We are particularly concerned with public perceptions of how well the parties are performing their representative functions, and citizens' views concerning whether the parties should be maintained as a central institution in the process of representative democracy. Additionally, we evaluate how individual-level identification with or disaffection from political parties relates to broader feelings about parties.

We build upon and expand our previous examinations of these issues. We have examined several dimensions of partisan disaffection from the perspective of antipartyism (Dennis and Owen 1997). Here we attempt to specify these dimensions of public attitudes toward parties in greater detail. In addition, we seek to uncover more clearly some main sources of these sentiments, particularly in relation to political, economic, demographic, and mass media factors.

In this study, we identify three broad categories of citizens' attitudes toward the party system. One simple distinction we make follows roughly from what Easton (1965, 1975) characterized as "diffuse" versus "specific" support. The part of that distinction that we use here has to do with supporting a political object for its own sake, versus supporting it because of its performance. While these two aspects of support are no doubt reciprocally connected over the longer term, in the short term they may be quite disconnected. One suspects, over the long haul, that people's experience with the performance of the party system will feed back upon their vision of the role that parties ought to have, and vice versa. When investigating attitudes toward the party system, it is necessary to provide measures of both "diffuse" and "specific" support. In addition, political parties historically have been associated with various types of reform. Currently, calls for reform in areas such as campaign finance frequently have strong connections to political parties. Thus, our third general attitudinal dimension is associated with party reform.

The Data

The evidence for this study comes from a national probability telephone survey of 566 adults conducted during the three summer months of 1997. The data were collected by the University of Wisconsin Survey Center as part of its continuous, computer-assisted National Omnibus Study of adults in the forty-eight continuous states. The WISCON Survey's true response rate for this complex sampling design is approximately 50 percent.

Two of the present authors (Klofstad and Dennis) developed a series of questions pertaining to citizens' attitudes toward political parties and the party system that expanded upon our earlier work, which we were able to include on the WISCON Survey. Some of these questions, or variants of them, previously appeared in the 1980 National Election Study (NES), the 1993 NES Pilot Study, the NES 1994 Congressional Election Study, and the 1996 NES. In addition, several new questions were devised for the WISCON Survey with the goal of developing more refined measures of party system attitudes, which we present below.[1]

The WISCON Survey also contained a variety of other political variables, including measures of party identification, political ideology, institutional support, and mass media attitude items. Though the WISCON Survey does not provide as wide a range of political variables as the NES, we are better able to approach our task of giving a more refined account of the public's attitudes toward the party system using these questions than is possible with the NES questions. To explore some basic trends in citizens' attitudes toward political parties, we employ NES data from 1993, 1994, 1996, and 1998. Our analysis is limited, however, by the availability of questions asked over time and changes in question wording.

Dimensions of Party System Attitudes

In an effort to explore more fully the dimensions of citizen attitudes toward the party system, we began by analyzing a group of twelve variables included on the WISCON Survey. Our first step was to perform an exploratory factor analysis. Five dimensions emerged initially, which we labeled antiparty sentiments, party system support, party performance evaluations, party cues, and party reform. (Results of the exploratory factor analysis are in the Appendix and Table 4.7.) Antiparty sentiments and party system support fall into our general categorization of "diffuse support." Party performance evaluations and party cues are indicators of "specific support." A confirmatory factor analysis performed using AMOS revealed that our indicators of party reform split into two fairly distinct dimensions—one that advocates reform by strengthening the existing party structure and another that calls for the growth of third parties.

In addition, we identified a separate partisan independence dimension of party system attitudes. As we will discuss below, independence is used as both a dependent and an independent variable in our analysis. Thus, we did not include it in our exploratory factor analysis. (The Appendix contains a complete listing of the variables used in this analysis, a description of the indexes that we constructed, and their scale reliabilities. The results of the confirmatory factor analysis describing the relationship of the observed variables to the underlying dimensional constructs are presented in Table 4.1.)

Diffuse Support

Antiparty Sentiment   Antipartyism constitutes the most negative set of attitudes toward the existing political party system. Antiparty sentiments go beyond mere indifference to outright rejection of the two major parties. These hostile attitudes are epitomized by the belief that political parties are no longer needed, and that the political system would be better off without parties.[2]

We use three items to tap antiparty sentiments. Respondents were asked if political parties are needed in America anymore, if parties are necessary to make the political system work, and if it would be better if there were no party labels on the ballot in elections. The variables are scored so that a high value indicates the antiparty response. As our confirmatory factor analysis demonstrates, these items are rather strongly related to the underlying antipartyism construct, especially the marker variable, parties are no longer needed. The scale reliability (alpha = 0.71) also indicates a good fit.

Party System Support   The party system support dimension is the antithesis of antipartyism. Supporters identify with political parties, believe that the party system works well, and feel that it should be maintained.

TABLE 4.1
Confirmatory Factor Analysis (AMOS) in Party-System Attitudes

	Standardized Regression Weights	Unstandardized Regression Weights	S.E.
Antiparty Sentiments	0.807	1.144	0.093
No parties	0.583	0.489	0.044
Parties necessary	0.695	1.000	
Support			
Party supporter	0.600	1.109	0.120
Parties serve well	0.585	1.000	
Performance			
Parties care	0.444	0.639	0.086
Party job rating	0.651	1.480	0.163
Parties—gov't attn.	0.607	1.000	
Party Cues			
Disregard parties	0.347	0.872	0.213
Parties confuse	0.464	1.000	
Strengthen Parties	0.448	1.000	
Third Parties	0.890	1.000	
Independence			
Strength ind.	0.645	0.594	0.100
Folded PID	0.410	1.000	

Note: Coefficients are maximum likelihood estimates.

The WISCON Survey contains two questions that measure party system support. The first item asks respondents if it is better to be a firm party supporter than to be a political independent. The second measures whether or not citizens believe that the existing two-party system serves the country well. These items are scored so that a high value indicates support for the party system. Confirmatory factor analysis and scale reliability analysis (alpha = 0.52) demonstrate that these variables do a relatively good job of representing the party support construct, although the internal consistency is not as high as for the antiparty sentiment dimension.

Specific Support

Party Performance Evaluations   Another way in which citizens view parties is in terms of their performance. The party performance attitudinal dimension indicates how good a job people perceive the two major political parties are doing in general, and how successful citizens feel parties are in representing them in political affairs.

The WISCON Survey included three questions that together provide people's party performance evaluations. The first had respondents rate the job that the Democrats and Republicans are doing. Another tapped whether or not they feel that political parties care what ordinary people think. The final item asked if the political parties make the government pay attention to what the people think. These questions tap part of what Easton termed specific support, in that one's evaluations are tied directly to perceived outputs, benefits, or performance. A high score on these questions indicates a negative rating of the parties' performance. The results of the confirmatory factor analysis corroborate our decision to treat these three items as indicators of party system performance. The question about whether the parties care about ordinary people is the least strongly related to the underlying construct. The scale reliability is moderately strong (alpha = 0.57).

Party Cues   Traditionally, American political parties have served as central cue givers for citizens, providing guidance and a short-cut method for decision making about candidates and issues. Cue giving has been an important feature of the parties' performance of intermediary or linkage functions (Campbell et al. 1960). This attitudinal dimension indicates the degree to which individuals perceive that the parties are useful in this cue-giving role.

Two questions in our survey are associated with the party-cues dimension. One measures whether respondents feel that the best rule in voting is to pick the candidate regardless of the party label.[3] The other asked them to agree or disagree with the statement that parties do more to confuse the issues than to provide a clear choice. A high score on these variables indicates that the parties do not provide useful cues. As Table 4.1 depicts, these two items are moderately related to the underlying construct of party cues, although there is room for improved measurement given that the scale reliability is somewhat low (alpha = 0.28).[4]

Party Reform: Strengthening Parties and Third Parties

In terms of diffuse versus specific support, one may envision a situation in which citizens may come to disapprove of the actual operation of the parties, and yet not conclude that the principle of competitive parties is no longer relevant. Thus, for those who are positive in terms of diffuse support yet negative at the level of specific support, the main alternative may be one of encouraging party system reform.

Reforms are no doubt complex, in that a whole variety of changes might be possible. Changing the underlying institutional structure of political parties, introducing specific regulations, such as those pertaining to election campaign finance, or altering the representational environment of the parties relative to other mechanisms of representation, such as legislative bodies, executive agencies, candidates' campaign organizations, PACs and other advocacy organizations, sociopolitical movements, and the mass media, might be contemplated. For reasons of lack of space on the survey, we could tap only a few of such matters.[5]

The WISCON Survey included two indicators of party reform. The first tapped respondents' belief that the role of political parties should be strengthened by reforms, such as better campaign financing, and the other their views about whether or not the system would benefit from the growth of new parties. The exploratory factor analysis indicated that these two variables loaded together and were strongly associated with the same factor (see the Appendix and Table 4.7). However, confirmatory factor analysis revealed that these variables are not a good measure of the same underlying construct.[6]

As Table 4.2 indicates, the correlation between these two items is a modest 0.220. In addition, these two aspects of reform are conceptually distinct. The first type of reform implies that the existing two-party structure of the party system should be strengthened. The second advocates a system that provides more party options to challenge the existing duopoly.

In light of our confirmatory factor analysis results, we consider strengthening of the existing party system and advocating the introduction of third parties to represent two different aspects of party reform. Thus, we treat these variables separately in our subsequent analyses. The strengthen-parties variable is coded so that a high score corresponds to agreeing strongly with the idea that parties should be strengthened by reforms. The new-third-party item is scored so that a high value indicates strong agreement with the need for new parties to challenge effectively the Democrats and the Republicans.

Political Independence

Political independence is in some ways more complicated to characterize within the context of the present discussion than are the six dimensions we have discussed thus far. In certain respects, independence exists on a different plane of meaning and feeling than does partisan preference (Petrocik 1974; Valentine and Van Wingen 1980; Weisberg 1980; Dennis 1988a, 1988b, 1992). Independence thus constitutes a separate dimension of attitudes relevant to the party system.

Prior work by one of the present authors suggests strongly that a significant minority, perhaps 15 percent of all American adults, do not place independence on the same bipolar scale as being Republican or Democratic, but indeed, regard themselves as *both* partisan and independent. Another nearly 30 percent of adults resonate to neither partisanship nor independence if they are asked the question in a way that allows them to choose nonattachment of either kind (Dennis 1988a). To the extent to which individuals treat independence as a way

TABLE 4.2
Correlations between Dimensions of Party-System Attitudes (AMOS)[a]

	Antiparty	Support	Perform	Cues	Strengthen	Third Party
Antiparty	—					
Support	−0.419	—				
Perform	0.426	−0.695	—			
Cues	0.602	−0.298	0.417	—		
Strengthen	−0.153	0.305	−0.206	0.073	—	
Third party	0.116	−0.369	0.309	0.190	0.220	—
Independ.	0.270	−0.814	0.561	0.251	−0.136	0.215

[a]n = 530

Model Fit: CMIN/df = 27

of keeping themselves separated from the two major parties, we can use independence indicators as dependent variables that measure party-system attitudes (Dennis 1988b).

In another sense, political independence may be, for many people, simply a
way station as they move to and from some sense of partisan identification. In
this sense, citizens are simply distancing themselves from the existing two major parties, if not from the party system, or partisanship per se. At this level of
individual self-image, the taking of a posture of partisan independence may
lead one to disapprove of the existing partisan duopoly. From this perspective
we want to see what predictive value independence has for broader party-
system attitudes, and thus treat it as an independent variable.

We measure political independence using two items—an index of strength
of independence and a folded version of the traditional seven-point party identification scale. On both measures, a high value equates with strong independence. Our confirmatory factor analysis demonstrated a fairly good relationship
between these indicators and the underlying construct. But the scale reliability
for these measures is only fair (alpha = 0.30).

Relationships among Dimensions of Party-System Attitudes

Given that all these partisanship attitudes are in the same general domain, we
need to be aware of the extent to which they are interrelated. We now examine the correlations among the dimensions we have identified—antiparty sentiments, party-system support, party performance evaluations, party cues,
strengthening parties, third parties, and political independence. The results of
the AMOS analysis computing the correlations among the various party system attitudinal dimensions are depicted in Table 4.2. The correlations among
the specific dimensions vary substantially in degree.

Strong correlations exist for the most part where we would expect them.
The largest correlation—an inverse relationship—exists between political
independence and support for political parties (−0.814). The party-system
support dimension also is inversely related to negative party performance evaluations (−0.695) and antiparty sentiments (−0.419). Antipartyism is most
strongly associated with the belief that political parties do not provide meaningful cues about candidates and issues (0.602) and low party performance
scores (0.426). In addition, negative performance ratings are correlated with
political independence (0.561) and with the belief that the existing parties are
not successful cue givers (0.417).

Weaker relationships exist among the two reform dimensions and the other
party system attitude measures. A desire to strengthen political parties is more
strongly associated with party performance than with the other dimensions, although the correlation is relatively modest (0.305). As one would anticipate,
the relationship between antipartyism and strengthening parties through reform is weak. The correlation between political independence and the desire
to strengthen parties through reform is weak and negative (−0.136). The association between strengthening parties and negative performance evaluations

also is anemic. There is only a very small association between strengthening parties and the party-cues dimension.

The relationship between antiparty sentiments and disagreement that third parties are needed is weak, although the positive coefficient indicates that individuals taking an antiparty position in general tend to support the development of new parties. In addition, the position that new third parties are needed is positively related to political independence. The moderate negative correlation between the third party and support dimensions (-0.369) indicates that those who advocate the growth of new parties tend to lack support for the existing two-major-party system. Similarly, the relationships between third partyism and the party performance and party cues dimensions demonstrate that those who support the creation of new political parties tend to evaluate parties negatively and also to believe that parties do not provide useful cues for decision making about candidates and issues.

Finally, the correlation between antipartyism and political independence (0.270) is less robust than we might have anticipated. Perhaps this is because antipartyism postulates a complete rejection of political parties, whereas some aspects of independence still permit political parties to serve as a point of reference (see Dennis 1988b). Our measure of independence to some extent assumes the latter since it incorporates independent Republicans and Democrats as points along the continuum.

Trends in Citizens' Attitudes toward Political Parties

Before proceeding with our analysis, which predicts attitudes toward the party system, we present some basic trend and cohort analyses using the NES. Data that allow for over-time comparison are available for four of our party attitude dimensions—antipartyism, party-system support, party cues, and support for third parties. We adopt the generational divides suggested by Strauss and Howe (1991) for the cohort breakdowns on the NES items. Citizens born between 1901 and 1924 constitute the "GI Generation"; between 1925 and 1942, the "Silent Generation"; between 1943 and 1960, the "Baby Boom Generation"; and between 1961 and 1981, "Generation X."

Antiparty attitudes are tapped by the question, "The truth is we probably don't need political parties in America anymore." As Table 4.3 depicts, there is a slight increase in the percentage of citizens who agree with this statement from 1980 to 1998,[7] indicating a trend toward greater antipartyism. There are significant generational differences in antiparty attitudes expressed by this measure. In 1980, Baby Boomers were only slightly more antiparty in orientation than members of the GI and Silent Generations. However, by 1998, Boomers were substantially more likely than older cohorts to believe that parties are not necessary. The attitudes of Generation X were similar to those of the Baby Boomers.

A single NES question captures the party-system support, party cues, and third-party support dimensions of citizen attitudes. "Which of the opinions do you prefer: (1) a continuation of the two-party system of Democrats and Republicans; (2) elections in which candidates run as individuals without party la-

THE STATE OF DEMOCRACY IN AMERICA

TABLE 4.3
Don't Need Political Parties (NES)

"The truth is we probably don't need political parties in America anymore."

	1980 (%)	1993[a] (%)	1998[a] (%)
Agree	25	33	29
Neither	29	—	14
Disagree	46	77	57
Total %	100	100	100
n	(1,471)	(625)	(1,246)

Percentage within Generation
"The truth is we probably don't need political parties in America anymore."

	GI (%)	Silent (%)	Baby Boom (%)	Gen X (%)
1980[b]				
Agree	23	22	26	—
Disagree	56	50	38	—
n = 1,443				
1998[b]				
Agree	16	19	34	33
Disagree	76	72	54	49
n = 1,251				

[a]In 1993 and 1998, the respondent had to volunteer the response of neither agree nor disagree. In 1993, fewer than 1% of the respondents answered this way. We do not present data for the 1993 survey because of the relatively small number of cases on this item and the lack of a neutral category.
[b]Chi-square statistical significance: p<0.01.

bels; or (3) the growth of one or more parties that could effectively challenge the Democrats and Republicans?"[8] Table 4.4 indicates that there is a fair amount of stability in these attitudes across the four years from 1994 to 1998. Around 40 percent of respondents supported maintaining the current two-party system, while between 32 and 37 percent favored no party labels on the ballot, and approximately 25 percent favored the proliferation of third parties. Though no directly comparable question was asked in 1980, the NES did include an item asking respondents whether they agreed or disagreed with the idea of putting no party labels on the ballot. Thirty-seven percent agreed with the statement, which is similar to the findings for this response to the three-part item asked in 1994, 1996, and 1998.

Perhaps more interesting than the overall findings are the generational attitudes about these issues. Since the findings were similar across years, we include data only for 1998 in Table 4.4. It is clear that younger people are far less supportive of the existing two major political parties and more open to changing the established system than are older citizens. Support for the two-party system declines in a linear fashion as we move from the oldest to the youngest cohort. Sixty-four percent of the GI Generation favor keeping the existing two-party system, compared with 56 percent of the Silent Generation, 34 percent of the Baby Boomers, and only 29 percent of Generation X. Just over 20

TABLE 4.4
Party-System Support, Party Cues, and Support for Third Parties (NES)

	1994 (%)	1996 (%)	1998 (%)
Two-party System	39	42	39
No party labels	37	32	35
Third parties	24	26	26
Total	100	100	100
n	(1,795)	(1,505)	(1,259)

Note: In 1980, the NES included the question: "It would be better if, in all elections, we put no party labels on the ballot." Thirty-seven percent of respondents agreed with this statement, 32% neither agreed nor disagreed, and 31% disagreed.

Generational Differences (1998 NES)

	GI (%)	Silent (%)	Baby Boom (%)	Gen X (%)
Two-party	64	56	34	29
No party labels	21	22	38	42
Third parties	15	22	28	29
Total	100	100	100	100
n	(102)	(237)	(468)	(437)

Note: Chi-square significance: $p < 0.01$.

percent of the GI and Silent generations feel that party labels should not appear on the ballot, while 38 percent of Boomers and 42 percent of Xers feel this way. Finally, only 15 percent of the GI Generation favor the emergence of third parties, compared with 22 percent of the Silent Generation, 28 percent of Baby Boomers, and 29 percent of Generation X.

The 1996 and 1998 NES data provide us with some intriguing clues about citizens' attitudes about the parties as cue givers through a battery of questions about whether respondents feel that the Democrats or Republicans do the best job of handling policies in particular areas, or whether there is no difference between the parties. As Table 4.5 depicts, there is a significant rise in the percentage of respondents claiming that there is no difference between the parties in their handling of crime (45% to 57%), the environment (43% to 49%), and foreign affairs (36% to 49%) in just this two-year period. There was virtually no change regarding Social Security and the economy, although close to 40 percent perceived no difference between the parties in each year. These data indicate that the two major parties' utility as cue givers on policy issues is declining, at least in several major issue realms.

Predicting Attitudes toward the Political Party System

Our next step is to examine some possible predictors of the seven dimensions of party-system attitudes that we have identified. We performed comparable OLS regression analyses for each party-system attitudinal dimension. Indexes were constructed for our dependent variables—antipartyism, party-system support, performance evaluations, party cues, and political independence. The

TABLE 4.5
See No Difference in the Major Parties' Handling of Specific Issues

	1996 (%)	1998 (%)	Change (%)
Crime	45	57	12
Environment	43	49	6
Foreign affairs	36	49	13
Social Security	39	38	−1
Economy	37	37	0

independent variables in the analysis included some basic demographic controls for sex, age, race, education, and income. We also incorporated political variables, economic outlook indicators, and mass media items into the equation. (A complete description of the variables appears in the Appendix.)

Our political variables include whether or not the respondents were registered to vote and whether they ever considered themselves to be supporters of Ross Perot and his third-party movement. Strength of political ideology is measured by folding the traditional seven-point ideology scale. A high score refers to a strongly ideological respondent. An index of support for government and institutions was created, with a high score corresponding to strong approval of their performance. Our measure of satisfaction with democracy is coded in an alienated direction, so that a high value indicates that the respondent is not at all satisfied with the way democracy works in the United States. We also use political independence as a predictor in the regression analyses for the other six dimensions of party-system attitudes.

Two economic outlook variables are included in the model. The first asked the respondents if they anticipated that their families would be better off financially in a year. A high score corresponds to negative predictions about the future state of one's family finances. The second is a measure of economic pessimism that taps individuals' expectations about the future economic condition of the country. This index includes perceptions about business conditions, unemployment, and interest rates. The higher the score on this index, the greater the level of macro-economic pessimism.

We also use a measure of perceived mass media performance. We created an index that measures respondents' rating of the job the national and local news media are doing. Higher scores on this index represent positive feelings about the media's job performance.

Hypotheses

At this stage in the process, our analysis is largely exploratory. We do, however, offer some basic hypotheses that we test with the regression analyses. We anticipate that individuals who hold negative attitudes about politics, economics, and the media more generally will not be satisfied with the existing political party system, which they may perceive to be part of the problem. Further, we expect that political independents and supporters of Ross Perot will not be favorably disposed toward the traditional party system, as they are interested in alternatives (Owen and Dennis 1996). Citizens with strong ideological orientations, however, may have more positive attitudes toward political parties, as they are more likely to align with the major Democratic and Republican party options (Dennis 1995). Thus, we examine the following propositions:

H_1: Individuals who hold negative opinions of political and mass media institutions, and who are not satisfied with the way democracy is currently working, are less likely to be supportive of the political party system.

H_2: Political independence is likely to be associated with negative attitudes toward the political party system.

H_3: Ross Perot supporters are more likely to be dissatisfied with the political party system as it is currently constituted, and to desire reform, especially the creation of third-party alternatives.

H_4: Individuals with strong ideological convictions will be more positively oriented toward the party system than people who are less ideological.

H_5: People whose personal financial future appears bleak, and who are more pessimistic about the nation's economic outlook, are less likely to be supportive of the party system.

Findings

Our analysis is to some extent limited by the items available in the WISCON Survey. We would have liked to have explored additional political factors, including political interest, trust, civic duty, and political efficacy. For example, it would be useful to explore the relationship between political participation and attitudes toward the party system in more detail. The only test of this relationship we could perform employs the single related measure included on the WISCON Survey—the voter registration status of the respondent. However, this item was not a significant predictor of party-system attitudes in any of the regression analyses. Despite such data limitations, our analysis reveals some interesting findings. The results of the regression analyses appear in Table 4.6.

Diffuse Support: Antipartyism and Party Support

The regression analysis for antipartyism reveals that the strongest predictor of antiparty sentiments is dissatisfaction with how democracy is currently working. Dissatisfaction with democracy is the only one of the political, economic, or mass media variables to achieve statistical significance. Among the demographic indicators, we find that women are more likely than men to hold antiparty attitudes. Although the relationships are not strong, age and education are negatively related to antipartyism. Younger and less educated people are more antiparty in orientation than other citizens.

TABLE 4.6
OLS Regression Analysis of Party-System Attitudes

	Antiparty	Support	Perform	Cues	Strengthen	Third Party	Independence
Sex	0.099[b]	−0.056	−0.012	−0.020	−0.161[a]	−0.086[c]	−0.149[a]
Age	−0.080[c]	0.276[a]	−0.030	−0.045	0.199[a]	−0.101[b]	0.088[c]
Race	0.022	0.164[a]	−0.009	0.019	0.075[c]	0.004	−0.041
Education	−0.079[c]	−0.063	−0.060	−0.041	0.067	0.036	0.119[a]
Income	−0.043	−0.005	0.022	−0.002	−0.054	−0.008	0.020
Register vote	−0.043	−0.033	0.019	−0.085	−0.029	−0.015	0.044
Perot	0.039	−0.009	0.000	−0.004	0.004	0.183[a]	0.154[a]
Ideology	−0.094	0.105[a]	−0.092	0.036	0.070	−0.004	0.007
Gov't support	0.035	0.175[a]	−0.260[a]	0.132[a]	0.047	−0.052	−0.107[b]
Democracy	0.244[a]	−0.117[a]	0.313[a]	0.090	0.024	0.127[a]	0.085[c]
Independence	0.073	−0.338[a]	0.143[a]	0.163[a]	−0.032	0.155[a]	
Personal finances	−0.003	−0.042	−0.079[b]	−0.052	−0.020	0.044	0.046
Economy	−0.014	0.062	−0.033	−0.058	−0.050	−0.091[b]	−0.115[b]
Media	0.055	0.090[b]	−0.144[a]	−0.078	0.088[c]	−0.009	−0.007
R^2	0.108[a]	0.302[a]	0.359[a]	0.055[b]	0.078[a]	0.128[a]	0.144[a]
n	439	445	433	449	443	449	453

Note: Standardized coefficients: [a]$p<0.01$, [b]$p<0.05$, [c]$p<0.10$.

A variety of factors included in our model predict support for the present political party system. Among the political variables, the largest regression coefficient is associated with political independence.[9] As we would expect, strong independence is associated with a lack of support for the party system. A high level of support for other kinds of government institutions corresponds to positive attitudes toward parties. In addition, individuals who are highly ideological are likely to be more supportive of the party system and to believe that it works well. Neither of the economic outlook indicators is a significant predictor of party support. A weak relationship exists for perceived mass media performance, in that a low evaluation of the media corresponds to a lack of party support.

Two of the demographic variables in this equation are statistically significant. As age increases, so does support for political parties. Race is also a significant predictor, in that whites are less supportive of parties on this dimension than are nonwhites.

Specific Support: Party-System Performance and Party Cues

Three of the political factors are significant indicators of party performance evaluations, the biggest of which is satisfaction with democracy. Respondents who feel that democracy is not working hold negative opinions about the job the parties have been doing. People who have poor evaluations of other government institutions' performance hold similarly low opinions about the parties' performance. The same holds true for ratings of the mass media, in that people who feel that the mass media are doing a bad job feel the same way about political parties. Political independence also is related to poor party performance ratings. In addition, the personal finances variable is statistically significant, if barely. There is a small tendency for people who rate parties low to perceive that they will be better off financially a year from now. None of the demographic variables is statistically significant in this equation.

Only two independent variables are significant in the party-cues equation—approval of government institutional performance and political independence. High levels of general institutional support are related to a belief that parties fail as cue givers. In addition, those who are politically independent are more likely to perceive that the parties do not help in distinguishing candidates and issues. None of the demographic, economic, or media indicators predict feelings about the parties as cue givers.

Party Reform: Strengthening Parties and New Parties

The political and economic variables in our model did not predict attitudes about proposed reforms to strengthen political parties. However, several demographic characteristics are statistically significant. Women are more inclined than men to believe that the parties are in need of strengthening. Younger people are more likely to disagree with the need to strengthen the role of parties than are older individuals. Though the relationship is not as strong, a racial as-

TABLE 4.7
Factor Analysis (Principal Component Analysis)
Party System Support Variables

Factor	Loading	Variance (%)
Support		
Party supporter	0.799	
Parties serve well	0.601	15.8
Antiparty		
No parties	0.846	
Parties necessary	0.753	
No party labels	0.656	12.6
Performance		
Parties care	0.800	
Parties' job rating	0.635	
Parties—Gov't attention	0.626	12.5
Reform		
Strengthen parties	0.725	
New parties	0.719	10.9
No Cues		
Disregard parties	0.679	
Parties confuse issues	0.673	9.8
Total		61.7
n		443

sociation is somewhat evident, as nonwhite citizens agree more with the idea of reforms to strengthen parties than whites. There is a weak relationship between perceived media performance and a desire to strengthen the parties.

As we expected, a desire for third parties is significantly related to political independence and to support for Ross Perot. In addition, respondents who are dissatisfied with how democracy is working are more likely to support the growth of new political parties. People who are pessimistic about the economy, however, are more inclined to disagree with the need for introducing third parties. Among our demographic predictors, older people are more likely than are younger citizens to disagree with the need for new parties. Men favor third parties more than do women.

Independence

Finally, we ran a model in which political independence was treated as a dependent variable. Our analysis reveals that support for Ross Perot is the strongest predictor of independence. In addition, independence corresponds to a lack of approval of other government institutions' performance, and it is weakly associated with dissatisfaction with democracy. Further, political independence is inversely related to macro-economic pessimism. In keeping with the findings for support for new parties, males are more likely than females to score high on the independence dimension. Education is also significantly and positively related to political independence.

Summary

In sum, we find support for our hypothesis that adverse opinions about political institutions and the current state of democracy are related to negative attitudes about the party system for all but the two reform dimensions. As hypothesized, support for Ross Perot was an important predictor of third partyism and political independence. However, Perot support was not significant for any other party-system support dimension. Ideology was significant solely in the party-system support equation, where the findings were as hypothesized.

Dissatisfaction with the performance of the mass media was a significant predictor in the expected direction only for the positive party-system support and party-cues dimensions, and it was weakly related to a preference for strengthening the parties. The economic outlook variables did not perform especially well in the analysis, although there is some limited support for our hypothesis that a pessimistic personal financial outlook corresponds to less favorable views of the party system in terms of party performance evaluations.

The demographic predictors revealed some patterns worthy of comment. Women are more likely than men to express antiparty sentiments and to advocate party reform. Men, however, are more likely to desire the introduction of third parties. The finding that age is inversely related to supportive attitudes toward political parties confirms previous research demonstrating that younger generations, especially Generation X, identify less with parties and have more negative feelings about the party system than their older counterparts (Dennis and Owen 1997; Miller 1992).

Conclusion

The most important extraconstitutional mechanism of representation to develop over the past two centuries in the United States has been the political party system. Although the constitutional framers did not deem parties to be a necessary, or even positive, form of representation of citizens either at the national or other levels of government, the party system has nonetheless come strongly into being (see Epstein 1986; McCormick 1986). In the present century, we generally have taken this idea for granted. As Schattschneider put it at the beginning of one of his works, "It should be stated flatly at the outset that this volume is devoted to the thesis that political parties created democracy and that modern democracy is unthinkable save in terms of the parties" (1942, 1–2).

As has been the case for legislatures (Davidson and Parker 1972; Dennis 1981; Hibbing and Theiss-Morse 1995; Patterson and Boynton 1974; Patterson, Hedlund, and Boynton 1975), popular attitudes toward political parties in this country—while fluctuating somewhat—have generally trended in a negative direction since the 1960s. Political parties have come under a cloud of public disapprobation (Dennis, 1966, 1975, 1980, 1986; Dennis and Owen 1997; and Owen and Dennis 1996). The gradual loss of institutional support by the party system is manifested at several levels. The most easily observed

65

sign of partisan alienation is the gradual aggregate subsidence of political party identification. Substantial time series data, such as those collected by the Gallup organization since the 1930s and the National Election Studies/Survey Research Center/Center for Political Studies at the University of Michigan since the early 1950s, suggest that partisan identification has declined. As each new cohort of Americans has reached political maturity, we have observed a weaker collective partisan impulse accompanied by an increasingly complex set of attitudes toward parties in general (Dennis 1988a; Miller 1992; Miller and Shanks 1996; Dennis and Owen 1997). These attitudes contain elements of both greater indifference and hostility toward the party system (Dennis and Owen 1994; also see Wattenberg 1990; and Craig 1985).

The rise in the relative numbers of self-styled Independents in the general populace has been an associated trend (Dennis 1988a, 1988b, 1993), even though in important respects partisan affiliation and political independence comprise two fairly separate dimensions of political attitudes and behavior (Petrocik 1974; Valentine and Van Wingen 1980; Weisberg 1980; and Dennis 1988a, 1988b, 1992; but see Keith et al., 1992). Independence and other forms of nonidentification with the two major parties may well suggest a general distancing of Americans from this usual means of political representation.

Such "dealignment" appears to be present in a variety of other comparable western systems, such as Canada and Great Britain (see Crewe, Sarlvik, and Alt 1977; Clarke and Kornberg 1996; Clarke and Stewart 1984, 1985, 1987, 1988). Antiparty movements of various kinds have accompanied such dealignment and are now increasingly recognized as such by scholars in a variety of countries (e.g., Pedersen 1988; Lawson 1988; Poguntke and Scarrow 1996). Thus, the loss of popular regard for the role of parties in representation goes beyond the phenomenon of partisan dealignment in the United States.

When people begin to question the present party system's ability to provide adequate representation of their demands, they may turn to alternative parties or to independent candidates, as occurred during the early 1990s with Ross Perot in the United States and Silvio Berlusconi in Italy. However, citizens may shift their focus to alternative organizations as well. Over the longer term in the United States, some of the party's representative role has devolved more upon candidate organizations that perform relatively separate electioneering and linkage functions while operating only nominally under a party's label.

Such candidate-centeredness may be further enhanced by direct financial support from interest or advocacy groups operating for the most part outside the aegis of the parties. Further, the competition for popular support also may enhance the role of other organizations, such as those associated with mass political or social movements and the mass media. These alternatives to parties begin to take on part of the representative function that was earlier reserved for the major parties. One might even argue that the modern-day presidency, as its powers have become enlarged, may also take up some of these functions, particularly under the stewardship of a president who puts great stress on maintaining an almost intimate connection to the general populace, as did Bill Clinton (Balogh 1998).

Such expansion may operate both within the context of elections and be-yond them. Both candidates and parties often have moved to recapture some of the earlier role played by the parties. Nonetheless, we see that advocacy groups and the mass media are able to reshape the content of campaigns and the process of informing, persuading, and mobilizing the public in a manner that often bypasses the wishes and efforts of both the candidates' organizations and the major parties. Thus, a more complex representative process has evolved—one in which the role of the parties under many circumstances may be increasingly constricted. (For arguments on each side of this issue see, for example, Maisel 1988; and Herrnson and Green 1997).

In this chapter, we have tried to advance the study of the public's degree of approval or disapproval of the political party system in the United States. As is the case for a variety of other party systems in present-day representative de-mocracies, the evidence collected since the early 1960s has suggested a gradual decline in public regard for, and thus legitimation of, the representative insti-tution of the party system. The somewhat scattered indicators and observa-tions that we have had available thus far in these studies, including the evi-dence we present here from the NES, still bear the symptoms of an early stage of research.

We have examined the problem more broadly than has been done thus far and have developed some more refined measures of this phenomenon. We find that a variety of connected, if still separable, types of public sentiments toward the party system exist, quite apart from a personal sense of attachment to a po-litical party. Using dimensional analyses, we have discovered that the phenom-enon of generalized support or lack of support for parties as representative in-stitutions takes on several more specific forms. On the side of what we have termed "diffuse support" for the party system, we have distinguished both a positive and an antiparty dimension of sentiment. In terms of what we might think of as more in the realm of "specific support," we have identified evalua-tions of the general performance of the parties, plus a more specific dimension that pertains to the "cue-giving" function of parties. Together, these constructs indicate how well people think the parties have been doing their job.

An area that no doubt connects diffuse to specific support is that of potential reforms. The only reforms that we were able to include on this brief round of questioning are strengthening the parties through improving their financial situation and introducing a viable third party to improve the degree of com-petitiveness of the party system as a whole, although a viable third party might well weaken the present two-party system. Changes brought about by reform might help the parties perform better, thus increasing specific support, and in time, regain a greater measure of generalized, or diffuse, support. In addition, we have treated independence separately, and considered its relationships both in an antecedent and in a consequent context.

We also have attempted to get a better sense of where some of the causal ex-planations for these phenomena might lie. We find that a number of different kinds of explanatory variables help us to explain some of the variance in our measures of party-system sentiment. The explanatory power of the various demographic, political, economic, and mass media independent variables differs somewhat for the specific attitudinal dimensions.

We have addressed seriously the question of better measuring the nature of public opinion regarding a primary device of representational democracy. At the end of the twentieth century we witnessed strains upon the legitimacy of political parties. Our task here has been to try to provide a more fine-grained analysis of the dimensions of this culture shift—one that we can then apply to subsequent sets of observations. We want to see more precisely the nature of change in public approval or disapproval of parties that goes beyond the mere observance of the decline in the levels of individual identification with one or the other of the two major parties in the United States. To accomplish this task, we have introduced our new battery of indexes.

Notes

1. The survey included not only our block of questions on partisan attitudes and other related variables, but also a set of core items. The latter is composed of a variety of demographic questions, a measure of personal sense of depression, relative approval of the performance of a variety of political institutions, such as Congress, economic outlook at both the micro and macro levels, feelings about the tax system, and other related matters.

2. Previously, we included a wider range of attitudes under the rubric of antiparty sentiments. These included dissatisfaction with the current status of political parties, but not with the concept of political parties per se, a preference for more options than the Democratic and Republican parties, as well as a desire to eliminate or minimize party's role in the political process (Dennis and Owen 1997). With the larger battery of questions available in the WISCON Survey, we are able to refine our analysis of antipartyism, both conceptually and empirically, to represent one extreme of a continuum anchored on the one end by a strong desire to maintain the existing political party system as it is, and on the other by a desire to eliminate parties altogether.

3. Though this question is similar to the one about party labels associated with the antiparty sentiments dimension, it differs in a fundamental way. The antipartyism question deals with the party system and the electoral process. The question corresponding to the party-cues dimension concerns the individual's use of the party label as a cue for selecting candidates. Both the exploratory and confirmatory factor analyses empirically support this conceptual distinction.

4. Attempts to treat these two indicators separately in the confirmatory factor analysis worsened the model fit substantially.

5. We did more extensive coverage of such possible reforms in our summer 1998 survey.

6. The results of this analysis are not reported here but can be obtained by contacting the coauthor (owend@georgetown.edu).

7. The data are not entirely comparable, as the "neither agree nor disagree" category was not offered to respondents as an option in 1993 or 1998 as it was in 1980. Respondents in 1993 and 1998 had to volunteer this response. It may be the case that in 1993 and 1998, the percentage of respondents who disagreed with the statement that we don't need political parties anymore may be inflated because of the absence of the neither-response category.

8. This question may underestimate the percentage of people who believe that candidates should run without party labels and who favor the growth of third parties, as

it requires respondents to choose between these options, which may not be mutually exclusive.

9. This relationship is to be expected, as the party-support index includes a variable that asks respondents to agree or disagree with the statement that it is better to be a firm party supporter than a political independent.

APPENDIX: Measures: National Study Version P8023

DIFFUSE SUPPORT

Antiparty

NO PARTIES — The truth is we probably don't need political parties in America anymore.

PARTIES NECESSARY — Some people say that political parties are necessary to make our political system work in the United States. Others think that political parties are not needed in the United States.

NO PARTY LABELS — It would be better if, in all elections, we put no party labels on the ballot.

Combined to create an additive index ranging from 1 (proparty) to 17 (antiparty).

Scale reliability — alpha = 0.71

Support

PARTY SUPPORTER — It is better to be a firm party supporter than to be a political independent.

PARTIES SERVE WELL — The two-party system that we have serves this country well.

Combined to create an additive index ranging from 1 (no party support) to 13 (strong support).

Scale reliability — alpha = 0.52

SPECIFIC SUPPORT

Performance

PARTIES CARE — Some people say that the political parties in the United States care what ordinary people think. Others say that political parties in the United States don't care what ordinary people think.

PARTY JOB RATING — How good a job do you feel that the two major political parties, the Democrats and Republicans, are doing?

PARTIES—GOV'T. ATTN. — How much do you feel that political parties help to make the government pay attention to what the people think, a good deal, some, or not much?

Combined to create an additive index ranging from 1 (negative rating of party performance) to 19 (positive rating of party performance).

Scale reliability — alpha = 0.57

Party Cues

DISREGARD PARTY — The best rule in voting is to pick a candidate regardless of party label.

PARTIES CONFUSE — The parties do more to confuse the issues than to provide a clear choice on issues.

Combined to create an additive index ranging from 1 (parties provide cues) to 13 (parties provide no cues).

Scale reliability — alpha = 0.28

REFORM

STRENGTHEN PARTIES   We need to strengthen the role of the political parties in American government through various reforms, such as better campaign financing. Ranges from 1 (disagree strongly with need to reform) to 7 (agree strongly with the need to reform).

THIRD PARTIES   We need the growth of one or more new parties that could effectively challenge the Democrats and Republicans. Ranges from 1 (disagree strongly with the need for new parties) to 7 (agree strongly with the need for new parties).

[Note: When reform1 and reform2 are combined to create an additive index ranging from 1 (reform parties) to 13 (no reform), the scale reliability is alpha = 0.30).]

INDEPENDENCE

STRENGTH IND   Index of strength of partisan independence ranging from 1 (not at all independent) to 8 (strongly independent).

FOLDED PID   An index of partisan strength created by folding the traditional 7-point party identification scale, ranging from 1 (strong partisan) to 4 (independent).

Combined to form an index ranging from 1 (not at all independent) to 11 (strongly independent).

Scale reliability   alpha = 0.30

DEMOGRAPHICS

SEX   1 Male; 2 Female

AGE   In years

EDUCATION   A scale ranging from 1 (less than high school) to 6 (doctorate, advanced degree beyond MA)

RACE   1 White; 2 Nonwhite

INCOME   Respondent's yearly income

POLITICAL VARIABLES

STRENGTH IDEOLOGY   Folded version of the traditional 7-point ideology scale, ranging from 1 (moderate) to 4 (strongly ideological).

REGISTERED TO VOTE   Registered to vote, 1 Registered; 2 Not Registered.

PEROT SUPPORTER   Have you ever considered yourself a supporter of Ross Perot's Reform Party, or United We Stand America? 1 No; 2 Yes.

INSTITUTION SUPPORT   How good a job do you feel the president is doing? The Congress? The Supreme Court? State government?

Combined to form an additive index ranging from 1 (low support) to 37 (high support).

Scale reliability   alpha = 0.69

SATISFIED DEMOCRACY   On the whole, are you very satisfied, fairly satisfied, not very satisfied, or not at all satisfied with the way democracy works in the United States? 1 (very satisfied) to 5 (not at all satisfied).

ECONOMIC VARIABLES

PERSONAL FINANCES   Now looking ahead—do you think that a year from now you (and your family) will be better off financially, or worse off, or just about the same as now? 1 (better off) to 3 (worse off).

ECONOMIC PESSIMISM

Now turning to business conditions in the country as a whole, do you think that during the next 12 months we'll have good times financially, bad times, or what?

Would you say that at the present time business conditions are better or worse than they were a year ago, or just about the same?

And how about a year from now—do you expect business conditions will be better or worse than they are at present, or just about the same?

How about people out of work during the coming 12 months—do you think that there will be more unemployment than now, less unemployment than now, or about the same?

During the next 12 months do you think that prices in general will go up, go down, or stay where they are now?

What about interest rates—do you think that during the next 12 months interest rates will go up, come down, or stay about the same as they are now?

Combined to form an additive index ranging from 1 (optimism) to 10 (pessimism).

Scale reliability   alpha = 0.69

MEDIA VARIABLES

MEDIA PERFORMANCE

How would you rate the job the national news media are doing?

How would you rate the job the local news media are doing?

Combined to form an additive index ranging from 1 (a terrible job) to 20 (a perfect job).

Scale reliability   alpha = 0.76

References

Balogh, Bruce. 1998. No small change: Clinton scandals aside, history is diminishing. *Milwaukee Journal Sentinel*, 9 August 1998, p. J1.

Beck, Paul Allen. 1997. *Party Politics in America*, 8th ed. New York, NY: Longman.

Burnham, Walter Dean. 1970. *Critical Elections and the Mainsprings of American Politics*. New York: Norton.

Campbell, Angus, Phillip E. Converse, Warren E. Miller, and Donald E. Stokes. 1960. *The American Voter*. New York: Wiley.

Chambers, William Nesbit, and Walter Dean Burnham. 1967. *The American Party Systems: Stages of Political Development*. New York: Oxford University Press.

Clarke, Harold D., and Allen Kornberg. 1996. Partisan dealignment, electoral choice and party-system change in Canada. *Party Politics* 2: 455–78.

Clarke, Harold D., and Marianne C. Stewart. 1984. Dealignment of degree: Partisan change in Britain, 1974–1983. *Journal of Politics* 46: 689–718.

———. 1985. Short-term forces and partisan change in Canada, 1974–1980. *Electoral Studies* 4:15–35.

———. 1987. Partisan inconsistency and partisan change in federal states: The case of Canada. *American Journal of Political Science* 31: 383–407.

———. 1998. The decline of parties in the minds of Citizens. *Annual Review of Political Science* 1: 357–78.

Craig, Stephen C. 1985. The decline of partisanship in the United States: A re-examination of the neutrality hypothesis. *Political Behavior* 7: 57–78.

Crewe, Ivor, Bo Sarlvik, and James Alt. 1977. Partisan dealignment in Britain, 1964–1974. *British Journal of Political Science* 7: 179–90.

Dahl, Robert Alan. 2000. *On Democracy*. New Haven, CT: Yale University Press.

Davidson, Roger, and Glenn R. Parker. 1972. Positive support for political institutions: The case of Congress. *Western Political Quarterly* 25: 600–612.

Dennis, Jack. 1966. Support for the party system by the mass public. *American Political Science Review* 60: 600–615.

———. 1975. Trends in public support for the American party system. *British Journal of Political Science* 5 (April): 187–230.

———. 1980. Changing public support for the American party system. In William J. Crotty (ed.), *Paths to Political Reform*. Lexington, MA: D.C. Heath, pp. 35–66.

———. 1981. "Public Support for Congress. *Political Behavior* 3: 319–50.

———. 1986. *Dilemmas of Pluralist Democracy*. New Haven, CT: Yale University Press.

———. 1986. Public support for the party system, 1964–1984. Paper delivered at the annual meeting of American Political Science Associataion (APSA), Washington, DC, August 28-31.

———. 1988a. Political independence in America, part I: On being an independent partisan supporter. *British Journal of Political Science* 18: 77–109.

———. 1988b. Political independence in America, part II: Towards a theory. *British Journal of Political Science* 18: 197–219.

———. 1992. Political independence in America: In search of closet partisans. *Political Behavior* 14: 261–96.

———. 1993. Do we believe Aristotle? A study of American beliefs about democracy. Paper delivered at the annual meeting of the Midwest Political Science Association, Chicago, April 15–17.

———. 1995. Political ideology in the 1992 presidential election. Paper delivered at the annual meeting of the Midwest Political Science Association, Chicago, April 7.

———. 1997. The partisanship puzzle: Identification and attitudes of Generation X. In Stephen C. Craig and Stephen Earl Bennett (eds.), *After the Boom: The Politics of Generation X*. Lanham, MD: Rowman and Littlefield, pp. 43–61.

Easton, David. 1965. *A Systems Analysis of Political Life*. New York: Wiley.

———. 1975. A re-assessment of the concept of political support. *British Journal of Political Science* 5 (October): 435–57.

Epstein, Leon D. 1967. *Political Parties in Western Democracies*. New York: Transaction Publishers.

———. 1986. *Political Parties in the American Mold*. Madison: University of Wisconsin Press.

Herrnson, Paul S., and John C. Green. 1997. *Mutiparty Politics in America*. Lanham, MD: Rowman and Littlefield.

Hibbing, John R., and Elizabeth Theiss-Morse. 1995. *Congress as Public Enemy: Public Attitudes toward American Political Institutions*. New York: Cambridge University Press.

Hofstadter, Richard. 1955. *The Age of Reform*. New York: Knopf.

Keith, Bruce, David B. Magleby, Candice J. Nelson, Elizabeth A. Orr, Mark C. Westlye, and Raymond E. Wolfinger. 1992. *The Myth of the Independent Voter*. Berkeley: University of California.

King, Anthony. 1969. Political parties in Western democracies. *Polity* 2: 111–41.

———, ed. 1997. *Culture, Globalization, and the World System: Contemporary Conditions for the Representation of Identity*. Minneapolis: University of Minnesota Press.

Lawson, Kay, 1988. When linkage fails. In Kay Lawson and Peter H. Merkl (eds.), *When Parties Fail*. Princeton, NJ: Princeton University Press, pp. 13–38.

Lawson, Kay, and Peter H. Merkl, eds. 1988. *When Parties Fail.* Princeton, NJ: Princeton University Press.

Maisel, L. Sandy. 1998. *The Parties Respond*, 3d ed. Boulder, CO: Westview Press.

McCormick, Richard L. 1986. *The Party Period and Public Policy: American Politics from the Age of Jackson to the Progressive Era.* New York: Oxford.

Miller, Warren E. 1992. Generational changes and party identification. *Political Behavior* 14: 333–52.

Miller, Warren E., and J. Merrill Shanks. 1996. *The New American Voter.* Cambridge, MA: Harvard University Press.

Owen, Diana, and Jack Dennis. 1996. Antipartyism in the USA and support for Ross Perot. *European Journal of Political Research* 29: 383–400.

Patterson, Samuel C., and G. Robert Boynton. 1974. *Citizens, Leaders, and Legislators: Perspectives on Support for the American Legislature.* Beverly Hills, CA: Sage.

Patterson, Samuel C., Ronald D. Hedlund, and G. Robert Boynton. 1975. *Representatives and Represented: Bases of Public Support for the American Legislatures.* New York: Wiley.

Pedersen, Mogens N. 1988. The defeat of all parties: The Danish Folketing election, 1973. In Kay Lawson and Peter Merkl (eds.), *When Parties Fail.* Princeton, NJ: Princeton University Press, pp. 257–82.

Petrocik, John R. 1974. An analysis of the intransitivities in the index of party identification. *Political Methodology* 1: 31–47.

Poguntke, Thomas, and Susan E. Scarrow. 1996. Anti-party sentiment—Conceptual thoughts and empirical evidence: Explorations into a minefield. Special issue of *European Journal of Political Research* 29 (3): 319–44.

Rosenthal, Alan. 1997. *The Decline of Representative Democracy: Process, Participation, and Power in the State Legislatures.* Washington, DC: Congressional Quarterly Press.

Sartori, Giovanni. 1987. *Theory of Democracy Revisited.* New York: Chatham House.

Schattschneider, E.E. 1942. *Party Government.* New York: Rinehart.

Sorauf, Frank J. 1976. *Party Politics in America*, 3d ed. Boston: Little, Brown.

Strauss, William, and Neil Howe. 1991. *Generations.* New York: William Morrow.

Valentine, David, and John R. Van Wingen. 1980. Partisanship, independence, and the partisan identification question. *American Politics Quarterly* 8: 165–85.

Wahlke, John C., Heinz Eulau, William Buchanan, and LeRoy C. Ferguson. 1962. *The Legislative System: Explorations in Legislative Behavior.* New York: Wiley.

Wattenberg, Martin. 1990. *The Decline of American Political Parties, 1952–1988.* Cambridge, MA: Harvard University Press.

Weisberg, Herbert F. 1980. A multidimensional conceptualization of party identification. *Political Behavior* 2: 33–60.

White, John Kenneth, and Jerome M. Mileur. 1992. *Challenges to Party Government.* Carbondale and Edwardsville: Southern Illinois University Press.

5

Party Relevance over Time

WILLIAM CROTTY

Introduction

A good deal of attention is paid to political parties and their operations on the assumption that they are important. The belief has even been put forward that they are critical actors in the democratic drama, crucial to the success of a vital democracy. Their job is to represent voters, meet their needs, and carry out their wishes through the selection of candidates for public office, the promotion of their candidacies in campaigns, and, once in power, the enactment of policies endorsed by the public in elections. The issues selected for attention by the parties, and through them the electorate, are considered to include the most pressing concerns facing the society.

These are the assumptions, endorsed by all who study political parties and democratic politics. The views of voters along these lines may be at considerable odds with such abstract conceptualizations as to the societal functions encompassed by these beliefs.

For some, such views are naïve; parties and candidates are seen as dedicated to the primary goal of winning office and exercising power in a form of a free-market free-for-all. Anything beyond this is fanciful; parties and candidates promote their own self-interests (seen as exercising power), and other pursuits are considered secondary and even accidental. Attention given to the quality and appeals of campaigns or the substance of debate over legislative actions might well reinforce such beliefs.

However, there is more to the story. The objective of winning is clear enough and indisputable; that is where the parties most visibly expend their energies and their resources. But to do so, they must market their views, and the candidates who commit to enacting these, to groups of voters in coalitions of sufficient size to assure a plurality of votes. Such marketing is neither easily entered into nor random in choice (Jackson and Crotty 2000). The coalitions that support the parties are remarkably stable over elections (and in broad outline even generations), and the issues that the parties commit to must resonate in given elections and over time with the core constituencies they count on for support (Miller and Shanks 1996). As a consequence, there is a broad consistency in party positions over elections, as well as a coherence in association of views between party supporters and elites on the policies of fundamental concern to the coalitions, and these are impressive (Crotty 2001; Crotty, Jackson, and Miller 1999). The process is far from random or arbitrary.

The crucial question may not be the distinctive policy positioning of the two major parties—this has been established—but the relevance of the parties and the party system as a whole as seen by the voters in performing the linkage functions outlined. How important are the political parties to the operations of the American democratic system? How clear are the differences between them as perceived by voters over time and in specific elections? How well received are the parties' candidacies for the nation's highest office, the presidency, and how clear and distinctive are their appeals? Do perceptions and evaluations along these dimensions change over time? Are they consistent among subgroups or does considerable variation in perceptions of salience and importance among social groups occur, either over a significant number of campaigns or in particular elections? What does all of this say to the relevance of political parties, as analyzed over the last half century, and what does it tell us about the positioning of the parties and their role in political representation upon entering a new century?

These are some of the questions we address. We do so by looking at measures of party and candidate salience taken from the National Election Studies for the period 1952–1992. The belief is that the election of 1996 in particular may have introduced a new era of party positioning, one that carried over into the 2000 contests and that would skew the analysis and deserves separate attention. The winning presidential candidate in 1992 and 1996 followed a self-consciously consistent strategy of presenting a centrist policy agenda and blurring the difference between the parties. Our concern is with the balance of voter perception over the four-decade period leading up to the Clinton presidency and its impact on the political system, although we will be speaking to some aspects of the 1996 results and of the Clinton years and their consequences.

Political Change in the Last Half of the Twentieth Century

The America of the early twenty-first century is not the America of the post-World War II era, and the political parties of the contemporary period are not the parties of midcentury America. Much has changed. A broad look at the dimensions of social and economic change that have occurred in the United States over the last five decades can be found in chapter 2. Transformations of a fundamental nature are also evident in the party system. The nature of what has taken place is not in question; most agree on this and see it as adaptations to an evolving social and political environment. There is considerably less agreement—more accurately, virtually none—on what these mean for assessing the importance of the parties in executing their democratic duties. The changes in the parties can be described. Several testimonials to the parties of the midcentury, followed by assessments of their relevance over time, can serve to make the point.

E. E. Schattschneider, writing in the early 1940s, compared the American party system to the British with its centralization of authority and national-level emphasis. In the United States, according to Schattschneider, there is the ideal and there is the reality:

> [T]here is the democratic system in which the local organizations participate by a broadly representative process in decisions made in a party conference acting with authority of the whole party. This is what the American system *seems* to be. Unfortunately, the democratization of the internal processes of the parties in the United States has been chiefly theoretical, and the practical results have not been important . . . the local organizations may seize power in the party, use this power for their own purposes, and refuse to recognize any superior party authority. This is the American system in fact. (1942, 171)

Schattschneider goes on to describe the real-world operations of a party boss-dominated system:

> The essential fact is that the local party machine is the seat of authority. The first mark of the boss is that he has power; he must be explained in terms of power. . . . The American party which seems unable to hold its lines at the national level is remarkably well disciplined at the level of the state and local bosses. This is the meaning of the statement that the American major party [sic] is decentralized. . . . The local boss is distinguished not merely by the fact that he has power, but more especially because he has power without responsibility. . . . The American local boss is remarkable for his success in exercising power for which he is accountable to no one. (1942, 171–72)

The American Political Science Association's 1950 report on the political parties of the day described them "as two loose associations of state and local organizations, with very little national machinery and very little national cohesion," essentially ill equipped and functionally incapable of governing with any degree of cohesion or programmatic unity at the national level.

Edward N. Costikyan, an officeholder and reformer in New York City, in reminiscing on his days in politics, explains the party practices of his time this way:

> [D]istrict leaders were the unpaid local directors of the Democratic party. . . . [U]nder them served enough captains to cover every election district . . . and each assembly district . . . had its own regular Democratic club, which was the local party headquarters. . . . [M]ost of these clubs were regarded by their

members as private membership and social as well as political organizations. Many were modestly wealthy, owning their own headquarters and possessing substantial investments. Newcomers to the Democratic Party—as voters—were welcome, but not as members of the local club—at least, not unless some member sponsored them. Certainly, no one coming in "off the street" was accepted without inquiry. Once in the club, a lengthy period of probation was appropriate before the new member was accepted, let alone heard from. (1966, 23–24)

Reform and the changing times, along with different voter expectations, paved the way for a new type of politics. Costikyan explains what "reform" meant in this environment and how much of a challenge practices we often take for granted today presented to the old ways of conducting party business:

"Reform" was generally used to describe any insurgent candidate for district leader whose club had a . . . constitution (membership control [of the party], open financial reports, control over the leadership by the club's executive committee and [its] membership). With this small-d democracy went a series of other distinguishing marks: regular monthly meetings of the membership to hear speakers on subjects from air pollution to U.S. foreign policy, forums, countless committees made up of members dealing with whatever problems they wanted to deal with (mental health, art tours, United Nations hospitality, problems of the aged), and a degree of self righteousness.

These clubs asserted a doctrine of party discipline that shocked the traditional Democratic Party worker—that discipline flowed from the bottom up—that the leader followed the dictates of the club—and that "the word" did not come down from the top. This idea, more than anything else, shook and shocked the party establishment, in essential implication (though hardly in scale) much as the Protestant Reformation shook the Catholic Church. (1966, 35–36)

Finally, in this context there is the judgment of Edward C. Banfield and James Q. Wilson in *City Politics* (1963) "that a system of government based upon specific, material inducements is wholly at odds with that conception of democracy that says that decisions ought to be made on the basis of reasonable discussion about what the common good requires. Machine government is essentially, a system of organized bribery" (1963,125).

The local party machine was a product of a historical era and the need to assimilate immigrant populations into the American political culture and to expand democratic participation. It was all done at a cost. By the late 1940s and early 1950s the political machine had become an anachronism and a general embarrassment, one that failed to adequately meet the demands of a changing society. The New Deal social programs had made it and the services it provided obsolete. Yet the traditions that it left behind of parochialism, localism, lack of a dominant national party presence, and a nationalized policy agenda ("issue-oriented parties") remained in the post–World War II period and set the tone for the politics of the day.

It is difficult to equate this picture with the national politics of the contemporary era: the media-fueled and high-finance campaigns, the dominance of the presidential (and, to a lesser extent, congressional) elections in the nation's political life, the atrophying of the state and local parties, and the impersonal, technology-driven corporate approach we are familiar with today.

The parties' role in all of this appears to have declined to the point that some have labeled the present parties as "candidate-centered" (as against "party-centered") (Wattenberg 1998). Each candidate is an independent entrepreneur attempting to amass the considerable funds needed for a serious campaign. The money is needed to subsidize pollsters, consultants, voter identification experts, experienced fund-raisers, and the political managers crucial to electoral success. The extent to which this improves upon the past and the costs in terms of services and personalized representation is an open question, although I suspect most would consider it—whatever its shortcomings—an improvement over previous practices.

The role of the political party—and in particular its relevance to the contemporary political scene—is debatable. Martin P. Wattenberg, in examining data relevant to the time period examined here, would argue that the relevance of the parties and their importance have eroded. Voters, he believes, are indifferent to parties; they do not see them as crucial to the political scene or of importance to their own decision making in elections (1998).

Walter Dean Burnham, as with many political scientists, has been anticipating a long-overdue realignment to reestablish the parties' vitality and their credibility in representing constituent groups, a regrouping that he feels now may be close at hand (1970, 1982, 2000).

Finally, in this regard, Diana Owen, Jack Dennis, and Casey Klofstadt, writing at the beginning of the new century (in chapter 4), report on their research on public attitudes toward, and public support for, the party system. Their study reports on surveys from the 1990s but also includes results from earlier research for a time period that roughly parallels the present analysis. After assessing the factors that have contributed to the parties' decline, mostly familiar—the money explosion; for-hire, instantaneous campaigns; the media's dominance of political discourse; the reduction in party affiliations; and the growing disaffection for politics among younger adults—they write:

> We suspect that a shift in the political culture that pertains to the party system has been underway for some time operating at several levels. This shift . . . is complex and not yet fully understood. Traditional formal institutions of representation, such as legislatures, and less formally constituted institutions, such as parties, apparently have become the main objects of declining popular support and legitimacy.

Basically, what could amount to a systemic repositioning of the parties in terms of their representative role in American politics could be in progress. If so, a declining legitimacy associated with the party system combined with the redefinition of their functional relevance could result in a less familiar, more stratified and, more than likely, less broadly inclusive or politically relevant party presence. Owen, Dennis, and Klofstad make a related point:

> When people begin to question the present party system's ability to provide adequate representation of their demands, they may turn to alternative parties or to independent candidates. . . . [C]itizens may shift their focus to alternative organizations as well. Over the long term in the United States, some of the party's representative role has devolved more upon candidate organizations that perform relatively separate electioneering and linkage functions while operating only nominally under a party's label.
>
> Such candidate-centeredness may be further enhanced by direct financial support from interest or advocacy groups. . . . [T]he competition for popular support also may enhance the role of other organizations, such as those associated with mass political or social movements and the mass media. These alternatives to parties begin to take on part of the representative function that was earlier reserved for the major parties. One might even argue the modern-day presidency, as its powers have become enlarged, may also take up some of these functions, particularly under the stewardship of a president who puts great stress on maintaining an almost intimate connection to the general populace, such as Bill Clinton did.
>
> . . . Thus, a more complex representative process has evolved—one in which the role of the parties . . . may be increasingly constricted.

An understanding of public attitudes toward the party system should then prove instructive, if not critical, in gauging their political health and potential staying power.

The Present Study

The foregoing provides a context for the assessment of political party relevance as seen by the voters. The years in question, as indicated, are 1952–1992, and the data used are from the quadrennial National Election Studies (NES) conducted by the Center for Political and Social Studies of the Survey Research Center of the University of Michigan. The indicators examined include measures of political party *salience*, the ability of voters to distinguish between parties and the importance they assigned to them and their activities. The second measure focuses on *affect*, the positive or negative feelings that voters associated with the party. The affect score presented in the following subtracts the negative from the positive and lists the remainder, with a negative score preceded by a minus sign. A third set of measures looks at salience and affect as they relate to both parties' presidential nominees. The differences and variations in these measures are less predictable between the parties and from one election to another and more varied than the other measures examined.

Party Salience

Table 5.1 presents the overall scores for the party system for the years 1952–1992 and by selected major population subgroups for the same time frame.

TABLE 5.1
Political Party Salience, 1952–1992

Grouping						Year					
	1952	1956	1960	1964	1968	1972	1976	1980	1984	1988	1992
Overall	**4.69**	**3.76**	**3.43**	**3.32**	**4.02**	**2.98**	**3.15**	**2.71**	**3.2**	**3.71**	**3.5**
Partisan Affiliation											
Democrats	2.62	1.93	1.76	1.88	2.31	1.5	1.62	1.49	1.63	1.84	1.77
Republicans	2.07	1.83	1.67	1.44	1.71	1.48	1.53	1.22	1.57	1.87	1.73
Sex											
Male	5.13	4.34	3.91	3.65	4.55	3.35	3.77	3.21	3.79	4.59	4.13
Female	4.31	3.29	3.04	3.05	3.61	2.71	2.7	2.33	2.75	3.05	2.96
Age											
1959–Present								1.9	2.56	2.89	2.99
1943–1958				2.5	3.26	2.45	2.74	2.45	3.51	4.28	4.08
1927–1942	4.47	3.3	3.09	3.06	3.76	3.15	3.22	3.33	3.58	4.01	3.6
1911–1926	4.48	3.73	3.46	3.47	4.4	3.46	3.67	2.89	3.16	3.53	3.34
1895–1910	4.99	4.08	3.6	3.61	4.27	3	3.36	2.5	2.23	2.68	2.92
Before 1895	4.75	3.72	3.61	3.21	3.79	2.19	2.65	2.33	2.25		
Race											
White	4.87	3.87	3.53	3.37	4.05	3	3.15	2.75	3.36	3.88	3.56
Black	3.1	2.58	2.55	2.93	3.79	3.07	3.14	2.37	2.3	2.8	3.08
Other Races	3.33	1.83	1.83	2.15	3.65	1.47	3.16	3.44	2.02	3.06	4.15
Education											
Only Grade School	3.84	2.98	3.16	2.62	3.23	2.35	2.46	1.88	1.64	2.09	2.35
Only High School	4.8	3.72	3.3	3.09	3.73	2.67	2.53	2.09	2.43	2.7	2.43
College Degree	6.8	5.13	4.07	4.56	5.24	4	4.42	3.84	4.51	5.19	4.72
Urbanism											
Central Cities	5.09	4.07	3.53	3.59	4.5	3.27	3.64	2.97	3.41	4.1	3.92
Suburban Areas	4.98	4.08	4.01	3.7	4.17	3.63	3.29	2.82	3.45	4.09	3.82
Rural	4.11	3.42	3.07	2.81	3.64	2.38	2.65	2.36	2.76	2.93	2.76

Table 5.1 *(Continued)*
Political Party Salience, 1952–1992

Location											
Non-South	4.91	4.03	3.59	3.43	4.07	3.08	3.27	2.78	3.46	4.06	3.7
South	3.96	2.91	2.95	2.95	3.89	2.72	2.79	2.54	2.55	2.94	3.08
Level of Income											
0–16th Percentile	3.58	2.63	2.88	2.76	3.28	2.55	2.49	2.03	2.26	2.61	2.63
17–33rd Precentile	4.03	3.31	3.05	3.13	3.45	2.65	2.8	2.18	2.63	2.98	2.75
34–67th Percentile	4.49	3.38	3.25	3.07	4.1	2.74	2.86	2.7	3.23	3.71	3.4
68–95th Percentile	5.55	4.56	3.86	3.75	4.61	3.73	3.81	3.43	4.15	4.78	4.38
96–100th Percentile	7.05	5.03	4.77	4.48	5.37	3.82	4.78	4.04	4.88	5.6	5.8
Occupation											
Professional/Manager	6.15	4.84	4.63	4.28	5.39	4.04	4.58	3.91	4.73	5.27	4.88
Clerical/Sales	5.37	4.09	3.52	3.66	4.18	3.02	3.13	2.62	3.12	3.96	3.36
Skilled/Semi-skilled	4.8	4.02	3.43	3.01	3.74	2.85	2.96	2.37	2.73	2.8	2.92
Laborers	3.62	2.98	3.3	2.69	3.22	2.96	2.25	2.23	2.25	2.8	2.93
Farm/Forest/Fishers	4.41	3.41	3.23	2.81	3.48	2.87	2.51	1.84	1.88	3.43	2.94
Homemakers	4.22	3.19	2.85	2.98	3.42	2.39	2.33	1.85	2.49	2.75	2.58
Union Membership											
Union	4.78	3.85	3.32	3.49	3.78	2.84	3.22	2.85	3.65	3.96	3.72
Nonunion	4.68	3.72	3.48	3.26	4.11	3.05	3.14	2.67	3.09	3.66	3.47
Religion											
Protestant	4.51	3.7	3.41	3.29	3.97	2.82	3.01	2.51	3.1	3.49	3.34
Catholic	4.96	3.92	3.59	3.32	4.11	3.33	3.22	2.93	3.18	3.92	3.68
Jewish	6.53	4.55	4.61	3.6	4.4	3.68	5.13	4.08	4.11	5.45	6.57
Other/None	4.85	3.09	3.58	3.69	4.68	3.25	3.46	2.89	3.62	4.32	3.55

The mean score for the eleven-election series is 3.50. The most pronounced indicators of salience were the Eisenhower–Stevenson elections in the 1950s (and especially the 1952 contest), 1968, and 1988. The lowest were the first Reagan election in 1980 and the Nixon–McGovern race in 1972. Basically, and this is the most impressive finding, the importance of the party system ranks high among voters, not a totally predictable outcome given the controversies and disruptions associated with the parties and the campaigns in given years.

When the major subgroup populations are assessed in terms of their perceptions of party salience, most parallel the overall trends indicated, falling slightly above or below the averages for all groups. These would include such social categorizations as males and females; most age cohorts; city and suburban dwellers; southerners and non-southerners; union and nonunion workers; Catholics and Protestants; clerical/sales, skilled and semi-skilled workers (professionals and managers are considerably more positive in their evaluations while laborers and farm workers are less so); those with more formal education (with college graduates more enthusiastic while those with a grade school education are less so).

There are exceptions to the broader patterns, and there are variations within categories. Figure 5-1 (party identification), Figure 5-2 (race), and Figure 5-3 (religion) illustrate some of the more significant differences. In Figure 5-1, the weaker assessments of both parties' membership are shown, a curiosity in the sense that party identifiers attribute considerably less importance to the party system than does the electorate at large. It may be that they are more demanding and more cognizant of what the parties do and do not do. Whites, in particular (Figure 5-2A), and blacks with more variation (especially during the Republican cycles of 1952–1956 and 1980–1988) (Figure 5-2B) follow the pattern of overall assessments of salience, while non-black minorities clearly do not (Figure 5-2C). The latter group exhibits significant fluctuation in their evaluations. Finally, those of the Jewish faith differ perceptibly from Catholics and Protestants (groups that are particularly close to the overall averages) in their more positive regard for party salience (Figure 5-3C).

In broader context, it is the constituents' positive assessments of salience that attract attention. The political parties and the party system more generally are seen as positive contributors to the quality of the democratic experience, a finding not necessarily predictable from the constant and frequently severe criticism leveled at the parties in individual elections and over time.

Party Affect

Party affect—the likes and dislikes in terms of emotion—that people direct toward the political parties (Table 5.2) ranges from strong positive associations (1956, 1964, 1976, and 1996) to those marginally above neutral (1952, 1980), to negative projections (relating to the bitter election battle of 1968). Here the subgroup evaluations are clearly distinctive and, as would be expected with emotional associations, show greater intensity and volatility relative to those associated with party saliency (a range of −0.131 to 0.642). The mean is 0.307.

PARTY RELEVANCE OVER TIME

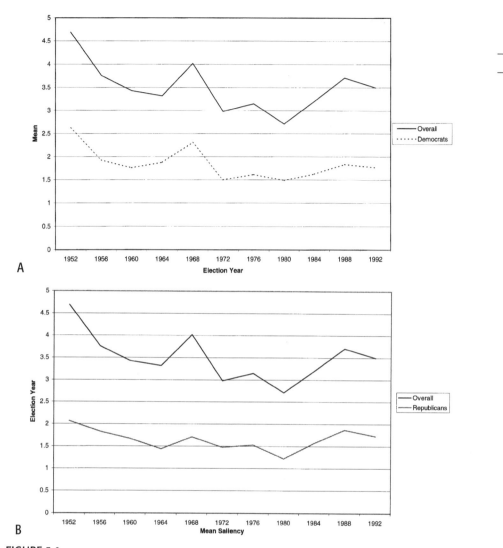

FIGURE 5-1

(A). Political Party Affiliation and Perceptions of Salience, 1952–1992: Democrats vs. Entire Population. (B). Political Party Affiliation and Perceptions of Salience, 1952–1992: Republicans vs. Entire Population.

Source: Adapted from the National Election Studies

In addition to evaluations in the election year of 1968, parties did less well in 1952 and 1980. They received strong positive emotional associations in 1992, 1964, 1976 and 1956. Regional (north/south), gender, age (with exceptions for two elections), and the oldest cohort of voters (the smallest in numbers) were unusually positive in 1980 and the youngest category entering the electorate in 1968 was again substantially more positive than other age cohorts. Suburban and rural areas (more negative) closely followed the general trend lines. High school graduates also mimicked the overall pattern, as did those with only a grade school education (although in more positive terms). College graduates

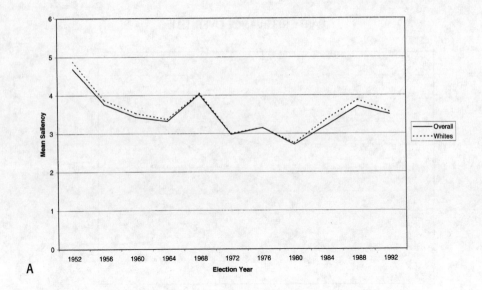

A

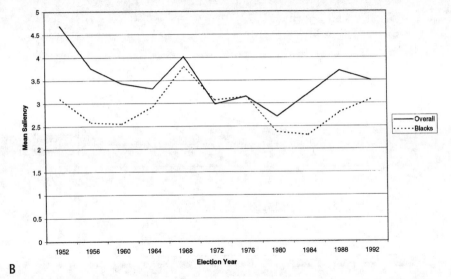

B

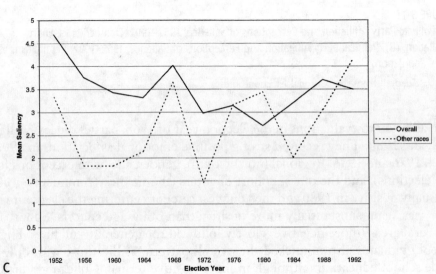

C

were far less predictable, falling well below others in 1952 and well above other categories in both 1964 and 1988. Middle- and upper-income respondents were again close to the averages for all groups, low-income voters scored above the collective mean, and the highest income category (those in the 96th–100th income bracket) most consistently below the mean.

Union and nonunion members followed the general pattern for each election with the former feeling more positive and the latter slightly more negative than the population as a whole. Occupational groups followed the general contour of the trend lines, again with the exception of laborers (more positive and more changeable) and farmers (more negative). Homemakers and those in professional/managerial classes and to a lesser extent those in clerical and sales positions were more negative than the average for the population as a whole.

Figures 5-4, 5-5, and 5-6 show some of the more interesting deviations. Republicans have considerably more negative associations with their party than do Democrats (Figure 5-4A); whites are somewhat more negative than the average score for all respondents, while blacks are substantially more positive, actually leading in this category (Figure 5-5B); and in terms of religious affiliation both Protestants (slightly more negative) (Figure 5-6A) and Catholics (slightly more positive overall and emotionally strongly committed in the John F. Kennedy race in 1960; Figure 5-6B) are close to the overall trend lines, while those of the Jewish faith are consistently well above the national average (Figure 5-6C).

The positive and negative associations with the parties do vary substantially from one election to another, presumably dependent on the candidates put forward, the issues of greatest relevance, and the parties' positioning on these. The "likes/dislikes" measures are clearly different in character from the more stable dimensions of salience, as would be expected, and, more than likely, a factor of greater consequence in short-term election outcomes. Stability of association is not the defining quality in relation to affective reactions to the parties, although some social groups do maintain (in relative perspective) a consistently favorable emotional association with the parties and others an equally consistent negative association. Overall, it cannot be argued that the parties are well received. Regardless of election, candidates, or the political context of the times, the negative appears to carry more weight than the positive.

Perceptions of Presidential Candidates

Table 5.3 presents a profile of measures of salience as these relate to both parties' presidential candidates for the eleven elections analyzed. Generally in re-

◀ FIGURE 5-2
(A). Race and Party Saliency, 1952–1992: Whites vs. the Entire Population. (B). Race and Party Saliency, 1952–1992: Blacks vs. the Entire Population. (C). Race and Party Saliency, 1952–1992: Non-Whites and Non-Blacks vs. the Entire Population.

Source: Adapted from the National Election Studies

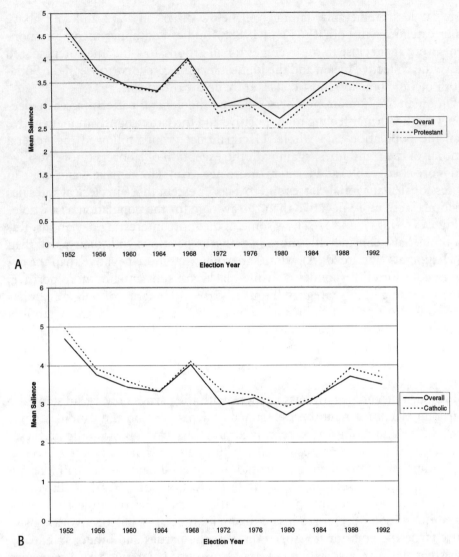

FIGURE 5-3

(A). Religion and Party Salience, 1952–1992: Protestants vs. the Entire Population. (B). Religion and Party Salience, 1952–1992: Catholics vs. the Entire Population.

lation to salience Republican nominees do better than Democratic nominees (an $\bar{x}$ of 2.496 for Republicans to 2.307 for the Democrats), although Kennedy, Johnson, Carter, and Dukakis were perceived in varying degrees in more positive terms than were their opponents. Conversely, Eisenhower, Nixon in 1972, Reagan in 1984, and Bush outscore their Democratic opponents.

In relation to affect, again there is significantly more variation from one election to the next and between the political parties. The Republican candidates on the average do better than their Democratic counterparts (an $\bar{x}$ of 0.227 compared to an $\bar{x}$ of 0.133), although the Republicans did have four

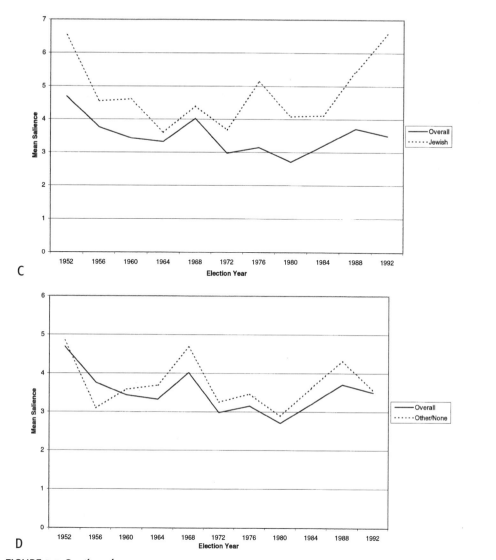

C

D

FIGURE 5-3 *Continued*
(C). Religion and Party Salience, 1952–1992: Jewish People vs. the Entire Population. (D). Religion and Party Salience, 1952–1992: People of Other or No Religion vs. the Entire Population.

Source: Adapted from the National Election Studies

nominees score in negative terms in the public's evaluations, including Ronald Reagan in both 1980 and 1984 (surprisingly) and his successor George Bush in 1988 (a high −0.606). The least-liked candidate of all the contenders, Republican or Democrat, was Barry Goldwater (−0.727). The most warmly received Republican was Dwight Eisenhower.

The Democratic Party's best candidate in terms of public reception was Lyndon B. Johnson in 1964, clearly a reaction in part to John F. Kennedy's assassination and the new president's success in pulling the country together and in part also to Johnson's success in positioning his opponent, Goldwater, as an

TABLE 5.2
Political Party Affect, 1952–1992

Grouping	1952	1956	1960	1964	1968	1972	1976	1980	1984	1988	1992
						Year					
Overall	**0.013**	**0.417**	**0.372**	**0.628**	**-0.131**	**0.227**	**0.486**	**0.187**	**0.293**	**0.243**	**0.642**
Partisan Affiliation											
Democrats	0.14	0.49	0.46	0.44	-0.18	0.07	0.16	0.16	0.28	0.27	0.25
Republicans	0.12	0.07	0.09	-0.19	-0.05	-0.16	-0.32	-0.02	-0.01	0.03	-0.39
Sex											
Male	0.032	0.68	0.507	0.588	-0.266	0.223	0.467	0.039	0.231	-0.029	0.443
Female	-0.004	0.204	0.26	0.66	-0.025	0.231	0.5	0.298	0.342	0.445	0.813
Age											
1959–Present								0.097	0.344	0.244	0.48
1943–1958				1.19	-0.217	0.342	0.664	0.162	0.193	0.062	0.74
1927–1942	0.207	0.518	0.621	0.581	-0.129	0.322	0.371	0.085	0.212	0.349	0.574
1911–1926	0.493	0.489	0.413	0.659	-0.025	0.196	0.441	0.306	0.504	0.485	0.829
1895–1910	-0.257	0.421	0.317	0.785	-0.157	0.182	0.363	0.275	0.35	0.327	0.718
Before 1895	-0.486	0.117	-0.019	0.223	-0.402	-0.769	0.026	0.333	1.75		
Race											
White	-0.193	0.316	0.29	0.419	-0.471	0.016	0.274	0.028	0.141	-0.013	0.473
Black	1.85	1.48	1.16	2.44	2.76	2.06	2.22	1.35	1.54	1.61	1.91
Other Races	2.67	1.5	0.722	0.923	1.95	1	0.431	0.667	0.102	1.24	0.108
Education											
Only Grade School	0.688	0.63	0.386	1.19	0.632	0.44	0.885	0.526	0.703	0.598	1.15
Only High School	-0.135	0.55	0.7	0.671	-0.104	0.255	0.539	0.278	0.284	0.352	0.722
College Degree	-1.46	-0.303	0.722	0.923	1.95	1	0.431	0.667	0.102	1.24	0.108
Urbanism											
Central Cities	0.5	0.799	0.947	1.042	0.374	0.741	0.966	0.76	0.766	0.978	1.32
Suburban Areas	-0.32	0.037	0.173	0.459	-0.27	0.04	0.343	-0.042	0.224	-0.073	0.52
Rural Areas	-0.153	0.428	0.224	0.444	-0.337	0.068	0.26	-0.015	0.061	0.11	0.267

TABLE 5.2 (Continued)
Political Party Affect, 1952–1992

Location											
Non-South	-0.138	0.246	0.423	0.624	-0.196	0.221	0.466	0.197	0.34	0.306	0.69
South	0.518	0.94	0.2	0.64	0.068	0.245	0.547	0.161	0.177	0.105	0.537
Level of Income											
0–16th Percentile	0.335	0.509	0.194	1.1	0.369	0.417	0.799	0.552	1.04	0.73	1.11
17–33rd Percentile	0.471	0.677	0.416	0.892	0.114	0.343	0.819	0.423	0.565	0.687	0.964
34–67th Percentile	0.39	0.672	0.718	0.839	-0.291	0.314	0.657	0.202	0.255	0.142	0.579
68–95th Percentile	-0.274	0.38	0.41	0.274	-0.338	0.132	0.354	0.125	0.104	-0.054	0.375
96–100th Percentile	-2.98	-1.12	-1.55	-0.538	-0.886	-0.887	-1.1	-0.87	-0.821	-1.38	0.285
Occupation											
Professional/Manager	-1.37	-0.118	-0.061	-0.191	-0.757	-0.119	0.137	0.01	0.36	0.125	0.551
Clerical/Sales	-0.221	0.506	-0.275	0.51	-0.47	0.117	0.466	0.071	0.064	0.021	0.696
Skilled/Semi-skilled	0.942	0.832	1.09	1.26	0.381	0.696	0.934	0.366	0.546	0.424	0.823
Laborers	1.24	1.37	0.162	1.81	1.67	0.783	1.08	0.104	0.981	0.722	1.35
Farm/Forest/Fishers	-0.321	0.699	-0.184	0.595	-0.15	-0.154	-0.024	0.156	-0.35	0.155	-0.075
Homemakers	-0.164	0.133	0.248	0.524	-0.199	-0.008	0.073	0.113	-0.118	0.229	0.406
Union Membership											
Union	1.14	0.99	1.29	1.77	0.41	0.703	1.15	0.515	0.805	0.659	1.12
Nonunion	-0.4	0.2	0.028	0.269	-0.312	0.065	0.277	0.07	0.156	0.145	0.551
Religion											
Protestant	-0.35	0.14	-0.046	0.445	-0.358	0.084	0.251	0.054	0.088	0.065	0.391
Catholic	0.677	1.04	1.72	1.11	0.415	0.526	0.827	0.295	0.445	0.384	0.807
Jewish	2.86	2.09	2.55	1.42	1.26	1.18	1.68	1.76	1.92	1.13	2.97
Other/None	0.55	1.18	-0.526	0.62	0	0.367	0.871	0.264	0.82	0.889	1.06

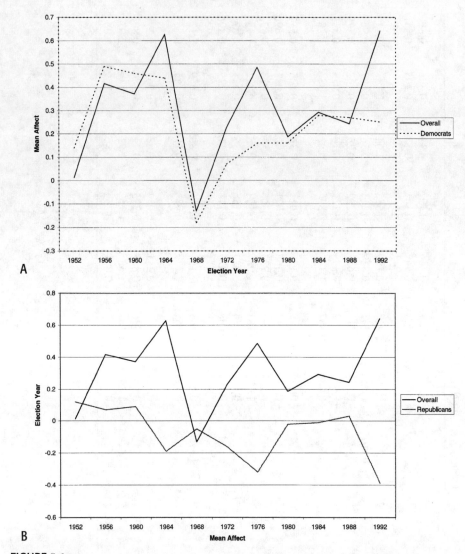

FIGURE 5-4

(A). Political Party Affiliation and Party Affect, 1952–1992: Democrats vs. the Entire Population.

(B). Political Party Affiliation and Pary Affect, 1952–1992: Republicans vs. the Entire Population.

Source: Adopted from the National Election Studies

FIGURE 5-5

(A). Race and Party Affect, 1952–1992: Whites toward Political Parties vs. the Entire Population.

(B). Race and Party Affect, 1952–1992: Blacks toward Political Parties vs. the Entire Population.

(C). Race and Party Affect: Non-Whites and Blacks toward Political Parties vs. the Entire Population.

Source: Adapted from the National Election Studies

PARTY RELEVANCE OVER TIME

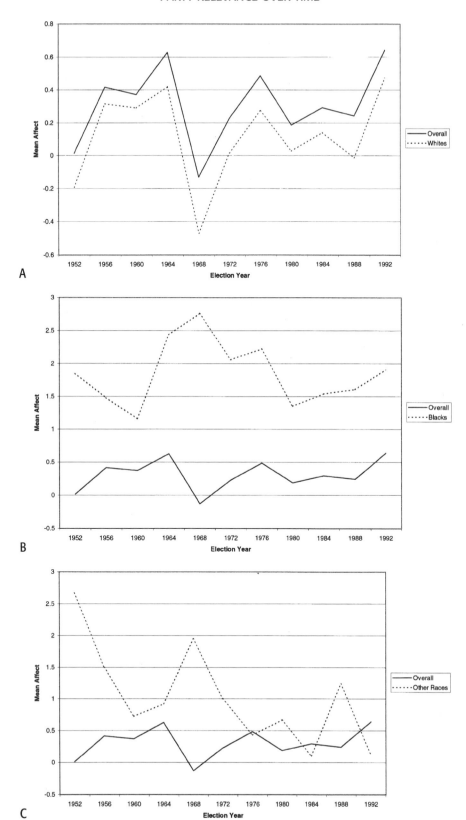

A

B

C

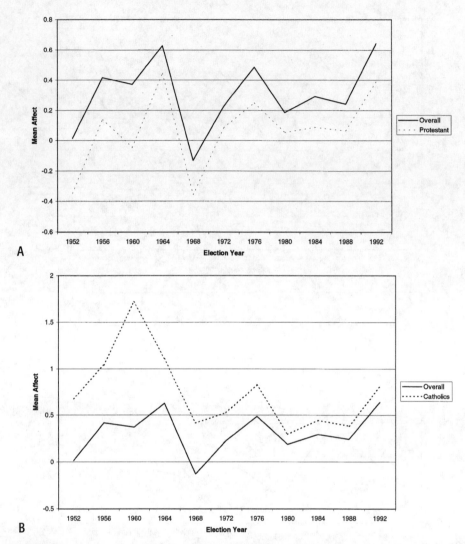

FIGURE 5-6
(A). Religion and Party Affect, 1952–1992: Toward Political Parties of Protestants vs. the Entire Population. (B). Religion and Party Affect, 1952–1992: Toward Political Parties of Catholics vs. Entire Population.

extremist helped solidify his own already positive image. Beyond Johnson, both Adlai E. Stevenson (1952) and Bill Clinton (1992) in their first races were well thought of. Of the five nominees who received negative responses, George McGovern encountered the strongest reaction (−0.641) in 1972, a year in which the Democratic Party split badly over the "New Politics" and the party reforms (recommended by a party committee initially chaired by McGovern and intended to avoid the chaos that marked the 1968 election year). The changes split the party and its coalition for over a decade and in some respects, as the Clinton presidency has shown (see below), have yet to be fully resolved. In addition, in the election of 1968 (Hubert H. Humphrey) and

PARTY RELEVANCE OVER TIME

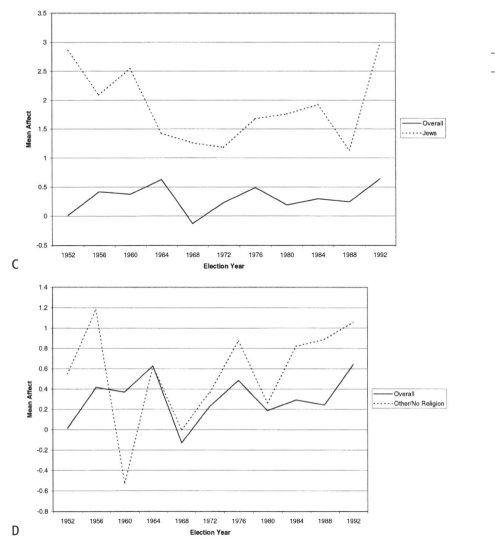

C

D

FIGURE 5-6 *(Continued)*
(C). Religion and Party Affect, 1952–1992: Toward Political Parties of Jewish People vs. the Entire Population. (D). Religion and Party Affect, 1952–1992: Toward Political Parties of Other or No Religion vs. the Entire Population.

Source: Adapted from the National Election Studies

during the Reagan–Bush era also Democratic candidates (Jimmy Carter in his reelection bid in 1980, his vice president, Walter Mondale, in 1984, and Massachusetts Governor Michael S. Dukakis in 1988) did poorly. Neither party's candidates were well received in the Reagan elections.

Overall then, the electorate could be said to do well in separating and distinguishing the candidates and their appeals and in evaluating them. The nominees, while still exhibiting some variation, are perceived as offering skills and programs of importance. More volatile and less predictable, the emotional associations with the candidates and the extent to which they are liked or disliked

TABLE 5.3A

Salience and Presidential Candidates, 1952–1992: Salience and the Democratic Party's Presidential Candidates

Salience Grouping	Year										
	1952	1956	1960	1964	1968	1972	1976	1980	1984	1988	1992
Overall	1.789	1.814	2.377	2.625	2.576	2.08	2.409	2.683	2.214	2.271	2.538
Sex											
Male	1.815	2.029	2.476	2.603	2.649	2.23	2.618	2.821	2.438	2.643	2.608
Female	1.767	1.639	2.296	2.643	2.519	1.968	2.257	2.579	2.039	1.994	2.477
Age											
1959–Present								2.39	2.122	1.941	2.426
1943–1958				2.731	2.48	2.155	2.517	2.69	2.343	2.549	2.796
1927–1942	1.673	1.725	2.448	2.79	2.648	2.257	2.462	2.875	2.269	2.415	2.549
1911–1926	1.824	1.934	2.557	2.614	2.728	2.12	2.403	2.834	2.229	2.175	2.358
1895–1910	1.926	1.782	2.298	2.6	2.397	1.8	2.106	2.195	1.695	1.558	1.826
Before 1895	1.611	1.609	1.966	2.149	2.152	1.231	1.966	2	1.5		
Race											
White	1.86	1.885	2.485	2.623	2.576	2.123	2.448	2.74	2.275	2.37	2.624
Black	1.123	1.027	1.337	2.669	2.664	1.761	2.101	2.26	1.928	1.699	2.069
Other Races	2	1.833	1.944	2.384	1.95	1.529	2.302	2.813	1.429	2.105	2.406
Education											
Only Grade School	1.304	1.238	1.823	2.113	2.131	1.454	1.698	1.883	1.265	1.427	1.473
Only High School	1.938	1.806	2.456	2.604	2.505	1.948	2.117	2.409	1.884	1.774	2.043
College Degree	2.714	2.776	2.991	3.231	3.097	2.758	3.206	3.332	2.846	3.017	3.192
Urbanism											
Central Cities	2.174	1.998	2.382	2.808	2.857	2.225	2.422	2.755	2.311	2.405	2.669
Suburban Areas	1.828	1.994	2.587	2.794	2.645	2.377	2.616	2.756	2.335	2.52	2.756
Rural Areas	1.423	1.622	2.263	2.35	2.36	1.792	2.204	2.539	2.004	1.861	2.115

TABLE 5.3A (Continued)
Salience and Presidential Candidates, 1952–1992: Salience and the Democratic Party's Presidential Candidates

Location											
Non-South	1.906	1.922	2.449	2.719	2.63	2.159	2.481	2.725	2.339	2.436	2.669
South	1.395	1.479	2.174	2.314	2.411	1.858	2.197	2.578	1.905	1.916	2.252
Level of Income											
0–16th Percentile	1.139	1.073	1.594	2.288	2.246	1.475	1.878	2.091	1.772	1.624	1.93
17–33rd Percentile	1.533	1.513	1.946	2.547	2.279	1.956	2.227	2.423	2.088	1.902	2.243
34–67th Percentile	1.768	1.791	2.522	2.666	2.69	2.09	2.347	2.734	2.303	2.292	2.66
68–95th Percentile	2.19	2.323	2.718	2.847	2.841	2.547	2.859	3.131	2.605	2.861	2.951
96–100th Percentile	3.031	2.948	3.33	2.981	2.911	2.79	3.051	3.507	3.045	2.979	3.716
Occupation											
Professional/Manager	2.395	2.513	3.003	2.943	3.09	2.684	3.122	3.262	2.994	3.112	3.265
Clerical/Sales	2.3	2.152	2.736	2.842	2.773	2.213	2.393	2.765	2.14	2.299	2.674
Skilled/Semi-skilled	1.669	1.778	2.267	2.409	2.388	1.868	2.275	2.396	1.996	1.822	2.115
Laborers	1.368	1.407	2.081	2.639	2.259	1.391	1.903	2.149	1.712	1.944	1.835
Farm/Forest/Fishers	1.282	1.354	1.679	1.932	2.483	1.718	1.578	2.094	1.513	1.931	1.878
Homemakers	1.694	1.574	2.186	2.657	2.339	1.837	2.092	2.49	1.83	1.814	2.247
Union Membership											
Union	1.897	1.877	2.399	2.759	2.51	2.061	2.459	2.867	2.544	2.541	2.68
Nonunion	1.76	1.792	2.376	2.586	2.601	2.094	2.402	2.623	2.13	2.21	2.514
Religion											
Protestant	1.643	1.775	2.298	2.559	2.516	2.002	2.318	2.576	2.107	2.183	2.469
Catholic	2.072	1.841	2.849	2.722	2.733	2.245	2.501	2.774	2.247	2.335	2.598
Jewish	2.966	2.554	3.016	3.178	3.381	2.786	3.378	3.471	2.887	3.065	4.129
Other/None	1.933	1.773	2.053	2.859	2.475	2.203	2.598	2.819	2.626	2.52	2.578

TABLE 5.3B

Salience and Presidential Candidates 1952–1992: Salience and the Republican Party's Presidential Candidates

Salience Grouping	Year										
	1952	1956	1960	1964	1968	1972	1976	1980	1984	1988	1992
Overall	**2.514**	**2.74**	**2.148**	**2.39**	**2.598**	**2.308**	**2.32**	**2.313**	**2.988**	**2.223**	**2.917**
Sex											
Male	2.541	2.923	2.274	2.434	2.652	2.475	2.575	2.51	3.284	2.556	3.055
Female	2.491	2.593	2.044	2.354	2.556	2.182	2.135	2.164	2.757	1.974	2.797
Age											
1959–Present								1.885	2.769	1.884	2.673
1943–1958				2.615	2.579	2.407	2.329	2.422	3.166	2.477	3.109
1927–1942	2.533	2.554	2.201	2.587	2.632	2.419	2.401	2.696	3.194	2.351	3.022
1911–1926	2.621	2.874	2.306	2.343	2.719	2.316	2.358	2.177	2.969	2.172	2.968
1895–1910	2.543	2.734	2.002	2.345	2.452	2.138	2.131	1.769	2.26	1.797	2.484
Before 1895	2.32	2.568	1.944	1.96	2.283	1.712	2.078	1.25	1.25		
Race											
White	2.65	2.844	2.226	2.463	2.708	2.355	2.372	2.403	3.093	2.367	2.053
Black	1.316	1.644	1.39	1.805	1.72	1.925	1.932	1.636	2.264	1.364	2.049
Other Races	0.5	1.667	1.833	1.615	1.55	1.941	1.879	2.063	2.714	1.896	3.001
Education											
Only Grade School	1.804	2.041	1.64	1.64	1.78	1.777	1.596	1.372	1.78	1.472	1.97
Only High School	2.841	2.804	2.191	2.373	2.587	2.134	2.054	1.945	2.563	1.66	2.35
College Degree	3.565	3.724	2.762	3.226	3.311	2.983	3.079	3.138	3.805	3.013	3.615
Urbanism											
Central Cities	2.711	2.913	2.097	2.473	2.695	2.397	2.36	2.38	2.951	2.233	2.944
Suburban Areas	2.669	2.968	2.457	2.71	2.826	2.683	2.538	2.434	3.167	2.518	2.228
Rural Areas	2.221	2.528	2.003	2.069	2.382	1.997	2.085	2.112	2.798	1.842	2.497

TABLE 5.3B (*Continued*)

Salience and Presidential Candidates 1952–1992: Salience and the Republican Party's Presidential Candidates

Location											
Non-South	2.702	2.913	2.22	2.537	2.707	2.414	2.389	2.403	3.154	2.453	3.084
South	1.881	2.21	1.94	1.904	2.262	2.008	2.118	2.082	2.578	1.724	2.553
Level of Income											
0–16th Percentile	1.659	1.974	1.632	1.938	2.025	1.892	1.733	1.617	2.234	1.508	2.18
17–33rd Percentile	2.123	2.373	1.915	2.022	2.196	2.051	2.029	1.861	2.804	1.85	2.64
34–67th Percentile	2.595	2.743	2.089	2.395	2.705	2.232	2.314	2.413	3.152	2.176	3.075
68–95th Percentile	3.029	3.258	2.407	2.796	3.055	2.768	2.712	2.915	3.486	2.873	3.334
96–100th Percentile	3.692	3.91	3.318	3.047	3.279	3.193	3.116	3.027	3.848	3.489	1.187
Occupation											
Professional/Manager	3.147	3.41	2.637	2.859	3.2	2.953	3.085	3.065	3.929	3.008	3.693
Clerical/Sales	3.137	2.989	2.617	2.683	2.991	2.345	2.471	2.431	2.934	2.352	3.025
Skilled/Semi-skilled	2.375	2.721	2.007	2.165	2.264	2.125	2.146	1.992	2.669	1.742	2.466
Laborers	1.617	1.824	1.838	1.333	1.815	1.522	1.8	1.9	2.634	1.537	1.894
Farm/Forest/Fishers	2.145	2.398	1.725	1.757	1.917	1.897	1.735	1.531	2.225	2.052	2.115
Homemakers	2.486	2.6	1.933	2.341	2.49	2.061	1.904	1.951	2.566	1.9	2.658
Union Membership											
Union	2.638	2.668	1.923	2.451	2.446	2.265	2.234	2.443	3.092	2.341	2.956
Nonunion	2.478	2.765	2.237	2.37	2.652	2.33	2.348	2.277	2.967	2.191	2.909
Religion											
Protestant	2.44	2.734	2.202	2.314	2.595	2.229	2.229	2.174	2.945	2.125	2.849
Catholic	2.677	2.753	2.039	2.438	2.608	2.503	2.412	2.433	2.962	2.272	3.063
Jewish	3.237	3.143	2.403	2.844	2.619	2.821	2.43	3.059	3.434	3.097	4.271
Other/None	2.35	2.364	2.553	3.07	2.593	2.392	2.424	2.644	3.234	2.53	2.836

TABLE 5.4A

Affect and Presidential Candidates, 1952–1992: Affect and the Democratic Party's Presidential Candidates

Affect Grouping	Year										
	1952	1956	1960	1964	1968	1972	1976	1980	1984	1988	1992
Overall	**0.464**	**0.018**	**0.45**	**1.002**	**-0.062**	**-0.641**	**0.284**	**-0.427**	**-0.014**	**-0.025**	**0.416**
Sex											
Male	0.531	0.052	0.503	0.913	-0.237	-0.762	0.195	-0.62	-0.226	-0.24	0.25
Female	0.407	-0.01	0.406	1.074	0.075	-0.552	0.349	-0.281	0.151	0.136	0.56
Age											
1959–Present				1.192	-0.191	-0.291	0.375	-0.266	0.116	0	0.375
1943–1958	0.313	-0.032	0.736	1.078	-0.109	-0.738	0.144	-0.499	-0.131	-0.129	0.342
1927–1942	0.601	0.052	0.532	0.977	0.058	-0.908	0.263	-0.763	-0.024	-0.007	0.391
1911–1926	0.459	0.013	0.267	1.003	-0.083	-0.653	0.314	-0.241	0.094	0.241	0.677
1895–1910	0.312	0	0.138	0.811	-0.109	-0.5	0	-0.018	-0.011	0.371	0.44
Before 1895								0.833	1		
Race											
White	0.412	-0.046	0.402	0.823	-0.32	-0.839	0.142	-0.594	-0.202	-0.226	0.275
Black	0.912	0.644	0.861	2.401	2.248	1.045	1.394	0.919	1.344	0.993	1.394
Other Races	1.667	1.833	1.167	1.079	0.65	0.235	0.526	-0.813	0.041	0.97	-0.163
Education											
Only Grade School	0.569	0.09	0.208	1.309	0.371	-0.326	0.687	0.309	0.587	0.563	0.774
Only High School	0.397	0.042	0.586	1.087	-0.044	-0.684	0.368	-0.335	-0.019	0.032	0.468
College Degree	0.363	-0.2	0.492	0.511	-0.452	-0.788	-0.06	-0.808	-0.17	-0.22	0.31
Urbanism											
Central Cities	0.792	0.235	0.91	1.218	0.537	-0.207	0.528	-0.04	0.471	0.49	0.882
Suburban Areas	0.286	-0.167	0.335	0.929	-0.127	-0.941	0.055	-0.614	-0.131	-0.245	0.244
Rural Areas	0.315	0.007	0.308	0.895	-0.375	-0.679	0.316	-0.523	-0.197	-0.119	0.272

TABLE 5.4A (Continued)

Affect and Presidential Candidates, 1952–1992: Affect and the Democratic Party's Presidential Candidates

Location											
Non-South	0.472	−0.31	0.56	1.072	−0.046	−0.658	0.203	−0.53	−0.065	−0.05	0.417
South	0.436	0.166	0.134	0.771	−0.113	−0.593	0.524	−0.166	0.111	0.031	0.415
Level of Income											
0–16th Percentile	0.367	0.121	0.198	1.323	0.449	−0.224	0.656	0.214	0.71	0.36	0.879
17–33rd Percentile	0.511	0.164	0.171	1.245	−0.443	−0.394	0.71	−0.205	0.384	0.268	0.729
34–67th Percentile	0.603	0.245	0.63	1.13	−0.251	−0.57	0.358	−0.468	−0.088	0.089	0.467
68–95th Percentile	0.48	−0.057	0.574	0.721	−0.09	−1.011	−0.018	−0.92	−0.381	−0.43	0.101
96–100th Percentile	−0.077	−0.276	0.375	0.302	−0.709	−1.56	−0.783	−1.48	−0.991	−1.106	−0.375
Occupation											
Professional/Manager	0.297	−0.137	0.521	0.471	−0.47	−0.957	−0.214	−0.744	−0.194	−0.102	0.333
Clerical/Sales	0.521	−0.163	0.238	0.852	−0.147	−0.569	0.105	−0.554	−0.228	−0.198	0.342
Skilled/Semi-skilled	0.653	0.182	0.611	1.396	0.044	−0.443	0.599	−0.304	0.232	0.101	0.574	0.577
Laborers	0.839	0.333	0.189	1.972	0.704	−0.435	0.936	−0.319	0.404	0.278	0.577
Farm/Forest/Fishers	0.275	0.044	0.101	0.905	0.017	−0.897	−0.072	−0.469	−0.388	−0.207	0.102
Homemakers	0.347	−0.04	0.441	0.994	0.059	−0.716	0.3	−0.109	−0.059	−0.048	0.334
Union Membership											
Union	0.853	0.178	1.062	1.698	0.167	−0.458	0.511	−0.232	0.364	0.218	0.78
Nonunion	0.328	−0.039	0.223	0.784	−0.134	−0.713	0.21	−0.507	−0.119	−0.082	0.354
Religion											
Protestant	0.249	−0.102	0.012	0.88	−0.246	−0.73	0.206	−0.371	−0.127	−0.163	0.266
Catholic	0.848	0.202	1.945	1.267	0.389	−0.548	0.469	−0.411	0.162	0.141	0.511
Jewish	2.19	1.339	1.661	2.067	1.333	0.214	0	−0.765	0.925	0.613	1.826
Other/None	0.7	0.364	−0.211	0.944	−0.068	−0.279	0.368	−0.644	0.059	0.399	0.675

TABLE 5.4B
Affect and Presidential Candidates, 1952–1992: Affect and the Republican Party's Presidential Candidates

Affect Grouping	Year										
	1952	1956	1960	1964	1968	1972	1976	1980	1984	1988	1992
Overall	**0.954**	**1.207**	**0.85**	**−0.727**	**0.413**	**0.526**	**0.07**	**−0.222**	**−0.022**	**0.076**	**−0.606**
Sex											
Male	0.821	1.06	0.752	−0.65	0.523	0.612	0.113	−0.14	0.134	0.127	−0.598
Female	1.065	1.327	0.932	−0.789	0.327	0.462	0.038	−0.284	−0.144	0.037	−0.614
Age											
1959–Present								−0.646	0.127	0.025	−0.619
1943–1958				−1	0.079	0.441	−0.114	−0.345	0.087	0.094	−0.683
1927–1942	1.027	1.157	0.667	−0.824	0.394	0.37	0.064	−0.111	−0.093	0.101	−0.513
1911–1926	0.852	1.219	0.879	−0.813	0.377	0.662	0.198	−0.119	−0.299	0.051	−0.696
1895–1910	1.028	1.135	0.858	−0.615	0.526	0.6	0.255	0.03	0.034	0.15	0.191
Before 1895	1	1.38	1.056	−0.284	0.848	1.019	0.888	−0.583	0.25		
Race											
White	1.072	1.298	0.878	−0.619	0.605	0.702	0.234	−0.13	0.159	0.23	−0.514
Black	−0.064	0.274	0.564	−1.667	−1.315	−1	−1.259	−0.988	−1.552	−0.695	−1.414
Other Races	−0.5	−0.333	0.944	−0.846	−0.05	−0.059	0.017	0.063	0.347	−0.851	−0.012
Education											
Only Grade School	0.52	0.875	0.714	−0.763	0.07	0.429	−0.081	−0.266	−0.579	−0.256	−0.268
Only High School	1.136	1.201	0.665	−0.739	0.43	0.547	−0.051	−0.154	−0.006	0.045	−0.602
College Degree	1.656	1.779	1.44	−0.656	0.666	0.548	0.333	−0.299	0.102	0.185	−0.65
Urbanism											
Central Cities	0.755	1.137	0.565	−0.981	−0.01	0.029	−0.238	−0.601	−0.676	−0.294	−1.01
Suburban Areas	1.214	1.547	1.12	−0.661	0.491	0.664	0.185	−0.148	0.163	0.187	−0.53
Rural Areas	0.925	1.059	0.832	−0.585	0.612	0.712	0.192	0	0.192	0.202	−0.388

TABLE 5.4B *(Continued)*

Affect and Presidential Candidates, 1952–1992: Affect and the Republican Party's Presidential Candidates

Location											
Non-South	1.024	1.347	0.869	−0.846	0.432	0.493	0.063	−0.276	−0.049	0.023	−0.75
South	0.719	0.781	0.798	−0.336	0.356	0.621	0.09	−0.086	0.043	0.189	−0.293
Level of Income											
0–16th Percentile	0.466	0.846	0.903	−0.715	0.153	0.278	−0.117	−0.383	−0.524	0.037	−0.67
17–33rd Percentile	0.899	0.987	0.982	−0.791	0.329	0.591	−0.111	−0.158	−0.526	−0.159	−0.837
34–67th Percentile	0.945	1.061	0.606	−0.946	0.561	0.396	0.004	−0.238	0.064	0.033	−0.691
68–95th Percentile	1.148	1.43	0.791	−0.584	0.498	0.747	0.174	−0.105	0.205	0.277	−0.427
96–100th Percentile	2.092	2.343	2.091	−0.481	0.468	1.263	0.928	0.069	1.152	1.404	−0.527
Occupation											
Professional/Manager	1.553	1.557	1.164	−0.589	0.7	0.694	0.356	−0.208	0.002	0.041	−0.668
Clerical/Sales	1.379	1.506	1.376	−0.644	0.45	0.467	0.276	−0.127	0.09	0.269	−0.543
Skilled/Semi-skilled	0.414	0.937	0.492	−0.926	0.233	0.408	−0.261	−0.312	−0.226	−0.045	−0.79
Laborers	0.176	0.491	0.919	−1	−0.482	−0.391	−0.239	−0.34	−0.365	0.093	−0.774
Farm/Forest/Fishers	0.771	0.628	0.661	−0.324	0.683	0.667	0.458	0.156	0.875	−0.017	0.034
Homemakers	1.155	1.575	0.849	−0.707	0.445	0.652	0.161	−0.154	0.17	0.212	−0.245
Union Membership											
Union	0.48	0.877	0.244	−1.294	0.205	0.242	−0.24	−0.458	−0.598	−0.244	−1.042
Nonunion	1.128	1.329	1.079	−0.551	0.479	0.635	0.165	−0.136	0.132	0.154	0.52
Religion											
Protestant	1.087	1.329	1.127	−0.557	0.637	0.669	0.201	−0.047	0.184	0.195	−0.404
Catholic	0.749	1.043	0.006	−1.006	0.104	0.419	−0.036	−0.295	−0.107	0.004	−0.609
Jewish	0.322	0.214	−0.436	−2.089	−1.429	−0.893	−0.719	−1.216	−1.472	−0.129	−2.641
Other/None	0.117	0.364	1.026	−1.155	−0.763	−0.139	−0.406	−0.756	−0.784	−0.47	−1.142

by the public fluctuate in relation to the qualities associated with the party nominees, what they represent, and the tenor of the times. Party affect in relation to individual candidacies exhibits the most pronounced variation of any of the measures.

The Presidential Election of 1996 and a New Course for Party Politics?

The Clinton elections, the first of which is included as the end piece of the foregoing analysis, may provide a dividing point in American politics. If so, it is likely to be one that (1) blurs the differences between the parties, making them less distinctive in the public mind and further removed from their core base and the types of policy themes that marked party appeals since at least the New Deal; and (2) capitalizes on a cumulative drift in American politics, which includes the graduated lessening of party ties; the increasing of freelance voting, marked by split-ticketing; the continued contraction of the American electorate in terms of active participation; a further decrease in representation of less economically well-off groups; an increasing polarization of high-income and lower-income groups; and the dominance in campaigns of consultants, media, and the money necessary to hire such professional services.

A stated objective of the Clinton campaigns, more evident in 1996 but also present in the earlier contest, was to project a centrist image, closer to middle-class values and more typical of Republican policy proposals, one removed from minority and explicitly working-class objectives. The intent was to appeal to the unaffiliated (or weakly affiliated) and the broad middle-class constituencies that participate in elections and decide outcomes. The appeals ranged from issues of economic expansion and tax relief to a family-values agenda and included the adoption of Republican initiatives on the budget, welfare reform, debt reduction, defense funding, and trade policies opposed by organized labor, a core Democratic constituency (NAFTA as an example). Much of this was done at the expense of social programming. Many of the policies supported were either adapted from previous Republican administrations or were designed to appeal to Republican and higher-income constituencies (Greenberg and Skocpol 1997).

The strategy worked for Clinton. Its greatest success, given the ethical and personal accusations made against the president and the continuing special counsel and periodic congressional investigations, came in the reelection effort of 1996. The Republican Party, of course, cooperated, putting forth a tired agenda of worn promises (tax relief) in both the congressional and the presidential races. In addition, the party experienced an intraparty, contentious series of contests in the primaries. The uninspired and poorly managed presidential race of Robert Dole in the 1996 general election did not help its cause.

Yet this was far from the whole story. While the Democrats were attempting to recast their appeal and restructure their core coalition, the Republicans were on a power trip. In an unusual (even, for American politics, "revolutionary") move, they set about to introduce a policy coherence and across-the-board conservative ideological commitment into party ranks. The most visible focal point for this new party orthodoxy was the "Contract with America," the touchstone for their 1994 off-year campaign and later the reference point for their legislative agenda.

They were spectacularly, and unexpectedly, successful. The party captured both houses of the Congress in the 1994 election and came to aggressively assert itself as the equals (or better) of the executive branch in setting the nation's policy agenda. One major consequence of all this was an unprecedented period of partisan strife, congressional and special counsel investigations of the president and his wife, continual accusations of unethical and even illegal behavior on the part of the chief executive, charges of sexual and personal misconduct, and a series of partisan-inspired court cases. In policy terms, outcomes included legislative gridlock, budget impasses, and shutdown of the federal government. It all culminated in the impeachment of the president and his later acquittal by the Senate.

How this will ultimately play out will not be known until some time in the twenty-first century. What is clear is that the nineties was a decade of unusual political stress, one presenting competing models of the American parties with the ultimate choices to be made somewhere down the line.

Political commentator E. J. Dionne, Jr. in *Why Americans Hate Politics* (1991) held out the promise that the nineties could "offer an opportunity for creative political thinking not seen since the industrial revolution ushered in new intellectual systems" that could result in approaches that "could rescue American politics from its current impasse" (353). In his later *They Only Look Dead* (1997), he laid out the dimensions of what this new political order (a revived "Progressivism") might entail:

> Progressives believe that the vast economic transformation now under way could confer large benefits. They do not seek to stop economic change. They accept the freedoms and the disciplines of the marketplace. They do not believe the government has infinite capacities, and they respect an American business system that Progressivism itself helped to build, save and nurture. . . . [N]either do Progressives believe that government can simply get out of the way, ignore the declining living standards of many American families or expect the free market to solve problems that the market has never been able to solve in the past. Progressives believe that government can help preserve a broad American middle class and expand the choices available to individuals. (1997,11)

It is fair to say that Dionne saw the Clinton policies as moving in this direction, setting new objectives, breaking old molds, and attempting to recast the fundamentals of American politics. How successful this proves to be in the long run and how deeply it takes root over the next generation or so are, of course, yet to be established. The 1990s appeared to be a period of experimentation with traditional forms of appeal and association and, in the most optimistic scenario, a revitalizing of political allegiances that sets a new course for party politics. If so, addressing the problems indicated above as to the polarization of society—economically and politically—does not appear to be a basic concern of either party. The politics and society that emerge over the next generation could have little in common with the New Deal base that gave them birth.

Conclusion

The American people distinguish between the major political parties and their offerings in terms of both their political agendas and their presidential nominees, and they assign them a relatively high and consistent grade in terms of importance. Their responses in relation to likes and dislikes of the parties and their candidates are another matter. These shift depending on the party and the election and are far less consistent in strength of appeal—in fact, both the parties and their nominees weigh in periodically with more debits than credits in public assessments. Overall, the emotional responses indicated are more than likely healthy and feed a skepticism in terms of party personnel and actions that in the four decades assessed was all too often justified. The line between skepticism and alienation is not clear; one may be reality-oriented, whereas the other clearly is deeper and, in systemic terms, more pathological. It both distracts from and serves to weaken the democratic experience. In a human endeavor, however, the ability to change perceptions and the associations made with the parties and candidates in relation to the context of individual elections is generally a good sign.

The most positive outcome from the analysis was the salience associated with the political parties and what they attempt to achieve. It may be that while electoral ties weaken and negative responses to the parties and their candidates are not uncommon, the parties continue to assume importance. This position if valid in turn offers grounds for reconsidering some of the more dire assessments of the parties' future and of their relevance. The electoral contests change. Voters can express strong personal reactions to individual candidates and what they see as the parties' goals in any given election, while still believing the parties themselves and the choices they offer are important for achieving broad social ends. If so, on a fundamental level the party system, for all the transformations presently underway, may be in better health than has been recognized.

References

American Political Science Association. 1950. *Toward a More Responsible Party System*. New York: Rinehart.

Banfield, Edward C., and James Q. Wilson. 1963. *City Politics*. New York: Vintage Books.

Burnham, Walter Dean. 1970. *Critical Elections and the Mainsprings of American Politics*. New York: W.W. Norton.

———. 1982. *The Current Crisis in American Politics*. Oxford: Oxford University Press.

———. 2000. Whole lotta shakin' goin' on: A political realignment is on the way. *Nation* 270 (15): 11–15.

Costikyan, Edward N. 1966. *Behind Closed Doors*. New York: Harcourt Brace.

Crotty, William. 2001. Policy coherence in political parties: The elections of 1984, 1988, and 1992. In Jeffrey Cohen and Paul Cantor (eds.), *Political Parties and the Future of American Politics*. Washington, DC: Congressional Quarterly Press.

Crotty, William, John S. Jackson III, and Melissa Kary Miller. 1999. Political activists over time: "Working elites" in the party system. In Biroz A. Yesilada (ed.), *Comparative Political Parties and Elites*. Ann Arbor: University of Michigan Press, pp. 259–86.

Dionne, Jr., E. J. 1996. *They Only Look Dead: Why Progressives Will Dominate the Next Political Era*. New York: Simon and Schuster.

_____. 1991. *Why Americans Hate Politics*. New York: Simon and Schuster.

Greenberg, Stanley, and Theda Skocpol, eds. 1997. *Toward a Popular Progressive Politics*. New Haven, CT: Yale University Press.

Jackson III, John S., and William Crotty. 2000. *The Politics of Presidential Selection*. 2d ed. New York: Addison Wesley Longman.

Miller, Warren E., and J. Merrill Shanks. 1996. *The New American Voter*. Cambridge, MA: Harvard University Press.

Schattschneider, E. E. 1942. *Party Government*. New York: Rinehart.

Wattenberg, Martin. 1991. *The Rise of Candidate-Centered Politics*. Cambridge, MA: Harvard University Press.

_____. 1998. *The Decline of American Political Parties, 1952–1996*. Cambridge, MA: Harvard University Press.

6

Does Congress Represent
the American People?

DONALD R. MATTHEWS

How well does the U.S. Congress represent the American people?[1]

This seems a good time to ask. We approach the end of the twentieth century and the beginning of the twenty-first, a natural time for taking stock. Confidence in the Congress eroded in the late twentieth century—presumably the institution's performance as a representative body had something to do with this. Congress has attracted the attention of many able political scientists over the last forty years—the literature on Congress is now immense and its quality is nearly as impressive as its bulk[2]—but this research has failed to yield a clear and widely accepted answer to our question: How well does the U.S. Congress "represent" the American people?

One major reason for this failure is that the concept *political representation* has no "clear and widely accepted" meaning. Virtually all contemporary governments *claim* to be representative, thereby muddying the conceptual waters. Competing definitions of representation abound in both theoretical works and empirical studies.[3]

Despite this terminological confusion, there is agreement that political representation involves, among other things, representatives *responding* to the interests and/or preferences of those persons they represent. But responsiveness is not an easy thing to study. The "law of anticipatory reaction" is a huge confounding factor. Agreement between representatives and their constituents is much easier to study than responsiveness.[4] Thus, most research on political representation settles for measurements of the congruence or agreement between representatives and the represented—the more agreement, the more "representation." But how is agreement reached? The usual assumption is that agreement results from legislators responding to the wishes of their constituents. But quite the opposite seems more plausible, given the limited interest and information of the mass electorate. The interactions of representatives and the represented need to be studied intensively,[5] not assumed to be dominated by the represented. That is what much legislative research implicitly does.

A final reason why we do not know how representative the Congress is is that most research in the field focuses on the behavior of individual members in the policymaking process, especially roll-call voting. The seminal work in this tradition is Miller and Stokes's elegant article on "Constituency Influence on Congress."[6] We have learned some things about legislative behavior from this line of research, but it has numerous limitations. It assumes that constituents have policy preferences, that these preferences can be made known to representatives in a timely fashion, that mass preferences can be compared to the highly specific and sometimes technical decisions that legislating involves, that the voters control the policy decisions of congresspersons, and so on.

Figure 6-1 presents an alternative conception of legislative representation that I feel does do justice to the complexity of the subject. There is nothing new or original about this typology; rather, it reflects my attempt to reduce the theoretical and empirical literature to a manageable number of categories. Members of Congress respond to constituents in three different realms—policy, service, and symbolic responsiveness.[7] Responsiveness within each realm can be examined on either the individual or the aggregate level. Illustrative kinds of behavior within each of the six cells are indicated in the figure. Until recently, almost all research on Congress has been concerned with individual-level behavior in the public policy realm—we know much less about the five other types of representation. If we focus our attention on the *collective* performance of Congress as a representative body, we begin to have some purchase on our question about representation. The independent variables that seem to shape that performance become features of the constitutional and political system within which the Congress exists.

| Level of Representation | Realm of Responsiveness | | |
	Policy	Service	Symbolic
Aggregate	Lawmaking Budgeting Oversight	Allocation of particularized benefits through collective action, "logrolling"	Symbolic legislation Symbolic representation of voters by members
Individual	Committee work of members Floor activities Voting	Services provided to constituents by individual members, "casework"	Position-taking Credit-claiming

FIGURE 6-1
Types of Legislative Representation

The Senate

The Senate of the United States is one of the most strangely apportioned democratic legislatures in the world. Because we are familiar with the origins of this arrangement, we tend to ignore its lingering effects. A legislature in which the largest states with 50 percent of the population have only 18 percent of the votes, while the eighteen smallest states with 36 percent of the population have 52 percent of the votes is a serious anomaly in a nation committed to the notion that equality of individual voting power is mandated by the Constitution!

My colleague Donald McCrone has come up with an ingenious way to grasp the magnitude of Senate misrepresentation.[8] He hypothetically reconstitutes the Senate into a 100-seat body with the states represented proportionally to their population. Then he looks at the magnitude of the shifts in seats from the status quo that this reconstitution creates. Some of his findings are below:

	Seat Change
The highest quartile of states in metropolitan population	+ 19 seats
The lowest quartile of states in metropolitan population	− 12 seats
The highest quartile of states in percentage of population Black	+ 2 seats
The lowest quartile of states in percentage of population Black	− 11 seats
The highest quartile of states in percentage Hispanic	+ 9 seats
The lowest quartile of states in percentage Hispanic	− 10 seats
The highest quartile of states in percentage Jewish	+ 8 seats
The lowest quartile of states in percentage Jewish	− 18 seats
The highest quartile of states in abortion rate	+ 14 seats
The lowest quartile of states in abortion rate	− 10 seats
The highest quartile of states in percentage foreign born	+ 16 seats
The lowest quartile of states in percentage foreign born	− 7 seats
The highest quartile of states for Reagan in 1984	− 9 seats
The lowest quartile of states for Reagan in 1984	+ 3 seats

Then he looks at roll-call votes, comparing his hypothetical Senate with the real thing on key votes for 1981 and 1982. The results are startling (Table 6.1). Of the sixteen *Congressional Quarterly* key votes in 1981, seven were converted from losses to wins by representing states proportionally. In 1982, there were fifteen key votes, and six losses would have been wins if the states had been proportionally represented.

Thus, under contemporary conditions the impact of the equal representation of the states on the Senate as a representative body is large and negative.

The House of Representatives

The House of Representatives does not labor under such a heavy constitutional burden. But the electoral system used to elect representatives—single-

TABLE 6.1

Change in CQ Key Votes of Shifting from State Equality to Proportional Representation by Year

Liberal Issue Shift	1981		
	Equality	Proportionality	Net
AWACS sale[a]	−4 (LOSS)	+22 (WIN)	+26
Busing closure[a]	−25 (LOSS)	−9 (WIN)[b]	+16
Tobacco support[a]	− 1 (LOSS)	+12 (WIN)	+13
Abortion funds[a]	−9 (LOSS)	+ 2 (WIN)	+11
Waterway funds[a]	−2 (LOSS)	+ 9 (WIN)	+11
Social Security reductions[a]	−1 (LOSS)	+ 9 (WIN)	+10
Limit tax cuts	−45 (LOSS)	−36 (WIN)	+ 9
Oil antitrust	−44 (LOSS)	−37 (LOSS)	+ 7
Budget cuts	−78 (LOSS)	−71 (LOSS)	+ 7
Nuclear plant cuts[a]	−2 (LOSS)	+ 3 (WIN)	+ 5
Index tax cuts	−17 (LOSS)	−12 (LOSS)	+ 5
MX missile cuts	−64 (LOSS)	−64 (LOSS)	0
Debt limit increase	−55 (LOSS)	−57 (LOSS)	−2
B-1 Bomber cuts	−38 (LOSS)	−41 (LOSS)	−3
Congressional pay hike	−4 (LOSS)	−7 (LOSS)	−3
Milk price support	−22 (LOSS)	−31 (LOSS)	−9
	1982		
FTC Medical Regulation	+22 (WIN)	+43 (WIN)	+20
Table Antiabortion Motion	+ 1 (WIN)	+18 (WIN)	+17
Farm irrigation	−36 (LOSS)	−19 (LOSS)	+17
Delete cap on COLA for government ret.[a]	−3 (LOSS)	+12 (WIN)	+15
Mortgage subsidy	+46 (WIN)	+55 (WIN)	+ 9
Balanced budget amendment[a]	−38 (LOSS)	−30 (WIN)[b]	+ 8
Budget resolution[a]	−6 (LOSS)	+ 1 (WIN)	+ 7
Tax increase, welfare cut[a]	−3 (LOSS)	+ 3 (WIN)	+ 6
Tobacco price support[a]	−2 (LOSS)	+ 4 (WIN)	+ 6
Clinch River nuclear reactor[a]	−1 (LOSS)	+ 4 (WIN)	+ 5
Delete public works	+ 4 (WIN)	+ 9 (WIN)	+ 5
MX missile temporary delay	−14 (LOSS)	−9 (LOSS)	+ 5
Veto override supplementary delay	+30 (WIN)	+34 (WIN)	+ 4
Transportation assistance	−22 (LOSS)	−22 (LOSS)	0
Abolish limit on outside income, senators	−16 (LOSS)	−18 (LOSS)	−2

Source: Donald J. McCrone, "The Representational Consequences of State Equality in the U.S. Senate" (paper presented at the meeting of the Western Political Science Association, 1990).

[a]Reversal of outcome, loss to win.

[b]Reversal due to special majority requirements.

member districts with plurality election—has several consequences on the performance of the House as a representative legislature.

First, single-member districts, when combined with weak political parties, result in close, direct, and personal ties between members and their districts. It is possible for members to increase their reelection chances substantially by aggressive and skillful servicing of the wants and needs of their constituents. Congressional staffs who do the vast majority of this "casework" have grown at almost cancerous rates in recent decades.[9] This provides sitting members with a core of grateful constituents who support the incumbent without much concern for his or her votes or policy pronouncements.

In Norway (the one non-American legislature I know reasonably well) members of the *Storting* are elected in multimember districts as part of a political party's electoral list.[10] The relationship between the member and his/her electoral district is less clear-cut and is mediated through the parties. Different members of the same party's slate "represent" different interests or aspects of the party—for example, women, or young people, or residents of different towns—since the party slate makers are devoted to "balanced tickets." Once elected, members of the *Storting* engage in "case work," too. The average (modal) *Storting* member reports spending 20 to 30 percent of the time on constituent service. But *Storting* members have almost no staffs, so the aggregate amount of constituency service provided by the legislature is small compared with that provided by the Congress. At service representation, the U.S. Congress shines.

The single-member-district electoral system has other representational effects. Members of minority groups are substantially underrepresented in the American Congress, compared with national legislatures elected in multimember districts with proportional representation elections.[11] Candidate-centered elections where the leadership has no control over nominations favor those with ability to raise and spend large sums of money, with name recognition and self-promotional skills. With party-controlled lists of candidates, minorities are needed to balance the ticket. Women have achieved near equality of representation in the *Storting*. This seems to result more from institutional arrangements than from any enthusiasm for sexual equality among Norwegian men.[12]

Since the Voting Rights Act of 1965 Congress and the federal courts have sought, with some success, to do something about the symbolic representation of minorities in the House. The principal mechanism has been to encourage states to create "minority-majority" districts, which could be expected to elect African Americans or Latinos to the House. By the early 1990s a total of thirty-two congressional districts could be counted upon to elect blacks and twenty, Latinos. However, this blatant racial gerrymandering quickly ran into serious opposition. It was clearly contrary to the equal voting power doctrine mandated by the Supreme Court. In *Miller v. Johnson* (1995) the Supreme Court rejected Georgia's districting, in which "race was a predominant factor." And in the wake of the '92 and '94 elections, the Democrats concluded (correctly) that the creation of majority-minority districts had contributed to Republican electoral success in the Senate. Minority-majority districts are no longer in vogue.

The bias of the American single-member district system against minority candidates (including women as well as blacks and Chicanos) is not easily changed. On this aspect of political representation, the House and Senate rate poor marks compared with other national legislatures.

TABLE 6.2
The Overrepresentation of the Democratic House Vote, 1954–1992

	Election Difference	Democratic Vote (%)	Democratic Seat (%)
1954	52.8	53.3	+ .6
1956	51.2	53.8	+2.6
1958	56.7	64.9	+8.2
1960	55.1	60.0	+4.8
1962	52.9	59.4	+6.6
1964	57.8	67.8	+10.0
1966	51.4	57.0	+5.6
1968	51.0	55.9	+4.9
1970	54.7	58.6	+3.9
1972	53.2	55.8	+2.6
1974	59.2	66.9	+7.7
1976	57.4	67.1	+9.7
1978	54.8	63.7	+8.9
1980	51.5	55.9	+4.4
1982	56.4	61.8	+5.2
1984	52.5	58.2	+5.6
1986	55.0	59.3	+4.4
1988	54.2	59.8	+5.6
1990	53.3	61.5	+8.1
1992	53.1	59.4	+6.4
Mean	54.2	60.0	+5.8

Source: Table 2.8 from James E. Campbell, *Cheap Seats: The Democratic Party's Advantage in U.S. House Elections* (Columbus: Ohio State University Press, 1996), p. 35.

Finally, there is a partisan bias in the electoral system for the House of Representatives. Between 1954 and 1992, the Democrats consistently won a larger share of the seats than of the votes in House elections (see Table 6-2). James Campbell's careful study of this partisan tilt concludes that about ten to twelve seats are typically lost to the Republicans and gained by the Democrats in each election.[13] The main culprit is the very different rates of voter turnout in congressional districts. The Democrats consistently win more of the districts with low turnout—"cheap seats"—than the Republicans do. This is the primary (although not the only) cause of the Democrats' advantage.

Some Concluding Thoughts

This brief examination of the collective representativeness of the American Congress shows much room for improvement. Both chambers have significant partisan and policy biases—the Senate toward Republicans and conservative policies, the House toward Democrats and more left-of-center causes. That these representational "errors" are in different directions is, perhaps, a good thing: to some extent they tend to cancel one another out. But this also means these representational biases contribute to divided party control of Congress and more policy conflict between the two chambers than would be the case if the two chambers were more representative.

The Congress spends a great deal of time and resources in "service" representation. No doubt this is one reason why Americans tend to like their individual congresspersons while holding negative views of the Congress. And the consequences for policy implementation of 535 legislators and their sizable staffs, aggressively championing the parochial concerns of the constituents, must be large.

Finally, a great deal of what happens on Capitol Hill is highly symbolic. However, the House and Senate fail to represent women and minorities adequately within their own ranks. There has been some improvement in recent years, but the Congress lags well behind other national legislatures in this form of symbolic representation.

Notes

1. I have drawn upon chapter 1 of Donald R. Matthews and Henry Valen, *Parliamentary Representation: The Case of the Norwegian Storting* (Columbus: Ohio State University Press, 1999), in the following discussion.
2. Those who doubt this statement should look at Gerhard Lowenberg and Samuel C. Patterson, *Comparing Legislatures* (Boston: Little, Brown, 1979); Gerhard Lowenberg, Samuel C. Patterson, and Malcolm E. Jewell, eds., *Handbook of Legislative Research* (Cambridge, MA: Harvard University Press, 1985); Malcolm E. Jewell and Samuel C. Patterson, *The Legislative Process in the United States*, 2d ed. (New York: Random House, 1973); Samuel C. Patterson and Anthony Mughan, *Senates: Bicameralism in the Contemporary World* (Columbus: Ohio State University Press, 1999); and Samuel C. Patterson and Gary W. Copeland, eds., *Parliaments in the Modern World: Changing Institutions* (Ann Arbor: University of Michigan Press, 1994).
3. Hannah F. Pitkin, *The Concept of Representation* (Berkeley: University of California Press, 1972).
4. Carl J. Frederick, *Constitutional Government and Democracy* (Boston: Little, Brown, 1941).
5. Walhke called for this many years ago.
6. Warren Miller and Donald Stokes, "Constituency Influence in Congress," *American Political Science Association* 57: 45–56 (1963).
7. This formulation has been taken, in slightly revised form, from the work of Heinz Eulau. See especially Heinz Eulau and P.D. Karps, "The Puzzle of Representation: Specifying Components of Responsiveness," *Legislative Studies Quarterly* 2: 233–54 (1977).
8. Donald J. McCrone, "The Representational Consequences of State Equality in the U.S. Senate." Unpublished paper presented at the 1990 meeting of the Western Political Science Association, March 22–24, 1990, Newport Beach, CA.
9. In 1996, the average House member's staff numbered about fifteen full-time employees. The Senate member's staff ranged in size from thirteen to seventy-one, the average being about thirty-five. Roger H. Davidson and Walter J. Oleszek, *Congress and Its Members*, 3d ed. (Washington, DC: CQ Press, 1998), 148–50.
10. Donald R. Matthews and Henry Valen, *Parliamentry Representation: The Case of the Norwegian Storting* (Columbus: Ohio State University Press, 1999), chapters 5 and 9.

11. Richard E. Matland, "Institutional Variables Affecting Female Representation in National Legislatures: The Case of Norway," *Journal of Politics* 55: 737–55 (1993).
12. Richard E. Matland, "Putting Scandinavian Equality to the Test: An Experimental Evaluation of Gender Stereotyping of Political Candidates," *British Journal of Political Science* 24: 273–92 (1994).
13. James E. Campbell, *Cheap Seats: The Democratic Party's Advantage in the U.S. House Elections* (Columbus: Ohio State University Press, 1996).

7

The Enduring Dilemma of Political Tolerance in American Political History

GEORGE E. MARCUS

Introduction

Many, perhaps most, people accept the claim that democratic regimes have an important stake in sustaining political tolerance (i.e., securing the political rights of all citizens). This should be so for a number of reasons. First, democratic regimes gain political legitimacy to the extent that the election of political leaders, the adoption of public policies, and the drafting of new laws are achieved by the deliberation and free choices of all citizens. This is often made apparent in acceptance speeches of politicians immediately following their election. Though politicians begin by thanking their followers for their successful efforts, they go on to assert their responsibility to act as elected leader for everyone, not just their supporters. Elected officials typically proclaim that they will make every effort to represent all their constituents. Politicians elected by the vote of most citizens seek to be seen as the legitimate representative of all citizens.

Second, though the majority has the constitutional responsibility for choosing among possible leaders and thereby which policy alternatives and legal statutes will be adopted or rejected, the power of the majority to make such determinations is bolstered by moral authority when the majority makes its choices with due consideration for the rights and interests of all citizens (Spitz, 1984). The fact of being a majority does not by itself ensure that a majority is just and public spirited. Having *most* citizens make the rules for *all* citizens is not a certain guarantee that those laws will be just and beneficial to everyone. It is too often tempting for a majority, especially one that is embattled, to act against those who oppose, or otherwise offend, the majority.

Thus limiting the ability of some to fully participate in politics, to hinder or restrict the ability of even the disparaged to be fully politically active has serious consequences and not only for those who might be excluded. How well has America succeeded in securing the political rights of all Americans? And what is the prospect for an ever more tolerant society? Americans are an optimistic people. That optimism is reflected in the conviction that all good things can be achieved. My central argument is that the effort to secure political tolerance must also be matched by efforts to enrich diversity and actualize liberal democracy. This will be far more difficult than we intuitively expect. Before making that argument in detail, I will first have to review the competing conceptions of how to secure political tolerance before going on to consider the relationship of political tolerance to diversity and the practice of liberal democracy. I will then review the empirical evidence on the current and future levels of political tolerance.

An essay meant to provide an overview of the struggle to secure political tolerance, like this one, might appropriately have been prepared for delivery at one of our important historical memorial celebrations, such as on the Fourth of July. Had it evolved for such a purpose, we would together find ourselves celebrating the many accomplishments of this remarkable republic and the wisdom of our Founding Fathers and the history of progress since 1787. We would no doubt speak on the struggle of so many in this nation to end slavery; to extend suffrage to non-property owners, former slaves, and women; to extend social and economic opportunity more widely; and to legalize the rights of labor to organize. These examples would be offered as appropriate demonstrations of the progressive character of our nation. Though such a litany might portray accurate, if incomplete, history and partial realization of the promise of the Declaration of Independence, there is a danger in imagining such an account as prologue to an ever more perfect union, at least with respect to political tolerance.[1]

What would a more measured consideration lead us to conclude about the future prospects of a more tolerant society? Further, since the past is often the best predictor of the future, it would not seem unreasonable to expect yet more progress in this realm. Although real progress has been secured in establishing the rights of American citizens, often at great costs, these gains come not from some inevitable "engine of history" but from the persuasive power of the ideals that set this nation into being and the concerted efforts of many people to protect their own rights, to complain loudly and effectively when their rights were not protected, and to join with others to protect the rights of at least some other citizens under duress. Yet if these ideals continue to direct our current efforts, we must regain the wisdom, now abandoned, that animated the expression of these ideals that gave birth to the government and regime within which those ideals were and are pursued, among other things. While we have retained our commitment to the ideals of the collective well-being, liberty and justice, we have largely abandoned the foundational beliefs that created the political regime, the Constitution and Bill of Rights. These beliefs have been replaced by more modern conceptions of politics that leave us less able to fully understand the problematic nature of political tolerance in liberal democracies such as ours.

The principal purpose of this chapter is to rearticulate the earlier foundational beliefs so we can compare and contrast them to our modern contemporary conceptions. Though our ideals of a just and liberal democratic society and a politics committed to realizing the common good have remained constant, the ways we expect to achieve them have changed. We have two different conceptions of how to achieve our ideals: one old and largely abandoned, and one we most currently rely upon. These two conceptions provide very different perspectives for judging the historical evidence on political tolerance and for plausible expectations of what we can anticipate for political tolerance in the future.[2]

The modern democratic understanding as outlined by Hanson (1985) contains a number of ideas that mark the democratic regime. The greatest benefit of liberty is understood to be its capacity to enable people to achieve their desires and talents, enabling at least those eager and assertive enough to claim for themselves the "pursuit of happiness." To all of us will come the full accomplishments that will flow from the application of our skill, talent, and the freedom to exercise the unique faculties of our minds. Taken together with the sheer abundance of land and natural resources, America offers the space and riches to enable everyone to pursue these lofty, self-realizing dreams. Of course, for at least some matters people in a liberal democratic society will have to come together to make collective decisions. Americans are a social people even if the vastness of space affords considerable room for the practice of Emersonian introspection and rugged individualism. Though the riches of America, amplified by technology and a liberal government, provide for great and widespread material satisfaction, we will often find ourselves having to come together to make political decisions that will establish uniform obligations and collective enterprises.[3]

Insofar as those collective decisions are meant to be borne by and benefit the public, who better than the public to make those decisions? The public is no longer merely the beneficiary of a democratic government but has taken on the responsibility for directing the course of democratic government. Lincoln's language resonates strongly today, a "government of the people, by the people, and for the people."(Wills, 1992). Democracy has come to mean that the public must be the judge of what is best, because it has the capacity to execute that responsibility.[4] After all, who else is better able to judge the consequences of public decisions than those who must bear them? Given that current conceptions of governance have focused on the essential capacity of the people to rule themselves, it is not surprising that research on political tolerance has been dominated by survey research. Though other research strategies are not precluded, the major projects in this area rely on survey research (Gibson 1988; Lawrence 1976; Nunn, Crockett, and Williams 1978; Prothro and Grigg 1960; Stouffer 1955; Sullivan, Pierson, and Marcus 1982). Insofar as the responsibility of governing is increasingly presumed to be properly dependent on public choices, the preservation of the political rights of minorities is thought to be essentially a matter of public determination and commitment.[5]

It is this perspective on contemporary politics that led Paul Sniderman (1989) to offer the following two arguments. First, given a diverse populace that will evince considerable variation in cultural backgrounds, interests, historical experiences, religious convictions, among many other disparate features, the basis for political tolerance in democratic society *ought* to be sustained by near-universal popular commitment to and sole reliance on democratic principles in making judgments of political tolerance. If the public understands and commits to democratic practices, the public will protect and extend the opportunity for democratic engagement to everyone. Second, his reading of the evidence shows that these normative expectations are in fact sustained by the data.[6] Sniderman's view reflects a standard conception that a tolerant society demands a tolerant public. Though I do not find Sniderman's evidence persuasive, it is not his reading of the empirical findings that is central to the argument I am advancing in this chapter.

If a democratic and tolerant society depends on the public's commitment to the principles of democratic tolerance, it would follow that if we find evidence that the public does support these principles, then unpopular groups that support unpopular causes should have no reason to be alarmed. The possibility of damage to the political rights of the minority that the majority could inflict is precluded not only by constitutional protections, the extended republic, but also by the public's tolerant convictions. Indeed, if the latter condition obtained, then we would have little need for the other Madisonian mechanisms. However, in spite of Sniderman's view that comprehension and support of democratic principles are the necessary and sufficient conditions for a more tolerant society, neither the evidence nor the argument is compelling. As to the evidence, it has been well established for many years now that democratic principles do not, in and of themselves, guarantee that people who hold to them will be guided solely by these principles when they have to make political tolerance judgments about concrete cases (Gibson 1987; Gibson and Bingham 1985; Lawrence 1976; Prothro and Grigg 1960; Sullivan et al. 1982; Sullivan, Piereson, and Marcus 1979). These studies demonstrate that political tolerance is one among many factors taken into consideration when citizens judge aspects of a particular case. Most notably, citizens react to the means "unpopular" groups employ to advance their causes (Marcus et al. 1995). Thus, generating a more tolerant society is not identical to and not as simple as generating better and wider understanding of democratic norms.

Even more important, the simple view that tolerance is the natural result of greater understanding precludes a more thoughtful consideration of the role of diversity and its consequences in a liberal democratic society. On the contrary, tolerance is a central feature of political life when people are *not* the same, do not hold to the same political, economic, religious, social, and moral views, and are willing to go to political battle over which of these views should be implemented as public policy or legal statute. The cleavages that diversity in a pluralistic liberal society breeds give rise to political conflict. Political con-

117

flict is animated by the sentiments that attach to our diverse beliefs. Sentiments such as loyalty and fervor cement people to their faction. Other sentiments, such as mistrust and enmity, motivate opposition to the efforts of other factions. Therefore, an inevitable accompaniment to political conflict, compelled by our pluralist democracy to clarify our otherwise misted vision, are the sentiments that animate political conflict and give rise to political intolerance. Though intolerance can be contained by means considered below, it cannot be eradicated without doing greater harm to our freedom.

Madison's Republican Politics and Political Tolerance

The original understanding of the foundations for a popular government was not premised on the natural capacity of the public to rule itself. Indeed, crucial to the Founding Fathers' understanding was a distinction between the *necessity* of popular sovereignty, which they endorsed as the sole basis for legitimate government, and the *meritorious ability* of popular rule, which they viewed with considerable caution. The Founding Fathers shared with the ancient Greeks a crucial taxonomy that has since been largely ignored. That taxonomy differentiated political regimes on two axes of classification. First, it classified who would rule: the one, the few, or the many. Second, the taxonomy classified rulers as worthy or unworthy based on whether their rule was guided by virtue (for the benefit of the public good) or by corrupt self-interest (for the advantage of some). It is important to note that the definition of corruption then used was somewhat different from today's focus on "immorality" or, more specific to the realm of politics, bribery. Corruption was simply the opposite of virtue. The latter was understood as "civic virtue," which demanded that the needs of the community have priority over all other considerations. Corruption involved favoring narrow parochial concern over those of the community. Thus, a person who fulfills Aristotle's definition of a "good person" (Aristotle 1983) who takes care of family, friends, and strangers is not, by these definitions, a virtuous person.

Combining these two axes gives the then standard array of regime types:

Rule by the one:	*Virtue* monarchy virtuous rule by one	*Corruption* despotism corrupt rule by one
Rule by the few:	*Virtue* aristocracy virtuous rule by the few (*aristos*, the best)	*Corruption* oligarchy corrupt rule by the few (the rich, the powerful)
Rule by the many:	*Virtue* democracy rule by a virtuous people	*Corruption* democracy rule by the people, *demos*

In practical terms democracy has historically been thought to be inevitably corrupt, since the many will rule on the basis of their interests.[7]

The common experience of the American rebellion, a popular uprising that defeated Britain, then the most powerful imperial power in the world, convinced all the Founding Fathers, even those most committed to monarchial forms of government, that it would no longer be possible to secure a legitimate government without the express and continual support of the public. Popular sovereignty was accepted as an essential requirement of legitimate government.

Since the Founders rejected locating virtue in the hands of a select few and chose instead to found a popular, if republican, regime, does that mean they expected to find virtue in the people?[8] The answer to that is a clear no. It was central to the Founders' conception that the rule of interest, even if widely shared, is fundamentally corrupt rather than virtuous. As Madison famously asserted, a faction is "a number of citizens, whether amounting to a majority or a minority of the whole, who are united and actuated by some common impulse of passion, or of interest, adverse to the rights of citizens, or to the permanent and aggregate interests of the community" (Madison, Hamilton, and Jay 1961). Further, Madison allows that only the occasional statesman will have the capacity to rise above the corrupt influence of passion and interest to act on the basis of the common good. Madison claims that statesmen will be too few in number and not always available. And, in any case, since this is to be a republic, governance will most often not be placed into the hands of statesman. Rather, Madison argues that it is unavoidable, in fact a necessary condition, that faction, interest, and passion be intertwined in politics.

Madison adds yet another element to his argument, an element that makes political tolerance an even greater challenge in the context of democracy. In his famous definition of faction, Madison (1961) provides his definition of a virtuous government. For him, a virtuous government is one that secures the "rights of . . . citizens . . . [and] the permanent and aggregate interest of the community." He provides this definition to ensure that the reader grasps the contrast of civic virtue with the naturally arising political impulses. The natural political impulses of interest and passion, which germinate from liberty, are what motivate political action. Madison does not cast aspersions on factions. Though he might wish that people be otherwise, he understands that it is natural, and therefore unavoidable, that people act on the basis of their interests, their beliefs and sentiments.[9] But, surprisingly, he takes into account the corrupt nature of the citizenry's motivations and still manages to create a model of democratic politics that when put into action is able to produce virtuous policies.

The obvious question comes to mind: If the public, and their elected leaders, are, at the outset, animated by corrupt motives, as Madison argues they naturally must be, how can virtue result? It is interesting to note that when Madison describes people and politics, he uses metaphors of the natural world. Throughout *Federalist* No. 10, popular government is represented in terms of disease, and faction is shown to be as necessary to liberty as "air is to fire." Madison again uses the language of fire when he argues that "the most frivolous and fanciful distinctions have been sufficient to kindle their unfriendly passions, and excite their most violent conflict." Madison makes use of these metaphors to reinforce his principal thesis that faction and political conflict are natural and therefore ineradicable and essential elements in human nature. Of course, all of this then reinforces his conclusion that the natural impulses of interest and passion, which drive democratic politics, are naturally corrupt.

Madison goes on to argue that we cannot expect statesmen will be available in sufficient numbers to "adjust these clashing interests, and render them subservient to the public good." Here again is an important, and too often ignored, point in Madison's thought: The average of all competing interests, or some other simple aggregation so that everyone gets "a piece of the action," is no less corrupt for being widely and even equally shared. In *Federalist* No. 10 Madison makes this crystal clear. He warns that we cannot expect to rely on statesmen because they are too rare. And this is cause for concern precisely because only *enlightened* statesmen would "be able to adjust these clashing interests and render them subservient to the public good."

In *Federalist* No. 37 Madison argues that even if reason were shielded from the corrupting and particularizing effects of passion and interest, reason remains a far weaker device for identifying the public good than we might expect. Madison must add the term "enlightened" precisely because reason by itself cannot identify the public good. Those statesmen who have the capacity to enact the common good must first see beyond the normal range of human perception. This is so because Madison's definition of the common good encompasses two essential qualities: the common good is both permanent and a reflection of the aggregate interest of the community. Since even statesmen will rarely be seers, he explicitly adds the capability of enlightenment for this mental experiment to work. That is, even if statesmen were enlightened so that they could see the future as well as the past and present, and even if they could accommodate all of the competing interests in some compromise, they would not be able to create the common good. For the common good does not lie among the natural interests as expressed by the various political factions.

For Madison, politics—as constituted by the republican principle, the institutions of government then being recommended, and the character of a liberal people in a large and resourceful land—is machinery for taking corrupt inputs and generating "common good" outcomes.[10] In Madison's language, democratic processes mirror the processes, constituting elements, and productive capacity of a refinery, and Madison wants his readers to see the parallels.[11] A refinery combines natural materials such as metallic ores and consumes them by applying heat, which allows pure metal to be extracted from crude and contaminated sources. Each aspect of the process of refining has its analogue in representative politics as envisioned by Madison. The natural interests (corrupt) are equivalent to the ore. Passion, attached to interests, beliefs and purposes, and diversity guarantee political conflict, the analogue to the fire that heats the elements in a refinery. The refinery, though a man-made construction, is designed to contain fire that would otherwise naturally destroy and consume everything in its path. Similarly, Madison hopes that the new federal government will share these same properties, containing the heat of political conflict and producing purified interests.

Among the metals a metal refinery yields are those that do not naturally occur, for example, bronze and steel. These products are not natural, yet they have valuable properties that greatly strengthen the cultures and peoples who have the good sense to make proper use of them. Steel and concrete, yet other unnatural materials, enable people to build far sturdier, and therefore enduring, buildings than can be built from found materials (rubble, mud bricks, timber, and hides). These are aggregates, products that are fabrications. Moreover, especially public facilities, such as bridges, roads, libraries, schools, and hospitals, are greatly improved, thereby meeting Madison's standard criteria for distinguishing the partial from the common good, the permanent and aggregate interests of the community.

Much as steel is obtained by combining the natural elements of iron ore, coke, and fire and the unnatural contribution of the technology of refineries, the common good can be obtained by combining the natural elements of factional interests, political and public conflict with the unnatural contribution of a political science that introduces political institutions, constructed by the principles of limited constitutional government, representation, separation of powers, a bicameral legislature, and so forth. We can extend the comparison yet further. Refineries often require combining different materials to make better products. Here again, the technical process mirrors the political. More factional involvement ensures a wider representation of diverse interests, a more lively "marketplace of ideas" and the more lively the public contention, the more likely a fuller consideration will yield a more mature result. Both processes are public, not private; the heat of a refinery lights up the area, revealing all that is going on. Similarly, political conflict reveals much of what is going on: the involvement of all principal actors, even those who might wish to remain inconspicuous, as well as insights into their motives and their claims, is more readily available for all to see.

Finally, in a refinery, heat is used to burn off impurities. How would this aspect of the process have an analogue in representative politics? The diversity of interests in the extended republic that is America would ensure that most proposals arising directly from interests and the public would not, at the outset, command a majority. Majorities supportive of the common good would have to be fabricated. Madison calls such groups coalitions (in contrast with factions, which by his definition are corrupt). Coalitions would seldom arise other than on "principles . . . of justice and the general good," as Madison says in *Federalist* No. 51. Why is that? Because interested claims would have to be made in public, to secure support from those who are at the outset either neutral or opposed to the interests who authored the proposal.

How might such an appeal be crafted? If a proposal is to have any prospect for success, it must be couched as one that will benefit the nation, for, given the great diversity of the society, a selfish appeal will not move a sufficient audience to form a majority. Moreover, every proposal can be expected to be attacked by those with opposing interests or conflicting proposals. For a proposal to survive it must meet the intellectual challenge of sustaining its claim of a substantial benefit for the public good, rather than the particular, and its capacity to advance justice, rather than any selfish interest.[12]

For any particular proposal to succeed it must gain the support of those who find its arguments compelling even though they themselves are not rooted in the interests that authored the proposal. Needless to say, a standard line of attack is that the public purpose of any such proposal is a Trojan horse for some darker purposes and hidden benefits. And many proposals fail because there may be much merit to such critiques, which is precisely Madison's expectation. This is an essential part of the political process. Critical attention is an essential feature if democratic publics are to know very much about the nature and prospects for any proposal under public consideration. Critical attention is also essential to defeat the "temporary or partial" proposals based upon public consideration of whether any proposal is "consonant to the public good" (Madison, *Federalist* Nos. 10 and 51).[13]

All of this brings us to the major theme of this chapter—political conflict and its consequences for political tolerance in a republican society. For political conflict to have the mobilizing and cleansing effects that Madison's scheme requires, it must be laden with animus. Not only must factions pursue the proposals dear to their interests and passions, and do so with zeal, they must also be suspicious of the proposals advanced by other interests. For it is the clash of interests that generates the heat of political conflict that in turn generates the light that reveals the strengths and weaknesses of different proposals.

When Madison considers the various forms of factions, forming yet another list (or taxonomy), he lists them in order of the zeal with which they are typically associated. He starts with the most zealous of factions, those associated with competing leaders and religion. He ends his list, famously, with the most common and enduring source of faction, the uneven distribution of property. Though this last item on his list is most common and enduring, compared with other kinds of factions, those based on property have less zeal than all others; hence the item's position in his listing. Nonetheless, property-based factions are energized by a goodly measure of zeal.

Although zeal is normally a measure of commitment either to a specific religion, leader, or propertied interest, it is no less associated with animus against contending religions, leaders, and propertied interests. Indeed, it would be hard to make sense of the zeal that bankers have for hard money and low inflation unless one is also mindful of the zeal that debtors have for soft money and high inflation. Innumerable examples come to mind: we value our friends in part to the degree we fear our enemies; we value our family in part as a measure of how much we fear strangers; we value our own nation in part to the degree we fear other nations. Given that political zeal will be attached to particular, rather than common, interests, groups, or leaders, then sustaining the political rights of all citizens will be an especially difficult task, a task that cannot be expected to be sustained by the natural impulses of the citizenry.[14]

Madison knew full well that the sentiments that attach themselves to our beliefs are a mixture of the positive attachments that embellish and burnish those whom we value and associate with and the negative attachments that degrade and distance those we devalue and estrange. He valued a liberal society because the kinds of attachments, positive and negative, would be less severe than those likely in regimes of honor or religion. But such attachments are crucial to animate the political machinery, the "springs," and they cannot be eradicated without a fundamental change in human nature or the elimination of liberty.

Thus a Madisonian understanding of liberal democracy and the means by which a government can secure justice and establish the common good confronts us with a draconian choice. We can choose the harmonious path to achieve a homogenous tranquility at the risk of giving up the very mechanisms that minimize the threat of a corrupt regime. Or we can choose the conflicted path that requires sufficient political contention to enable the mechanisms that convert corrupt impulses to virtuous practices. However, even if the latter pathway is sufficiently restrained from the excessive violence that leads to civil war and domestic turmoil, it will raise the risk of political intolerance.[15]

Forms of Tolerance Defined

It is an easy, and unfortunately erroneous, presumption to group political tolerance with social tolerance and civility. These three degrees of accommodation are readily grasped as different aspects of the same general phenomenon, different degrees of willingness to live with and among difference.

Political tolerance, social tolerance, and civility are quite different from one another. The last, civility, which has often gained a great deal of attention, is actually the least important. It is often raised in religious contexts, as a form of ecumenical palliation. Civility provides a mannered public space in which we apply formal relationships to secure a measure of polite interaction, a diffidence that will protect the social space by withholding the expression of real, or more aptly, private beliefs and feelings.[16] Though securing public pleasantries in public meeting spaces has its value, it has two drawbacks. First, civility normally doesn't intrude very far into the private realm. Second, Madison's requirements for an animated politics, a politics of conflict, limit the value of civility in the realm of democratic politics.[17] Though civility has some value, it has very much less value when greater issues are at stake. At such times we have a need for sufficient political conflict to sear away the pretensions, guises, and facades that often accompany political assertions.

Social tolerance is a more intimate form of accommodation than is civility. Social tolerance deals with the willingness of people from different, even contentious, groups to authentically welcome meeting people from across group boundaries. As such, social tolerance is compatible with a wide array of political regimes, including regimes that are neither liberal nor democratic.[18] Plural extended liberal democracies, of the sort that Madison argues is essential for a sound democratic politics, put people of different identities together. It seems a basic pattern of human nature that most people find a major part of their identity in group memberships and loyalties (Aboud 1988; Bogardus 1925). Yet liberal societies encourage individual autonomy. Thus, it can be expected

124

that successful liberal societies will gradually encourage people of whatever social identities to adopt more individuated identities. Yet we cannot expect social groups to go completely away or to abandon their concern for maintaining some degree of group autonomy and to protect group boundaries.

In the domain of social tolerance, the issue is: How welcoming to strangers should we be? Most communities have shared traditions, cultural practices and beliefs. Each community may willingly or unwillingly accommodate others from different communities, to come to its religious activities, to share in its culture, and to intermarry. Whether welcoming or not, each community does retain, if it is to continue, certain of its boundaries and its moral value. Being protective of its spaces and values against incursion from those who may disregard or disrespect its particular values is not at all surprising. What liberal societies do insist, however, is that no matter how stringent these convictions may be, or how differentiating these practices may become, all of its subjects retain their legal status as citizens. As such, they retain their rights to move in and out of various communities within the nation (though they do not secure thereby the right to gain admittance to any specific community). Social tolerance, then, is determined by the willingness of some extant community to be willing to interact with "guests," to allow strangers and nonbelievers to participate alongside, and engage with, members of its particular community.

Social tolerance is concerned with the question: How are the private realms of these groups and cross-group intermingling going to be policed? If animus and suspicion between different groups and individuals are too frequent consequences of the diversity that liberty affords, then Madison's system offers less protection for social than for political tolerance. At least the latter can be secured by the apparatus of government in all its various aspects. Unless public policy supports intervention to make private action publicly accountable, then group cultural values and beliefs often rule and shape when and how people from different groups will intermingle, if at all.[19]

Securing social tolerance is essential to liberal plural societies because increased individuality and social intermingling add to the liberal value of autonomy and enhance the willingness of individuals to join political coalitions based on political appeals rather than to remain fixed within cultural, religious, ethnic, or other identity-based groups. Hence, social tolerance is far more important to democratic societies than is civility because the extent of social tolerance can fundamentally alter how people know each other and how they view themselves. But securing social tolerance by benevolent means (e.g., positive education to accept and value difference) or by means that rely on penalty (e.g., making illegal the more outrageous consequences of social intolerance) is in tension with the value of a liberal society, which offers the prospect of greater personal liberty of belief and action.

Political tolerance is by far the more important form of tolerance for it helps secure the full and active practice of citizenship in all its legal, and even quasi-legal forms (e.g., civil disobedience). Unlike social tolerance, which has broad applicability, political tolerance is compatible only with democratic regimes. Of the three variants of tolerance, only political tolerance supports the active involvement of all citizens in politics, especially those who most need the opportunity of political participation. Political tolerance requires that those who wish the accolade "politically tolerant" support the legal political practices of those who propose policies they find abhorrent.[20] The doctrine of political tolerance demands that we support the full and active practice of citizenship of all citizens no matter who they are, what they believe, or what goals or programs they legally pursue.

It would seem probable that social tolerance, as a more general practice, and political tolerance, a more specific practice, go hand in hand. It would be nice and reassuring if that were the case. Additionally, if the factors that strengthened social tolerance also enhanced political tolerance, and vice versa, that also would lend support to the possibility of increasingly progressive development of tolerance.

The Public's Capacity for Sustaining Political and Social Tolerance

Perhaps the best available exploration of the relationships of interest with respect to social and political tolerance can be found in a national survey conducted in 1978 (Sullivan, Pierson, and Marcus 1982).[21] There are three particular features of this analysis that recommend themselves for this purpose.

First, the data include multiple measures of social tolerance (defined as the willingness of people to socially engage people from groups they dislike) and of political tolerance (defined as the willingness of people to support political actions by people from groups they dislike). Moreover, the data include measures of other major concepts, such as social status (e.g., income), education, religious conviction, ideology, and so forth.

Second, the mode of data analysis, path analysis, is of special importance for a number of significant reasons. Path analysis requires that the analyst specify precisely how different factors interact. For example, as we shall see below, education may have a number of theoretically distinct effects on each form of tolerance. One "path" might be a direct one. Education gives people qualities, among them greater tolerance, that arise from just being in school. Here the theoretical claim is one of a direct, causal path: more education, in and of itself, is sufficient to elevate levels of tolerance. Another path might be an indirect one. Education encourages development of various interpersonal skills, which in turn makes people more self-confident, and that in turn makes people more willing to be tolerant of others. Education in this pathway operates at a distance: by elevating self-confidence, which in turn elevates tolerance, education has an indirect effect on tolerance but only by its influence on self-confidence. Of course, education may have, as it does, other indirect effects that might bear on tolerance. And it is often the case that a factor, such as education, might have multiple paths, both direct and indirect. Finally, path analysis provides coefficients that enable us to venture forth on two important considerations.

Each path's coefficient provides a reliable estimate of how change in an antecedent factor is likely to influence a consequent factor. For example, a path coefficient of 0.50 means that changing the antecedent factor by one standard measure—one standard deviation, for example—will increase the level of the consequent factor by one-half a standard measure. And we can do so for an indirect path by multiplying the intervening path coefficients (for example, if the effect of education on self-confidence had a path coefficient of 0.50 and the effect of self-confidence on tolerance also had a path coefficient of 0.50, then the effect of a unit increase in education would have a 0.25 effect on tolerance, $0.50 \times 0.50 = 0.25$).

These numerical values can then be used to compare across various factors that we anticipate have an effect on tolerance. For example, a standard theme in democratic theorizing is that citizenship is enhanced by wider and better public education and more political experience and involvement. Thus, two factors, education and political involvement, can be expected to generate more political tolerance. But are these effects equal or is one more potent than the other? By comparing path coefficients we can provide a provisional answer.

Another important consideration is to provide a reasonable, though hardly infallible, basis for speculating on how things might change if the society were to become, for example, even more educated, as has been the historical trend. If, as has been the trend this century, political involvement continues to decline, then we can estimate what consequences this might have for tolerance in the society.[22] Path models provide a method for comparing across factors and for speculating on how changes in the underlying factors might change the overall pattern of tolerance.[23]

Third, this study included all the theoretically relevant factors traditionally thought to influence tolerance, including social status, ideology, psychological makeup (i.e., propensity to be self-reliant, confident, and secure), education, political involvement (i.e., level of political activity), political information, and support for the general principles of democracy (e.g., majority rule, minority rights, etc.).[24] In addition, we included a factor we called "perceived threat." This factor proved to be influential on both facets of tolerance, social and political. Though not to the same degree, as perceived threat was far more potent in shaping social tolerance than political, perceptions that the group in question is a threat proved to be a common causal influence (i.e., a shared antecedent to both forms of tolerance).

There is one substantial drawback to relying on survey data. These data provide a reasonable ability to speculate about effects that are stable and enduring. However, survey data, unless experiments are embedded within (Kinder and Palfrey 1993; Piazza, Sniderman, and Tetlock 1990), are not very useful for estimating how strongly people hold to their convictions and how readily they are influenced by public discussions and elite opinions. We have conducted experimental studies, with student and adult samples that do enable estimates to be drawn, but we will postpone the consideration of these findings until we discuss the role of elites in the section that follows.

With respect to the other antecedent factors, two points are important to underline. First, common to each model, the conventional accounts of the factors thought to enhance tolerance (education, political involvement, and political information) do not have the same influence in each model. In the case of social tolerance, none of these factors have *any* substantive impact. Thus, changing the level of political engagement and experience, or improving the level of educational achievement, based on these results, will have negligible consequences. For social tolerance only two factors have any consequential influence, and both of these are direct effects. Those who are more supportive of the general principles of democracy are very modestly more socially tolerant (the path coefficient = 0.14). And perceptions of threat, defined as perceptions that the group in question is violating norms of decorum (being perceived as being overly belligerent and treacherous), dominate willingness to be socially tolerant (path coefficient = -0.65; i.e., the more threatened, the less socially tolerant).

Clearly the factor of perceptions of threat plays the most influential role in each model. It is important to note that in each instance that factor is exogenous. That is, other factors in the model, such as education, social status, and psychological security, do not account for variations in perceptions of threat. This is surprising because the most obvious presumption is that our fear of others is a reflection of our background and circumstances. These null relationships suggest a different explanation: perceptions of threat are contemporary observations of the activities of others being judged, and since contemporary observations are driven by contemporary circumstance, fears are exacerbated or assuaged by how those being judged behave. Our experimental work on tolerance judgments (Marcus et al. 1995) supports that interpretation. In any case, to the extent that perceptions of threat are not solely a projection of group stereotypes but are substantively based on group activity—most often political activity initiated to gain attention and support, the kind of activity essential to liberal democratic politics—then it is precisely such activity that is likely to stimulate greater political and social intolerance.

The two path models are displayed in Figure 7-1.

Consider what would happen if one were magically able to induce fundamental improvements in the social status of this society, in the ideological direction, psychological makeup (were that possible), or political experience of the populace. For social tolerance, the implications seem clear and straightforward; these findings suggest that there is little prospect for making this society more socially tolerant because none of these determinants have any substantive influence on social tolerance. The reason we don't "just get along" is because too many of us perceive "them" as overly belligerent and treacherous, the single but very influential antecedent of social intolerance. Absent a profound change in how we perceive groups different from ourselves, social intolerance is likely to be an enduring feature of American society.

For political tolerance the story is more complex and marginally more encouraging. Though the conventional factors thought to enhance political tolerance have no direct effect, and, in the case of education, only very modest indirect effects, there are other factors that do shape political tolerance judgments. Thus, though it is disappointing that conventionally identified factors seem largely irrelevant to political tolerance, it is comforting that encouraging people to learn and then come to rely upon general principles of democracy

I. Social Tolerance–Path Model

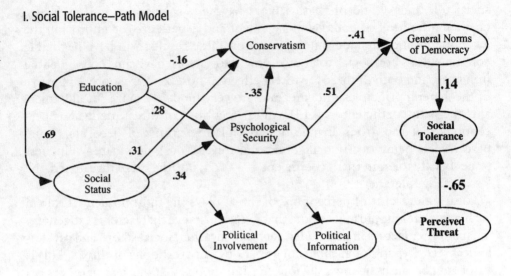

II. Political Tolerance–Path Model

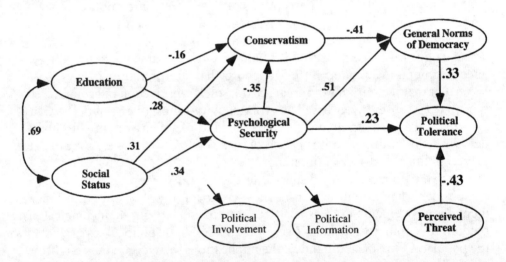

FIGURE 7-1
Comparing Political and Social Tolerance: Antecedent Factors
Source: 1978 NORC, Sullivan, Piereson, and Marcus 1982.

can elevate the overall level of political tolerance (a point to which we will return later in this chapter). It is encouraging that elevating the overall sense of
security and self-confidence in the society, by elevating levels of educational
accomplishment and social achievement, will also have a beneficial effect.

Having explored these results, it is worth noting the differences across the
two path models. One conclusion that seems to flow from such a comparison is
that improving the overall material condition of the society (i.e., increased educational opportunity, improved job conditions, and social well-being) may

well have some modest benefits for the level of political tolerance, though none can be expected for social tolerance. In part, this is so because people rely on their belief in democratic principles to make political tolerance judgments. Yet with regard to social tolerance judgments, decisions as to whether to become more socially intimate with members of disliked groups, democratic principles are far less weighty an influence. Indeed, though statistically significant, the effect of democratic beliefs in social tolerance judgments is largely inconsequential. What we find suggests that the distinction between public and private, a distinction central to liberal theorists, seems to powerfully resonate with the public. Political tolerance involves public rules about political processes. On the other hand, social tolerance involves what we do in the immediacy of our home and neighborhood. Democratic principles are accepted as applying to the political realm but are largely ignored in the private realm.[25]

Thus, social tolerance judgments are shaped by judgments relying on the apprehension that the "others" in question accept the norms of good behavior and on the degree of comfort born of similarity. On the other hand, political tolerance judgments are shaped by greater psychological self-confidence, commitment to democratic principles, and, to a lesser extent than in the case of social tolerance, the norms of trustworthiness and compliance.

The contemporary presumptions that improvements in social conditions, better understanding, and more political experience will engender a more tolerant society seem not well supported by these findings. There is another robust body of research findings that is also a cause for some pessimism regarding the possibility of a more enlightened populace. One facet of the broad personality dimension we have labeled psychological security is authoritarianism. Those high on authoritarianism generally value order more than disorder, value compliance with social norms rather than being rebellious, and tend to value conservative authority figures over more radical leaders (Adorno et al. 1950; Duckitt 1989; Ekhardt 1991; Sanford 1973). Authoritarians, or rightwing authoritarians, as Altemeyer (1988) has labeled them, are ill disposed to support democratic principles generally, or, more specifically, those they find objectionable.

One widely reliable finding has been the strong association between those who are more authoritarian and greater prejudice against liminal groups, a relationship that does not augur well for greater social tolerance (Altemeyer 1994; Haddock, Zanna, and Esses 1993; Meloen et al. 1988). More troubling still is recent work suggesting that those who hold authoritarian values are more likely to express and act on those attitudes in times of crisis and stress, precisely the moments when political tolerance is most required (Altemeyer 1994; Doty, Peterson, and Winter 1991; Sales 1973). If authoritarian individuals were inclined to act in safe periods, or were constant in their views and actions, that would be a modest problem for diverse liberal societies, societies that value and must protect the political activity of even those who are not inclined to express the democratic personality and its associated values. However, it appears that the circumstances that most require political tolerance, such as periods of economic dislocation, war, or other sorts of turmoil, are precisely those circumstances that appear to make manifest authoritarian expression and action that are not apparent in more tranquil moments.

Thus, the evidence on the determinants of social and political tolerance suggests that social and political intolerance will not disappear, at least not any time soon. Madison's perspective requires the enduring necessity of factions, sustained by the ever greater diversity that has resulted from liberty. Political conflict will lead to perceptions of greater, rather than lesser, belligerence between groups in conflict. Political conflict is also likely to increase the perception that treachery is a common motive in politics (Goertzel 1994; Hofstadter 1966). These are conditions that suggest that intolerance—the animus that divides groups from one another, that generates the sentiments that favor and despise—will be enduring as well. So neither perspective offers much hope for eradicating the problem of political and social intolerance. But can we perhaps keep it in check?

Nonpublic Sources of Political Tolerance: Elites and Institutions

As Russell Hanson has pointed out, "the characteristics of a political system are not the orientations of its citizens writ large" (1993, p. 285). As the Founding Fathers understood, the protection of political rights and practices would require "auxiliary precautions" such as a limited democratic government, augmented by a bill of rights to secure those limitations, the republican principle that would provide elevated leadership, as well as an independent judiciary instituted in part to secure liberties not sufficiently safeguarded by other means. Thus, it is less of a problem that citizens may not sufficiently protect the political rights of all fellow citizens, especially when they see some others not as citizens like themselves but as objectionable people who are sufficiently different as to warrant exclusion.

If citizens cannot be expected to be the sufficient bulwark for political rights, then we can count on political elites, those leaders selected because of their superior character and understanding, as well as their willingness to act with political courage, to do what is right especially when what is right may antagonize the citizens who have elected them.

And if we cannot count on citizens and their elected leaders to be the sufficient shield protecting the political rights of other citizens, then surely we can count on judges, especially those of the highest quality, such as we can find on the Supreme Court. The Supreme Court, because its jurists are selected on the basis of their competency in the law, their commitment to legal norms, their understanding of constitutional issues, and their security from political pressure, is aptly constructed to provide additional safeguard to the political rights of the despised and disparaged even when the public and political leaders may come to some malevolent agreement to restrict the rights of some citizens.[26]

A review of the history of political tolerance in the United States with special attention to the role of political leaders and the Supreme Court suggests that the difficult task of joining popular sovereignty with the protection of minority rights has been only partially been achieved. The effort on the part of political leaders to secure the government's authority against attack from the public, especially during and following times of war and crisis, has been more of a constant feature of American history than we would like to acknowledge. The Alien and Sedition Acts of 1798 were not exceptional excesses that occurred in the "crawling stages" of the newly born American republic. The declaration of martial law by Lincoln to suppress the Copperhead opposition to the continuation of the Civil War can of course be treated as an exceptional and necessary act to preserve the Union. However, what are we to make of the Sedition Act of 1918? This act was passed in both legislative branches and signed into law by President Woodrow Wilson. Moreover, the United States Supreme Court affirmed the constitutionality of the law in the Abrams case. The Sedition Act, among other provisions, made it a crime to "say or do anything" with the intent to block the sale of war bonds; to "willfully utter, print, write, or publish any disloyal, profane, scurrilous, or abusive language" about the United States form of government, Constitution, military or naval forces, or flag, or about the uniform of the Army and Navy; or to use any language designed to bring any of these things "into contempt, scorn, contumely, or disrepute" (Polenberg 1987). This act had the express purpose of suppressing anarchist, socialist, and antiwar activity. Moreover, these activities were well within the domain of conventional and legitimate political action. This legislation was enacted into law by highly experienced legislators and signed into law by a former university president who could hardly, given his training, have claimed ignorance as a defense. Apparently, the threat of war, in this case, generated a claim of necessity that succeeded in persuading all three branches of the United States government to agree to repress the political and civil rights of American citizens.

There have been more recent experiences of government-led repression. Among those since World War I that come to mind are the forced evacuation of American citizens of Japanese ancestry to concentration camps in World War II; the next period of anticommunist fear, during the Red Scare period of the fifties and the role of the HUAC, the presidency, and the courts to repress communists and "fellow travellers" (Fried 1990); and the effort of President Richard Nixon to use the FBI and IRS to go after antiwar activists. These instances all suggest that political leaders will pursue the goal of securing public order by restricting the rights of at least the more liminal of political movements and groups no less in the future than in the past.

Thus, institutional barriers to repression can be breached even by those who least expected to join such efforts. It may well be the case that citizens, by themselves, cannot be expected to secure political tolerance. But it is also clear that political elites and democratic institutions are not certain guarantors either (Searing 1982).

Moreover, it is also clear that leaders can present an issue in a fashion that may effectively shape the public's response. When political leaders call for repression, those calls may be generally well received, not just by those already partial to calls for order. Studies have demonstrated that people are attentive and responsive to the views of others when making judgments about how to respond when the issue is one of protecting or restricting the rights of objectionable people, groups, movements, or ideas (Marcus et al. 1995; Nelson, Clawson, and Oxley 1997). When the conflict is presented with a call to "protect the rights of everyone," people respond with greater tolerance than they otherwise would. However, when the issue is presented as one demanding the protection of the society and the normative values of the society against the forces of disorder, then those calls are also influential.[27] The rhetoric of democracy is sufficiently plastic that it can be used to protect civil rights or to accommodate the claims of majorities and leaders for social order and compliance. The rhetoric political leaders use is important because their choice of argument is going to have some measure of influence for at least some citizens. As has often been the case, especially in times of crises, when elected political leaders argue for order and for restrictions to democracy, it is not only the Supreme Court but also the public that may comply.

Conclusions

A harmonious politics, however appealing that vision of a more tranquil society might be, has severe consequences for the prospects for justice and the common good. Yet we are often drawn to "end of conflict" visions, such as those presented by Rodney King ("Why can't we just get along") or more eloquently by Martin Luther King ("I have a dream"). Politics must be vigorous, and it must be animated by the passions that generate action (after all, the word "emotion" means, literally, a state of being in motion). It would be nice if leaders, citizens, and institutions would differentiate between, on the one hand, their support for the political prerogatives afforded to all citizens that require universal application and, on the other, their pursuit of their beliefs and interests that require at least some measure of zealous attachment to a particular leader, group, and proposal. And to a degree the evidence supports such a possibility.

However, the connection between the sufficient degree of zeal necessary to mobilize political action and the attendant partisan attachments and animosities, so central to Madison's conception of human nature, suggests political intolerance is also a likely consequence.

Political intolerance is also a likely recurring problem for liberal plural societies because they are diverse and diversity often leads to at least some animus (Aboud 1988; LeVine and Campbell 1972). A liberal society is one that accepts, indeed applauds, the evolution of individuals according to their talents, inclinations, and personality. It is also clear that some recurring personality traits make some people more and others less predisposed to greater political intolerance. Liberal political philosophies encourage support for doctrines that seek to protect the civil and political rights of all citizens. Yet the liberal society will find itself populated by some who are less inclined to endorse or be bound by such doctrines. As a consequence, any liberal society will find itself populated with a segment of people who are ill disposed, by nature, to endorse the premises of liberality and who will be inclined to accept nativist and xeno-phobic appeals.

Normal politics, the everyday politics of confrontation, mobilization, and compromise, puts people and groups into political action and conflict. At least some political activities are intentionally and necessarily designed to attract attention, to be sufficiently outrageous as to draw public attention. It is just such activity that is likely not only to gain attention but also to stimulate greater intolerance among those who find the purposes and methods of such political action objectionable (Feldman and Stenner 1997; Marcus et al. 1995). Since the ebb and flow of threatening circumstances—both domestic, such as economic crisis, and foreign, such as war—will be an ineradicable aspect of democratic politics, we can also anticipate that the problem of political tolerance will also be more or less severe depending on the character of the times. We can also expect that the targets of political intolerance will also change as circumstances and the changing character of diversity in the society make different groups in our society, at different times, more despised or more accepted (Sullivan and Marcus 1988; Sullivan, Piereson, and Marcus 1979; Sullivan, Piereson, Marcus, and Feldman 1979). As different crises arise, and as new groups with different values and goals emerge or immigrate to our society, political intolerance will be an always lurking dilemma.

Research has shown that an effective middle school curriculum can strengthen students' understanding of democratic principles and the obligations of political tolerance (Avery et al. 1992; Bird et al., 1994; Sullivan et al. 1994; Thalhammer et al. 1994; Wood et al. 1994). However, one interesting finding of this research is that while the curriculum strengthens understanding of and reliance on democratic principles by the students in making political tolerance judgments, it also strengthens the animus that students have against the groups they are most likely to target for intolerance.[28]

And even though this curriculum seems to have some capacity to have enduring impact, it cannot, by itself, do more than ameliorate the problem of intolerance in a liberal democracy. Recall that democratic norms are not applied to social tolerance judgments. Thus, it is unlikely that this kind of curriculum, which attempts to strengthen reliance on democratic principles, can have much impact on the willingness of people who are members of different and antagonistic groups to intermingle.

It seems most prudent, then, to conclude that political and social intolerance will be recurring problems for a liberal society such as ours. We need not despair, for there is much that we can do. We can remind ourselves, especially in moments of crisis, that political tolerance serves all of us. And, we can take on the important responsibility to take up public action in support of political tolerance.[29] If we do so, if we speak out, we can expect that others will be similarly reminded and that such reminders are influential. Further, we can, as my colleagues have done, help prepare our next generation by teaching our children of the central vital importance of sustaining our commitment to democratic practices especially when it is not natural or easy to do so. Though I am dubious that such practices can eliminate the risk of political intolerance in America, they can mitigate the damage that political intolerance can inflict. Such efforts will not produce a final solution, but they are an important and enduring if nonetheless partial solution. We may not be able to accomplish more than that. But we should not aspire to do any less.

Notes

A number of colleagues have been kind enough to offer insightful criticisms of earlier drafts of this chapter. Among them are James Gibson, Russell Hanson, James Kuklinski, Gary Jacobsohn, and J. Russell Muirhead. In addition, the members of my course on Intolerance and Political Tolerance also provided valuable comments for which I am also grateful. Needless to say, their cautions and suggestions made this a more carefully reasoned discussion, though the positions taken and arguments advanced are my own.

1. In the West, at least since the period of the Enlightenment, the idea of progress has changed from a biological conception, one that mimics the rhythms of life (birth, maturation, decay, death, and rebirth), to a linear model that presumes that a process of change, if properly initiated and sustained, will yield ever greater degrees of progress (Arendt 1963). Hence, if progress is linear, then once a regime of democracy is put into motion, and the public is given more political experience, supported by improved public education, the public's appreciation of and commitment to democracy will continue to be strengthened (Barber 1984; Pateman 1970; Thompson 1970).

2. I don't mean to suggest that only two conceptions exist for how to achieve a just society, or even that there is universal agreement as to the proper goal for politics. I have restricted the considerations of this chapter to a comparison of what I take to be the modern understanding of the machinery of democratic politics with the understanding that Madison and his colleagues, in the main, shared. It is well worth expanding this comparison to integrate yet other considerations; however, that is beyond the scope of this chapter.

3. These will involve domestic and legal issues (e.g., to sustain or restrict the right of a woman to choose an abortion) and international decisions (e.g., to engage in "peace-making" or war or to secure trading agreements). And, the Constitution mandates that we must choose our elected leaders frequently and continually.

4. Gordon Wood (1992) has persuasively shown that the adoption of a more democratic and a less deferential politics took place with surprising rapidity.

5. For a thoughtful dissenting view read Hanson (1993). Hanson argues, in part, that other factors protect minority group rights and that therefore the public is not solely or even primarily responsible for ensuring political tolerance in this society. Hanson is certainly correct in that assertion, and we shall review some of these ancillary sources of protection below. However, insofar as explicit public support is the principal source of legitimacy, and insofar as protecting political tolerance in concrete circumstances is important, then ignoring or downplaying the public's responsible role in securing political tolerance for despised minorities and unpopular causes seems to suggest the need to limit the public's responsibilities in authorizing democratic choices.

6. Sniderman argues that people making political tolerance judgments eschew affective considerations, though elsewhere he has argued that people effectively rely upon affective cues to make political judgments (Brady and Sniderman 1985).

7. A city state, organized as a democracy, could be virtuous if all its people, or at least all its citizens, were sufficiently homogenous in their common convictions and

commitments to a collective way of life that placed the needs of the society as preeminent.

8. The classic taxonomy, too briefly summarized above, suggests that the principal task of founding a virtuous regime is to properly assign the responsibilities of governance to those (one, few, or many) who have the requisite virtue for the task. This is the point at which the Founding Fathers reject classic understandings. Madison himself provides much of the effort to create a new "science of politics" that he himself calls for.

9. The rarity of disinterested statesmen is one problem. However, in *Federalist* No. 37, Madison points to another problem. In this paper Madison gives an account of the limitations of reason, suggesting that the ability to correctly perceive the common good, even among those who are not disabled by self-interest or passion, is far more limited than we might suspect.

10. I do not mean here to assert that Madison believed that this new politics could absorb *any* form of conflict or interest. In *Federalist* No. 10, Madison makes clear that some forms of conflict, those most zealous (such as religious strife) are likely beyond the capacity of this system to manage. But as the United States has a multiplicity of religious sects, is large and diverse, and seems willing to accept proscription against state involvement in religion, the forms of factional activity most likely to engage politics, such as the distribution of property, are sufficiently moderate that they can be properly contained.

11. Madison had yet another reason for choosing his central metaphor from the realm of technology. We often concern ourselves, in matters of corruption and civic virtue, with intention. But here Madison wants us to focus on the real material consequences of proposals. That good should come of good intentions, and bad from those with malevolent purposes, is no doubt an association we hope will be robust, but far more important is the observation that consequences of political actions are often quite different from those intended. For more on the role of technology in the enrichment of cultures and greater dominance over nature and other competing societies, see Diamond (1997).

12. Of course, any claim, even one that gains substantial public support and becomes law may nonetheless be a flawed and corrupting policy. Madison does not offer a certainty about the process; he recommends only the greater *probability* of success. And, of course, frequent elections and a dynamic society with fragile coalitions ensure a measure of reconsideration of policies, even of those that were once popular.

13. Of course, such tactics as horse trading, pork-barrel legislation, and hidden portions of large omnibus legislation can defeat the benefit of public political conflict. And it is just such tactics that enable private interests to secure private, i.e. corrupt, benefits. Madison, of course, knows this. He promises that the machinery he advances is *generally* going to work, as he understands that there remain opportunities for corrupt interests to gain political advantage even in this system. That he was certainly correct on that score is amply demonstrated in such venues as the *NBC News* regular feature "The Fleecing of America," itself a reprise of Senator Proxmire's Golden Fleece Award.

14. Hence, Madison's use of "auxiliary precautions."

15. Madison would have had in mind the religious wars of Europe, such as the Thirty Years' War, but even since, we have had our own civil war. Plural democracies have a difficult task, creating sufficient political conflict to make the system work but not so much conflict that it provokes a level of violence that could overwhelm the political apparatus.

16. Perhaps the best observer of the practices of civility remains Erving Goffman (1959; 1971).

17. Though, of course, in many societies, civility may be a far more precious commodity. See Walzer (1997).

18. Though more widely available than political tolerance, social tolerance is not compatible with totalitarian regimes that attempt to atomize groups so that individuals have no source of affiliation other than with and to the state.

19. The attempts to end discriminatory practices have been a major component of the civil rights movement—for example, to make illegal deed restrictions that preclude selling of a property to someone who does not belong to the favored group, or racially dedicated scholarships, or to make illegal the prerogative of landlords to rely on local mores or prejudices to withhold rental apartments from those they disparage.

20. And, of course, political tolerance established an obligation to support the rights of those whom one dislikes quite independent of any specific political views or beliefs.

21. These findings have been replicated, in the main, in the United States by Jim Gibson (1992) and in other countries by John Sullivan and colleagues (1985).

22. Why not assess trends on political tolerance by comparing the proportions of the United States population that express tolerant attitudes at different periods? This approach would appear to provide direct evidence on the historical trends that are central to this discussion. Moreover, studies have produced just these sorts of comparisons (Mueller 1988; Nunn et al. 1978). But interpreting such evidence is fraught with problems of interpretation (Sullivan and Marcus 1988; Sullivan, Piereson, and Marcus 1979). Most important, political tolerance at any historical moment depends on a number of factors, one of which is the number and salience of despised groups. And, as is clear with attitudes toward communists, these attitudes can change in more than one direction. For example, at the turn of this century, as evidenced in the Sedition Act of 1918, communists were intensely disliked by many, yet twenty years later, they became our friendly allies in the effort to defeat the Axis powers, only, yet again, to become feared in the period, following World War II, during the "Red Scare."

23. The fact that we can generate numbers does not warrant treating these analyses and comparisons as any more than grounded speculations. These assessments are no better than the data that generate them and are constrained to the time and place and procedures that generated them. However, though considerable caution should be retained, they do force us to consider theoretical and empirical implications by virtue of the mathematical expression of these findings that a less precise articulation would not enable.

24. In each path model, in order to keep the models from being overly cluttered, I have not detailed how the various antecedent factors influence political involvement and political information. Because neither of these factors influences either social or political tolerance, the subject of this chapter, there is no need to elaborate the role of education, as well as other factors, in accounting for variations in these two political variables (for those interested in those relationships, see Sullivan, Pierson, and Marcus 1982).

25. One implication of this distinction is that we now can offer an account of why many people so resisted court-ordered busing to achieve racial integration. Though the courts were acting as agents of a democratic government, though of the judiciary, many people may have felt that the decision of which school their child should attend was essentially a social rather than a political matter. And in the social realm different rules apply.

26. I have put the case in its strongest form. Of course, in many instances there are good reasons to expect that the Supreme Court, lacking any enforcement mechanism of its own and having no direct means other than by appealing to public understanding for securing public endorsement of its actions, may find it necessary to tactically withdraw or delay until a more propitious time before acting to protect the rights of those who seek the Court's protection. But even if our expecta-

tions of the Court's capacity should be more qualified, that does not alter the basic conclusion, judging from the history of the Court, that securing universal political rights is beyond the power of the Court, especially at those moments when such rights are most at risk.

27. James Gibson (1998) reports that his surveys, conducted in the United States, South Africa, and Russia, in which persuasive appeals are experimentally embedded, reveal that "the tolerant can be converted to intolerance at twice the rate at which the intolerant can be converted to tolerance." This asymmetry is, of course, troubling, as it suggests that the commitment of the tolerant is more fragile and less dependable than that of the intolerant (an interpretation that is also corroborated by our work showing that the intolerant are more inclined than the tolerant to act in support of their beliefs). See Marcus et al. 1995.

28. This is less surprising when you consider that most of us, if we are given even more contact with or information about a group we already despise to some extent, are likely to find our antagonistic convictions strengthened as a result.

29. Though the evidence is not sufficient to be definitive, it suggests that the politically intolerant are more intense in their beliefs and are more inclined to act in support of them than are the tolerant (Marcus et al. 1995).

References

Aboud, F. 1988. *Children and Prejudice*. Oxford: Basil Blackwell.

Adorno, T., E. Frenkel-Brunswick, D. Levinson, and R. N. Sanford. 1950. *The Authoritarian Personality*. New York: Harper and Row.

————. 1988. *Enemies of Freedom: Understanding Right-Wing Authoritarianism*. San Francisco: Jossey-Bass.

Altemeyer, B. 1994. Reducing prejudice in right-wing authoritarians. In M. P. Zanna and J. M. Olson (eds.), *The Psychology of Prejudice: The Ontario Symposium*, volume 7 (chapter 6). Hillsdale, NJ: Lawrence Erlbaum.

Arendt, H. 1963. *On Revolution*. New York: Viking Press.

Aristotle. 1983. *The Politics* (Sinclair, Trans.). Rev. ed. New York: Penguin Books.

Avery, P., K. Bird, S. Johnstone, J. L. Sullivan, and K. Thalhammer. 1992. Exploring political tolerance with adolescents. *Theory and Research in Social Education*, 20 (4): 386–420.

Barber, B. 1984. *Strong Democracy: Participatory Politics for a New Age*. Berkeley and Los Angeles: University of California Press.

Bird, K., J. L. Sullivan, P. G. Avery, K. Thalhammer, and S. Wood. 1994. Not just lip-synching anymore: Education and tolerance revisited. *The Review of Education/Pedagogy/Cultural Studies* 16 (3–4): 373–86.

Bogardus, E. S. 1925. Measuring social distance. *Journal of Applied Sociology* 9: 299–308.

Brady, H., and P. Sniderman. 1985. Attitude attribution: A group basis for political reasoning. *American Political Science Review* 79: 1061–78.

Diamond, J. 1997. *Guns, Germs, and Steel: The Fates of Human Societies*. New York: W. W. Norton & Co.

Doty, R. M., B. E. Peterson, and D. G. Winter. 1991. Threat and authoritarianism in the United States, 1978–1987. *Journal of Personality and Social Psychology* 61 (4): 629–40.

Duckitt, J. 1989. Authoritarianism and group identification: A new view of an old construct. *Political Psychology* 10 (1): 63–84.

Ekhardt, W. 1991. Authoritarianism. *Political Psychology* 12 (1): 97–124.

Feldman, S., and K. Stenner. 1997. Perceived threat and authoritarianism. *Political Psychology* 18 (4): 741–70.

Fried, R. M. 1990. *The McCarthy Era in Perspective*. New York: Oxford University Press.

Gibson, J. L. 1987. Homosexuals and the Ku Klux Klan: A contextual analysis of political tolerance. *Western Political Quarterly* 40: 427–48.

———. 1988. Political intolerance and political repression during the McCarthy Red Scare. *American Political Science Review* 82 (2): 511–29.

———. 1992. Alternative measures of political tolerance: Must tolerance be "least-liked"? *American Journal of Political Science* 36 (2): 560–77.

———. 1998. A sober second thought: An experiment in persuading Russians to tolerate. *American Journal of Political Science* 42 (3): 819–50.

Gibson, J. L., and R. D. Bingham. 1985. *Civil Liberties and Nazis: The Skokie Free-Speech Controversy*. New York: Praeger.

Goertzel, T. 1994. Belief in conspiracy theories. *Political Psychology* 15 (4): 731–42.

Goffman, E. 1959. *The Presentation of Self in Everyday Life*. Garden City, NY: Doubleday & Co.

———. 1971. *Relations in Public*. New York: Basic Books.

Haddock, G., M. P. Zanna, and V. M. Esses. 1993. Assessing the structure of prejudiced attitudes: The case of attitudes toward homosexuals. *Journal of Personality and Social Psychology* 65 (6): 1105–18.

Hanson, R. L. 1985. *The Democratic Imagination in America: Conversations with Our Past*. Princeton, NJ: Princeton University Press.

———. 1993. Deliberation, tolerance and democracy. In G. E. Marcus and R. L. Hanson (eds.), *Reconsidering the Democratic Public*. University Park: Pennsylvania State University Press, pp. 273–86.

Hofstadter, R. 1966. *Anti-Intellectualism in American Life*. New York: Vintage Press.

Kinder, D. R., and T. R. Palfrey (eds.) 1993. *Experimental Foundations of Political Science*. Ann Arbor: University of Michigan Press.

Lawrence, D. 1976. Procedural norms and tolerance: A reassessment. *American Political Science Review* 70 (1): 70–80.

LeVine, R. A., and D. T. Campbell, 1972. *Ethnocentrism: Theories of Conflict, Ethnic Attitudes and Group Behavior*. New York: John Wiley and Sons.

Madison, J., A. Hamilton, and J. Jay. 1961. *The Federalist Papers*. Cleveland: World Publishing.

Marcus, G. E., J. L. Sullivan, E. Theiss-Morse, and S. Wood. 1995. *With Malice toward Some: How People Make Civil Liberties Judgments*. New York: Cambridge University Press.

Meloen, J. D., L. Hagendoorn, Q. Raaijmakers, and L. Visser. 1988. Authoritarianism and the revival of political racism: Reassessments on the Netherlands of the reliability and validity of the concept of authoritarianism by Adorno et al. *Political Psychology* 9 (3): 413–29.

Mueller, J. 1988. Trends in political tolerance. *Public Opinion Quarterly* 52: 1–25.

Nelson, T. E., R. A. Clawson, and Z. M. Oxley. 1997. Media framing of a civil liberties conflict and its effect on tolerance. *American Political Science Review* 91 (3): 567–83.

Nunn, C. Z., H. J. Crockett, and J. A. Williams. 1978. *Tolerance for Nonconformity*. San Francisco: Jossey-Bass.

Pateman, C. 1970. *Participation and Democratic Theory*. Cambridge: Cambridge University Press.

Piazza, T., P. M. Sniderman, and P. E. Tetlock. 1990. Analysis of the dynamics of political reasoning: A general-purpose computer-assisted methodology. In J. A. Stimson (ed.), *Political Analysis*. Ann Arbor: University of Michigan Press, pp. 99–119.

Polenberg, R. 1987. *Fighting Faiths: The Abrams Case, the Supreme Court, and Free Speech*. New York: Viking.

Prothro, J. W., and C. W. Grigg. 1960. Fundamental principles of democracy: Bases of agreement and disagreement. *Journal of Politics* 22: 276–94.

Sales, S. M. 1973. Threat as a factor in authoritarianism: An analysis of archival data. *Journal of Personality and Social Psychology* 28: 44–57.

Sanford, N. 1973. Authoritarian personality in contemporary perspective. In J. Knutson (ed.), *Handbook of Political Psychology*. San Francisco: Jossey-Bass.

Searing, D. B. 1982. Rules of the game in Britain: Can politicians be trusted? *American Political Science Review* 76 (2): 239–58.

Sniderman, P. M., P. Tetlock, J. Glaser, D. P. Glaser, and M. Hout. 1989. Principled tolerance and the American mass public. *British Journal of Political Science* 19: 25–45.

Spitz, E. 1984. *Majority Rule*. Chatham, NJ: Chatham House.

Stouffer, S. 1955. *Communism, Conformity and Civil Liberties*. New York: Doubleday.

Sullivan, J. L., P. G. Avery, K. Thalhammer, S. Wood, and K. Bird. 1994. Education and political tolerance in the United States: The mediating role of cognitive sophistication, personality, and Democratic norms. *Review of Education/Pedagogy/Cultural Studies* 16 (3–4): 315–24.

Sullivan, J. L., and G. E. Marcus. 1988. A note on "Trends in Political Tolerance." *Public Opinion Quarterly* 52: 26–32.

Sullivan, J. L., J. E. Piereson, and G. E. Marcus. 1979. An alternative conceptualization of political tolerance: Illusory increases 1950s–1970s. *American Political Science Review* 73 (3): 781–94.

———. 1982. *Political Tolerance and American Democracy*. Chicago: University of Chicago Press.

Sullivan, J. L., J. E. Piereson, G. E. Marcus, and S. Feldman. 1979. The more things change, the more they stay the same: The stability of mass belief systems. *American Journal of Political Science* 23 (1): 176–86.

Sullivan, J. L., M. Shamir, P. Walsh, and N. S. Roberts. 1985. *Political Tolerance in Context*. Boulder, CO: Westview Press.

Thalhammer, K., S. Wood, K. Bird, P. G. Avery, and J. L. Sullivan. 1994. Adolescents and political tolerance: Lip-synching to the tune of democratcy. *Review of Education/Pedagogy/Cultural Studies* 16 (3–4): 325–47.

Thompson, D. 1970. *The Democratic Citizen: Social Science and Democratic Theory in the Twentieth Century*. New York: Cambridge University Press.

Walzer, M. 1997. *On Toleration*. New Haven, CT: Yale University Press.

Wills, G. 1992. *Lincoln at Gettysburg*. New York: Simon and Schuster.

Wood, G. S. 1992. *The Radicalism of the American Revolution*. New York: Alfred A. Knopf.

Wood, S., K. Thalhammer, J. L. Sullivan, K. Bird, P. G. Avery, and K. Klein. 1994. Tolerance for diversity of beliefs: Learning about tolerance and liking it too. *Review of Education/Pedagogy/Cultural Studies* 16 (3–4): 349–72.

8

The Future of Racial Politics: Beyond Fatalism

EDWARD G. CARMINES AND PAUL M. SNIDERMAN

It is easy to be fatalistic about the politics of race in the United States today. Although no one doubts that racial progress was made in the 1960s and to a lesser extent the 1970s—indeed this may have been the crowning achievement of these years—the politics of race seems to have been fixed in place now for more than a decade. No genuine, large-scale initiatives were launched in the 1980s. On the contrary, the largest part of the political energies of racial liberals has been devoted to defensive battles, to hanging on to the gains of the 1980s and 1970s. Worse, it is widely argued that unless and until the hearts and minds of ordinary white Americans can be transformed, progress in achieving racial equality is not possible. "Without affirmative action," declares Cornel West, "racial and sexual discrimination would return with a vengeance." (West 1993, 95). Jonathan Coleman, a white liberal, is certain that even in the hearts of whites most sympathetic to blacks, there remains the incubus of bigotry (Coleman 1997). And this is the explicit theme of Andrew Hacker's best-selling book *Two Nations: Separate, Hostile, Unequal* (Hacker 1992). We agree that the constraints on progress are real, and indeed one of our objectives in this chapter is to explore the political roots of the contemporary impasse over race. But our primary objective is different. It is to indicate how, notwithstanding the tangle over racial politics nowadays, there may be a possible way forward.

To accomplish both these aims, we are going to rely on a series of national surveys that we have conducted over the last decade (see Sniderman and Carmines 1997). Funded by the National Science Foundation and carried out by the Survey Research Center at the University of California at Berkeley, these surveys have had a unique feature. By taking advantage of computer-assisted interviewing, it has been possible to develop a new approach to the study of public opinion that combines the external validity advantages of representative surveys with the internal validity strengths of complex randomized experiments (see Sniderman and Grob 1996).

Our argument is two-pronged. We argue, first, that race-conscious policies, notably affirmative action, cannot be the centerpiece of a successful racial politics strategy. The reason is simple: affirmative action lacks requisite public support. As we demonstrate, it is not just that strong opposition to affirmative action is found among the policy's presumed enemies—Republicans and those on the right. When measured appropriately—which in this case means unobtrusively—it turns out that white liberals and Democrats are equally angry and upset over affirmative action. If affirmative action is treated as the new benchmark of racial progress, fatalism may indeed be in order. For there is no more public support for this race-centered policy today than there was a decade or two ago. But the second part of the chapter shows that racial progress still may be possible in spite of the overwhelming white opposition to race-conscious policies. The key is to move beyond race-centered policies to programs that benefit the badly off, whether black or white, and, perhaps more important, to policies that can be justified in racially inclusive terms. Public support depends on not only who gets what but why.

Contemporary Cleavages: The Politics of Affirmative Action

We begin with what is arguably the most prominent of the many faces of the issue of race today—notably, the anger and resentment over racial politics that is so evident, so palpable. Race, it is worth remembering, was once supposed to be an issue that we would put behind us: never entirely perhaps, but it would surely abate with progress. But race has not receded into the background of American life. On the contrary, it is obvious, even to the casual observer, that there are gaping cleavages over racial issues, and not only at the margins of American society, among the poorly educated and the poorly off, but at its center. The issue of race remains divisive, in some ways more than ever, and the question we want to examine is why.

This manifestly requires considering affirmative action, and we want to begin consideration of it by taking note of the standard account of the contemporary politics of race (Carmines and Stimson, 1989). It runs, briefly, like this. For a generation the issue of race has served as a fulcrum of the party system. In 1964, the Republican Party, which had been the champion of racial liberalism under Abraham Lincoln, became, with the nomination of Barry Goldwater, the party of racial conservatism. At the same time, the Democratic Party, formerly the party of slavery and segregation became, under the leadership of Lyndon Johnson, the party of racial liberalism. The consequence, according to the standard account, has been a steady defection of whites, particularly southerners, the working class, and those less attached to the Democratic Party's main principles, to the Republican side of the political ledger. On the standard account, then, in response to a series of racially divisive issues, affirmative action most recently, for a generation the Democratic Party has suffered defection from its periphery.

And there is substantial backing for the standard account. Whether one looks at our surveys or the disciplinary series—the National Election Studies for political science and the General Social Survey for sociology—one can see an obvious ideological division over affirmative action. Conservatives are significantly more likely to oppose it, liberals significantly more likely to support it. Yet it surely is not necessary to belabor the problem of validity. The standard approach in public opinion surveys presupposes that people will say how they honestly feel, or more exactly, that those who refuse to say candidly how they feel are a random set of the sample as a whole and their refusal therefore does not bias the results. But why is this presupposition reasonable? Race is a controversial issue, and affirmative action particularly so. Why suppose that everyone will simply say what he or she thinks? Why not take seriously the possibility that people instead will say what they think they should say?

These are old questions in survey research, but we have tried to tackle them in new ways. One of these new ways is the List Experiment. The design of this experiment can be complex, but its logic is perfectly straightforward. We randomly divide a representative sample of the country into two halves, which we refer to as the baseline condition and the test condition, respectively. In the baseline condition, the interviewer begins by saying:

> I'm going to read you a list of three things that sometimes make people angry or upset. After I read all three, just tell me HOW MANY of them upset you. I don't want to know which ones, just how many.

Then, the interviewer reads a list of three items:

> The federal government increasing the tax on gasoline; professional athletes getting million-dollar-plus salaries; large corporations polluting the environment.

In the test condition, very nearly everything is the same. But this time the interviewer reads a list of four items. The first three are the exactly the same. The fourth item is "black leaders asking the government for affirmative action."

If some people in the test condition are upset that athletes make too much money and if they also cannot abide affirmative action, they can feel free to say that two things make them angry, since the interviewer cannot tell that affirmative action is one of them. But since the two conditions differ only with respect to the inclusion of affirmative action in the test condition, the difference in the proportions of the two half samples that say they are angry has to be due to affirmative action. In other words, once the interviews are completed, we can calculate the difference between the number of angry responses in the two experimental conditions to estimate the proportion of whites angry over affirmative action.

TABLE 8.1
Covert White Anger over Affirmative Action, by Ideology and Partisanship (List Experiment)

Respondents, by Ideology and Partisanship	No. of Items That Anger Respondents		
	When Affirmative Action Is Not on the List	When Affirmative Action Is on the List	Difference[a]
Liberals	1.97	2.54	0.57
Moderates	2.04	2.59	0.55
Conservatives	2.18	2.68	0.50
Democrats	2.23	2.88	0.65
Independents	2.17	2.57	0.40
Republicans	2.19	2.83	0.64

Source: 1991 Race and Politics Study. Number of respondents for ideology, from 92 to 159; for partisanship, from 173 to 201.
[a]Difference is significant at .001 level for all items.

What do the politics of affirmative action look like when people feel free to say what they think? Table 8.1 compares the rate of anger over affirmative action for whites of different political orientations. The results, obviously enough, are quite different from those of conventional public opinion surveys. As Figure 8-1 shows, interviewed in the conventional way, with the interviewer manifestly knowing the position that respondents take, liberals are significantly less likely to oppose affirmative action than conservatives. But when they believe that they can express how they feel without anyone, including the interviewer, being able to tell how they feel, liberals turn out to be just as likely to be angry over affirma-

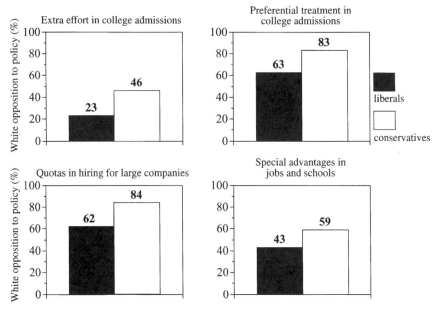

FIGURE 8-1
White Opposition to Affirmative Action, by Ideology
Source: 1991 Race and Politics Study. Number of respondents ranges from 78 to 313.

tive action as conservatives, and Democrats as likely to be upset over it as Republicans.

144

This is a result that, if valid, is exceedingly important. So we have gone to unusual lengths to validate it, including conducting an entirely independent national survey in order to replicate it. Part of the reason that it seemed worth the effort of cross-validation, which imposed a substantial cost in terms of years to complete the study as well as funds to carry it out, is that the initial affirmative action condition is potentially ambiguous. The item "black leaders asking the government for affirmative action" encompasses two referents—attitudes toward black leaders and attitudes toward affirmative action. It is possible that the high rates of anger in the List Experiment reflect not just the unpopularity of affirmative action but also of black leaders. So in the follow-up study an additional experimental condition was added, using as a test item "awarding college scholarships on the basis of race."

The replication of the List Experiment strongly confirms the results from the original experiment. In the original experiment 55 percent of whites were angry or upset over "black leaders asking the government for affirmative action." In the follow-up study 49 percent were angry over this identical item and 61 percent were angry over "awarding college scholarships on the basis of race." Thus, it was not the black leader referent in the wording of the original affirmative action item that elicited white anger but the actual practice of the policy.

What does the replicated List Experiment show about the ideological and partisan divisions over affirmative action? Again, the results shown in Table 8.2 closely parallel those in the original experiment. When we ask about affirmative action overtly, liberals seem less angry about it than conservatives (33 percent compared with 51 percent). But when reactions are measured unobtrusively this difference vanishes—56 percent of liberals and 59 percent of conservatives express anger. Thus, a large proportion of liberals (41 percent) are suppressing their anger over affirmative action.

Similar results are found when we look again at party affiliation. When asked directly about affirmative action, Republicans seem more angry than Democrats (37 percent versus 48 percent). But just as in the original experiment, when we ask about affirmative action covertly, Democrats are just as angry as Republicans; indeed, in the replication they are more so (52 percent of Democrats, 43 percent of Republicans).

One additional finding in the follow-up study casts new light on the contemporary politics of race. If liberals and Democrats are especially prone to suppress their anger over affirmative action, should this not also be the case for those most committed to racial equality? Figure 8-2 examines this proposition by comparing the reactions to affirmative action of whites who are most and least committed to racial equality, measured both directly and covertly. It shows two things are true. First, it is those who care about racial equality, not those who are indifferent or opposed to it, who hold back on their anger to affirmative action when asked directly. Second, they are, when they believe that they can express how they feel without anyone's knowing it, just as likely to be angry and upset over affirmative action as those who do not care about racial equality.

TABLE 8.2
Overt and Covert White Anger over Affirmative Action,
by Ideology and Partisanship (List Experiment)

By Ideology	Liberals (%)	Conservatives (%)	Difference (%)
A. Overt measure of affirmative action attitudes	32.7	50.9	18.2[a]
B. Covert measure of affirmative action attitudes	55.8	59.1	3.3
C. Difference (B−A)	23.1[a]	8.2	
D. Unacknowledged anger (C/B)	41.4	13.9	

By Partisanship	Democrats (%)	Republicans (%)	Difference (%)
A. Overt measure of affirmative action attitudes	36.6	48.1	11.5[b]
B. Covert measure of affirmative action attitudes	52.0	43.5	−8.5
C. Difference (B−A)	15.4[a]	n.s.	
D. Unacknowledged anger (C/B)	29.6	n.s.	

Source: 1994 Multiple Investigator Study.
[a]$p<.05$.
[b]$p<.01$.

These results thus suggest that the standard account of the politics of race is potentially quite misleading. The civil rights coalition itself—liberals, Democrats, and those whites most committed to racial equality—is divided over race-conscious policies not at its edges but at its center.

Group-Exclusive vs. Group-Inclusive Policies

But if a deep cleavage over affirmative action runs not merely between the left and right, but right through the left itself, is there a way forward? Is there a

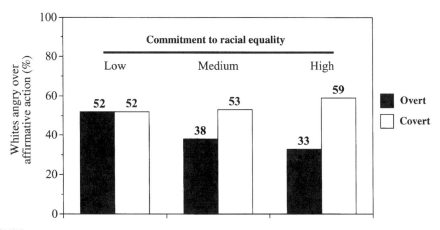

FIGURE 8-2
Whites' Anger over Affirmative Action, by Commitment to Racial Equality
Source: 1994 Multiple Investigator Study. Number of repondents ranges from 134 to 277.

way of building public support for policies to relieve the real and persisting problems of race?

The argument has been made, most powerfully by William Julius Wilson (Wilson 1978, 1987, 1996, 1999), that a possible way forward is to move from a race-centered politics to a racially neutral one. It is this idea that we want to explore.

It is now well established that the same policy framed in race-neutral terms is markedly more popular among whites than when it is presented in racially specific ones, that is, targeted to help blacks specifically (Bobo and Kluegel 1993). The crucial question, however, is why?

Three explanations have most commonly been given. The first emphasizes the continuing power of white racism. On this idea, racism may not be as freely or as crudely expressed as a generation ago. It may have become less blatant, more subtle, more covert. But it has not disappeared. And it has not lost its power to drive the emotional reactions of whites. On the contrary, according to this account, the very fact that you can increase the popularity of a policy merely by omitting to say that it is intended to help blacks is proof of the continuing strength of racism. The second explanation, by contrast, points to the anger and resentment swirling over race now, and in particular, to a perception of many whites that blacks are at the moment getting special treatment while, at the same time, continuing to complain vocally about being treated worse. Finally, in addition to the "racial prejudice" and the "racial backlash" hypotheses, there is the "group interest" argument. The notion here is that the reason why whites are readier to support racially neutral policies than racially specific ones is not that racially specific ones permit blacks to benefit, but that they prohibit whites from doing the same. White Americans, on this view, are reluctant to support race-centered policies because, though they too may need help from them, as whites, they can't get it.

To test the three hypotheses we focused on a particular policy issue—whether school taxes should be increased in order to improve public schools. One half of the time the issue was framed in terms of helping minorities; the other half, in terms of helping all children in public schools. Consistent with previous research, there was substantially more support for school assistance when the issue was framed in group-inclusive terms than when it was framed in group-exclusive terms, with 66 percent of whites favoring the former compared with 49 percent favoring the latter.

Why is the same policy more popular among whites if framed in racially neutral rather than racially specific terms? According to the first hypothesis, the reason is racial prejudice. To measure prejudice, we counted the number of negative characterizations of blacks that whites endorsed (e.g., aggressive or violent, boastful, lazy, irresponsible, complaining) and the accuracy with which they believed that each of these negative qualities characterized most blacks. Taking advantage of this measure of prejudice, Figure 8-3 compares the level of support for the two formulations of school policy as a function of the degree of white Americans' hostility to black Americans. If racial prejudice indeed is

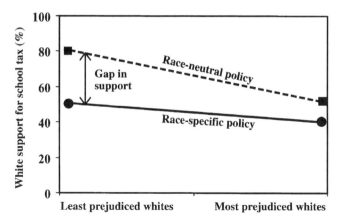

FIGURE 8-3
School Tax Experiment
Source: 1991 Race and Politics Study.

the reason for the greater popularity of racially neutral over racially specific policies, then the more prejudiced that whites are, the greater should be the difference in their level of support for racially neutral as compared with racially specific policies. But, as Figure 8-3 shows, things are just the other way around. Rather than the gap in support between racially neutral and racially specific policies widening the more racially intolerant whites are, it widens the more tolerant they are. The racial backlash hypothesis also fails (results not shown). Those who are angry over the special treatment that they perceive blacks to be getting are neither more nor less likely to favor racially neutral policies over racially specific ones than those who reject the idea that blacks are getting special treatment.

This leaves the "group interest" explanation. But if whites object to government assistance being targeted for blacks because they, as whites, cannot benefit, those whites who are most likely to benefit from such policies should be the most likely to object. But as Table 8.3 shows, however one operationalizes material interest—whether in terms of family income, self-assessment of financial condition, or security of employment status—none of these indicators of being badly off helps in any substantial way to account for the greater popularity of race-neutral over race-specific policies.

But if the difference in support for race-neutral as against race-specific policies is not attributable to racial attitudes or to group interest, then to what is it attributable?

What we want to suggest is that race-specific policies are less popular not mainly because they are racial, but more fundamentally because they are group-specific. The idea is that any policy framed in group-exclusive terms—that is, framed to benefit a specific, limited group—will be less popular than the same policy framed in broader, more inclusive terms. What limits the appeal of racially specific policies, on this line of argument, is not primarily that

TABLE 8.3
White Support for Race-Neutral versus Race-Specific Policies to Aid Schoolchildren,
by Self-Interest of Respondents

Measure of Self-interest	White Support for Public Schools (Race-neutral)		White Support for Minorities (Race-specific)	
Financial status[a]				
Improved	70%	(442)	50%	(421)
No change	59	(200)	46	(187)
Worse	62	(296)	42	(258)
Family income[b]				
Under $10,000	60%	(57)	42%	(53)
$10,000–19,999	63	(120)	47	(108)
$20,000–29,999	57	(156)	49	(135)
$30,000–39,999	68	(154)	53	(144)
$40,000–49,999	63	(126)	51	(127)
$50,000–69,999	71	(154)	45	(137)
$70,000+	69	(132)	44	(120)
Employment status[c]				
Full time	66%	(556)	47%	(521)
Part time	68	(104)	56	(76)
Laid off	73	(14)	48	(6)
Unemployed	82	(23)	31	(18)
Retired	58	(126)	42	(139)
Disabled	47	(13)	36	(10)
Keeping house	52	(72)	45	(77)
Student	86	(27)	77	(17)

Source: 1991 Race and Politics Study.

[a]Interaction between type of tax and financial status: not significant

[b]Interaction between type of tax and income: not significant.

[c]Interaction between type of tax and employment status: not significant.

they aim to benefit blacks, but more fundamentally that they aim to benefit only a limited group.

If so, then policies aimed at an equivalently particularistic group of whites should be similarly limited in their appeal. To test this prediction we carried out the Helping Hand Experiment. In the Helping Hand Experiment, we independently vary three aspects of a poverty policy: (1) who is to be helped: blacks and minorities or new immigrants from Europe; (2) how they are to be helped: through job training programs or welfare; and (3) why they might be entitled to be helped: because they are "people who have shown that they want to work their way out of their own problems," as opposed, in the contrasting experimental condition, to being "people who have had trouble hanging on to jobs." Since there are three aspects of the policy simultaneously being varied, and each of the three can take on one of two values, then all in all there are eight versions of the policy. The particular version a respondent is presented with is, of course, determined on a random basis, but then, whatever version they have been presented with, all are asked the same question: "Are you

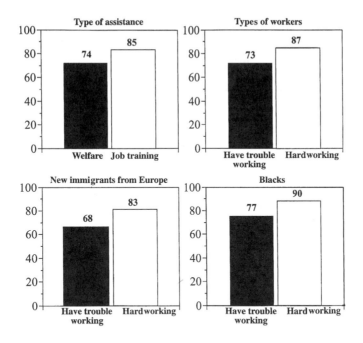

FIGURE 8-4
Helping Hand Experiment

Source: 1991 Race and Politics Study. Number of respondents ranges from 388 to 1011.

strongly in favor, somewhat in favor, somewhat opposed, or strongly opposed to these programs?"

Our hypothesis on particularlism suggests that the primary consideration is not whether blacks are to be helped but instead that only a limited, specifically defined group is to benefit. If the particularism hypothesis is true, then the policy should not be markedly more popular when a limited, particularlistically defined group of whites is to be assisted—even though they are white—than when minorities are to be assisted. As Figure 8-4 shows, not only is there not significantly more support for the policy when whites are to benefit than when blacks are to benefit; there is in fact significantly less. In addition, and not surprisingly, there is more support for assistance for the poor when it takes the form of job training rather than welfare and when it is to be directed toward those who are trying to help themselves rather than those who are failing to take advantage of the chances that come their way. But what is surprising is that this universalistic argument of self-effort—that one should try to help those who are trying to help themselves—carries just as much weight, creates just as much support for a program of assistance, when it is made in behalf of a black as when it is made in behalf of a white.

The Helping Hand Experiment thus suggests two points worth consideration. First, framing the beneficiaries of a policy in racial terms may be costly, not primarily because it is racial, but more fundamentally because it is particularistic. And second, whether a policy is targeted in racial terms or not, it can be argued for on grounds that go beyond race. This distinction between how a policy is targeted—and whether that is racial or not, and how it is justified, and whether *that* is racial or not—is, we think, crucial.

To demonstrate this, we first carried out the Regardless of Race Experiment. In this experiment we examined reactions to a policy supporting job-training programs, organized by the federal government and directed at reducing unemployment among blacks. The objective of the policy was always the same and always racially targeted—to promote employment for blacks—but the arguments made in its behalf varied. In one experimental condition the argument made in behalf of the policy was racially-centered—namely, that "because of the historic injustices that blacks have suffered," this program deserved support. In the other experimental condition, by contrast, the argument was expressly universalistic—namely, that the program merited support "because the government ought to help people who are out of work and want to find a job, whether they're white or black."

Our hypothesis, suggested by the Helping Hand Experiment, is that the nature of the argument made in behalf of a policy matters quite apart from the identity of the beneficiary of a policy. In Figure 8-5, therefore, we have plotted levels of support for this job-training program for blacks, first, as a function of the nature of the argument made in its behalf, then as a function of citizens' political orientation, too. Looking at the results in Figure 8-5, one can see that there is significantly more support for the policy when the policy is advanced with a color-blind justification than with a race-centered one. No less telling is where this increase is won on the political spectrum. The character of the argument—whether it is race-neutral or race-centered—makes no difference to conservatives. And it shouldn't. From a conservative point of view, this is ex-

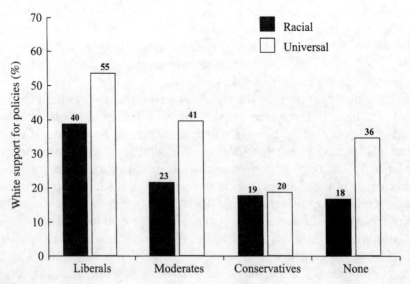

FIGURE 8-5
Regardless of Race Experiment

Source: 1994 Multiple Investigator Study. Number of respondents ranges from 599 to 649.

actly the kind of policy that, if you are a conservative, you should oppose. Where the gain in support comes from is in other places—among those without an ideological precommitment, moderates, and, no less important, on the political left, among those who see themselves as liberal in their political orientation.

The results of the Regardless of Race Experiment point to the possibility of putting together a coalition in behalf of policies to support those who are badly off by broadening the arguments made in their behalf. To try and determine how much weight should be attached to these findings, we conducted the Color Blind Experiment. In its essential design the Color Blind Experiment aims at replicating the Regardless of Race Experiment. In the baseline condition, a policy is presented that is racially targeted—aimed specifically at helping blacks and minorities, and racially justified—argued for on grounds specifically tied to race. Specifically, respondents in the first condition were asked:

> Some people believe that the government in Washington should be responsible for improving the social and economic condition of blacks who are born into poverty. They say that *because of the continuing legacy of slavery and discrimination we have a special obligation to help blacks to get ahead.* Other people believe that the strength of the American way of life is that people should deal with their problems on their own. If you had to choose, would you say the government should take responsibility for improving the social and economic conditions of blacks who are born into poverty, or should the government stay out of it?

In the second condition the policy again is racially targeted but now it is universalistically justified—argued for on grounds that apply to everyone in need regardless of race. Specifically, respondents in the second condition were asked:

> Some people believe that the government in Washington should be responsible for improving the social and economic condition of blacks who are born into poverty. They say that *we ought to try to make sure that everyone has an equal opportunity to succeed.* Other people believe that the strength of the American way of life is that people should deal with their problems on their own. If you had to choose, would you say the government should take responsibility for improving the social and economic conditions of blacks who are born in to poverty or should the government stay out of it?

Notice that everything is the same except for the argument in justification. Instead of attempting to win support by emphasizing the historical injustices that have been done to blacks, there now is an appeal made to the value of equal opportunity.

So far the second experiment exactly parallels the first. But in the Color Blind Experiment there is a third condition. Our aim is to find out how much support can be won for a policy if it reaches beyond race in terms of both who is to be helped and why they should be helped. So in the third experimental condition the policy now is presented in terms that reach beyond race with respect to both how it is targeted and how it is justified. Specifically, respondents were asked:

> *Some people believe that the government in Washington should be responsible for improving the social and economic conditions of people who are born into poverty. They say that we ought to try to make sure that everyone has an equal opportunity to succeed.* Other people believe that the strength of the American way of life is that people should deal with their problems on their own. If you had to choose, would you say the government should take responsibility for improving the social and economic conditions of people who are born into poverty, or should the government stay out of it?

The results of the Color Blind Experiment, analyzed in detail, back up those of the Regardless of Race Experiment in all points. The second experiment, however, adds a crucial finding that the first could not. Figure 8-6 reports the proportions of white Americans—and for the final experimental condition of the sample of as a whole—who support the policy as a function of its framing. Racially targeted and racially justified, only about one in every three whites favors government action. If the policy is universalistically justified, the proportion in support goes up to 42 percent, even though it is racially targeted. Finally, if it is both universalistically targeted *and* justified, the level of support reaches 49 percent of whites and 57 percent of the public as a whole.

It of course would be a mistake to equate the results of a public opinion survey and the play of actual politics. The numbers in an opinion survey have only a comparative, not an absolute, meaning, and in any event the opinion interview is designed to eliminate, or at any rate minimize, the impact of factors at work in everyday life. But it would, we think, be a still greater mistake to dis-

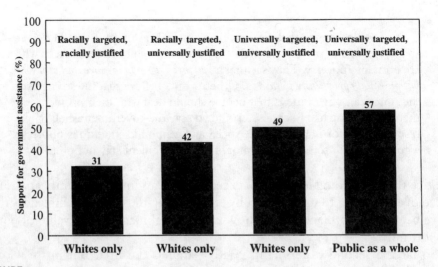

FIGURE 8-6
Color-Blind Experiment

Source: 1994 Multiple Investigator Study. Number of respondents ranges from 399 to 415.

miss the implications of the Color Blind Experiment for real politics. If it is impossible to say exactly how many in the public would support policies that reach beyond race, it is quite possible to say with assurance that markedly more will support them than policies confined to race. So understood, we wish to underline the distinctive lesson of the Color Blind Experiment. By reaching beyond race it is possible to turn a policy to assist those who are badly off that has the support of only a minority into one that has the backing of the majority.

A Final Word

At the close of the twentieth century the politics of race in America stands at a political crossroads. Down one road is the path that we have been following so far during the post-civil rights era. This has been a path in which race-conscious policies—notably affirmative action—have been put at the top of the racial policy agenda. The idea has been to provide special benefits to African Americans because of the special burdens they have had to endure. This is a noble impulse, but it leads to a political impasse because affirmative action lacks public support. Moreover, although it is tempting to see the overwhelming resistance to affirmative action as being due to the tenacity of racial prejudice in white America, there is a fundamental difficulty with this argument—there are far more opponents of affirmative action than there are racial bigots. Indeed, as we have shown, even most liberals are upset with affirmative action once they feel they can reveal their preferences without anyone's knowing their true feelings. Opposition to race-conscious policies, in other words, is both intense and widespread.

We suggest going down a different political path based on our findings on the role of political argumentation in building support for public policies. What we find is that public support to assist the badly off can be dramatically increased if the policy is not only inclusive in terms of its beneficiaries but justified on universalistic rather than particularistic grounds. It makes a difference whom a policy is going to benefit, but the basis for justifying the policy makes even more of a difference. Without minimizing the power of racial prejudice, we want to suggest that the deeper problem is instead one of political leadership. A winning coalition of the public can be won in support of policies to assist the badly off, our results suggest, provided that we remember what we once knew: Politics is a matter of argument. And as the civil rights movement in the 1960s itself taught, the strongest arguments—even in behalf of policies centered on blacks—are those that reach beyond race to the moral considerations that give the issue of race itself a moral claim upon us.

References

Bobo, Lawrence, and James R. Kluegel. 1993. Opposition to race-targeting: Self-interest, stratification ideology, or racial attitudes. *American Sociological Review* 58: 443–64.

Carmines, Edward G., and James A. Stimson. 1989. *Issue Evolution: Race and the Transformation of American Politics*. Princeton, NJ: Princeton University Press.

Coleman, Jonathan. 1997. *Long Way to Go: Black and White in America*. New York: Atlantic Monthly Press.

Hacker, Andrew. 1992. *Two Nations: Black and White, Separate, Hostile, Unequal*. New York: Charles Scribner's Sons.

Sniderman, Paul M., and Edward G. Carmines. 1997. *Reaching Beyond Race*. Cambridge, MA: Harvard University Press.

Sniderman, Paul M., and Douglas Grob. 1996. Innovations in experimental design in general population attitude surveys. In John Hagan and Karen Cook (eds.), *Annual Review of Sociology*. Palo Alto, CA: Annual Review.

West, Cornel. 1993. *Race Matters*. Boston: Beacon Press.

Wilson, William Julius. 1978. *The Declining Significance of Race*. Chicago: University of Chicago Press.

———. 1987. *The Truly Disadvantaged: The Inner City, the Underclass and Public Policy*. Chicago: University of Chicago Press.

———. 1996. *When Work Disappears: The World of the New Urban Poor*. New York: Alfred A. Knopf.

———. 1999. *The Bridge over the Racial Divide: Rising Inequality and Coalition Politics*. Berkeley: University of California Press.

9

The Limits of the Market: New Examinations of an Old Problem

BETTY GLAD

The development of the global economic order and the booming stock market in the United States, when combined with the clear failure of communism in Russia and Eastern Europe, has created a broad receptivity to the notion that unregulated markets provide the best of all possible worlds for people. This assumption has provided impetus for dismantling the mixed economy Americans built during the first three-quarters of the twentieth century. Recently, however, we have seen a renewal of the debate begun more than a hundred years ago over the nature of the market and its relationship to the government. The outcome of the debate will determine whether or not the American people have the will and the knowledge to control in some ways the economic order upon which so much of their lives depends.

At the presidential level Jimmy Carter began the process of cutting back on governmental involvement in the economy with the deregulation of trucking and airline industries. It was President Reagan, however, with his rhetorical attacks on what he saw as the welfare state, who provided the widespread legitimization for the idea that the best government is the one that governs least. During his and subsequent administrations the banks and the communications industries have been deregulated and mergers have flourished.[1] The safety net that was constructed since the New Deal to protect individuals against the vagaries of the market and private misfortune has been cut back. The reform of welfare (the Personal Responsibility and Work Opportunity Act of 1996) was based on the assumption that only the worthy poor deserve our support, that we should provide welfare to people who, for some reason or another, cannot work because they are in bad health or otherwise incapacitated. Even women who have some children should get off welfare as soon as possible.[2] Endeavors to privatize primary and secondary schools, garbage collection, bus systems, and other enterprises originally run by governmental bodies have been rampant, the argument being that any private enterprise is bound to be more efficiently run than a public one. Recent attempts to privatize Social Security are based on arguments purporting to show that an individual would be better off engaging in private investments in the stock market than depending on the Social Security program.[3] Finally, through the creation of the North America Free Trade Agreement (NAFTA) in 1994 and the embrace of the World Trade Organization (WTO), which in 1995 replaced the General Agreement on Tariffs and Trade of 1948 (GATT), most trade barriers have been eliminated. With rates that are allowed to fluctuate in accord with the operations of the market, the United States is now tied to the vagaries of the world economic system.

The Chicago School

Members of the Chicago School of economics have provided the rationale for these changes. Their ideas were most widely popularized in Milton and Rose Friedman's book *Free to Choose*. The genius of Adam Smith, according to the Friedmans, was "his recognition that the prices that emerged from voluntary transactions between buyers and sellers . . . in a free market could coordinate the activity of millions of people, each seeking his own interest, in such a way as to make everyone better off" (Friedman and Friedman [1979], 1990, 13). This pricing system is not only effective for making decisions in the realm of production, but the tacit assumption is that it rewards individuals in terms of their actual contribution to production. Otherwise, one could not assume, as the Friedmans do, that any effort to redistribute income via taxes is a violation of individual liberty of those who are taxed for the benefit of others. If production were seen as a genuinely group enterprise in which the distribution of income is in some sense based on one's power and place in the system, then those who were particularly well rewarded would not have an absolute right to all the profits or wages they make.

The Friedmans do recognize that individuals in the system do not always start from the same playing field. But in the long run, they argue, the openness of the American economic order provides the opportunity for those with initiative and skill that start from behind to rise quickly up the economic and social ladder. The rapid rise in the economic and social position of various less privileged groups demonstrates that these obstacles were by no means insurmountable. To impose goals of fairness on the system, they argue, is to get us into the swamp of deciding what is fair. Such a standard, they suggest, is likely to commit us to measures providing compensatory education for those who are the least talented, while giving special attention to those who lack natural talents. Indeed, if we take that concept of "fairness seriously, youngsters with less musical skill should be given the greatest amount of musical training in order to compensate for their inherited disadvantage, and those with greater musical aptitude should be prevented from having access to good musical training and similarly with all other categories of inherited personal qualities" (Friedman and Friedman [1979] 1990, 134–36).

The role of government, then, should be primarily restricted to achieving goals such as national security and public order. Generally, private enterprise is better than governmental (Friedman and Friedman [1979] 1990, 27–32). This is because the governmental officials spend someone else's money and thus have little incentive either to economize or to try to get the best value out of what they spend. Indeed, bureaucrats tend to use the government to benefit persons like themselves—middle- and upper-income groups rather than the poor for whom the benefits are supposedly intended. Welfare programs are even bad for those they are purported to benefit because they promote passivity. The individuals on these programs "would have become self-reliant individuals instead of wards of the state" (pp. 117–19). Programs that redistribute income are especially suspect. Social Security, for example, they see as a system providing for a nonvoluntary transfer of funds between the generations (pp. 103–4).

It is not surprising, then, to see that the Friedmans have practically never met a government program they liked. United States expenditures on medicine and health, for example, have simply resulted in the rise of the costs of medical and health services without any corresponding improvement in the quality of medical care. Housing, they claim, "is better and more widely distributed in the United States today than when the public housing program was started, but that has occurred through private enterprise, and despite the government subsidies." Spending on education has been skyrocketing, yet by common consent the quality of education has been declining. The result has been that today many parents lack control "over the kind of schooling their children receive either directly, through choosing and paying for the schools their children attend, or indirectly, through local political activity. Power has instead gravitated to professional educators" (pp. 110–15, 151–52).

Social Darwinist Roots: William Graham Sumner

The Social Darwinist roots of this conservative perspective were provided more explicitly over one hundred years ago in the writings of William Graham Sumner.[4] Essentially, Sumner argued that the free market is a law of nature, that it provides for the survival of the fittest, and any kind of intervention in that law of nature results in the survival of the less fit. The people with the most skill, with the most ability to compete and accumulate capital, rise to the top of the system. But his definition of the best is not people who are artistically talented, who make new inventions, or who have concern for others. They are, instead, the entrepreneurs who contribute to economic production. The inheritance of great sums of wealth would seem to run counter to this argument. But Sumner gets around the problem by arguing that the accumulation of capital in the hands of one person or one center is a requisite for the development of a capitalist society, which the United States was becoming at that time (Sumner 1963, 150–57).

What is even more interesting is Sumner's pitting of the "forgotten Americans"—the blue-collar worker in the city—against the very poor. The former are hardworking, God-fearing individuals who fulfill their contracts, provide **158** for their families, and preserve the institutions by which their lives are governed. The latter, he implies, are often where they are because of personal failings. "The paupers and the physically incapacitated are an inevitable charge on society," he concedes. "But the weak who constantly arouse the pity of the humanists and philanthropists are the shiftless, the imprudent, the negligent, the impractical, the inefficient, or they are idle, the intemperate, the extravagant, and the vicious" (p. 118). These people should be left to the discipline of nature, he suggests: "[A] drunkard in the gutter is where he ought to be. Nature is working away at him to get him out of the way, just as she sets up her process of dissolution to remove whatever is a failure in its line" (p. 122).

Governmental programs for the poor are paid for by these so-called Forgotten Americans. There is only so much capital in the system and whatever goes to the poor is taken away from the more productive workers. The Forgotten Man, in short, is " the victim of the reformer, social speculator, and philanthropist" (Sumner 1963, 111). Whatever transfers are made to the poor, he suggests, should be made by private charities, where individuals who are so inclined can contribute to the well-being of the worthy poor (p. 121).[5]

The "glory" of the 'United States, Sumner argues, is that it has shown "what self-reliance, energy, enterprise, hard sense men can develop when they have room and liberty and when they are emancipated from the burden of traditions and faiths which are nothing but the accumulated follies and blunders of a hundred generations of 'statesmen'" (Sumner 1963, 103). But government has a very limited role to play in society. When governments attempt to engage in public works and social services, they only pit those who control the government against the legitimate interests of those whom they tax. The bureaucrats obtain jobs for themselves and their friends, and the reformers, the busybodies, promote unproductive services—all impediments to those civil liberties that "leave each man to run his career in life in his own way, only guaranteeing to him whatever he does in the way of industry, economy, prudence, and sound judgement, etc., shall redound to his own welfare and shall not be diverted to someone else's benefit" (p. 117).

Lester Ward's Critique

Lester Ward challenged Sumner's basic assumptions in the late 1880s and 1890s. He argued that nature could not be the moral standard we must follow. "Those who survived have simply prove their fitness to survive; and the fact which all biologists understand: viz. that fitness to survive is distinct from real superiority is of course ignored. . . . " Indeed, all social classes are in some respect natural. Even the reformers at whom Sumner sneers are products of society and natural. They "belong to society as much as the hated paupers and worthless invalids whom he would turn over to nature" (Ward [1884] 1967, 66–67).

However, the kind of competition we see in nature prevents any form from attaining its maximum development, but rather maintains a comparatively low level of development for all forms that succeed in surviving. Art, however, can improve on nature. Scarcely anything has value until it has been transformed from the natural into the artificial state. Wherever competition in nature is wholly removed, as through the agency of man, the protected forms flourish. Such has been the case with cereals, fruit trees, and domestic animals (Ward [1886] 1967, 102–3, 156–57).

In terms of the human species, the great men of history have been protected from the forces of a raw nature. The true promoters of civilization have been men with leisure, educated and reared in a supportive environment. These benefactors of mankind have been in possession of rare opportunities. They have either been "entirely free from the distractions of want and the necessity of toil," or they have found themselves in situations that "furnish the incentive to the effort, however great, which they must put forth in order to achieve success." The stultifying effects of working against great odds are evident in the characteristic of the self-made man. Those who burst the bonds do so at an immense cost in energy and will. All this narrows the mental horizon and renders the results superficial. "There is no more vicious popular fallacy than that the powers of the mind are strengthened and improved by adversity. Every one who has accomplished anything, against adverse circumstances, would have accomplished proportionately more had such circumstances been removed" (Ward [1886] 1967, 100–101).

But because that kind of leisure and education has been limited to a small group of people, the leadership of most groups has been drawn from a small pool. Indeed, he notes, one half of the human race, namely womankind, has been kept out of the picture. Universal education for women as well as for men, he concludes, is a requisite for widening the talent pool from which leaders can be chosen (Ward [1906] 1967, 357–59).

For Ward, the laws of nature as exemplified in the laissez faire economic system have borne down especially hard on the very blue-collar worker that Sumner idealized. "The world appears to be approaching a stage at which the laborer, no matter how skilled, how industrious, or how frugal, will receive, according to an oft-quoted law of political economy, only so much for his services as will enable him to 'live and reproduce.'" These, Ward suggests, are great evils, in comparison to the individual crimes—"mere trifles" that the state usually prosecutes (Ward [1887] 1967, 112).

Anticipating the demand-side arguments of later economists, Ward ([1889] 1967, 125) contends that the actual raising of wages could have a positive effect on profits. The workers are also consumers and as they go into the market to purchase the products they have produced, prices are sustained, though no one will claim that they consume as much per capita as the rich, and of many products they consume none. But here we may ask, why is this so? "The obvious answer is, because they have not the means" (Ward [1889] 1967, 125).

Government, Ward ([1887] 1967, 111) suggests, is itself an art—a form of collective action to protect the vulnerable against "the evils of organized aggrandizement, the abuse of wealth, and the subtle processes by which the producer of wealth is deprived of his share in it." This has been recognized in the common support for governmental management of the public finances, the transmission of letters and packages, and the administration of criminal law. "What the laissez faire economists have done is simply to focus on a relatively small number of relatively unimportant governmental actions which they declare to have been failures or to be doing harm to society" (Ward, [1906] 1967, 345–47).

Limits of the Market

The relevance of Ward's kind of analysis to the U. S. economy became evident as various vulnerabilities of the system were manifested in the late nineteenth and first three-quarters of the twentieth century. Overall giant strides were made during this period in terms of raising the Gross National Product, advancing medical and other technologies, and connecting the nation through new transportation and communication industries. However, the unregulated free market did not seem to reward individuals automatically in accordance with their contribution to the overall working of the economy. In the late nineteenth and early twentieth century the railroads, the oil, and other giant industries engaged in conspiracies to restrict competition and engage in discriminatory pricing practices. Meats and other food were produced in processes that were cruel and unsanitary, and drugs were compounded with unidentified ingredients. Depressions in the latter part of the nineteenth century and right after World War I and from 1929 to 1935 meant that hard-working farmers could not sell their goods at prices that covered their costs. Blue-collar workers also had difficulty finding employment during these slumps. During the Great Depression of 1929–1935, 15 million persons were unemployed. Later, natural resources were wantonly destroyed by some industrial giants, particularly in the post-World War II epoch, and poisonous waste products were put into the air and the waters of the nation.

Holding views similar to Ward's—that the people could act through the government to correct some of these evils—the Populists and the Progressives at the turn of the century called for and were able to bring about governmental actions to regulate the trusts, break up some of the worst monopolies, preserve the natural environment, and control the money supply in ways that would minimize the business cycle. Then, by the time of Roosevelt's "New Deal," the government was seen as the institution of last resort in providing a safety net for the unemployed, the sick, and the elderly and the institution that could promote some equality of opportunity in education. A movement that was bipartisan in its origins (Theodore Roosevelt's "Square Deal" and Woodrow Wilson's "New Freedom"), with only the brief hiatus of Republican "normalcy" in the twenties, still retained its bipartisan support on most issues as late as the early seventies. As Richard Nixon once said, "We are all Keynsians now."[6]

As suggested above, the contemporary backlash to the mixed economy can be dated back to the late 1970s. Recently, however, several latter-day Lester

Wards have raised some of the old issues as well as noting the new problems rising out of the present global economy. Their concerns may be summarized as follows.

First, the market, as Schmookler points out in *The Illusion of Choice* (1993, 40–41), has a "natural tendency to undermine the very competitiveness on which its virtues of efficient allocation depend. Competition produces winners and losers, and the losers tend to disappear." However, if a single producer or group of producers

> could gain control over the supply side of the market for some important commodity, the price will cease to represent that optimal balance between costs and bents that economist celebrate. What one gets, then, is the worst aspect of the public and private spheres combined. Instead of the impersonal forces of the market, decisions are imposed, but these are the decisions of a private, wholly self-interested party.

Second, the assumption of Sumner and the Friedmans that an increase in gross production benefits all productive people in the community is questionable. At the most abstract level, the very way we quantify such growth is being debated. The Gross Domestic Product, the GDP, it is argued, in effect measures money changing hands. What it leaves out of the equation is the quality of the transaction and the distribution of income that results. If both parents have to work to make ends meet, the GDP looks better. If they divorce and need two houses, the GDP increases. But deterioration in family life is not the only symptom of a growing GDP. The destruction of natural resources may also "boost" the economy by increasing the need for pollution-control measures. Moreover, when those whose health is damaged by the pollution go for medical treatment, and pay for it, the GDP is again raised. In short, the GDP, as its critics suggest, ignores the costs of fixing environmental and social blunders of the past, borrows resources from the future, and ignores the transfer of service from the household and community to the realm of the market (Cobb, Halstead, and Rowe 1995, 66; Rowe and Silverstein 1999, 17ff).

Over 400 economists (including Herbert Simon and Robert Eisner) have suggested that another measure, the GPI (Genuine Progress Indicator), would provide a better indicator of economic and social progress. From current transactions they would subtract the cost of environmental and social degradation. To that figure they would add nonmarket efforts such as charitable activities to improve neighborhoods and support the elderly (Baker, 1999, 36) The goal of a broader indicator, as the Harvard economist Amartya Sen has suggested, is to measure the extent to which an economy reaches the desired ends of a people. Welfare should be measured through the attainment of these goals, rather than the means, such as income, for achieving those ends (Cohen 1994, 53–54).

Along these lines we should note that the GDP also does not measure the distribution of income. The much-used metaphor that a rising tide lifts all boats does not seem to apply during this recent period of growth. From a low in

1973 of 11.1 percent, the proportion of the population below the poverty level increased gradually to 12.8 percent at the end of the Reagan years (Greenbook 1991, cited by Sloan 1999, 253). The measure of wealth of the richest one-fifth of all households increased 14 percent from 1984 to 1988, while there was hardly any change in the net worth of the remaining four-fifths (Robert Pear, cited by Sloan 1999, 251). By 1995, the minimum wage had suffered an almost 30 percent drop in real terms from its 1979 level (Mishel 1995, 62).[7]

The increasing inequality is particularly demonstrated by the disparity in incomes of CEOs and the average worker. According to the Institute for Policy Studies, top executives in 1980 earned 42 times more than factory workers. By 1998 this disparity had increased almost tenfold, to 419 times (cited by Wolfe 1999, A27). During the eighties, the increase in the amount spent on salaries above $1 million was 2,200 percent, an increase 50 times greater than that for salaries between $20,000 and $50,000 (Reilly 1995, 27). In the one-year period from 1994 to 1995, the average CEO's compensation increased by 23 percent.[8] By 1999, the average CEO compensation package at the largest public firms exceeded $10.9 million, representing a 16 percent increase from the previous year and a 50 percent increase from 1995 (Pearl Meyer 1999).

This disparity as suggested above is also manifest in the reduction of benefit packages going to various segments of the working population. The switch of corporations such as IBM from the traditional pension plan for their employees to a cash-balance plan reduced the benefits of midcareer workers by 20 to 50 percent (Armour 1999, 1B). The proportion of workers with employer-paid pension plans fell by 25 percent in the period from 1979 to 1988. By the early 1990s such plans covered less than a quarter of those workers without high-school degrees (Reich, cited by Sloan 1999, 253). Workers under 65 with employer-paid health care declined from 63 to 56 percent of the total in the period from 1979 to 1988 (Reilly 1995, 27). For workers without high school degrees, employer-sponsored health coverage fell from 53 to 36 percent of the total in the period from 1979 to 1993 (Reich, cited by Sloan, 1999, 253). A U.S. Census Bureau study estimates that in 1998 16.3 percent of the population, or 44.3 million people, had no health insurance, even though 58 percent of these uninsured had full-time employment or did some work (Toner 1999, 16).[9]

As the above benefits figures suggest, there also has been an increasing stratification among the workforce, with the gap between the better-educated workers and those with lesser qualifications increasing in income, home ownership, and access to health care (Reich, cited by Sloan 1999, 253). Over the last two decades, the wages of workers without college degrees have decreased by 20 percent in real terms, while the incomes of almost 20 percent still leave them below the poverty line (Reilly 1995, 27).

This decline in returns to labor is based on several factors. The weakening of labor unions has undermined the bargaining position of workers in major industries. Privatization and "downsizing" have enabled companies to reduce benefits to workers in the name of greater efficiency. But globalization of the world economy has had perhaps the most important impact. Wages are not based simply on what an individual produces but on his or her marginal productivity. As the supply of labor increases, its marginal productivity decreases and wages go down correspondingly. The globalization of the economy presents particular problems for the U.S. workforce along these lines. The mobility of capital and raw materials is such that they can move across national boundaries to areas where there is a cheaper labor supply. The result of this, of course, is that firms can easily relocate to areas where labor costs are lower than in the United States, thus undermining the position of U.S. laborers.

The highly inflated salaries of corporate executives, on the other hand, are based, in part, on a soaring stock market. One deep truth about such "top hogs" is that for them "pay isn't really a reward for performance; it is a measure of their status." But their rewards do not seem to be directly related to productivity. Many corporate executives are pocketing above-average salaries while their companies underperform relative to their competitors (McLean, 1998, 129). Certainly, there seems to be no "productivity" rationale for the size of the differentials between American CEOs' pay and the wages of their workers as contrasted to those differentials in other industrial countries. In Japan, for example, the ratio is 17 to 1. In Germany, the figures are 23–25 to 1 (Will, cited by Sloan 1999, 252).

Third, the existence of externalities raises the issues of third-party costs. As Herman Daly and John Cobb in *For the Common Good* (1989, 51–61) and Andrew Bard Schmookler in *The Illusion of Choice* (1993, 55–59) point out, many costs of production are borne by the public or other bystanders, not the contracting parties themselves. Thus waste products that are put into the air, oceans, or rivers of the world cost people as a whole, though the company does not have that cost factor on its own balance sheet. So how do you put this into the basic accounting system? Daly and Cobb argue that the public as a whole has to step in (via their governments) to place limitations on what can be dumped into rivers and the air, or charge the costs to those who are responsible for this dumping. The costs will be calculated against the goods they produce. This means there has to be some outside regulation for the market to actually work in any realistic way.

Fourth, the assumption that private enterprises are always superior to public ones overlooks differences in types of relationships between producers and consumers. The privatization of prisons, for example, places undue power in the hands of the providers. With a price for their activities set by their contract with a governmental body, they have motives to skimp on what they provide their consumers—that is, the prisoners. But the latter is not the usual consumer. He or she cannot choose a better place to spend his or her time. In other fields private producers may lower their costs relative to governmental programs, by hiring younger people and part-timers and limiting benefits to their employees, thereby contributing to the further inequalities in wages. Most private schools, for example, pay lower wages to their teachers than public schools and provide smaller benefit packages (Lowe 1995, 198).

Indeed, certain broad social goals may be met only by governmentally based programs. To privatize Social Security, for example, one must subject citizens to the vagaries of the market. Moreover, as the much-touted Chilean program suggests, large groups of people will not be covered at all and the returns will be less than the earnings made in the market because of higher charges for processing the investments and giving advice to the clients. Unlike the government, the middlemen in the market must make a profit.[10] Another proposal—that primary and secondary school students be provided with vouchers so that they can go to a school of their choice—overlooks the important role the public schools in the United States have provided for the creation of a public culture that is supportive of democratic values, compromise, and a nonsectarian approach to the issues of truth. Persons of diverse religious and national backgrounds have gone to schools with one another and learned American values of compromise and the commitment to truth via the route of science. If the voucher program were to become widespread, however, ethnic and religious divisions in an already diverse population would very likely be intensified. Moreover, the very best schools would still be off limits to the poor, as the voucher programs could never meet the elevated tuition costs charged by such institutions.[11]

Fifth, another assumption that deserves revisiting is the law of comparative advantage as it works in multilevel global trading today. David Ricardo said some time ago that two countries, A and B, which were potentially productive in two lines of production, could trade to their mutual advantage even if one of them, A, had no absolute advantage in either of those goods. If A had a relative advantage in one of those goods, even if its overall costs for both products were higher than the other country's, it could still specialize in the product in which it had a relative advantage and trade with the other. However, this simple model may not cover a situation when you are dealing with a multinational global trading market in which Country A does not have the market power to influence the price of the *good* in which it has a comparative advantage. It still may not be able to produce that *good* for the world market at a price that covers their costs. This is what has happened in Russia recently, in terms of oil. The Russians have a major resource, but the price of oil is such that they cannot market one of their most valuable resources. Indeed, as Daly and Cobb point out, Ricardo himself emphasized that the principle of comparative advantage could not work within one country—that is, a market system in which capital could flow freely. Today, however, the absence of inhibitions to the flow of capital across national boundaries has erased the differences between national and international trade. So to take Ricardo's example, if Portugal today had an absolute advantage in the production of both wine and cloth relative to England, then English investors would join Portuguese investors in the production of both cloth and wine. The only alternative to this kind of lopsided development, Daly and Cobb suggest, is for England to insist upon measures that would create some balance between its exports and imports, at least in the long run (1989, 213–15, 229–35).

Sixth, the concept of market equilibrium must also be revisited. General equilibrium theories suggest that all the particular markets within a trading system come into some kind of balance that guarantees that the GNP has been maximized. Yet at the empirical level it is evident that capital markets sometimes do not clear in ways that maximize productivity. Foreign exchange markets, as George Soros points out in his book *The Crises of Global Capitalism*, are inherently unstable.[12] When capital flight begins in one country, for example, investors call on their loans to other countries and capital flight can spread to others in a kind of domino effect. Thus Soros argues that Indonesia's financial collapse in 1997 led to problems in other Asian countries, then Russia, and finally Latin America (Soros 1998, 148–59; Soros and Madrick 1999, 36). New regulatory obligations should be imposed on bank and hedge funds, he suggests, and there should be penalties for the "errant behavior of creditors," instead of the usual bailout when they get into trouble. He concludes that the introduction of international and national controls is a requisite for the stability of the entire global system (Soros 1998, 179–201; for Soros's similar position in the late 1980s see Greider, 1997a, 319–20.)

Attempts to impose fundamentalist notions of free-market discipline on troubled economies, as the International Monetary Fund (IMF) has attempted to do, contributed to this problem. In exchange for desperately needed loans from the IMF, several countries already in economic difficulties were required to drive interest rates to sky-high levels and cut their budgets. As Paul Krugman notes, this is "almost exactly the reverse of what the United States does in the face of a slump" (Krugman 1999, 103). As Bluestein's (1999, 33) summary of Krugman's position puts it, "countries facing investor panic should eschew IMF style austerity and slap emergency controls on the outflows of capital." Rather than blindly following the prescriptions of the Hoover era, they should consider the strategy adopted by Malaysia, where investors were prohibited from withdrawing their money for a year.

Related theories suggesting that imports must equal exports over the long run also ignore the fact that there may be some pretty long-term asymmetries along these lines. Moreover, the "corrections" necessitated by a long-term need for balance between exports and imports could be very disruptive of the entire world trading system.

For a time, the United States has been able to provide crucial support as a buyer of last resort for the world trading system. Writing in 1997, William Greider pointed out that since 1980 Americans bought $1.5 trillion more than they sold in their merchandise trade with foreign nations. "The great wealth of American economic life serves as a kind of safety valve of the global marketplace, reducing conflict, keeping it afloat" (Greider, 1997b, 73, 75). In one year alone, 1995, the United States had a $111.04 billion trade deficit (Crutsinger 1996, D1). Yet it is not clear that the United States can continue to perform this role in the long run. The result of the trade imbalance has been an increase in U.S. foreign indebtedness (Greider 1997b, 74). Moreover, as Dean Baker (1997, 81) has pointed out, the present economic well-being of the United States has been provided not by soaring domestic investment but by soaring consumption. This spur to consumption was due to the enormous increase in stock prices. Since 1993, more than $8 trillion has been created in new wealth. This is what supported the spending spree among the segment of the population that owns significant amounts of stock.

166

If the correction of this situation led to a sharp fall in the U.S. stock market, consumers would have to cut back in America and the entire world would go into a recession. This in turn would create an increased demand for protection, which would cut down on U.S. imports, making it even more difficult for the Asian nations to rebound. They in turn would be even less able to buy U.S. exports, causing more difficulties here (Soros and Madrick 1999, 40).

Finally, the economic theories of Sumner of yesterday and the Friedmans of today neglect the significance of shared values to the whole functioning of the economic order. The short-term selfish interests of the entrepreneurs cannot provide a basis for an efficient and stable market system. For the market to work as it should, the entrepreneurs will have to honor contracts they have entered into, let the market rather than side deals and criminal actions determine the money they receive, and invest back in the enterprises they head. We can see what happens if these factors are not present by looking at the business market in Russia. Cronies took over private enterprises, milked them to their own benefit, often murdered or engaged in other practices to keep others out of the competition, and did not spend the capital they obtained on investments in Russia but deposited it in private accounts outside the country (Glad 1999, 119–32; Kuns 1999, 75–94; Kelley 1999, 10A; Myre 1999, 10A). The effective operation of the free market, in short, assumes that there is a commitment on the part of the major entrepreneurs to the principles of honoring contracts, of making their decision on the bases of market prices, and of not engaging in practices to conspire against free trade, upon which their operations are purportedly based.

We also know that the very values of the consumers are not a simple "given," that what they want beyond the basics of food, safety, and shelter is shaped by the culture in which they live.[13] Indeed, many people do not focus on private action to obtain more material goods, but value the sense of community that the sharing of public goods (e.g., parks, national monuments, beaches) and altruistic acts generally bring. Moreover, those who live a community with a Judeo–Christian set of values must consider other human beings in terms other than their worth or lack of it as a factor of production. What do we do with marginal workers? In times of recession or depression can they simply be allowed to lie fallow as factories and mines and farmland might be? What do we do if the supply of unskilled labor drives wages down to a level that provides for them and their families only at a subsistence level? What do we do with people who through mental or physical disability are incapable of going to work or providing for themselves? Unlike Sumner, many of us would not leave them to die in the gutters of the world. Moreover, we realize that there is a cost in human dignity if we are always poking into the lives of the poor to make sure they are worthy of support.[14]

Then there is the issue of generational selfishness. To satisfy its current need, is one generation free to destroy forests and wildlife, and pollute large bodies of water upon which future generations will depend? And what do the young adults owe to those who have labored for years?

The Friedmans deal with this latter issue with a suggestion that the present Social Security system is a one-sided transfer of payments of the present generation to themselves at the expense of generations yet to come. Workers paying taxes today, they argue, have no assurance that they will receive benefits when they retire. Any assurance derives solely from the willingness of future taxpayers to impose taxes on themselves. The Friedmans realize that to some extent such a transfer has occurred throughout our history—the young supporting their parents, or other relatives, in old age. Indeed, in many poor countries with high infant death rates, like India, the desire to assure oneself of the survival of progeny who can provide support in old age is a major reason for high birth rates and large families. The difference between Social Security and earlier arrangements is that Social Security is compulsory and impersonal whereas earlier arrangements were voluntary and personal. Indeed, they conclude that "moral responsibility is an individual matter, not a social matter" (Friedman and Friedman 1990, 106).

Yet the elderly, whether or not their claims are based on a public-supported program such as Social Security, or private savings and pension plans, shift goods from a producing generation to that which has retired. Moreover, private pension plans are similar to governmental plans in that they carry no absolute warranty that as participants in a program they will receive, when they retire, the benefits that they think they have purchased. Insurance companies can go out of business, as did Mutual of New Jersey, and the worth of pension plans can dissipate if the stock markets take a downward dive. The real issue is whether or not we want the poor to bear the full responsibility of providing for the elderly in their own families. Moreover, many may not see the personal dependence of an older generation on the generosity of their young as psychologically or morally better than an impersonal entitlement based on contribution to a governmental program.

Conclusions

What is needed, then, at this point is some serious rethinking about how the American people can regain some control over the operation of the economy that has so much impact on their lives. The globalization of major manufacturing and the new information industries presents challenges for how those regulations might be exercised in the twenty-first century, a topic only lightly touched upon in this chapter. Recent developments in Washington suggest where we should *not* go. The Banking Reform Act signed into law by President Clinton on November 12, 1999, will knock down the firewalls between banking, insurance, and brokerage enterprises and thus contribute to the ever-greater concentration of power in the financial world. During the floor debate on the conference report in the Senate, Senator Paul Wellstone noted that "the problem with [the act] is that its regulatory reach does not match the size of the new conglomerates. . . . [We] seem determined to unlearn the lessons from our past mistakes" (*Congressional Record* 1999, S13872).

But worldwide competitive concerns undercut these considerations. Senator Charles Schumer explained his support of the measure in these terms: "If we don't pass this bill, we could find London or Frankfurt, or years down the road, Shanghai becoming the financial capital of the world" (*Congressional Record* 1999, S13880). As William Safire has noted, "Today's lust for global giantism has swept aside the voice of prudence; generous financial lobbies have persuaded our leaders that in enormous size there is strength." And he quotes Federal Reserve Board Chairman Alan Greenspan's observations that megabanks are becoming "complex entities that create the potential for unusually large systemic risks in the national and international economy should they fail." That is a risk, as Safire suggests, that most Americans should not have to bear (Safire 1999, A15).[15]

In short, many Americans have been riding an economic bubble, forgetting much of our past experience with the unregulated free market. Lester Ward, in his debate with William Graham Sumner over a hundred years ago, warned that the market on its own led to inequities that could be corrected only through governmental action. The experiences of Americans through the first three-quarters of the twentieth century led them to see the need for measures to counter these vulnerabilities (albeit with some countermovements in the twenties). The result was a system that operated with greater justice and stability. The rationale for the recent attempts to cut back on these measures was provided by the Friedmans and others associated with the University of Chicago School of Economics. Countering their views, today, a few economists and political scientists are once again pointing out the old vulnerabilities in the market, as well as some that are new. These include the shortcomings of the market in maintaining competition, providing an equitable distribution of scarce resources, managing public goods, preserving the environment, and assessing the costs of industrial wastes. Indeed, the very stability of the market system depends on external regulations to maintain the competition and the rules of the game upon which it relies. As George Soros has recently noted,

> the truth is that market fundamentalism is itself naïve and illogical. Even if we put aside the bigger moral and ethical questions and concentrate solely on the economic arena, the ideology of market fundamentalism is profoundly and irredeemably flawed. To put the matter simply, market forces, if they are given complete authority even in the purely economic and financial arenas, produce chaos and could ultimately lead to the downfall of the global capitalist system. (Soros 1998, xxvii)

Notes

I am indebted to Shafqat Chaudhuri, Eunro Lee, Jennifer Lightweis, and Jack Lechelt for their research and editorial assistance with this project.

1. The causes of the savings and loan industry debacle in the 1980s, estimates of whose cost to the taxpayer range from $100 billion to $500 billion, can be traced to deregulation measures that led to a "casino mentality" on the part of owners and operators, whose recklessness was based on the expectation of a government bailout (Sloan 1999, 191–92). For recent mergers see Roberts (1999), Barringer (1999), Holson (1999), Mifflin (1999), and "Control of the Electronic Highway" (1999).

2. With welfare reform, more of the burden of providing services has fallen on charitable organizations, yet the resources and subsidies available to the latter are shrinking. In many cities, food assistance programs have no choice but to turn away hungry people they would have fed in the past. At present, 76 percent of the cities receiving HUD support for homelessness programs have a shortage of emergency beds and transitional housing. A 1996 study projected that the homeless population would increase by 5 percent annually (Abrams 1999, 78).

3. For an analysis of types of enterprises and the prospects of each type of privatization by a proponent of such policies see Savas (2000).

4. Sumner wrote prolifically in the late 1880s and 1890s and was published in popular journals of the time. After his death, his essays were collected in the following volumes: *War and Other Essays* (1911), *Earth-Hunger and Other Essays* (1913), *The Challenge of Facts and Other Essays* (1914), and *The Forgotten Man and Other Essays* (1919). The quotes herein cited are culled from a more recent volume, *Social Darwinism: Selected Essays*.

5. But for Sumner even private charity is suspect. Thus, he gives the following advice:

   The next time you are tempted to subscribe a dollar to charity, I do not tell you not to do it, because after you have fairly considered the matter, you may think it right to do it, but I do ask you to stop and remember the Forgotten Man and understand that if you put a dollar in the savings bank it will go to swell the capital of the country which is available for division among those who while they earn it, will reproduce it with increase. (Sumner 1963, 123)

6. For the role of private money and various research institutes in the promotion of current conservative free-market ideas, see Stefancic and Delgado (1996), Callahan (1999), Gans (1997), and Cockett (1994).

7. The rise in the inequality of income became a global phenomenon in the 1980s, when many developing countries were forced to adopt privatization and market-driven policies, or opted to do so. During the decade, average incomes declined by 10 percent in Latin America and by 20 percent in sub-Saharan Africa, while the real minimum wage in many urban areas fell by as much as 50 percent. The World Bank estimated that the number of people suffering long-term malnourishment doubled over a decade to 950 million (United Nations Children Fund's 1990 annual report, cited by Broad, Cavanagh, and Bello 2000, 393).

8. Even those whose salaries were cut gained in stock options: thus Robert Allen, the Chairman of AT&T, took a pay cut of $512,000 in 1995 but received stock options valued in 1996 at some $ 9.7 million ("CEO 1995 Earnings," 1996, B10).

9. For the less wealthy, even the stock market bonanza has had a limited impact, though higher than in earlier decades. Those families holding stocks, including indirectly through retirement and savings plans, amount to less than half of the total, and their median holding is less than $20,000 (Baker 1999).

10. In Chile, for example, only about 43.4 percent of the workers contribute to the program, and their average taxable income is $460 per month. Men and women are categorized differently, and because women earn less and spend a great deal of time working inside the home, they systematically benefit less than men. In addition, even that which is contributed does not go entirely to the worker—management costs have been enormous: at times 20 percent of the contributions have gone to middlemen. Between 1982 and 1995 the annual return investment average was 12.7 percent. But as a World Bank study notes, the individual worker's return after commissions would have been 7.4 percent. Between 1991 and 1995 a 12.9 percent return was only 2.1 percent after commissions. The American worker, in a fiscally solvent system, pays less than 2 percent for administrative costs (Kay 1997, 48–51). For other critiques of privatization see Dean Baker, "The Privateers' Free Lunch" (1997), and Lieberman (1997).

11. The evidence on certain attempts to privatize the school system has been mixed. The initial Milwaukee school voucher program was actually very limited in scope, targeting about 1,000 of the almost 100,000 students of the district. Contrary to the forecasts of the supporters of school voucher programs, Wisconsin's official evaluator of the program from 1990 through 1995, John F. Witte, reported that there were no worthwhile differences between the achievements of public school students and those going to choice schools under the voucher program. Indeed, data from Milwaukee's Catholic schools showing a wide performance gap between those serving affluent and low-income neighborhoods, suggest that private schools do not achieve good results just through their status (Lowe 1995, 196–97, and "Voucher Students" 1999, 19).

12. For a general critique of equilibrium theories, see Soros 1998, 36–58.

13. For Joe Stiglitz's contribution to the limits of rationality in consumer choice due to information asymmetries, as well as his opposition to many of the free-market verities held by other economists in the Clinton administration, see Chait, 1999, 52–56; for more detailed discussion of relevance of norms to the market, see Kuttner 1997, 39–67.

14. "One of the best-documented findings from a long series of game-theory experiments is that most people, surprisingly, will contribute a share of windfall winnings to the public good, even though economic theory would predict that each rational individual would 'free-ride' and hope that somebody else will worry about the general welfare. The major exception occurs when the experiment is conducted among economics students, who have evidently been conditioned by their training to prize egoist behavior." See Kuttner 1997, 62.

15. The bipartisan support for the legislation may be due, in part, to political contributions made by the banking, insurance, and securities industries. Stephen Labaton in the *New York Times* (1999, 2) notes that they spent, in 1997 and 1998 alone, over $300 million in contributions to political candidates, and soft money contributions to political parties and lobbying activities.

References

Abrams, Stacey Y. 1999. Can a charity tax credit help the poor? Yes. *American Prospect*, vol. 10, no. 45 (July–August): 78–81.

Armour, Stephanie. 1999. Pension debate is heating up. *USA Today*, 21 September, 1B.

Averting a death foretold. 1994. *Newsweek*, 28 November, 72–73.

Baker, Dean. 1997. The privateers' free lunch. *American Prospect*, vol. 8, no. 37 (May–June): 81–84.

———. 1999. Bull market Keynesianism. *American Prospect*, vol. 10, no. 42 (January–February): 78–81.

Baker, Linda. 1999. Real Wealth: Use of Gross Domestic Product Figures as Economic Indicator May No Longer Be Valid. *E*, 10 (May): 3641.

Barringer, Felicity. 1999. CNBC invests in electronic stock trader. *New York Times*, 15 September, sec. C1.

Blustein, Paul. 1999. Stock options. *Washington Post*, national weekly edition, 14 June, 33.

Broad, Robin, John Cavanagh, and Walden Bello. 2000. Development: The market is not enough. In Jeffry A. Frieden and David A. Lake (eds.), *International Political Economy: Perspectives on Global Power and Wealth*, 4th ed. Boston: Bedford/St. Martin's Press.

Callahan, David. 1999. $1 billion for conservative ideas. *Nation*, 26 April, 21–23.

CEO 1995 earnings continued to soar amidst downsizing. 1996, *State*, 5 March, B10.

Chait, Jonathan. 1999. Shoeless Joe Stiglitz: Renegade at the top. *American Prospect*, vol. 10, no. 45 (July–August): 52–56.

Cobb, Clifford, Ted Halstead, and Jonathan Rowe. 1995. If the GDP is up, why is America down? *Atlantic Monthly*, October, 59–78.

Cockett, Richard. 1994. *Thinking the Unthinkable: Think Tanks and the Counter-Revolution, 1931–1983*. London: Harper Collins.

Cohen, Andrew. 1994. The hunger economist. *Lingua Franca* (May/June): 50–56.

Congressional Record. 1999. Vol. 145, no. 154, Nov. 4, S13871–S13917 ("The Financial Services Modernization Act of 1999—Discussion of Conference Report").

Control of the electronic highway. 1999. Editorial, *New York Times*, 10 October, Week in Review sec. 14.

Crutsinger, Martin. 1996. Trade deficit hits seven-year high: Data give ammunition to free-trade opponents. *State*, 29 February, D1.

Daly, Herman E., and John Cobb. 1989. *For the Common Good: Redirecting the Economy toward Community, The Environment, and a Sustainable Future*. Boston: Beacon Press.

Friedman, Milton. and Rose Friedman. [1979] 1990. *Free to Choose: A Personal Statement*. New York: Harvest/Harcourt Brace Jovanovich Publishers.

Gans, Herbert J. 1997. Tanking the right. *Nation*, 27 January, 28–30.

Glad, Betty. 1999. Yeltsin and the new political [dis]order. In Betty Glad and Eric Shiraev (eds.), *The Russian Transformation*. New York: St. Martin's Press.

Greider, William. 1997a. *One World, Ready or Not: The Manic Logic of Global Capitalism*. New York: Simon and Schuster.

———. 1997b. Who governs globalism? *American Prospect*, vol. 8, no. 30 (January–February): 73–80.

———. 1999. Curious George talks the market. *Nation*, 15 February, 25–28.

Holson, Laura M. 1999. The deal still rules: Mania for mergers defines the market. *New York Times*, 14 February, sec. 3, pp. 1, 10.

Kay, Stephen. 1997. The Chile con: Privatization of Social Security in South America. *American Prospect*, vol. 8, no. 33 (July–August): 48–51.

Kelley, Jack. 1999. GAO to study loan procedure in $90 billion sent to Russia. *USA Today*, 16 September, 10A.

Krugman, Paul R. 1999. *The Return of Depression Economics*. New York: W.W. Norton.

Kuns, Brian. 1999. Old corruption in the new Russia. In Betty Glad and Eric Shiraev (eds.), *The Russian Transformation*. New York: St. Martin's Press.

Kuttner, Robert. 1997. *Everything for Sale: The Virtues and Limits of Markets*. New York: Alfred A. Knopf.

Labaton, Stephen. 1999. Agreement reached on overhaul of U.S. financial system. *New York Times on the Web*, 23 October, 1–6.

Lieberman, Trudy. 1997. Social insecurity: The campaign to take the system private. *Nation*, 27 January, 11–16.

Lowe, Robert. 1995. The perils of school vouchers. In David Levine, Robert Lowe, Bob Peterson, and Rita Tenorio (eds.), *Rethinking Schools: An Agenda for Change*. New York: New Press, 191–204.

McLean, Bethany. 1998. Where's the loot coming from? *Fortune Magazine*, 7 September, 128–30.

Mifflin, Lawrie. 1999. $37.3 billion deal—Purchase would create an entertainment and advertising giant. *New York Times*, 8 September, 1.

Mishel, Lawrence. 1995. Rising tides, sinking wages. *American Prospect*, vol. 6, no. 23 (fall): 60–64.

Myre, Greg. 1999. Prosecutor: Most of loan diverted to Russian banks. *USA Today*, 16 September 16, 10A.

Pearl Meyer and Partners. 1999. *Executive Pay Report*. www.execpay.com

Reilly, Sean. 1995. The case for unions. *Washington Monthly*, July/August, 26–31.

Roberts, Wallace. 1999. Power play. *American Prospect*, vol. 10, no. 42 (January/February): 71–76.

Rowe, Jonathan and Judith Silverstein. 1999. The GDP myth. *Washington Monthly*, March, 17ff.

Safire, William. 2000. Mergers leave us naked to prying eyes, *State*, 3 November, A15.

Savas, E. S. 1999. *Privatization and Public-Private Partnerships*. New York: Chatham House Publishers.

Schmookler, Andrew Bard. 1993. *The Illusion of Choice: How the Market Economy Shapes Our Destiny*. Albany: State University of New York Press.

Sloan, John W. 1999. *The Reagan Effect: Economics and Political Leadership*. Lawrence: University Press of Kansas.

Soros, George. 1998. *The Crisis of Global Capitalism: Open Society Endangered*. New York: BBS/Public Affairs.

Soros, George, and Jeff Madrick, 1999. The international crisis: An interview. *New York Review of Books*, 14 January, 36–39.

Stefancic, Jean, and Richard Delgado. 1996. *No Mercy: How Conservative Think Tanks and Foundations Changed America's Social Agenda*. Philadelphia: Temple University Press.

Sumner, William Graham. 1963. *Social Darwinism: Selected Essays*, William E. Leuchtenburg and Bernard Wishy (eds.), Englewood Cliffs, NJ: Prentice-Hall.

Toner, Robin. 1999. Fevered issue, second pinion. *New York Times*, 10 October, Week in Review sec. 1, p. 16.

Voucher students show no academic gains, Milwaukee study says. 1999. *Church and State*, October, 19–20.

Ward, Lester Frank. 1967. *Lester Ward and the Welfare State*. Indianapolis: Bobbs-Merrill.

Wolfe, Alan. 1999. The new politics of inequality. *New York Times*, 22 September, A27.

10

Crossroads Blues: Business Representation, Public Policy, and Economic Growth for the Twenty-First Century

CATHIE JO MARTIN

Introduction

At the dawning of the twenty-first century, American capitalism exhibits the same type of schizophrenia that it did in the twenties. On the one hand one sees some real strength in the system. The stock market demonstrated unprecedented growth during the past decade. Corporate profits surged from 8 percent of national income in 1990 to 11 percent during the 1990s.[1] Unemployment has fallen below 6 percent, the lowest it has been in a quarter century, and this has been much lower than the double-digit unemployment rates found in many other advanced democracies.[2] American firms seem to have a commanding presence in international markets, and the United States continues to lead in productivity. These features of economic life have prompted all sorts of congratulatory self-adulation in the business press. For example, in May 1997 *Business Week* described ours as the "wonder economy."[3]

On the other hand, signs of real weakness in the economic system may be cause for alarm. Productivity was languid through much of the 1990s.[4] Although the United States leads in aggregate productivity, Japan has higher productivity than the United States in key export sectors such as machinery, electrical engineering, and transport equipment.[5] Corporate well-being has had very little impact on workers, and real wages have been flat or negative since the early seventies. Indeed, wages have been so flat that there actually was rejoicing in the business press over the recent *increase* in real wages for workers—a modest 1.4 percent and the biggest rise in two decades.[6] There has also been a growth of marginal workers in part-time or temporary jobs, positions usually without benefits and employment security. Those uneasy about America's economic future worry that U.S. firms will not have the people resources to stay competitive in a capitalism dominated by information technology.

These schizophrenic signs in the economy suggest that American capitalism is at a crossroads. The future could find U.S. firms more successful in the international marketplace or could reveal structural weaknesses in the American model and an erosion of our competitive position.

Economic analysts disagree about the role of government in assuring future prosperity and about the public policies necessary to fostering economic growth. This chapter considers one set of policies included in this debate: those to encourage investment in human resources such as training, health care, and other social supports linked to worker productivity. Laissez-faire economists view human resource investment policies as unnecessary and potentially detrimental to market efficiency, profitability, and capital investment funds. In stark contrast, high-performance-workplace advocates think that these investments are essential to growth and that government intervention is essential to getting enough of these kinds of investments. They fear that unless we invest in the necessary social infrastructure, the current surging prosperity will be as ill fated and unsustainable as its predecessor was in the 1920s.

The central question of this chapter is how our system of political representation might contribute to the resolution of this struggle over public policy, and thereby to the future of American capitalism and democracy. I focus especially on business representation, since managers are a big part of this debate.

I argue that there is considerable support for the high-performance-workplace approach even in the business community, but business representation diminishes the support for the high-performance-workplace package in three ways.[7] First, the American business community is deeply fragmented and is thereby less capable than employers elsewhere of thinking about its collective long-term interests. Second, a legacy of private-sector provision makes it even harder for employers as a group to formulate positions about collective human resource investment supports. Large firms have historically themselves provided social benefits linked to productivity when the state has failed to act in these areas, and today providers have very different interests from nonproviders in human resource investment policy. Third, major small business organizations have struggled to overcome this bias against collective political action; indeed, these are a major powerhouse in Washington today. But these groups are also the ones least likely to favor high-performance-workplace policies, both because they have close ideological ties to the Republicans and because they are dominated by domestic-producing, low-waged firms with little interest in expanding worker skills.

This chapter does not present an argument for a centrist or a business mobilization political strategy; rather, it explores how business representation affects public policy. Yet the analysis may help us to anticipate the consequences of centrist strategies. An accurate appraisal of the corporate political landscape may bring social policy activists to agree with Robert Reich that courting big business will ultimately deliver a limited payback and will only discourage the core constituents of the Democratic Party.[8]

An Ideological Debate

The debate over the role of social investment policies in fostering economic growth gravitates toward two crudely drawn views: the laissez-faire and the high-performance-workplace approaches. Laissez-faire or neoclassical economists consider social investment policies detrimental to market efficiency and profitability. Government regulations interfere with price competition, the best mechanism for distributing information about goods.[9] Government efforts to compensate for market failures are inevitably distorted by the demands of special interests; therefore, political solutions have pernicious unintended consequences and impede the natural course of entrepreneurship.[10] Social regulations limit companies' ability to hire and fire in downturns, the minimum wage allows workers to stay unskilled, and social benefits swell the cost of labor.[11] Mechanisms for skill development will emerge if the market demands this service.

Laissez-faire economists also believe that social spending hurts capital formation. Capital accumulation measured properly explains most productivity growth, making essential the creation of conditions for unfettered capital investment.[12] Social programs (even those devoted to improving the productivity of the workforce) require resources that could be devoted to economic accumulation in this zero-sum world; therefore, the proper course of action should be to cut private and public social spending in order to reduce labor costs and to free up investment capital.

By comparison, advocates of a high-performance workplace or a high-skill equilibrium consider social investment a necessary component to growth. Rationalizing, targeting, and often expanding social investment spending by governments and/or firms are necessary to develop the competent, productive workforce needed in knowledge-intensive, high-tech production.[13] Social and labor market regulation providing employment security makes it easier for workers willingly to embrace the technical change and industrial restructuring often so necessary to productivity growth.[14] Thus, the Council on Competitiveness worried in the late 1980s that the U.S. slow productivity growth was related to a lack of training.[15] Although global competition rewards lower labor costs, it demands efficient social reproduction of the workforce. Lower labor costs may motivate a movement away from the paternalistic firm with cradle-to-grave benefits, but efficient social reproduction may justify increasing investment in a highly skilled workforce.[16]

High-performance-workplace advocates feel that our nation currently underinvests in human resources, thus potentially damaging our ability to compete. To survive in high-end, lucrative sectors requiring highly skilled workers, employees need to have available to them programs for education and training. Yet firms spend little on training in the United States: only 1.2 to 1.8 percent of total employee compensation.[17] Company training budgets actually declined in 1991, and growth rates in training have barely kept up with inflation since.[18] Less than 10 percent of all companies do most of the spending of the $30 billion a year on training, and, according to some, most of this is spent on executives and managers.[19] Training in the United States. also tends to be more heavily concentrated in job-specific efforts, which are less transferable to new jobs and skills.[20]

Even business managers routinely complain that skills and training are undersupplied in the United States. In a National Association of Manufacturers (NAM) study, firms rejected five-sixths of their applicants because of inadequate skills and found one-third lacking basic reading and writing skills. Worker skill deficiencies prevented 40 percent of the companies from upgrading technology.[21] Of course, many multinational companies have simply shifted production to other countries, but this is not the optimal outcome for those seeking to enhance national fortunes.

Another area in which human resource investment is at risk is medical care. In the past, the linkage between a healthy workforce and productivity has prompted firms to provide medical insurance to employees. But today the uncontrollable costs of the American health system are killing employers. Health care adds enormously to the costs of U.S. goods, especially in comparison with countries where comprehensive health systems have greatly restrained costs. For example, health care is said to add $700 to the price of an American-made car, but only $200 to an auto made in Japan.[22] Health costs for each hourly Canadian steelworker are $3,200 a year; the American counterpart costs $7,600 a year.[23] Managed competition is currently working for some companies, but many wonder how long these savings will last without some rationalization of the total health system.[24] Many firms are simply dropping benefits, a practice often linked to reducing the permanent workforce through downsizing and outsourcing.

That American business managers may actually want more government meddling may be tough for some readers to swallow, especially those who think of America as a uniformly live-and-let-live kind of place. Lockean liberalism permeates our nation's collective political thought and has kept a host of social democratic inventions off the law books.[25] The Rube Goldberg quirks in our political system give businessmen good reason to distrust their state.[26] In all industrialized nations the need to appease corporate investors sets parameters on the art of the possible, whether managers use direct opposition to government initiatives or the more subtle structural power to keep things off the public agenda.[27] In the United States a weak labor movement and fragmented government enhance the structural power of business.[28] Since American social spending has always been limited, we should be all the more willing to jettison it in a time of anxious economic growth.

But several factors have increased corporate interest in human resource investment. First, as early as the 1970s productivity growth rates declined.[29] Some economists linked the drop-off to a mysterious decline in the advance of knowledge and to inadequate research and development.[30]

Second, a period of extremely rapid technological change signaled significant economic restructuring. Suddenly a burst of innovations, especially connected to microprocessors, made managers rethink their needs for high-skilled workers. Automation was projected to eliminate many of the most mundane tasks in direct labor, leaving workers to carry out more complicated, abstract, and challenging aspects of work.[31] Technological change can give workers more responsibility to learn, to adapt, and to manage.[32] These new technologies created a need for government interventions that enhanced worker capacities.[33]

Third, international competition made it more difficult for U.S. companies to hawk their wares, as firms in newly industrialized countries joined in the scramble for world market shares. The U.S. merchandise trade balance first went into deficit in 1972; by 1984 it was in the red by $140 billion.[34] Foreign multinationals obtained a powerful beachhead in the United States: the value of direct foreign investment in the United States jumped from $20.5 billion in 1973 to $403.7 billion by 1990.[35] At the same time U.S. companies increasingly engaged in outsourcing, whereby components of supposedly domestically produced goods were manufactured elsewhere; 20 percent of what we consider American output is actually produced by foreign workers.[36] In the new competitive context, standard price competition was seen by many as a dead end for companies in high-wage countries because these firms can never hope to undersell their third-world opponents.

Finally, firms began experiencing greater difficulty in providing company benefits. Corporate America has long been a major provider of social benefits, filling in the vacuum left by the very limited government welfare state.[37] Yet globalization and the beggar-thy-neighbor scrambling for a lower wage rate has made it much harder for multinational firms to fund their workers' social needs. In 1989 the average hourly wage was $17.58 in Germany and $2.32 in Mexico.[38]

Thus corporate America has come to human resource investment policy from many vantage points and a variety of motives. Some managers believe that a coherent government policy could rationalize the current system of social delivery and encourage greater provision of human resource investment in areas such as employment and training. Company providers would like government to force their competitors to offer benefits and to end cost shifting. Some big corporate spenders (often with fast commitments to their unions) would like the government to *bail them out* by assuming some of the costs of social provision. Big business managers do not want broad new government programs of the New Deal vintage; rather they look for solutions that work through existing private markets and do not interfere with their own private programs.

Business opinion polls confirm that social investment policies (at least conceptually) command quite a bit of interest from the business community. Although business managers often favor the general Republican goal of reducing aggregate public social spending, many promote specific social investment policy initiatives that promise to increase economic growth. For instance, 80 percent of a *Business Week* 1000 sample wanted new education and training programs, and 65 percent were even willing to pay higher corporate taxes for educational improvement.[39] Another study found 70 percent of the employers in its sample desiring increased federal spending on training.[40] In a NAM study 64 percent were interested in "a national, business-run remedial education program."[41] In my study of high-level managers from randomly sampled Fortune 200 companies, over half of the business respondents (54 percent) supported mandates and another 19 percent were mixed on the subject.[42] A NAM survey in the late summer of 1993 found a clear majority of its members supporting mandates and health alliances for firms with over 500 employees.[43]

The Least-Common-Denominator Business Community

Despite many managers' attraction to the high-performance-workplace logic, human resource investment policies are unlikely to command much support from the big business community. Several features of the U.S. system of business political representation diminish support for these policies.

First is the fragmented system of interest representation that I refer to as the least-common-denominator business community.[44] Interest group liberalism across private society makes it difficult for our society to work toward long-term collective goals, a category that includes the kind of social investment policies sought by high-performance-workplace advocates. American managers suffer from the interest-group-liberalism ailment: weak business political organizations make it much harder for U.S. employers to think about their collective long-term interests than their counterparts elsewhere. Unlike business managers in many advanced industrialized countries, U.S. businesspeople have no single peak association to aggregate their interests at a class level.[45] Rather, the Chamber of Commerce and the National Association of Manufacturers compete to represent the entire business community, and the Business Roundtable claims to represent big business.

The increased fragmentation of corporate political representation in the past few decades has made employers today less capable than ever of finding common ground. For example, Schlozman and Tierney found that between 1960 and 1980 there was a tenfold increase in the organizations listed in the *Congressional Quarterly* as representing a business.[46] Firm development of in-house political expertise further fragments the business voice. Companies today think more in terms of their individual interests than their industry interests, much less general business system interests. As Howard Vine (NAM) put it, "Associations used to be clubs on long leashes—you shared their theology, so you gave." This has changed to an attitude of "What's in it for my company?"[47]

Competition for members makes groups risk-adverse and unwilling to alienate their constituents with controversial stands. Because umbrella associations lack jurisdictional monopoly, they act more like sales organizations than like decision-making bodies and tend to cater to minority preferences. Unable to make difficult choices, employer organizations tend to defer to vocal minorities and to neglect the sentiments of the more silent majority. Since change always offends somebody, groups find it easier to voice short-term objections than to endorse positive policy change. The art of offending no one leaves big business groups in a kind of political limbo. Like feisty two-year-olds, they are very good at saying no to regulations that offend their narrow self-interests, but very bad at saying yes to policies that further their long-term, collective concerns. This least-common-denominator politics makes it hard for business groups to take long-term affirmative positions on policy change.

These constraints typically do not affect action toward the narrowly targeted self-interests of companies. In areas where a few large firms or even sectors have very direct economic interests, producers tend to dominate the policy process.[48] But when a wide spectrum of companies shares a broad collective goal, such as a skilled workforce, employers are hard-pressed to find common ground. Lacking assurance of one another's participation, firms find it difficult to take long-range, potentially punishing positions. If they train workers, they run the risk that these workers will be raided by other companies. If they offer health benefits, they may be undersold by companies not offering these benefits. As one manager lamented, "Big business will never do anything voluntarily for the collective good. They will only train after they have suffered." Thus companies are very good at securing their narrow self-interests but less good at expressing collective concerns.[49] Much has been made of the short-term perspective in economic investment; a similar dynamic constrains business managers' perceptions of their social interests.[50] Thus Vernon Loucks, Jr. (CEO of Baxter) despaired:

> While business may enjoy a measure of economic power, most businessmen don't have true political power and don't purport to understand it or use it. No change will come to our schools that isn't approved in some form by our political process. Yet put us in the political arena on a public policy question like education, and we in business are often totally in the dark.[51]

The fragmentation of power and leadership within government has only accentuated the fragmentation in interest representation. Congressional power has become less concentrated, the efforts of former Speakers Jim Baker and Newt Gingrich notwithstanding, and members need individualized attention. In the old days a few well-heeled CEOs could consult with the president or key congressional leaders and purport to represent the perspective of their sectors. Today this closed Washington community is a feature of the past, and interest groups must cultivate a broader array of legislators.[52]

Health Reform and the Least-Common-Denominator Politics

One sees an example of this least-common-denominator politics in the intra-corporate debate over the Clinton health reform bill. Health reform certainly died for many reasons, not the least of which was the problematic nature of the plan offered by the Clinton administration. Business supporters joined other analysts in considering the minimum benefits package excessive, the funding arrangements inadequate, and the plan too bureaucratic.[53]

But policy contradictions only partly explain the failure of big business to fight for health reform. The administration assured corporate allies that their concerns could be addressed. In addition, the initial bill was much closer to large employers' preferences than were later versions, because Democratic legislators kept offering subsidies to small business. An Association of Private Pensions and Welfare Plans (APPWP)/Wyatt study of the bifurcated mandate (not applicable to firms with fewer than a hundred employees) showed that under a partial mandate large employers would cover 14.7 million more individuals than they would under a full mandate; in other words, these extra lives would be cost-shifted from the small employers allowed to escape the mandate.[54] One wonders why big business wasn't more influential in protecting its turf to make the bill meet its interests.

The disappointing showing by large firms was also related to the failure of big business organizations to represent broad corporate concerns about health financing. Business groups helped to make health reform a top political issue but were unable to get business consensus for a specific legislative proposal. None of the umbrella associations ultimately supported the bill: each was crippled by internal divisions and resorted to a lowest-common-denominator politics.

The experience within the National Association of Manufacturers exemplified how difficult it was for umbrella organizations with a strongly opposed minority to exert leadership in health care reform. NAM members are big losers in the cost-shifting game: 99.3 percent offered benefits in 1988, and a NAM-commissioned Foster Higgins study found health care costs increasing 29.6 percent on average in 1989 (37.2 percent of employers' profits).[55] Consequently, many NAM members were very interested in a comprehensive reform bill. In a 1992 study 55 percent of NAM members favored a play-or-pay approach (complete with employer mandates) as part of overall system reform.[56] A NAM survey in the late summer of 1993 found a clear majority of its members supporting mandates and health alliances for firms over 500.[57]

Ira Magaziner met with the NAM in the early stages of the health reform planning effort and found the group very sympathetic to the administration's ambitions.[58] Jerry Jasinowski (NAM president) was one of the first individuals to see the draft in the summer of 1993. A deal was struck: Jasinowski agreed to take the plan before the board if the administration would fix five issues troubling to large employers. Referring to a September 1993 press release praising the Clinton plan, Jasinowski wrote, "I avoided any mention of mandates in order to imply that they may be a cost that business has to pay to get comprehensive reform; and to signal that mandates are not likely to be a top priority concern to manufacturers."[59] The administration calculated that 60 percent of the board was sympathetic to health reform.

But despite initial interest in the bill and considerable support from its members, NAM eventually rejected the president's approach. Before an important board meeting in 1994 the companies against reform secretly contacted board members and urged them to reject outright a Clinton-style plan. Providers and fast food magnates in the board's minority managed to prevent the association from supporting the proposal.[60] The reversal was rather sudden; indeed, NAM staff remember going into a board meeting in February 1994 having "good things to say about the Clinton bill and having the board do a 180-degree turn."[61]

Legacy of Private-Sector Provision

Second, a legacy of private-sector social provision further fragments corporate interests and makes it difficult to get a cohesive corporate view even among those who agree on the need for expanded social investment benefits. At earlier critical junctures large employers were unable to persuade their peers to support the social props they felt were necessary to the survival of capitalism. As a result these companies developed their own social programs, such as health care and pensions, that they believed had an impact on productivity.[62] Today where other countries have public health insurance, training programs, child allowances, and pensions, the United States has a patchwork system of benefits provided largely through our jobs. Business is at the heart of the health care system: almost two-thirds of our nonelderly population are covered through employers.[63] Companies spent $50.6 billion training their workers in 1994.[64] Even the biggest government benefit program, Social Security, has enormous help from the private sector in funding retirement income: in 1993 Social Security old age benefits (combined with disability insurance) paid individuals $297.9 billion, and private employer pensions paid out $192.6 billion.[65] The legacy of private-sector provision makes it difficult for a broad group of employers to articulate a collective position on social investment. First, it separates providers from nonproviders: those currently providing benefits would like to have their competitors forced to assume a share of the costs. Thus when Clinton proposed employer mandates as a means of achieving his social goals, many firms offering health benefits saw this as an opportunity to alter the competitive balance within their industries.

Second, the legacy of private provision creates a category of personnel within the firm with vested interests in the perpetuation of the status quo, even when the current system is hard to sustain. These personnel, found in human resource and benefits departments, are ironically often the most liberal people in the companies; yet they are also the least likely to support a radical new direction in public policy such as a comprehensive government system that might threaten the existing private systems of provision.

The policy legacies of the employer-based health system circumscribed the options considered by the Clinton administration in formulating its health plan. Employers were interested in health reform because of a failure of private firm-level solutions. But they were unwilling to deviate too far from the status quo and demanded that they retain benefits accorded to them in the current employer-based system. The Clinton administration complied in its desire to appeal to big business providers of health, and designed its proposal with the legacies of the employer-based system in mind, a move that single-payer advocates believed fatally flawed the plan.[66] Political expediency demanded that health reform be packaged to further growth, to level the global and domestic playing fields, and to protect the employer-based system. (Health alliances were to be quasi-public entities to negotiate rates with providers; large employers could opt out and continue to provide their current benefits package.)[67]

Perhaps not surprisingly, the goals of preserving the interests of large employers in the current job-based system and achieving real cost containment and expanded access came into conflict. The alliances needed to be big enough to have market leverage to restrain providers; yet business managers pushed for smaller alliances, worrying that ones covering entire regions would erode company purchasing power. The administration wanted fairly stringent rules for companies choosing to opt out of the alliances in order to ensure that firms did not move in and out of the public entities. Yet managers feared that these stringent rules would push many employers permanently into the public pool. As the reform process continued, many of the points of conflict were resolved in favor of employer interests in their private programs and to the detriment of the broader goal of cost control.

The Political Strength of Small Business

A third dynamic of business representation working against support for the high-performance-workplace approach concerns the pockets of strength in employer political organization. There are exceptions to the general rule of a least-common-denominator politics in which firms demonstrate more collective organizational power, but these tend to be concentrated among opponents of the high-performance-workplace perspective. The most important exception (and one that contradicts popular perceptions) is the small business lobby.

Political scientists often discount the power of small business: small firms have historically given much less money to political candidates, generally enjoy less prestige, and are too numerous to produce the star-quality CEOs offered by large corporations. Interest group theory predicts that widely dispersed interests (such as the multitude of small companies) should have a more difficult time overcoming collective action obstacles to the mobilizing and exercising of political power.[68] Large firms in industries are thought to control their smaller brethren; in interfirm alliances large manufacturers are considered to coerce their small business suppliers and customers.[69]

But although this perception of the economic distribution of power may be correct, small business is a political powerhouse in Washington today. Before delving into the reasons for this small business power, let me make clear that I am talking about the primary small business trade associations, the groups described as the small business lobby in the popular press. Small firms are a varied lot, and I do not wish to imply that all small business managers share the same interests. The entrepreneurial, high-tech software company is unlikely to have much in common with the corner mom-and-pop store in social investment. A skilled workforce obviously matters much more to small manufacturers in cutting-edge technologies than to low-wage service enterprises. But the primary trade associations in the small business lobby, such as the National Federation of Independent Business (NFIB), generally reflect the interests of the mom-and-pop-store contingent over the high-tech entrepreneurs. Small entrepreneurial firms do not have a very effective system of political representation and have little voice in national politics in more than a few issues in specific industries such as biotechnology and semiconductors.

What gives small business its political strength? One might assume that small business groups are more homogeneous, and therefore find it easier to take action. But opinion polls show small business to be fairly polarized. Some want no government interventions in areas such as health and family policies; others want even more government involvement than that desired by large employers, believing that small firms cannot hope to offer social investment support on their own. Thus NFIB found a quarter of its members favoring a government single-payer plan in health reform.[70] In a *New York Times*/CBS business poll, although more small employers believed that their labor costs would increase a lot during the Clinton administration, 52 percent of the firms with sales less than $99 million supported an employer mandate for health and 29 percent favored the Family and Medical Leave Act.[71]

Despite the plural character of small employers, their representative associations have an easier task of wielding political power in Washington. Their position on most issues of social policy is to oppose government intervention, and it is easier to oppose than to promote. Small employers also see their interests as more directly affected by human resource investment policies. They perceive family leave and health mandates as payroll deductions directly linked to their bottom line rather than as social supports with productivity implications; consequently, they are more strongly committed to political action in these areas than their big business counterparts, whose interests are more ambiguously linked to these initiatives. Under conditions of high capital mobility and possibilities for multinational production, large companies can move operations elsewhere; thus, there has been something of a division of labor between large, multinational companies' interest in trade and small domestic producers' interest in social issues.[72] Small firm PACs have been limited, but these are growing, and small business groups tend to target their funds to legislators who share their policy predilections.[73] Small firms exercise considerable leverage on large companies as customers; large companies have no such reciprocal power.

In addition to these other factors, small business has an unambiguous organizational advantage over large firms in the political arena. The major small business groups have several qualities that give them this comparative advantage. First, as media and public appeals have come to dominate modern political life, the ability to exercise spin control and to shape public perception of an issue is extremely important to political outcomes. Small businesses evoke the same kinds of nostalgic reminiscences as farmers do; this mom-and-pop-store profile allows the little guys to win very favorable approval ratings from outside publics. For example, small-firm proprietors were found credible by 71 percent of journals in 1982, but only 50 percent believed CEOs of big corporations.[74]

In this going-public world the ability to demonstrate a public show of organizational force carries more weight than it did when Washington was a closed community. The very weakness of small employers in the old days—their numbers, diversity, and lack of prestige—is a source of strength today. The well-heeled corporate lobbyist that wielded such power behind closed doors lacks the television charisma of hundreds of restaurateurs storming Congress. Innovations in computer technologies have augmented the advantage of small business groups: grassroots computer mailings first made popular by public interest groups are perfectly suited to their large and varied membership.

Second, these groups have developed organizational decision rules to augment the natural advantages of a broad-based, numerous membership. Thus NFIB avoids the least-common-denominator-politics of larger umbrella groups by grounding policy positions in regular membership polls. The association polls its 500,000 members every two months and immediately makes the data available to legislators. This practice lets them claim a mandate for action and makes it much easier to justify positions that hurt a minority subset of members. In 1995 *Roll Call* called NFIB the most powerful group in Washington.[75]

Third, small business groups have overcome the least-common-denominator-politics syndrome with single-issue coalitions. Large employers sometimes join these coalitions; for instance, Pepsico was an important actor in the Health Equity Action League to defeat the Clinton health plan. But groups such as the National Federation of Independent Business, the National Association of Wholesaler-Distributors, the National Restaurant Association, and the National Retail Association are typically at the core of these coalitions and are the leaders in organizational efforts. Indeed, the small business lobby has explicitly tried to establish itself as an independent voting block. In the words of NFIB's grassroots organizer R. Marc Nuttle, "Christians did not realize how big they were. Pat Robertson put a face on them and I intend to do that for small business."[76] NFIB recently passed on to its members David Broder's rhetorical question, "Is there a small business voting bloc?" The association's response was predictable: "Your personal involvement can help make the answer 'Yes.'"[77]

Coalitions happen because managers are dissatisfied with the stalemate in large umbrella groups and believe that a new forum dedicated to a single issue can make tougher decisions.[78] They typically address a single issue, although some outlast their precipitating legislative initiatives. Not all coalitions achieve the desired discipline, but the most successful have developed decision rules to keep participants committed to general objectives. Naturally, members demand specific benefits, but they must pledge in return to back and to mobilize behind all parts of the legislative package. Side deals are deemed especially egregious, and Washington players have a long memory when they feel betrayed by former allies. Thus, participants can hope to see movement on issues near and dear to their hearts, but in return they must promise to support the entire package and to restrain individual issues in favor of the broad legislative agenda.

Thus, the major small business associations have been able partially to overcome the least-common-denominator politics that handicaps much of the rest of the business sector. Because large employers are more likely supporters of social investment, small business power decreases the legislative potential for these initiatives.

Small Business Opposition to the Family and Medical Leave Act

An important example of small business use of coalitions to fight human resource investment initiatives was the fight against mandated family and medical leave. The Family and Medical Leave Act (mandating companies with over fifty workers to provide twelve weeks of unpaid leave to new parents) was signed into law in 1993, but only after enduring seven years of legislative failure and two presidential vetoes. As Senator Christopher Dodd pointed out, before the passage of the act, the United States joined only South Africa among industrialized nations in failing to mandate unpaid family leave.[79] According to pollster Ethel Klein, by 1989, 93 percent of Americans believed that individuals should have a right to take a leave to care for a newborn or sick parent without the threat of losing their jobs.[80] The delay in enactment is rather astounding, given the high level of public support and the ubiquitous presence of leaves in the industrialized world; small business groups may take full credit for the procrastination.

Small business predicted dire economic impacts to companies from the family leave legislation; thus, the U.S. Chamber of Commerce originally estimated that employers would spend an extra $16.2 billion a year on labor costs should leave be mandated, later revising this figure to $2.6 billion. (The General Accounting Office argued that the Chamber had overstated the number of individuals who used the leave, the number who would be replaced, and the cost of hiring replacements, and figured the leave mandate's cost at $147 million.)[81] Small business sought to frame the policy as a new entitlement, as when Mike Rousch (NFIB) worried that the family leave act set a precedent for mandates and promised to be a first step in a slippery slope toward an expanded welfare state.[82] Opponents also feared that the requirement for unpaid leaves would become the ubiquitous camel's nose under the tent leading to paid leaves. The Chamber's Virginia Lamp was to caution, "Mandating unpaid leave is only the first step; clearly, proponents seek to mandate paid leave."[83]

But supporters of the legislation pointed out that the legislation did little to change the status quo because it built on private-sector programs, ratifying what large firms were already doing and exempting small employers. A Families and Work Institute implementation study found that although only 14 percent of the firms had preexisting policies as extensive as the federal law, only 9 percent found implementing the leave policy to be difficult and only 6 percent cut health benefits in response to the act.[84]

Big business had little involvement with the family and medical leave dispute, but small business made it a cause célèbre for seven years. The U.S. Chamber of Commerce initially led the attack on family leave policy, organizing fifty associations and companies to oppose family leave.[85] But in 1987 others in the antileave coalition began to resent the Chamber's high visibility and felt that it was stealing the spotlight. John Motley (NFIB) complained, "A number of us got frustrated over that type of positioning by the chamber—insisting that their name be attached to every issue and insisting that they have to run the show." Mary Tavenner of the National Association of Wholesaler Distributors added that coalitions "work best when everyone in the group has an equal say. The majority should always rule, like any democracy."[86] Participants also felt that their association with the Chamber could tarnish their ability to influence moderate Democrats. Mary Tavenner remembers visiting Senator Jim Cooper (D-TN) to discuss the family leave bill. Cooper explained that he would not talk to her if she was part of the Chamber group.[87]

The discontented, some fifty-eight companies and groups, formed a new coalition, the Concerned Alliance of Responsible Employers (CARE). Mary Tavenner (National Association of Wholesaler Distributors) took the lead in organizing CARE, but in order to foster a sense of "ownership" and to avoid domination by any group, the members rotated the hosting of meetings. The coalition met on a weekly basis to discuss new information, tally congressional positions, and distribute assignments. Each association was expected to organize its own grassroots lobbying.[88]

Both the Chamber coalition and CARE fought to defeat family leave with the usual arsenal of coalition strategies: spin control, mailgrams, and media events. Presented with formidable public enthusiasm for family leaves, the small employers sought to put a less advantageous spin on the issue. CARE conducted its own public opinion poll showing that even while many Americans supported family leaves, they remained ambivalent about mandating this benefit. In addition, the organization cited a 1989 Washington Post/ABC poll that found leave not to be a high-priority issue.[89] Small business managers also picked up Phyllis Schlafly's (Eagle Forum) refrain that family leave was a "yuppie" issue.[90]

Small business opponents did a series of massive direct mail campaigns urging members to contact legislators each time the bill seemed to progress. In the fall of 1987 CARE geared up for a major offensive, and the family leave bill lost legislative sponsors. CARE's Mary Tavenner quipped, "We've been all over those guys like a cheap suit." The bill got stuck in the House Education and Labor Committee until the members exempted firms with fewer than fifty workers; the bill then made it out of committee, but small business continued to oppose the measure.[91]

In August 1988 the Chamber urged members to "blitz" legislators with mailgrams and phone calls.[92] By October the Senate had killed the family leave bill with very few moderate Republicans defecting from their party's majority. Senator Christopher Dodd (D-CT) blamed business lobbying for the defeat, angrily adding that "groups that support parental leave or child care don't have any political action committee money."[93]

The 1988 election, however, expanded the contested terrain as George Bush began to play both sides in the leave battle. Worried that Michael Dukakis would seize control of the family issue and capture the female vote, candidate Bush promised to diverge from Reaganomics with a kinder, gentler approach to public policy. At a meeting of Illinois Republican women he even seemed to lean toward mandated leave by stating, "We need to assure that women don't have to worry about getting their jobs back after having a child or caring for a child during a serious illness. That is what I mean when I talk about a gentler nation."[94] This campaign strategy prompted Linda Dorian (National Federation of Business and Professional Women) to comment, "We think the Bush campaign is showing some very good signs. There is room for some productive dialogue on this."[95] Business became skittish about the nominee's buying into the Democratic terms of the debate, and CARE's Mary Tavenner warned, "To keep from being on the defensive, Vice President Bush will have to come up with ammunition to combat Democratic proposals, and the sooner the better."[96]

In May of 1990 after both houses had passed the bill, the struggle for the heart and soul of George Bush intensified. Moderate Republicans tried to prevent the president's veto, pointing out that the action was inconsistent with the "family values" theme of the party. Representative Marge Roukema (R-NJ) went so far as to call the bill "a defining issue for the Republican Party" and "an economic necessity" for a majority of American workers. Representative Bill Green even quoted the 1988 Republican Party platform in his defense of family leave.[97]

Meanwhile, enemies of the legislation pumped up the volume. During the SBA's Small Business Week, employers stormed Washington and the White House to make their case against mandated leave. John Sununu (White House chief of staff) was sympathetic to their position and promised a presidential veto.[98] Bush himself continued to seem deeply ambivalent. When asked at a press conference whether he would veto the bill, the president couldn't get the answer out, but press secretary Marlin Fitzwater immediately answered in the affirmative.[99]

Where were big business managers while this struggle against family leave was unfolding? The Women's Legal Defense Fund (WLDF) tried hard to bring corporate leaders who supported private-sector leave policies into their reform coalition but were largely unsuccessful. The organization sent letters to the CEOs that headed a Working Women's list of best companies. The overwhelming response to this exercise was, "We agree with you but we can't alienate our colleagues."[100] The CARE opponents of leave also failed to win much big business support with the exception of large, labor-intensive, low-wage firms such as Pepsico. As Tavenner put it, "During the legislative activity, big business stayed in the background."[101]

In the endgame the big umbrella associations moved into a position of neutrality. After Clinton's election the Chamber decided to abstain from the Family and Medical Leave Act. The Chamber's chair for labor relations explained that the bill was less threatening than other labor initiatives: "We did not support it, but we decided that because over 70 percent of our members give [leave] and because there is a Democrat in the White House who will sign it, we could not develop a veto strategy. We also had to realize that as bad as family leave is, it is not going to kill American industry." NAM also abandoned its oppositional stance and concentrated on ensuring that employers and employees together negotiated changes in the work schedule. The neutrality game infuriated critics to the right. Grover Norquist (President of Americans for Tax Reform) colorfully denounced the Chamber's decision to sit out the battle:

> When you don't fight and stake out a position against it, you let the other side have a victory at no cost. It doesn't work for high school girls and it doesn't work for trade associations: You don't get respect by giving in a few times every once in a while. That doesn't make you reasonable; it makes you easy to have, and it makes you had. It doesn't get you invited to the prom. The problem with pragmatism is that it doesn't work.[102]

Family leave was ultimately signed into law, but only after immense effort and only with the arrival of a Democratic president. Even its opponents recognized that their opposition was somewhat overdrawn: at one point a Chamber lobbyist remarked, "This is almost an issue whose time has come and gone."[103]

Implications for Public Policy and American Democracy

I have argued that the big business community's incapacity to act for collective goals works against national legislation of high-performance-workplace policy initiatives. This chapter will conclude by speculating on what this system of political representation means for growth and democracy if the high-performance-workforce logic is correct.

First, the political dynamics discussed here have implications for competition in high-end markets. The rise of small business as a political force is gradually transforming the regulatory system, biasing fiscal and social legislation toward petit bourgeois sectors that are far from the cutting edge of global competitiveness. Today small business is exempted from a host of social, environmental, and safety protections, and thus about a third of American workers are left uncovered.[104] We are creating a dualistic regulatory framework that benefits small, domestic producers over big, international ones.

In today's fierce competitive environment, this two-tiered policy system is making large, paternalistic firms less willing to provide social investment benefits such as training and health care because they fear they will be punished for such behavior. Their goods will cost more; small companies may take advantage of their health plans (as, for example, when large firms pay for spouses' benefits); and nonproviders may raid the trained talent of large companies. For example, after national health reform failed, more firms returned to cost shifting as a way to cut costs: 78 percent of firms considered this in 1995 while only 48 percent thought that this was appropriate in 1991.[105] The increasing unwillingness of large firms to provide benefits is directly linked to their own political incapacities to get the human resource investment policies they need from government.

A resulting deficit in human resource investment may make it harder for firms to compete in high-skill equilibrium markets. This will only strengthen the recent trend toward concentration of a large proportion of new U.S. jobs in service sectors.[106] The absence of a national policy for human resource investment may lead to greater regional disparities. Insufficient human resource investment may ultimately hurt productivity; for example, Freeman believes that the United States already has slower *hourly* productivity growth than other advanced industrial nations. Freeman also finds misleading the widely touted claim that the American per capita GDP is higher than that of other advanced nations: the U.S. GDP advantage narrows when evaluated per worker and declines even more when you factor in that Americans work more hours.[107]

Second, the relative scarcity of human resource investments should only accelerate the income polarization between rich and poor. Severely skewed income distribution could precipitate a crisis of underconsumption. Thus the business press has periodically worried that deflation is becoming a real concern.[108]

Third, the popularity of the laissez-faire perspective and the parallel rosy scenario about our current economic conditions may be creating a time bomb for the future. Politicians of all political stripes love this rosy scenario because the booming economy makes the budgetary stranglehold seem less severe. For example, the 1997 budget accord achieved nearly half of its budget reduction by altering economic forecasts: adjusting the anticipated rise in the consumer price index permitted much more fiscal slack.[109] Consequently, the budgetary negotiations were concluded in a much more peaceful atmosphere than those of the year before. Yet critics suggest that these assumptions about the deficits were anything but probable, and that the bipartisanship was won at an excessive price because Clinton accepted the Republican constraints of a balanced budget that would greatly curtail future initiatives. In addition, a great irony of the exchange was that Clinton traded benefits for the middle class for a lessening of some of the draconian measures of the welfare reform bill. Thus the president reinforced the perception that the Democratic Party is the representative of the have-nots and moved away from the earlier claims of the New Democrats that they sought to represent the broad interests of the middle class. At the same time his brand of bipartisanship collaborated in the elimination of social supports that have been around for fifty years.[110]

Finally, the system of business representation has implications for political stability. Social tensions depend in part on the extent to which economic growth creates resources for resolving zero-sum conflicts. But if the current rosy views are incorrect, we may very well go back to the zero-sum deficit conflicts of the 1980s. As Eugene Steurele and others have argued, the fiscal stranglehold created by tax indexing in the 1980s has made it much harder for the national government to respond to new social needs.[111] When this current happy-face period is over, we could end up with continuing budget deficits, scaled-back entitlements, greater income polarization, reduced worker skills, and lack of an infrastructure to support firms moving into lucrative niches.

At this point we must worry about political stability. If the revolution comes, it may come from the trailer parks and pickup trucks of the Archie Bunkers of the world, the semiskilled workers who have lost big time in the global fight and flight. Regardless of what one thinks of Ross Perot, his use of the phrase "giant sucking sound" to describe the movement of American jobs to other countries struck a responsive chord in the hearts of many Americans, and he might win the prize as the most memorable politician of the late twentieth century.[112]

Notes

1. "Deciphering the Profits Puzzle," *Business Week*, September 29, 1997, p. 26.
2. Aaron Bernstein, "Sharing Prosperity," *Business Week*, September 1, 1997, p. 64; Commission of the European Communities, *Growth, Competitiveness, Employment: The challenges and ways forward in the 21st century*, Supplement 6/93, pp. 11, 40.
3. "New Thinking about the New Economy," *Business Week*, May 19, 1997, p. 150.
4. Stephen Oliner and William Wascher, "Is a Productivity Revolution Under Way in the United States?" *Challenge*, vol. 38, no. 6 (Nov.–Dec. 1995), pp. 18–30; "When Wage Gains Are Good News," *Business Week*, September 1, 1997, p. 104.
5. McKinsey Global Institute, *Manufacturing Productivity* (Washington, DC: McKinsey and Co., 1993), pp. 1–6. Also the lead in productivity is least impressive in areas such as steel, autos, consumer electronics, auto parts, and metalworking, so that aggregate figures mask threats to the United States in key sectors.
6. "When Wage Gains Are Good News," *Business Week*, September 1, 1997, p. 104.
7. See Cathie Jo Martin, *Stuck in Neutral: Business and the Politics of Human Capital Investment Policy* (Princeton, NJ: Princeton University Press, 2000).
8. Robert Reich, "Up from Bipartisanship," *American Prospect* (May–June 1997): 26–32.
9. F. A. Hayek, "The Use of Knowledge in Society," *American Economic Review* 35 (4) (September 1945): 519–30.
10. Dwight Lee and Richard McKenzie, *Failure and Progress* (Washington, DC: Cato Institute, 1993), pp. xi, 13; James Buchanan, *The Limits of Liberty* (Chicago: University of Chicago Press, 1975).
11. See, for example, Organisation for Economic Co-operation and Development, *Flexibility in the Labour Market* (Paris: OECD, 1986), pp. 111, 91. F. A. Hayak, "The Use of Knowledge in Society," *American Economic Review* 35 (4) (September 1945): 519–30.
12. Jeffrey Fuhrer, "Technology and Growth: An Overview," *New England Economic Review*, 21 November 1996, 3.
13. Wolfgang Streeck, *Social Institutions and Economic Performance* (Newbury Park, CA: Sage Publications, 1992), pp. 32–34.
14. Work in America Institute, *Employment Security in a Free Economy* (Elmsford, NY: Pergamon Press, 1984), pp. 323–45; Paul Osterman, "Work/Family Programs and the Employment Relationship," *Administrative Science Quarterly* 40 (1995): 681–700.
15. Council on Competitiveness, "Analysis on US Competitiveness Problems," *America's Competitive Crisis* (April 1987).
16. Thus, Dunning points out that modern conservative governments are both expounding a political philosophy of reducing state intervention and quietly pursuing activities that have a rising impact on firms and markets. John Dunning, *The Globalization of Business* (New York: Routledge, 1993), pp. 326–28.
17. Office of Technology Assessment, *Worker Training: Competing in the New International Economy* (Washington, DC: U.S. Government Printing Office, 1990), pp. 13, 15.
18. "Industry Report," *Training* 31 (10) (October 1994): 37.

19. Rochelle Stanfield, "Quest for Quality," *National Journal*, 8 August 1992), 1832.
20. Lisa Lynch, "Payoffs to Alternative Training Strategies at Work," in Richard Freeman, ed., *Working Under Different Rules* (New York: Russell Sage Foundation, 1994), pp. 68, 72–77, 81–85.
21. Produced by Towers Perrin for the National Association of Manufacturers, "Today's Dilemma: Tomorrow's Competitive Edge" (November 1991), obtained from Towers Perrin.
22. William Schneider, "Is There a Cure for America's Medical Inflation?" *National Journal*, 21 April 1990, 983.
23. Walter Williams, "United States Senate Committee on Finance Hearing on Health Care Costs, April 16, 1991," *Healthwise* 2 (2) (May 1991): 2.
24. Towers Perrin, "1996 Health Care Cost Survey," Towers Perrin Employee Benefit Information Center (March 1996).
25. Louis Hartz, *The Liberal Tradition in America* (New York: Harcourt, Brace, 1955).
26. David Vogel, "Why Businessmen Distrust Their State," *British Journal of Political Science* 8 (1) (January 1978): 45–78.
27. Charles Lindblom, *Politics and Markets* (New York: Basic Books, 1977).
28. Mike Davis, *Prisoners of the American Dream* (New York: Verso, 1986).
29. Edward Wolff, "The Magnitude and Causes of the Recent Productivity Slowdown in the United States," in William Baumol and Kenneth McLennan, eds., *Productivity Growth and U.S. Competitiveness* (Oxford: Oxford University Press, 1985), pp. 32, 36.
30. Edward Denison, *Trends in American Economic Growth*, 1929–1982 (Washington, DC: Brookings Institution, 1985), pp. 28–29, 100; Ramchandran Jaikumar, "Postindustrial Manufacturing," *Harvard Business Review* (Nov.–Dec. 1986): 70–71.
31. Shoshana Zuboff, "New Worlds of Computer-Mediated Work," *Harvard Business Review* (Sept.–Oct. 1982): 144–48.
32. Larry Hirshorn, *Beyond Mechanization: Work and Technology in a Post-industrial Age* (Cambridge, MA: MIT Press, 184), p. 73.
33. Anthony Carnevale, *America and the New Economy* (San Francisco: Jossey-Bass Publishers, 1991); George Lodge, *Perestroika for America* (Boston: Harvard Business School Press, 1990).
34. President's Commission on Industrial Competitiveness, *Global Competition: The New Reality* (Washington, DC: U.S. Government Printing Office, 1985), p. 13.
35. Robert Walters and David Blake, *The Politics of Global Economic Relations* (Englewood Cliffs, NJ: Prentice Hall, 1992), p. 107.
36. Robert Reich, *The Work of Nations* (New York: Alfred Knopf, 1991), p. 120.
37. Beth Stevens, *Complementing the Welfare State* (Geneva: International Labor Organisation, 1986).
38. Walters and Blake, *The Politics of Global Economic Relations*, p. 129.
39. Louis Harris and Associates, "A Survey of the Reaction of the American People and Top Business Executives to the Report on Public Education by the Task Force on Teaching as a Profession of the Carnegie Forum on Education and the Economy," Study No. 864011, Roper Library, "Harris for Carnegie Forum 08/1986" file.
40. Prepared for the Nightly Business Report by Yankelovich Clancy, Schulman, "Health Care and Health Insurance," June 10-19 (1992), obtained from the Roper Center, "Yankelovich for the Nightly Business Report Surveys of Executives 01/93" file.
41. Produced by Towers Perrin for the National Association of Manufacturers, "Today's Dilemma: Tomorrow's Competitive Edge," obtained from Towers Perrin (November 1991), p. 30.
42. Visits to corporate headquarters of these firms were made in the fall of 1992 and the spring of 1993 with follow-up interviews in the spring of 1995. Sixty-six per-

cent of a sample of eighty-nine companies participated. Cathie Jo Martin, "Nature or Nurture?"*American Political Science Review* (December 1995).

43. Unpublished survey provided by the administration.

192

44. Business is consistent in this way with other interest groups in the United States. Ian Maitland, "House Divided: Business Lobbying and the 1981 Budget," in *Corporate Social Performance and Policy*, vol. 5 (Greenwich, CT: JAI Press, 1983), pp. 1–25; Graham Wilson, "American Business and Politics," in Allan Cigler and Burdett Loomis, eds., *Interest Group Politics* (Washington, DC: CQ Press, 1986), pp. 227–31; Tim McKeown, "The Epidemiology of Corporate PAC formation, 1975–1984," *Journal of Economic Behavior and Organization* 24 (1994): 153–68.

45. Graham Wilson, *Business and Politics* (Chatham, NJ: Chatham House, 1990).

46. Kay Lehman Schlozman and John Tierney, *Organized Interests and American Democracy* (New York: Harper and Row, 1986), pp. 75–77.

47. Kirk Victor, "Step Under My Umbrella," *National Journal*, 23 April 1988, 1063.

48. James Q. Wilson, *The Politics of Regulation* (New York: Basic Books, 1980).

49. See also Wilson, *Business and Politics*.

50. Robert Hayes, Steven Wheelwright, and Kim Clark, *Dynamic Manufacturing* (New York: Free Press, 1988).

51. Vern Loucks, Jr., "Business and School Reform," *Vital Speeches* 59 (15) (May 15, 1993): 466.

52. Samuel Kernell, *Going Public* (Washington, DC: Congressional Quarterly Press, 1986).

53. Richard Smith, "Getting Business Support for Health Care Reform," *Washington Post*, 13 June 1994, p. A18.

54. Prepared by the Wyatt Company for APPWP, "Unintended Consequences of Excluding Small Firms from an Employer Mandate, Association of Private Pension and Welfare Plans," Washington, DC (May 1994).

55. Donna DiBlase, "Group Health Bills Equal a Third of Profits," *Business Insurance* 23 (22) (May 29, 1989): 37–38.

56. Foster Higgins/NAM, "Employer Cost-Shifting Expenditures" (November 1992).

57. A June 1994 Washington Business Group on Health survey of large firms showed 72 percent supporting a requirement that all companies offer insurance, 59 percent wanting firms to pay a portion, and 71 percent objecting to an arrangement that allowed small business to escape the mandate. NAM survey described in interview by Ira Magaziner; "Washington Business Group on Health," paper provided by the administration, no date.

58. Interview with Ira Magaziner (September 1993).

59. Memo to Magaziner from Jerry Jasinowski, "Administration Health Care Plan," September 15, 1993.

60. Interview with Ira Magaziner, September, 1993.

61. Interviews with NAM staff.

62. Edward Berkowitz and Kim McQuaid, *Creating the Welfare State* (New York: Praeger, 1988).

63. Marilyn Field and Harold Shapiro, "Summary," in Field and Shapiro, eds., *Employment and Health Benefits* (Washington, DC: National Academy Press, 1993).

64. "Industry Report," *Training* (October 1994), p. 30.

65. Caroly Pemberton and Deborah Holmes, "Benefits Received by Individuals," in Pemberton and Holmes, eds., *Ebri Databook on Employee Benefits* (Washington, DC: Employee Benefit Research Institution, 1995), p. 14.

66. For excellent discussions of the political sources of the Clinton plan and its weaknesses see Theda Skocpol, *Boomerang* (New York: W. W. Norton, 1996); and Tom Hamburger, Ted Marmor, and Jon Meacham, "What the Death of Health Reform Teaches Us about the Press," *Washington Monthly*, November 1994, 35–41.

67. Also the big insurers were the primary organizers of managed care networks for corporate purchasers, and hoped to administer the new Clinton system. Interviews with industry representatives (September 1992).

68. Mancur Olson, *The Logic of Collective Action* (Cambridge, MA: Harvard University Press, 1971).

69. See Neil Fligstein, *The Transformation of Corporate Control* (Cambridge, MA: Harvard University Press, 1990), pp.1–2.

70. Interview with NFIB staffer (June 1992).

71. *New York Times/CBS News* Business Poll, "Business Executives Survey" (1–9 December 1992), in Roper Library, "CBS News and CBS News/The New York Times Poll Releases—1992 (2)" file.

72. Interview with industry respondents.

73. Charles Brown, James Hamilton, and James Medoff, *Employers Large and Small* (Cambridge, MA: Harvard University Press, 1990), p. 70.

74. Brown et al., *Employers Large and Small*, p. 73.

75. "NFIB Named 'Most Powerful,'" *Capitol Coverage*, Washington, National Federation of Independent Business (December 1995).

76. Cindy Skrzychi, "Dome Alone II," *Washington Post*, 6 January 1995, p. B1.

77. "Building Bloc?" *Capitol Coverage*, Washington: National Federation of Independent Business (December 1995).

78. William Lanouette, "Chamber's Ponderous Decision Making Leaves It Sitting on the Sidelines," *National Journal*, 24 July 1982, 1298.

79. "Selected Statements on the Family and Medical Leave Act Delivered February 2, 1989, to the Senate Labor Subcommittee on Children, Family, and Alcoholism," *BNA Daily Labor Report*, no. 22 (February 3, 1989): E-1.

80. David Anderson, "Survey: Government, Business Should Take on Family Issues," *BC Cycle* (June 20, 1989).

81. Statement of William J. Gainer, U.S. General Accounting Office, "Statements on Parental Leave Act (S 249) before Senate Labor Subcommittee on Children, Families, Drugs and Alcoholism," *BNA Daily Labor Report*, no. 78 (April 24, 1987): D1.

82. Michael Verespej, "Clinton's First Legislative Child," *Industry Week* 242 (5) (March 1, 1993): 57.

83. William Miller, "Employee Benefits," *Industry Week* 234 (1) (January 12, 1987): 48.

84. James T. Bond et al., *Beyond the Parental Leave Debate:The Impact of Laws in Four States* (Watertown, NY: Families and Work Institute, 1991), pp. ii–viii.

85. Cindy Skrzycki and Frank Swoboda, "Child Care Issue Emerges as Focus of Legislative Efforts," *Washington Post*, 8 February 1988, p. A1.

86. Kirk Victor, "Step under My Umbrella," *National Journal*, 23 April 1988, 1063–67.

87. Interview with Mary Tavenner, formerly at the National Association of Wholesaler Distributors (July 1996).

88. Interview with Mary Tavenner (July 1996).

89. Respondents were asked to choose whether the federal government should mandate fringe benefits or allow employers and employees flexibility in choosing benefits. "American Public prefers Flexibility to Federal Mandates According to the Society for Human Resource Management," *PR Newswire* (February 28, 1991).

90. "Sen. Cochran Will Lead Opposition to Mandated Parental Leave," *PR Newswire* (July 25, 1988).

91. Carol Matlack, "Mobilizing a Multitude," *National Journal*, 17 October 1987, 2592.

92. Pamela Brogan and Judy Sarasohn, "Parent's Leave May Hinge on Dukakis," *Legal Times*, 29 August 1988, 8.

93. Joyce Barrett, "Democrats Claim 'Pro-Family' Political Victory," *American Metal Market*, 12 October 1988, 7.

94. Margaret Wolf Freivogel, "Supporters of Bill on Family Leave Try to Head off Veto," *St. Louis Post-Dispatch*, 16 June 1999, p. 1B.
95. "Women's Groups Begin Push for Parental Leave Measure," *New York Times*, 9 September 1988, p. 22.
96. Joani Nelson-Horchler, "The Politics of Child Care: What Business Can Expect from Bush, 'Duke,'" *Industry Week* 237 (2) (July 7, 1988): 20.
97. William Eaton, "Bush Warned by GOP Leave-Bill Backers," *Los Angeles Times*, 9 May 1990, p.18.
98. Jane Applegate, "Small Businesses Gain New Clout in Washington," *Los Angeles Times*, 10 May 1990, p. 1.
99. Margaret Wolf Freivogel, "Supporters of Bill on Family Leave Try to Head off Veto," *St. Louis Post-Dispatch*, 19 June 1990, p. 1B.
100. Interview with Donna Lenhoff (March 31, 1995).
101. Interview with Mary Tavenner (July 1996).
102. Kirk Victor, "Deal Us In," *National Journal*, 3 April 1993, 805.
103. Karl Vick, "The Principle behind the Family Leave Bill," *St. Petersburg Times*, 9 May 1990, p. 7A.
104. Brown et al., *Employers Large and Small*, pp. 82–84, 90.
105. Wayne Guglielmo, "Business Has a Mixed Message for Doctors," *Medical Economics* 73 (1) (January 15, 1996): 180; "National Executive Opinion Poll," *Business and Health* (1993).
106. Eileen Applebaum and Ronald Schettkat, "Employment and Industrial Restructuring in the United States and West Germany," in Egon Matzner and Wolfgang Streeck, eds. *Beyond Keynesianism* (Brookfield, VT: Edward Elgar, 1991): 137.
107. Richard Freeman, "How Labor Fares in Advanced Economies," in Freeman, ed. *Working Under Different Rules* (New York: Russell Sage Foundation, 1995), pp. 9–10.
108. "When Wage Gains Are Good News," *Business Week*, 1 September 1997, 104.
109. Julie Kosterlitz, "Betting on Good Times," *National Journal* 29 (25) (1997): 1266.
110. Judith Feder, "Double Whammy for the Elderly," *Washington Post*, 20 December 1995, p. A25.
111. Eugene Steurele, *The Tax Decade* (Washington, DC: Urban Institute, 1992).
112. Critical realignment theory predicts that midcycle protest candidates often anticipate the most salient issues of the next realignment cycle. See Walter Dean Burnham, *Critical Elections and the Mainsprings of American Politics* (New York: W. W. Norton, 1970).

11

Blowing Smoke: Impeachment, the Clinton Presidency, and the Political Economy

THOMAS FERGUSON

If Mr. Clinton is unable to shape the debate, prospects for certain industries may brighten, Mr. Gabriel said. For example, shares of tobacco companies and health maintenance organizations, two industries on Mr. Clinton's hit list, could benefit if he is distracted. Retailers and fast-food concerns could be helped if Mr.Clinton's plan to raise the minimum wage is undone by scandal. (*New York Times*, Dec. 20, 1998)

Ten minutes before the impeachment trial of President Clinton resumed yesterday, Senate Minority Leader Thomas A. Daschle and Senator Edward Kennedy convened a news conference to address the "matter of the moment." Health care. "We know you are dying to ask questions about the Patient's Bill of Rights," Daschle said, "so we are making ourselves available." The laughs quickly subsided. So, too, did curiosity about the state of health care legislation. (*Boston Globe*, Jan. 16, 1999)

Hillary Clinton sounded hollow yesterday when she said, as she introduced her husband at a gun-control rally: "Part of growing up is learning to control one's impulses." . . . After Bill Clinton sold the Lincoln bedroom to Hollywood buddies, after Hillary became a Miramax flak, after Al Gore and Jeffrey Katzenberg hugged, after Tipper soft-pedaled her crusade to raise PG kids in an X-rated society for a decade after Hollywood honchos told her husband it would hurt fund-raising, they should spare us their outrage. (Maureen Dowd, *New York Times*, April 28, 1999)

With so much of the world languishing in a ghastly and (at that time) still spreading depression, most of the human race is unlikely to commemorate 1998 as a banner year. But one set of people in particular is likely to shudder forever at memories of the year's congressional election campaign: "post-modernists" and other champions of the idea that society is to be understood primarily in terms of language or—in the expression now equally fashionable on both the Left and the Right Banks—"discourse."[1]

No profound enigmas of "signifiers" or "signified" in that campaign. In its "discourse" only one question ever mattered: Did he, or didn't he? Never mind that Asia was collapsing; that Russian debt default was triggering a credit crunch in what used to be called the Third World; or that in September, barely a week after Federal Reserve Board Chair Alan Greenspan solemnly assured a congressional committee that he knew of no imminent threats to the U.S. financial system, the appearance of the Angel of Death over a Greenwich, Connecticut, hedge fund co-owned by two Nobel prize winners and a former Federal Reserve vice-chair threatened briefly to drag down the world financial system. Save for summer snickers about *Wag the Dog* and, in the final weeks, when even hairdressers knew for sure, by gasps that a gentleman would offer something besides a Tipparillo to a lady, the rhetoric never varied. As far as anyone could glean from watching TV, listening to the radio, or reading newspapers or the Internet, the only suspense left was how many new Republicans it would take for the next Congress to render a last judgment on the First Fornicator.[2]

But election night brought a stunning surprise: the Senate elections were a wash, with the New York Republican Senator Alphonse D'Amato yielding his grip on the seat he had held for eighteen years. For only the fourth occasion in the history of the United States, and the first time since 1934, an incumbent president's party actually gained seats in the House of Representatives.[3]

This near-perfect inversion of conventional discourse was quickly followed by others even more surreal. A few days after the election, a major national political leader did indeed announce his resignation—but it was Newt Gingrich, not Bill Clinton. Amid a riot of press notices hailing the GOP's return to the pragmatic "center," Louisiana Republican Robert Livingston, a self-proclaimed consensus builder putatively less connected to the far right, laid claim to the Speaker's gavel. House Republicans began crawling away from the impeachment issue and casting about for a graceful way to abort the House Judiciary Committee's scheduled hearings. When Special Prosecutor Kenneth Starr's own ethics adviser resigned in protest over Starr's decision to appear before the committee, the inquest seemed on the verge of foundering.[4]

Then something peculiar happened. With things falling apart, the new GOP center suddenly could not hold. In fact, it didn't even try. In the face of polls showing Americans overwhelmingly opposed to impeachment, Republicans on the Judiciary Committee railroaded through four articles of impeachment on a straight party-line vote. The new leadership refused to permit a House vote on the milder penalty of censure, and Republican "moderates" joined the rush to judgment.[5]

On the eve of the now certain vote for impeachment, life imitated Hollywood, if not exactly art. *Wag the Dog* stopped being funny, as the president ordered air strikes and missile attacks on Iraq. The GOP followed with an unprecedented maneuver: With split screens on televisions around the world memorably realizing American public life's "doublethink," they livened up their own party by blowing out another Speaker.[6]

Back in October *Hustler* magazine publisher Larry Flynt had placed a full-page ad in the *Washington Post* offering up to a million dollars to women who could testify personally to the power of Republican family values. As Flynt and the Capitol Hill daily *Roll Call* trained their crosshairs on him, House Speaker-designate Livingston prudently elected to parry their volleys by confessing that he, too, had sinned—with at least four different women, according to Flynt. The gambit failed. In the GOP, where many of the most ardent cadres may well hope someday to replace *Entrance of the Elephants* as the party's song with *A Mighty Fortress Is Our God*, the prospect of the next GOP convention opening with the overture to *Don Giovanni* was simply too much. Confronted with a wafer-thin margin in the next House and active protests from the right—including, it appears, some followers of Gingrich, who already harbored doubts about him—Livingston was in trouble. Protests from leaders of the religious right such as Phyllis Schlafly, Jerry Falwell, and the Reverend Lou Sheldon, chair of the Traditional Values Coalition, added fuel to the fire. Claiming to have made the decision on his own, Livingston committed ritual suicide. He announced he would not run for Speaker and would leave Congress. He also invited Clinton to follow him into oblivion. A stunned House swiftly approved two of the four articles of impeachment.[7]

The "historic" Senate trial proved something of an anticlimax. With the elite media dropping strong hints that the public was weary of the whole spectacle, Senate Republicans insisted on calling witnesses. One after the other, Monica Lewinsky, Superlawyer Vernon Jordan, and White House aide Sidney Blumenthal all duly appeared to record testimony on videotape. No bombshells burst. As all chances vanished that enough Democrats would ever defect to reach the required magic number of two-thirds of the Senate voting to convict, the debate droned on. Finally, with the GOP leadership still adamantly opposed to a separate censure resolution, and the Republican Party dropping in the polls like a runaway elevator, the Senate voted to acquit the president on both counts.

Though a federal judge announced her intention to hold the president in contempt for his testimony in the Paula Jones case, and Special Prosecutor Starr hinted broadly that he might someday indict the president, the immediate crisis dissipated.[8] But the dizzying concatenation of events left many observers shaking their heads. How can one possibly explain how the government of the world's sole superpower came so close to melting down, in the political equivalent of Chernobyl or, at least, Three Mile Island, less than a decade after winning the Cold War, amidst relative prosperity at home, if not abroad?

Certainly not by pointing to that hardy perennial of traditional American political science—the will of the electorate. Postelection analyses of the '98 vote were mostly instrumental and unilluminating: Liberal Democrats ascribed their party's relatively strong showing to success at turning out its traditional bases among labor, women, and minorities. Conservative Democrats countered by pointing to evidence that relative prosperity attracted upper-income groups and white males back to the party. Conservatives blamed the Republican debacle on Gingrich's failure to act like a conservative when he dodged another government shutdown and compromised on the budget. "Moderate" Republicans, at least until the impeachment vote, pointed to the baleful influence of the far right within the GOP, etc. None of these "establishment" analyses paid much heed to the evidence—manifest in the close-to-record-low turnout of approximately 36 percent—that the ship of state currently floats in a sea of apathy. Or to the strong hint from Minnesota, where voters searching for someone to wrestle with their problems opted for a trained professional running on a third-party label and the slogan "Retaliate in '98," that beneath the surface apathy runs a powerful current of disgust and anger.[9]

But for assessing public opinion's role in driving the impeachment process, none of this matters. The congressional elections manifestly did not tap a riptide of public anger toward Bill Clinton. Exit polls indicated that the president's travails with Monica Lewinsky cut little ice with most voters as they cast their ballots. The relative minority who indicated that the issue figured in their voting decisions split almost down the middle between the major parties, in effect canceling each other out. Polls also suggest that in a strong U.S. economy, Jesus saves, but as Commerce Department data forcibly remind us, almost no one else does: Preelection forecasts that an army of Christian soldiers would power the GOP to victory proved hollow. With income rising a touch for many voters, Yahweh evidently lost out to the Golden Calf, or perhaps, mundane concerns about Social Security, health care, or education.[10]

Survey evidence once the GOP impeachment effort roared back in high gear after the election is even more compelling. While the electorate had deep misgivings about the president personally, all polls indicated that voters lopsidedly opposed impeachment, with the ranks of the disaffected swelling steadily in reaction to events on Capitol Hill. Voter perceptions of the GOP also fell sharply, in fact to a record low (though the data go back only fourteen years). A trickle of people were even said to be changing their party registrations in favor of the Democrats in some states.[11]

Perhaps most telling of all, however, were explanations put forward by prominent Republicans. With startling candor—so startling that an outlandish repair effort was briefly mounted—many openly mocked the idea that myopic, self-centered voters would ever hold them responsible, or indeed, ever could. As former Republican Senator Alan K. Simpson (who now runs the Institute of Politics at Harvard, a post that brings him into close touch with many on Capitol Hill) memorably expressed the sentiment: "The attention span of Americans is, 'Which movie is coming out next month?' and whether the quarterly report on their stock will change."[12]

This leaves only the "cultural wars" argument as a halfway plausible line of argument within the framework of conventional discourse. William Pfaff, for example, has argued that "Today's partisan war is trivial in cause—the Lewinsky episode and the president's pathetic lies about it—but it is in a way more dangerous than the Nixon or Johnson impeachments. Today's is a war not of politics but of cultures, social values, and to an extent, even of religion provoked by the generational value shift that took place in the 1960s." The "battle issues," claims the former analyst for the Hudson Institute and trenchant critic of "globalization," "are named feminism, abortion, homosexuality, multiculturalism, fundamentalism."[13]

This argument is just close enough to the truth to be seriously misleading. First of all, some clouds do in fact have silver linings. Though his influence pales beside that of such transnational institutions as Hollywood, consumer capitalism, organized gambling, or the television industry, Larry Flynt has done about as much as any single person to coarsen public life. But the campaign he and others waged to "out" prominent Republicans points up both the hypocrisy that sustains the Republican leadership's alliance with the Christian Right and the elaborately staged nature of the clash in "values." House Judiciary Committee Chair Henry Hyde's long affairs with both a savings and loan and a mistress, Congressman Dan Burton's "love child," Idaho Representative Helen Chenoweth's affair with a married man, Livingston's four (alleged) partners, the "Big Fish" and shoal of lesser fry that Flynt claimed to have netted— these may indeed reflect traditional values, but if so, they are the ones memorably depicted by Procopius or for that matter in *Elmer Gantry*. Together with the almost endless series of financial scandals that has engulfed the Republican leadership—such as Newt Gingrich's corrupt book contract from media tycoon Rupert Murdoch, or the fund-raising violations that finally did lead to his censure by a House committee he controlled, or Tom DeLay's apparent perjury in a business lawsuit related to campaign financing—they demonstrate that religious convictions explain very little about the GOP leadership.[14]

What is true of the formal party leaders holds in the main for the network of think tanks, foundations, Forbes 400 donors, and legal institutes that pushed along the impeachment issue for so many years. Some of these—notably, the Rutherford Institute, which helped finance the Paula Jones lawsuit—are indeed linked to major Christian Right donors, such as Howard Ahmanson, Jr. But most of the heavyweights are not. For example, though they may both say nice things about the Christian Right from time to time (especially as elections approach), neither of the two national journals that probably spilled the most ink about Whitewater or Monica Lewinsky—the *Wall Street Journal* and the *American Spectator*—has any significant religious identity. Though they could perhaps be said to have made a religion out of the free market, their kingdom is definitely of this world. The *Weekly Standard*, another prominent organ promoting impeachment, is owned by Rupert Murdoch, a broadcasting mogul with a long history of secular political concerns.[15]

Richard M. Scaife, who probably invested more money in efforts related to impeachment than anyone else (including at least $1.8 million in the *American Spectator*'s "Arkansas Project," which delved into the Clinton family's affairs, in many senses) has few ties with the religious right. Neither does David Koch, another member of the Forbes 400 whose sometimes contentious family has long supported a bevy of think tanks (including the Cato Institute and Citizens for a Sound Economy) and who publicly cheered on the push on impeachment. The Bradley Foundation, of Milwaukee, Wisconsin, which helped promote the Whitewater investigations, is also clearly secular in its orientation.[16]

200

It is true that the *Washington Times*, which vigorously puffed Whitewater and impeachment, is controlled by the Reverend Sun Myung Moon, head of the Unification Church. But this is the sort of exception that proves the rule. Many questions have been raised about possible ties between Moon and his secretive cult to right-wing Japanese businesses, the Korean Central Intelligence Agency, and other organizations not noted for their religious zeal. Moon has also encountered certain unusual problems in rendering unto Caesar—he was convicted of tax fraud and served time, after the Reagan administration tried but failed to stop prosecution by federal prosecutors in New York. His former daughter-in-law also has recently leveled charges in regard to indulgence in sex and drugs that, if true, would place the self-styled "Emperor of the Universe" not that far out of the Capitol Hill mainstream.[17]

None of this implies that leaders of the Christian Right did not fairly consistently favor impeachment. But except when the question dominated the national agenda (as it did in much of 1998), the issue typically figured merely as one more item on their rather long wish lists. By comparison with, say, Scaife or the *Wall Street Journal*, the Christian Right played mainly a supporting role. It was not chiefly responsible for pushing the impeachment issue to the top of the partisan agenda. William Kristol, editor of Rupert Murdoch's *Weekly Standard*, was only telling the truth when, after Pat Robertson suggested calling off the Senate trial for the sake of the GOP, he told the media that the preacher "has not been an influential voice on Clinton's impeachment."[18]

So what does explain the long-running meltdown? In a political system where it is accepted practice to sell nights in a White House bedroom, but consensual sex near there can bring down the regime, the answer is obvious: money. Or, more precisely, what I call the "investment" theory of political parties. A blunt rejection of conventional fantasies about the "median voter" and similar approaches to understanding political dynamics, this approach emphasizes that the critical factor in shaping public policy is normally the process of bloc formation among major investors. In countries like the United States, where most voters are unorganized, desperately pressed for both time and money, and often minimally informed or interested in politics, a political party's real market is defined by major investors, who generally have good and clear reasons for investing to control the state. In analyzing political outcomes, accordingly, the place to begin is with a systematic study of blocs of large investors. In most cases in the modern era—and certainly during the Clinton presidency—this requires a careful assessment of the regime's macroeconomic policies, since these usually relate very closely to the hopes and fears of both friends and foes of the ruling political coalition. One also pays heed as a matter of course to the subsidized "politics of ideas" and domestic social conflicts, particularly as these are affected by a changing world economy.[19]

This chapter draws liberally from my previous efforts to trace the workings of the "golden rule" in earlier stages of the Clinton administration. Thus it relies in part on my earlier analyses of Federal Election Campaign data for the 1992 and the initial stages ("early money") of the 1996 elections.[20] But this chapter also presents a fresh analysis of newly compiled FEC data for the entire '96 campaign and traces political contributions of certain key actors through (most of) the 1998 election cycle.

Taken together, these data show a striking pattern, against which the impeachment controversy stands out in bold relief: In the midst of a recession, Bill Clinton captured the White House by relying on a powerful but very thin wedge of support within big business, a wedge so exiguous that I compared it at the time to the Seattle Space Needle (Ferguson 1995, 322). But despite his loudly advertised efforts to walk away from the legacy of the New Deal, the "New Democrat" Clinton was unable to expand that base. Instead, most of American business opposed him from his earliest days in office, when he proposed a small raise in taxes on wealthy Americans to help close the deficit. That remarkably bitter clash prefigured the willingness of the GOP (including the so-called moderates) to threaten the administration with historically unusual (critics increasingly charged: "unconstitutional") tactics of opposition. By the middle of Clinton's first term, his administration was virtually at war with many major American industries, including health care, pharmaceuticals, chemicals, fast food, retailing, firearms, and—most fatefully of all, in the long run—tobacco. Flush with campaign funds and press support, the GOP pursued radical parliamentary tactics and other stratagems designed to make life unbearable for the White House. At the same time, the administration's inability to move the Japanese led it to adopt international economic policies that eventually seriously eroded its original core support.

The resulting catastrophe in the 1994 elections set off a desperate search for campaign funds for the '96 race by the White House and the Democratic National Committee—a search that eventually became notorious when the less than artful dodges of John Huang and other party operatives came to light. Prodigious White House fund-raising efforts, a substantial political business cycle, timely policy changes, but most of all the administration's efforts on behalf of the Telecommunications Act of 1996—which, in effect, brought Mickey Mouse (Disney and many others) to the president's rescue—pulled the administration through the election. But the triumph did little to enlarge the president's base in the business community or conciliate the Republicans and their affluent supporters.

In the fall of 1997, as Asia collapsed, the administration made a bold effort to pry open to American businesses the extensively closed economies of what had until then been the fastest-growing region in the world. As the Starr investigation engulfed the presidency, these efforts attracted significant political support—support that assuredly contributed to rescuing the party from what appeared to be certain disaster. But the campaign to force Anglo-Saxon style capitalism on the rest of the world engendered powerful opposition from foreign business circles, particularly in Japan, Germany, and the Third World. The continuing stalemate with the Japanese, a breathtaking series of financial disasters, along with the collapse of American policy toward Russia, eventually bogged down this effort, leaving Bill Clinton's elite support as thin as ever, just as the Republicans were cranking up the Lewinsky affair.

202

1992—Back to the Future

Bill Clinton's conquest of the presidency in 1992 was the culmination of more than a decade of effort by center-right business groups to remake the Democratic Party. Because my *Golden Rule* and earlier studies analyzed both these efforts and the 1994 debacle in detail, the treatment here will be summary.

As all the world—save perhaps some innocents within the political science fraternity—now recognizes, the *fons et origio* of Bill Clinton's national campaign was a bloc of investment bankers, led by Robert Rubin of Goldman, Sachs. Direct contributions to the 1992 Clinton campaign from Goldman personnel alone, for example, totaled well over $100,000, with substantial portions of that money arriving very early. Partners from that firm and several others, including the Blackstone Group, also helped raise many times that amount. Ranged alongside the financiers were prominent business figures from a limited number of other industries (Table 11.1): aircraft, oil and gas (the latter appears to have been particularly active), transportation, utilities (which at that time included important parts of telecommunications), computers, and a group of firms best characterized as capital-intensive exporters. A substantial number of high-tech executives also ended up noisily endorsing Clinton.[21]

TABLE 11.1
Industries Significantly above the Mean
in Support of Clinton, 1992

(Mean = 21%, N = 948)	
Investment banking N = 50	46% (0.00)
Transportation N = 33	33% (0.08)
Computers N = 16	38% (0.12[a])
Aircraft N = 13	54% (0.00[a])
Capital-intensive exporters N =7	43% (0.17[a])
Oil and gas N = 65	28% (0.18)
Tobacco N = 4	50% (0.20[a])

Source: From Ferguson (1995, pp. 291 and 300); computed from FEC data.

Notes: Figures in parentheses are significance levels. Note text caution about utilities industry (not shown above).

[a]Expected value of cell in chi-square less than 5 is warning of low power. Significance levels reported in such cases are results of Fisher's Exact Test.

This bloc shared many policy commitments of the vastly larger Bush coalition, including, notably, a confident belief in the superiority of free trade and an open world economy. Many of its members, however, did not share the Republican conviction—famously expressed by Bush Council of Economic Advisers Chair Michael Boskin—that distinctions between potato chips and microchips were irrelevant for government policymaking in a free-market economy. Many also doubted that trade with the heavily state-directed economies of East Asia, particularly Japan, could any longer be left to chance. Not only Rubin (who chaired a committee that put out a report coauthored by economist Laura Tyson recommending a more activist technology policy just as Clinton took office), but many high-tech executives were quite willing to say so in public—in some cases as they endorsed Clinton. Representing mostly sectors with some direct tie to the government or lively hopes for profit from export promotion incentives, technology subsidies, or action to balance trade with foreign competitors, they were prepared to countenance a carefully delimited break with laissez-faire. Some were also sympathetic to efforts to rationalize the fantastically expensive U.S. health care system, though most of the energy for that initiative came from parts of the health care industry that were likely to lose heavily if the existing anarchy continued. These latter included, notably, many research hospitals, some nonprofit HMOs, nursing homes, physicians' groups anxious about the specter of "industrialized medicine," and many providers of services that the Bush policies had left out, such as home health care or mental health.[22]

With the United States mired in recession as the election approached, such appeals only gained force. The Clinton campaign, of course, assiduously fanned the impression that voters would also benefit from the policy initiatives it promised. This it did by the usual Democratic double strategy of vague hints (of "real change") combined with a full-court press on heads of labor unions, women's groups, and other prominent progressives (including some who had known Clinton since school days) to endorse his candidacy. Leading Democrats, assisted by timely foundation grants, also opened a few counterparts to conservative policy journals. In the end, the recession proved crucial; exit polls indicate that the poor performance of the economy counted heavily in the calculations of many voters, making 1992 an election that Bush (or perhaps more accurately, Alan Greenspan) lost rather than Clinton won.[23]

The Path to the Abyss

Literally the morning after the election, the signals emanating from the Clinton camp switched dramatically. The people who had won the election by focusing on "the economy, stupid" began trying to lower expectations that "real change" would happen anytime soon. Over the next few months, the incoming president announced that reducing the deficit would have to be his top priority. Rejecting appeals for a quick devaluation of the dollar against Asia, Clinton and his spokespersons, including Robert Rubin, declared in favor of a strong dollar. With help from leaders of two major unions, the Clinton team helped derail an initiative for Canadian-style "single payer" health insurance popular with many of his supporters. The president also abandoned the fight for a tiny budget stimulus that the American economy's subsequent record strongly indicates would have posed no threat at all of a resumption of inflation.[24]

Though bond markets, which rallied euphorically, picked up the shift, the public mostly did not. Who now remembers that in the weeks before the inauguration, public hopes for the new administration were soaring even among people who had not voted for Clinton, and that optimism was particularly marked among African Americans and people making less than $15,000 a year?[25]

The mushrooming public sentiment brushed past crucial signals coming from the Republicans. The most important of these was probably George Bush's own troubled history of dealings with congressional Republicans. By comparison with most post–New Deal presidents, Bush was a very conservative president. His administration, like Ronald Reagan's before it, worked tirelessly to roll back regulation, weaken unions, chop social spending, reduce taxes, extend free trade, and cultivate a vast military establishment in a world with no obvious need for one so large. Not surprisingly, in both 1988 and 1992, his presidential bids attracted massive support from businesses, particularly the multinationals. Nevertheless, the Texan's relations with the Republican right were frequently very rocky. Many self-styled conservative "revolutionaries" and their affluent backers regarded the president's "Tory wet" conservatism as hopelessly timid, almost dishonest.[26]

Eventually, on a matter of the highest importance to the White House—the famous "Read my lips" budget climb-down of 1990, which Bush embraced to open the way for Federal Reserve rate cuts that were vital to his hopes for re-election—relations between the Right and the president broke down entirely. To public cheers from super-rich backers of deep slashes in capital gains tax rates, such as financier Theodore Forstmann, Newt Gingrich and other insurgents broke with the administration's tax bill. A political disaster of almost mythic dimensions resulted (Ferguson, 1995, 288–89). For anyone who wanted to see, the lesson was plain: Right-wing Republican congressional leaders were quite prepared to push *Republican* presidents into the abyss.

Other portents were equally ominous. In a generous spirit of "majority rule" on election night 1992, "moderate" GOP Senate Leader Robert Dole suggested that the Senate Republicans might filibuster major legislation that the new Democratic president-elect proposed, forcing the Democrats to find sixty votes to pass anything.[27]

Dole's outburst could perhaps be dismissed as frustrated election night bluster. But when the new president proposed his scaled-down, conservative "New Democratic" tax plan designed to close the budget deficit, a storm of titanic proportions broke over the White House. The tax proposals called for a very modest rise in taxes on Americans in the highest income brackets. With a straight face (the Reagan and Bush administrations had, after all, presided over one of world history's greatest peacetime upward shifts in income redistribution), Republicans accused the administration of waging "class war," while at the same time claiming (falsely) that the bill raised taxes on most working Americans.[28]

Though in many cases the administration bent over backwards to compromise and enlist support from industry, virtually every other new measure it contemplated only fanned the flames of *jihad*. Despite major concessions to insurers and initial support from some industrial interests, the administration's much-touted health care initiative launched one of the most expensive lobbying battles in American history. The president's effort to regulate firearms (as promised during the campaign) by passage of the so-called Brady Bill drew bitter, lavishly financed attacks from the National Rife Association and firearms manufacturers. Proposed new rules by Interior Secretary Bruce Babbitt to control grazing by western ranchers on federal lands at below market rates ignited a firestorm. Oil companies opposed new taxes on energy, while seeking drilling rights in Alaskan wildlife sanctuaries. Most firms in oil, paper, chemicals, electric power, and related industries were up in arms over a proposed treaty on global warming. Despite a much-touted effort to revise the government's approach to regulation along lines many industries had been demanding, efforts to put across legislation for environmental cleanup (via a so-called Superfund) went nowhere, despite some significant business support.[29]

Though the Brady Bill and a compromise tax measured finally passed, a long series of defeats and scandals threw the administration into a tailspin. Clinton tried to quiet the firestorm by bringing in David Gergen, a Republican who had advised Ronald Reagan, as a special counselor. This won him plaudits from the press, who extolled the *USA Today* executive's communications skills and center-right impulses. But Gergen's communications skills left the general populace cold—the resident's polls did not move a jot (Ferguson 1995, 277). And they certainly did little to calm Republican attacks on the administration.

The Path to the Abyss—Down Tobacco Road

These were increasing rapidly. All the battles over taxes and regulation and the administration's occasional talk—it was just talk, though the Democrats then controlled both houses of Congress—of raising the minimum wage sent enormous, gushing streams of money from anxious businesses to the GOP. The sums involved were truly staggering. What is perhaps the best available index, the Federal Election Commission's final report on the two-year "cycle" leading up to the 1994 elections, takes no account of the millions of dollars' worth of "issue-oriented" advertising by the pharmaceuticals, insurers, and medical instrument companies. But it does indicate that total spending in congressional races was soaring—amounting to the record-breaking sum of $724 million, "with increased activity by Republican candidates . . . entirely responsible for the growth." Spending by the national parties, which the FEC tallies separately, was equally astronomical, amounting to more than $372 million—well above the $304 million reported in the 1989–90 off-year election cycle—again with a heavy GOP tilt.[30]

206

A rough calculation based on my sample of large concerns and investors for the 1996 election makes the point more starkly. Lumping together (most) firms in the pharmaceutical, insurance, and health care sectors with those in branches of industry most directly involved with the environmental concerns the administration was raising (paper, chemicals, etc.); and then adding in enterprises in firearms, and the retail and wholesale sectors (whose tumescent growth during recent merger waves had major political implications, since such firms are usually acutely sensitive to questions of minimum wages and mandated benefits), one arrives at the very conservative estimate that by the middle of his first term, the New Democrat, self-consciously pro-business Clinton administration was essentially at war with well over half of the largest investors in the United States. The sum total of opponents with less immediately drastic interests at stake, of course, would run far higher.

This calculation, however, leaves out of account one very special case: tobacco. Here, relations with the new administration were initially tense but rapidly became apocalyptic. Because the logic of this shift is central to understanding the most critical single episode in the long impeachment drama and because the oceans of ink spilled by the U.S. press on Kenneth Starr's investigation have unaccountably submerged the heart of the matter, the facts about the tobacco industry's long war with the Clinton administration require a careful look.[31]

Pressures on the big tobacco companies of course long antedated Bill Clinton's arrival in the White House. In the face of overwhelming evidence of smoking's deadly health effects and gigantic economic toll, even some Reagan appointees, such as Surgeon General C. Everett Koop, had occasionally spoken out against the industry. In the waning days of the Bush administration, the Environmental Protection Agency also began trying to rein in smoking in public places. Nevertheless, the industry's political efforts, which were massive—and quite bipartisan, though with an elective affinity to the GOP's laissez-faire traditions—gave it formidable protection. Though one of Clinton's first acts as president was to ban smoking in the White House, the evidence is that the administration was not then looking for a major confrontation. Dr. David Kessler, whom the administration retained as the head of a Food and Drug Administration already under siege from many other industries, only slowly decided to broaden the campaign against tobacco, which his agency traditionally had not sought to regulate.[32]

Several developments slowly changed this situation. An inevitable consequence of bringing together the advocates of sweeping health care reform was the bringing together of the advocates of a wider campaign against the tobacco industry, since the health care complex—including not only its professional but even some business components, such as insurance—is uniquely situated with respect to evaluating and developing new medical evidence. In addition, the logic of the administration's health plan ran sharply counter to the interests of the industry. As a proven cause of massive medical expenditures, the industry was naturally suspect. No less important, however, the industry was a vulnerable source of new tax revenues in a period when raising taxes was politically very costly. Indeed, to fund the health plan, the White House proposed a huge increase in excise taxes on cigarettes, from twenty-four cents a pack to ninety-nine cents.[33]

This proposal immediately sent the industry to battle stations. What happened next, however, moved the conflict—and in the end, American politics— to a whole new level of vehemence. Studies suggesting that smoking might fall sharply if nicotine were reduced persuaded the FDA's Kessler that nicotine might in fact qualify as an addictive substance in the technical, legal sense of the Food, Drug, and Cosmetic Act. This had sweeping implications, for regulating tobacco would then fall squarely within the FDA's purview. As one analyst (unconnected to the industry) put it, in part citing Kessler's own words:

> If the FDA successfully claims jurisdiction over tobacco, the agency could not only determine how much nicotine would be allowed in cigarettes but also how they are labeled, marketed and distributed. In short, the FDA would gain virtual control over cigarette production and could even totally ban tobacco products. FDA regulation "could mean, ultimately, removal from the market of tobacco products containing nicotine at levels that cause or satisfy addiction," Kessler wrote in February [1994]. "Only those tobacco products from which the nicotine had been removed or, possibly, tobacco products approved by the FDA . . . would then remain on the market."[34]

In the spring of 1994, Kessler testified to Congress that the industry had known for decades that nicotine was addictive and had hid that fact from the public. He also argued that tobacco companies had calibrated levels of nicotine in cigarettes to keep smokers hooked. Executives of the major tobacco companies responded in "an unprecedented joint appearance, insisting that nicotine levels are adjusted solely to enhance cigarette flavor and that they didn't think nicotine was addictive."[35]

Already at war with another of the administration's pivotal support groups, trial lawyers, whose proliferating suits were a major headache for the companies, the tobacco industry mobilized on a gigantic scale. Taking out full-page ads in newspapers and turning loose a legion of lobbyists, it fought back on many fronts. But while it succeeded in scaling back the proposed cigarette tax even before the Clinton health care plan's fiery crash landing, the industry's efforts to ward off the FDA were unavailing.

At the end of June talk of the industry's sweeping campaign and possible compromises surfaced in the national press. In July, however, the *New England Journal of Medicine* brought out a major study by two researchers whose previous work, according to the *Washington Post*, "had been heavily relied on by the FDA." The new study, which the *Post* suggested "also could prove influential" in shaping a forthcoming report by an FDA advisory panel, presented a case for compelling cigarette makers to reduce the nicotine content of their products by about five-sixths over a period of years. The newspaper report noted that the study's authors readily conceded that such proposals "might seem drastic to some." Quoting an FDA spokesperson's praise for the report as providing "the kind of information that the advisory committee will be working with in August," the story reported that the FDA group planned to begin hearings into "nicotine addiction and dosage" on the first of August.[36]

That report, and an accompanying denunciation by the Tobacco Institute, appeared in the *Post* on July 14, 1994. That very day, Jesse Helms and Lauch Faircloth, the two very conservative Republican senators from the state with the biggest stake of all in tobacco, North Carolina, met Judge David Sentelle for lunch in Washington. Sentelle, like Faircloth (who had once headed North Carolina Democrats for Helms before switching parties and winning election to the Senate) a Helms protégé, had formerly chaired the Republican Party of Mecklenburg County there. He had also served as a delegate to the 1984 Republican Convention from the Tarheel State and named one of his daughters "Reagan" in honor of the President.[37]

Because of a quirk in the law governing special prosecutors, Sentelle had recently regained a position of extraordinary sensitivity. In early 1992, as Special Prosecutor Lawrence Walsh's investigation of the Iran-Contra neared its climax, Chief Justice William D. Rehnquist had suddenly named the very junior Sentelle to replace moderate Republican Judge George MacKinnon as head of the three-judge panel that supervised special prosecutors. Subsequently, however, the law had lapsed; thus when the Whitewater scandal first burst upon the American political scene, Attorney General Janet Reno had named the first special prosecutor, Republican Robert Fiske. Thanks to the reinstated statute, Sentelle and his two other colleagues once again had authority over investigations by special prosecutors. Faircloth and Sentelle subsequently denied that the then widely discussed Whitewater investigation figured as a topic at their lunch. Soon thereafter, however, Sentelle's panel rejected Janet Reno's request that Fiske be allowed to continue and replaced him with Kenneth Starr.[38]

The appointment was a milestone, in many senses. Starr worked in the Washington office of Kirkland & Ellis, a prominent corporate law firm. Among other clients, he represented the tobacco industry; he was also peripherally involved in friend-of-the-court activities on behalf of the lawsuit filed by Paula Jones against the president. Subsequently, while conducting his investigation of the president, he continued to do legal work for Brown & Williamson, a leading tobacco firm.[39]

As his investigation proceeded, the battle between the industry and the Clinton administration escalated. One careful, though necessarily incomplete, attempt to estimate total contributions by the industry in American national politics noted that in the 1991–92 election cycle contributions by the industry totaled at least $5.7 million, of which about 57 percent went to Republican candidates for president or Congress. Total contributions during the 1993–94 election cycle—the Clinton administration's first two years—ran at roughly the same level despite the absence of a presidential campaign (which normally swells expenditure levels), while the percentage of contributions in favor of the *then completely out of power* GOP rose to 68. Thereafter, both total contributions and the percentage in favor of GOP candidates exploded, while Democratic campaign rhetoric increasingly singled out tobacco for special attention.

In the 1995–96 election cycle, the tobacco industry donated over $10 million to national political campaigns, with over 80 percent of the funds headed for Republicans. Incomplete figures for the 1997–98 cycle (which again, does not include a presidential campaign) show the industry giving more than $7 million, with about 78 percent of that going to GOP candidates. Lobbying expenses, it should be noted, normally run many times the level of an industry's formal political contributions.[40]

The 1994 Election and the Wall of Money

By the fall of 1994, the administration's political position was desperate, though most analysts underestimated the gravity of the situation. The failure of the much-touted health plan and the president's earlier refusal to stimulate the economy left the administration with little to point to that would easily impress ordinary voters. Indeed, polls taken as the off-year elections approached indicated that as many as half of all voters were unable to name even one achievement of the Clinton administration. Though many aggregate economic statistics suggested a recovery of respectable dimensions, complaints about the weak, "jobless" recovery multiplied. This was not simply hype: some analysts suggest that in 1994 as many as four out of every five households may well have been worse off than they had been in 1989, before the start of the recession that cost George Bush his job.[41]

The most immediate threat, however, came from another quarter: A dual squeeze was developing on the administration's supply of campaign finance. While its opponents anted up at breakneck pace, some of Clinton's most important allies were closing their checkbooks. After more than a half a century, the tectonic plates of American political life appeared on the verge of an epochal shift. Wall Street, which in 1992—as in many other presidential elections—had provided a plenary share of funds for the Democratic candidate, was abandoning the party.

This event—it was really a process—cast a shadow over everything the administration subsequently attempted. In all probability, it was also the final cause of the fund-raising scandals that subsequently convulsed the White House and the Democratic National Committee. But for peculiar reasons it all but disappears from the aggregate data presented in the FEC's final report on the 1996 presidential election. It becomes visible only if one carefully reconstructs the flow of funds within the usual reporting cycle.

In the background, probably, were several long-running trends—chiefly, the rise of mutual funds and the expanding importance of individual portfolio accounts; perhaps also the declining importance of some classical issues of financial regulation, such as the Glass-Steagall Act, which separated investment from commercial banking. What abruptly brought matters to a head in early 1994, however, were two fresh developments. The first was the administration's running battle to roll back the Japanese trade surplus and open Japanese markets to American producers. Exasperated by what they regarded as Japanese stonewalling, the Clinton economic team began trying to "talk down the dollar" (i.e., talk up the yen) in February 1994. The idea, which was immensely appealing to American producers of automobiles, semiconductors, telecommunications, and other tradable goods, was to make Japanese wares so expensive that Japan would have to open up out of sheer self-preservation.[42]

This strategy, however, implied a sharp drop, at least for a time, in the international value of the dollar. In New York financial circles, notions of this sort are pure poison. No matter how clever and intricate arguments from pure economic theory may occasionally be, international financial centers are generally unwilling to risk sustained declines in their currencies. Too many asset holders and traders start shifting out, with the perceived risk of the currency's irrevocable decline rising sharply the longer such episodes continue and the more frequent they become.

That the administration's shift caught much of Wall Street off guard added fuel to the fire. Some houses that had bet the wrong way briefly endured spectacular losses and sold out of bonds they had bought on credit. After central banks around the world began raising interest rates (or, as in the case of the Bundesbank, signaled an unwillingness to continue lowering them), havoc spread to many other bond markets.[43]

The second factor in Wall Street's estrangement from the Clinton administration grew out of the search for scapegoats that followed the turmoil in world financial markets. With some encouragement from rival financial concerns and regulatory authorities in and out of the United States, congressional Democrats (who then controlled Congress) briefly held hearings into so-called hedge funds (offshore vehicles for wealthy investors that frequently augment their own very considerable resources by borrowing). Though this effort was soon abandoned, the damage was done. Importuned by Democratic National Committee officials to open their wallets, Wall Street's Masters of the Universe nearly all refused. Some even walked out of earlier six-figure pledges. The immediate result was a sharp drop, many months before most Americans had ever heard of Newt Gingrich or the "Contract with America," in the pace of DNC soft-money receipts at precisely the moment they should have been rising.[44]

The Gingrich "Revolution": Big Business from Small Business?

The media firestorm that followed the GOP's takeover of the Congress in 1994 suggested that some new, elemental political force had mysteriously risen up—perhaps from the grass roots—to overpower existing political structures. A common theme, nourished by the GOP leadership itself, was that the new GOP coalition represented a coalescence of the forces of "small business."[45]

This is pure propaganda. As part of a survey of "early money" in the 1996 election, I examined who among my sample of America's largest firms and the Forbes 400 richest Americans donated to Gingrich or a handful of fund-raising vehicles that he directly controlled during 1995 and early 1996.

Though one has to be cautious about comparing apples with oranges (the Speaker was, after all, only a prospective candidate for the top spot), some pat-

TABLE 11.2
Industries within Big Business above Average in Support
for Newt Gingrich

(Mean = 21%, N = 875)	
Pharmaceuticals	47% (0.02[a])
N = 17	
Insurance	37% (0.01)
N = 43	
Oil and gas	28% (0.21)
N = 53	
Aircraft	36% (0.19[a])
N = 14	
Chemicals	32% (0.17)
N = 28	
Trucking/ground trans.	41% (0.07[a])
N = 17	
Accounting	50% (0.11[a])
N = 6	
Tobacco	50% (0.20[a])
N = 4	
Glass	60% (0.07[a])
N = 5	

Source: Calculated from FEC data as described in text.

Note: Numbers in parentheses are significance levels.

[a]Expected value of cell in chi-square less than 5 is warning of low power.
Significance levels reported in such cases are results of Fisher's Exact Test.
Period covered is "early money" for 1995–96, as in text.

terns are so obvious they scarcely require comment. As Table 11.2 indicates, the Speaker's strongest supporters came from precisely those sectors indicated earlier as the eye of the anti-Clinton hurricane: pharmaceuticals, insurers, and firms in sectors where environmental regulation is a high priority, notably chemicals. Gingrich, who has in the past been closely associated with various firms, notably in metal fabrication, with obvious labor problems, also drew support from parts of manufacturing recently marked by some high-profile labor disputes.[46]

A segment of Wall Street that strongly champions lower taxes, deregulation, and privatization was also very enthusiastic. Among retailers and wholesalers who contributed to Republicans, support for Gingrich was relatively strong, though his overall level of backing from these sectors was not as strong as, for example, Robert Dole, who later, as Senate Majority Leader in 1996, at one point refused even to permit a vote on legislation to raise the minimum wage.[47] Some firms in the transportation sector were also prominent (most notably ground transportation firms, such as those in trucking, but also including Atlanta-based Delta), where an interest in (de-)regulation seems patent.

The Georgia congressman also drew relatively heavy backing from segments of the oil industry. Some of this perhaps reflected routine policy considerations, such as environmental regulation, where the Speaker championed positions popular with the industry. But Gingrich, whose famous "Contract with America" contained a little-noted clause advocating a rapid expansion of NATO to the East and who vigorously promoted projection of American power on the periphery of the former Soviet Union, also received support from a number of the multinationals most deeply involved in the titanic struggle already underway for control of Transcaucasian oil, including Amoco, Chevron, and Mobil. The same question of how much influence Russia will finally wield over its former dependencies was also of burning interest to another constituency that then strongly supported the Speaker—the defense industry, whose increasingly vital export business can hope to flourish only where links to former Russian military suppliers are broken.[48]

But while the Super Speaker was unlikely ever to run out of money, his position was not impregnable. Though for most of 1995 the mass media pretended otherwise (just as they had with Ronald Reagan during the 1980s), the evidence from even the earliest polls was conclusive that the Republican agenda was not popular with voters. If the president could somehow contrive to stave off challenges from inside his own party and raise the funds for a counterattack, Gingrich and the GOP were vulnerable.[49]

The Comeback Kid

Though virtually no one noticed, Bill Clinton began his long climb out of the crypt by breaking the hold the Republicans were attempting to establish on contributions from two powerful constituencies: defense and oil.

A few weeks after the 1994 election, as pundits vied with one another to write off his chances for reelection, the president surprised everyone by declaring in favor of increased defense spending. With the United States already spending more on defense than the next six countries in the world combined, and polls showing that the public ranks military spending at the very bottom of its list of new spending priorities, this step made little sense in electoral terms. Brushing aside doubts expressed by the foreign policy establishment and the military, the administration also loudly advertised its devotion to rapid NATO expansion.[50]

Leapfrogging congressional Republicans, who were beginning to tout the former Soviet Republic of Georgia as a vital U.S. interest, the administration also threw its weight behind the American oil firms negotiating over rights in Transcaucasia. Though constrained by its strong commitment to the Yeltsin regime (which, as the eminently conservative *Frankfurter Allgemeine* observed, appears to have ordered its troops into Chechnya in response to an oil exploration agreement struck between Azerbaijan and a multinational consortium of oil firms involving several large U.S. firms), the Clinton team moved on several fronts at once. The United States intensified its already close relations with Turkey, which holds a pivotal position in the region. Clinton also personally telephoned the president of Azerbaijan to win support for a pipeline leading down through Georgia and eventually through Turkey, instead of one running only through Russian-controlled territory. American diplomats also backed Chevron in its struggle for a mammoth oil concession in Kazakhstan. The White House also vigorously promoted expansion of American exports abroad, in many instances apparently linking its support to contributions to the DNC.[51]

By the middle of 1995, this "multinational pork barrel" strategy was bringing some real advantages to the president. Though he continued to languish in the polls, Clinton and his advisers had begun taking the initiative away from Gingrich and the GOP, in a way that plainly paid off in a modest number of campaign contributions and applause—at first grudging, but eventually much warmer—from foreign policy elites.

Not surprisingly, the Clinton team soon experimented with activist strategies in other areas. Earlier inhibitions about deploying U.S. power abroad abruptly disappeared. In spite of the Somalian fiasco, the administration committed U.S. troops to Bosnia and Haiti. It helped mediate conflicts in Northern Ireland. In the face of major pressures from parts of the Pentagon and the more hawkish parts of the foreign policy establishment, the White House negotiated to de-escalate tensions with North Korea. And acutely aware that any more tremors in Mexico could shake its own reelection chances, the administration followed up its famous bailout with vigilant, if carefully modulated, support for the hard-pressed government of President Ernesto Zedillo.

Transforming the world into an electoral Potemkin Village, however, hardly sufficed to secure renomination, let alone reelection. To secure these, two additional steps were required. First, the president needed to amass a much larger war chest, both to scare off potential Democratic challengers and to pay for an advertising blitz as elections approached. Second, some way to dramatize Clinton's differences with Gingrich had to be contrived that would not frighten off potential investors in the campaign. In 1995, reconciling these two contradictory imperatives was an even taller order than usual. As one Clinton adviser confessed to the *Philadelphia Inquirer* in August 1995, "Lately we've been cowed into the position of not sticking up for working people, because we've been looking increasingly to wealthy interests in order to fund our campaign. You end up spending time with wealthy people who say, 'Let's not make this a *class* thing.'"[52]

Gifts from the East

The administration's struggle to crack open Japanese markets set off distress flares around the world. Criticism of the administration's new course was fierce—from financiers and multinationals concerned about threats to the world trading system; from the immense "Japan lobby"; from other countries, which sometimes moved to seize trading advantages from the situation. Over time, these pressures mounted. Alarms sounded that some Asian central banks were selling dollars and that members of OPEC were exploring the idea of pricing oil in some other currency. Some Europeans ostentatiously dramatized their efforts to forge a common currency less dependent on the dollar. The Japanese, who had for some time been repatriating funds from the United

States to shore up balance sheets at home, also reportedly rattled American policymakers with veiled threats to increase the pace of their bond sales.[53]

Though pure economic theory suggests that the administration's anxieties were overblown, there is no doubt that fears of Japanese bond sales weighed on American policymakers, as did fears of a complete meltdown of the Japanese economy. It is also clear, however, that the administration was not getting the political benefits it might reasonably have expected. Though the Semi-Conductor Industries Association and similar groups mostly cheered the policy, Silicon Valley wanted still more—above all, legislation limiting investors' rights to sue. But this demand put them on a collision course with another constituency that funneled millions of dollars into the Democratic Party—trial lawyers. White House hesitations translated into Silicon Valley reservations: In my sample of early money in the 1996 election (covering all of 1995 and the first couple of months of 1996), computers and software contributed virtually nothing to Clinton (compare Table 11.3).[54]

Most of the auto industry, which the administration made other special efforts to support, also hung back. In the early giving in 1995, most major executives opted for Republican Robert Dole, a likely challenger of the president's. It cannot have helped either that while during much of this period the dollar was indeed weak against the financial key currencies (deutsche mark and yen), it was high or rising against several of the United States' largest trading partners, such as Mexico and Canada.[55]

Not surprisingly, in the late spring of 1995 the administration declared victory and reversed course. It struck a deal with the Japanese calling for improved market access and additional purchases of American auto parts. Well-informed observers in both Japan and the United States also suggest that the accord embraced an understanding for continued Japanese purchases of Amer-

TABLE 11.3
Industries Significantly above the Mean in "Early Money" Support
for Clinton, Plus Investment Banking, 1995–1996

(Mean = 19%, N = 875)	
Telecommunications N = 62	42% (0.00)
Oil and gas N = 53	30% (0.05)
Aircraft N = 14	57% (0.00[a])
Accounting N = 6	50% (0.09[a])
Investment banking	26% (0.27)

Source: Calculated from FEC data as described in text.

Note: Numbers in parentheses are significance levels.

[a]Expected value of cell in chi-square less than 5 is warning of low power. Significance levels reported in such cases are results of Fisher's Exact Test

See also text, note 40, on tobacco.

ican bonds. These would help stabilize the U.S. bond market (thus keeping interest rates low) as the election approached. The Federal Reserve also struck a formal agreement with the Bank of Japan to keep American government bonds from coming on the market in cases of distress selling by Japanese firms.[56]

With the regularity of a *Glockenspiel*, Rubin and other members of the Clinton economic team thereafter began issuing pronouncements that the United States would welcome a stronger dollar. But my survey of early money indicates that neither this belated profession of faith nor even the Mexican bailout immediately turned Wall Street around. Instead the fallout from 1994 lingered. In my sample of "early money" for the 1996 election, the level of Clinton's contributions from investment houses was statistically indistinguishable from average—virtually the same rate, in fact, at which Michael Dukakis, without any of the advantages of White House incumbency, had raked in contributions at a comparable stage of the 1988 primary campaign.

But my sample for this industry is rather small and breaks the data into only two periods, determined more by accident than by design.[57] A much sharper focus on the stages of Wall Street's rapprochement with the Clinton campaign can be derived by analyzing data kindly supplied me by the Center for Responsive Politics. The Center undertakes the Sisyphean task of actually identifying all individual contributors to both parties. Center researchers are well aware of the pitfalls of such identifications (which are some of the reasons why I generally stick with my own survey practice, which begins from lists of known executives from large firms for analyzing political coalitions). But the Center's data include the dates of each contribution. That and the fact that these data are compiled quite independently of any theory of mine make them an excellent vehicle for my purposes here.[58]

Table 11.4 displays the key points. First, the rate at which contributions poured in from investment bankers differed sharply from the rate at which the rest of the sample contributed. There is a clear trend in the data: the rate of giving increased markedly over the course of 1995, eventually taking off like a rocket. Something, or some things, evidently happened that persuaded investment houses to loosen their wallets to the Democrats again. Was the dramatic change in U.S. policy to Japan a factor? In assessing this, it is well to remember that the abandonment of the high yen policy was more a process than an event, for it involved agreements in several different policy areas. A truce had to be negotiated in the noisy "auto war," but also two financial agreements (only one of them formal) were struck: an agreement between the Fed and the Bank of Japan to prevent Treasuries sold by the Bank of Japan in conditions of financial exigency from depressing the rest of the market and the celebrated "understanding" about continued Japanese bond purchases of U.S. bonds. Integral to all of these were policy changes designed to stimulate the Japanese economy at home.

All these events occurred in the first nine months of 1995, but they did not happen all at once. Perhaps the best-known part of the package, the understanding on auto parts and cars, came to a public climax in late June, though the basic policy change had to be in the planning stage not later than May, as U.S.

TABLE 11.4
Investment Banker Money to Rest of Clinton Campaign, 1995–1996

	Investment Banking $	Total $	Percent
Jan. 95	0	238,102	0.0
Feb. 95	25,250	954,500	2.6
Mar. 95	25,750	1,126,071	2.3
Apr. 95	38,750	2,114,683	1.8
May 95	93,725	1,879,783	5.0
June 95	491,199	8,862,055	5.5
July 95	75,250	1,674,231	4.5
Aug. 95	13,750	1,670,613	0.8
Sep. 95	217,134	6,815,426	3.2
Oct. 95	221,250	3,960,230	5.6
Nov. 95	472,799	5,241,075	9.0
Dec. 95	194,383	4,947,306	3.9
Jan. 96	203,500	1,906,316	10.7
Feb. 96	291,000	3,047,384	9.5
Mar. 96	319,860	5,154,099	6.2
Apr. 96	476,150	9,670,797	4.9
May 96	508,356	8,579,509	5.9
June 96	779,000	7,964,862	9.8
July 96	502,419	7,053,710	7.1
Aug. 96	356,850	5,393,603	6.6
Sep.96	252,050	8,412,803	3.0
Oct. 96	520,653	7,639,490	6.8
Nov. 96	88,000	3,854,523	2.3
Dec. 96	84,700	304,421	27.8

Source: FEC, as reworked by Center for Responsive Politics.

officials laid their plans for the upcoming G7 summit.[59] The financial parts of the accord appear to have been concluded slightly later (though at least the Fed-BOJ agreement had surely been under consideration since the spring, when anxieties about the Japanese financial system ran rife), while the Japanese moved clearly to stimulate their economy (with, eventually, only modest success) in late summer after the ruling LDP suffered losses in an election.[60] Depending on precisely what one believes about elite perceptions in this tumultuous period, one could envision a range of points in which it would make sense to divide the time series into two and test to see if the respective segments exhibit statistically significant differences. Probably the first plausible point would be in late April, when the yen began depreciating (rather rapidly in parts of May). The last might be in late summer, when the Japanese were obviously trying to reflate at least a bit. The striking point is this, however. No matter how one divides the time series, all plausible statistical tests for differences between two periods (t-tests, or any of several nonparametric tests, such as the Mann-Whitney U, Kolmogorov-Smirnov Z, or Wald-Wolfowitz) yield the same answer. The results appear truly robust. Substantial differences between the two data series persist, however they are defined. (Note that the Center was unable to identify a single contribution to the Clinton campaign in the month of January 1995—this from the sector that led the president's fund-raising in 1992 and that of so many other leading Democrats in years past!). Hypothesizing a lag (or lags), for the policy change to become truly credible to many investment bankers just adds realism: The money really began to roll in during the winter of 1995–96, most probably as time lent credibility to Rubin's policy pronouncements. But that was a half a year or so later.[61]

In the meantime, the White House struggled to cope with the nightmare scenario of American politicians—the prospect of running low on money in the midst of a battle with powerful, lavishly financed opponents. Some of the 1995 shortfall appears to have been made up by firms in industries the White House was clearly courting, notably oil and, especially, defense. Firms involved in various Commerce Department export schemes also appear to have helped out. Additional funds also arrived from trial lawyers, particularly as Clinton made up his mind to veto proposed legislation curbing lawsuits. A comparatively modest amount of money also arrived from unions. (Union donations amounted to approximately 10 percent of the DNC's soft money accounts for the 1995–96 election cycle. On the other hand, union contributions bulked considerably larger in some congressional campaigns, and the AFL-CIO also waged a sizable drive around "issues" nominally unconnected to the election. In the general election, unions also mounted important "get out the vote" drives.) [62]

Though details are likely to remain shrouded in darkness for all sorts of reasons—including Justice Department foot dragging, strong instincts for self-preservation on the part of key witnesses (some of whom disappeared for long stretches into China or other parts of East Asia), and fears among foreign policy elites in both parties that the China connection is too important to become a political football—it certainly appears that for the Clinton campaign, the East was green. For many years, influential American business groups have sponsored or informally encouraged entrepreneurial organization among immigrants and ethnic groups—if not, perhaps, West Coast Buddhist cults—as a form of bridge-building to foreign business communities. And both major political parties have recurrently sought support and funds from abroad. In 1995, the East Asian trade surpluses comprised one of the largest pools of liquidity in the world, and the Clinton administration was putting in play the whole question of trade with Asia. Considering that, as the U.S. government a few years later for its own reasons would come to remind us, Asian capitalism is extensively crony capitalism, the real surprise would be that the White House and DNC did not look there for money.[63]

In the last stages of the '96 campaign, part of Silicon Valley did finally come to support the president. Though small numbers preclude any credible statistical tests (and keep the industry as a whole out of my Table 11.5), the identities of the larger firms are striking indeed: executives from Netscape, Oracle, and Digital—all firms in intense rivalry with giant Microsoft, which stood to gain immensely from the now celebrated antitrust suit the Clinton Justice Department brought right after the election. High-tech support snowballed after Clinton reversed course and came out in favor of a California referendum lim-

TABLE 11.5
Industries Significantly above the Mean in Support for Clinton,
1995–1996 as a Whole

(Mean = 29%, N = 875)	
Telecommunications	53% (0.00)
N = 62	
Investment banking	45% (0.03)
N = 38	
Oil and gas	40% (0.08)
N = 53	
Aircraft	86% (0.00[a])
N = 14	
Accounting	83% (0.00[a])
N = 6	
Beverages	56% (0.02[a])
N = 16	
Transportation—Airlines	60% (0.04[a])
N = 10	
Glass	80% (0.03[a])
N = 5	

Source: Calculated from FEC data as described in text.

Note: Numbers in parentheses are significance levels.

[a]Expected value of cell in chi-square less than 5 is warning of low power.
Significance levels reported in such cases are results of Fisher's Exact Test.

iting shareholder suits. Wall Street, too, eventually pitched in, as Table 11.5 indicates. But public exposure of "Asian" and other foreign sources of Democratic fund-raising (including Latin America and the Middle East) assuredly put a crimp into any hopes the White House entertained of turning the whole world into a campaign cash machine. Thus it was that the best-kept secret of the 1996 election became the grand coalition forged of necessity between the White House and Mickey Mouse—that is, much of the telecommunications sector.[64]

Considering that as the race got underway, well-informed observers were confidently predicting that the lion's (or, perhaps, the Lion King's) share of contributions from this quarter would go inevitably to someone like Senator Robert Dole, this outcome is remarkable. In my sample of large firms, this then staggeringly profitable sector (which I treat as distinct from both the computer and software industries) stands out in its support for Clinton: Within my survey of "early money" some 42 percent of the firms contributed to the president's reelection campaign either through individual contributions from top executives or via soft money.[65]

This is a level matched by no other comparably large industry. And the level of contributions from individual concerns is sometimes remarkable. Over the course of 1995, for example, Miramax, a Disney subsidiary, alone contributed more than $250,000 to the DNC's soft-money accounts, while various Disney executives made personal donations to the Clinton campaign. By the end of the campaign, according to one estimate, total contributions by the Disney organization to the Democrats totaled over a million dollars.[66]

The reasons for such generosity are not complicated, though one could spin whole books out of details and qualifications that must perforce be neglected here. Hollywood, cable TV, over-the-air ("network") free television, book publishers, news concerns, radio stations, computer companies, software establishments, and phone companies had all separately been making vast sums of money for many years. By 1993–94, however, changes in technology (particularly the so-called digital compression revolution, which makes it possible to cram many more TV channels into homes with minimal new investment in equipment) and regulatory practice were bringing these industries together at an explosive pace.[67]

Virtually everyone was on fire to capture huge "synergies" from using TV and magazines to push movies that would sell books that would promote videos that would send droves of paying customers rushing to buy other "tied in" products from proprietary theme parks, toy stores, retail houses, restaurant chains and on-line home shopping networks. The result was a merger frenzy and massive pressure for sweeping changes in law and regulatory policy.[68]

With visions of sugar plums dancing in their heads, but enormous uncertainty about which technologies would ultimately prove out, almost everyone wanted legal rights to get into everyone else's (often, though not invariably, highly regulated) business. The administration's point men for telecommunications, Vice President Al Gore and his long-time associate, Federal Communications Commission Chair Reed Hundt, were not in principle opposed to such demands. "Competition" after all, was the public name of the New Democratic game.

As the Microsoft trial eventually demonstrated, however, the real game was still monopoly, with winning moves typically constructed out of subtle combinations of economies of scale, adroit legal and regulatory maneuvers, and technological virtuosity, not least in software. The initial charge for what became the Telecommunications Act of 1996 was led mostly by congressional Republicans, on behalf of the regional Bells and a handful of other companies responsible for local telephone service. The phone companies wanted the right to sell long-distance services currently offered by so-called long-line companies such as AT&T, Sprint, and MCI. Having long ago wired up nearly every home in America (and, as a result, looking at big bills for modernizing their systems with coaxial or fiber optic cable), they thought it was only natural that they should also be allowed to compete for subscribers with cable TV companies and even go into programming. Since their specialty was communication, they also saw no reason why they should not be allowed to offer wireless telephone and data services.[69]

After the cable companies won a promise of rate deregulation, they mostly fell in behind the proposed legislation. Early (largely Republican) versions of the bill, however, alarmed many producers of "content," including notably, many media companies whose core businesses often included news gathering and transmission. These latter were generally enthusiastic about provisions raising the ceiling on the number of stations they were allowed to own and weakening restrictions on cross ownership of other forms of media. But they feared that the Bells could use their huge cash flows from their regulated "captive" local phone customers to endlessly subsidize new lines of business. They were also alarmed by prospects of mergers between phone and cable companies. Like the long-line companies, they were apprehensive that the Bells would only grudgingly open up their systems to rivals.

These big media concerns accordingly joined with the long-line companies to battle the bill. Other broadcasters also weighed in, happy to support raising the ceiling on channel ownership, but also anxious to safeguard how their programs and software (the "menus" from which viewers choose) would be displayed on channels controlled by their rivals.[70]

In the end the Clinton administration's notion of appropriate "competition" reflected a relatively keen awareness of the danger that horizontally integrated ("monopoly") owners of lines running into the house (and wireless services) might abuse their privileged access to squeeze the content producers and the long-line service providers. By contrast, Clinton, Gore, Hundt & Co. appeared much less anxious about the dangers of Hollywood's integrating vertically with networks or cable concerns (as, for example, in the "mega-merger" of Time-Warner with Turner Communications). Only rarely troubled by concerns about public access, they did not appear to lose sleep over the possibility that news organizations and other content producers may profit substantially from economies of scale, so that distinctions between, for example, web sites and television networks, are unlikely soon to disappear.

The Clinton administration—which did not have firm control of the FCC and of course did not control Congress after 1994—thus tilted away from the Bells, among whose champions happened to be one Robert Dole, and the cable companies, in the direction of the sometimes conflicting interests of Hollywood; the networks (which produce vast amounts of programming); and the newspapers (though not radio stations, whose campaign to lift all ownership restrictions was linked closely with GOP congressional interests). In part thanks to White House efforts, the final version of the bill was much kinder to the content providers, though virtually everybody won some outcome important to them, and the Bells and GTE were regarded by some equity analysts as having come off best of all.

With the passage of the Telecommunications Act in early 1996, the action shifted to the FCC, which must issue new regulations to implement the law, and to battles over questions of "intellectual property" at home and abroad. Here again, the administration favored the large content providers. It firmly rejected suggestions that the FCC be abolished, as suggested by policy analysts close to Gingrich, or its role greatly reduced, as Senator Dole urged. Both of these prescriptions, like recent policy proposals floated by some Brookings analysts in the name of "competition," would probably make it much easier for local oligopolies to emerge via mergers of all "incoming wires," which might threaten even big, vertically integrated producers of content. The Justice Department also promised strict antitrust scrutiny of proposed phone company mergers.[71]

The administration also pushed along another bill, what might be termed the "Great Brain Robbery." This legislation aimed to tighten enforcement of royalties and copyrights on the Internet as well as over air, and sharply cut back traditional rights of "fair use." The draft bill would also have made owners of on-line systems responsible for copyright abuses by network users. And of course, for the producers of content, and no one else, the administration was willing to go the wall—the Great Wall—and threaten sanctions on the Chinese if they did not cease pirating that sector's products (videotapes, CDs, etc.).[72]

The Unmaking of the Co-President, 1995

Within the Democratic Party, the Clinton strategy of winning through intimidation worked very well. With contributions racing far ahead of the president's standing in the polls, potential Democratic challengers first paused and assayed their wallets. Then they thought better of the whole idea.

Unlike the left wing of the Democratic Party, however, Gingrich and the Republicans were never going to run out of money. As the Speaker roared through American public life like the White Tornado during most of 1995, many wondered when he would tire of playing "co-president" and turn the cyclonic energies of his movement for a "New American Revolution" down the road to the White House. Though the Speaker was coy, repeated visits to New Hampshire indicated he was evaluating his options.

In the end, however, the White House triumphed. What finally turned the tide was a dual strategy. To square the circle and satisfy both investors and potential voters, the president first broad-jumped to the right yet again, and endorsed the Republican goal of balancing the budget. The White House also began tiptoeing around the question of privatizing Social Security.[73]

Brushing aside the cuts that his own budget plan entailed after the 1996 election, the president spotlighted areas where his budget priorities clashed with those of the Republicans: health, education, Medicare and Medicaid, the environment. This sudden willingness to stand "firm" was not motivated purely by moral principle: Reductions in Medicare and Medicaid involve not just patients, but the medical industrial complex, which was willing to fight (and help pay) to defend the program. Fearful that the White House might fold completely, lobbyists for the National Education Association (whose organizational network probably matters more in presidential campaigns than its money) also warned the White House not to take its support for granted.[74]

As is usual when the Democrats stand up for something that the population wants, the strategy worked. Clinton refused further compromises on the budget. Instead he dared Gingrich and the GOP to shut down the government. Delighted to dramatize their differences with the president, Gingrich and the Republicans plunged ahead. They refused to pass a budget the president would sign. For a few heady days, they brought all but essential government functions to a screeching halt. But the consequences of living the fantasy of so many on the right were disastrous. With even *Time* wounding heels (on a notorious cover), Gingrich abruptly became radioactive. His poll ratings, never high, tumbled still further. Public impressions of Congress and the GOP nosedived.

Trying to Be Right and President

As Gingrich went down, disappointment in some parts of American big business was almost palpable. Talk about a "vacuum" in the GOP grew louder. This was not just media hype: While total contributions in the early stages of the '96 campaign ran well ahead of 1992, my survey of "early money" among large investors indicates that this group's average level of contributions to GOP candidates, though still quite high and far above that for Bill Clinton, was down appreciably from comparable stages of past races—probably more than could be explained by the simple fact that the Democrats now controlled the White House. In some industries—for example, computers and software—the fall-off in the rate of contributions was remarkable. In the absence of any plausible business reason (profits were doing fine) for the drop, it is hard not to suspect that with Gingrich out of the race, the remaining front-runner—for most of 1995, Senator Robert Dole—simply did not excite many leading business figures.[75]

The reasons why are subtle, and worth exploring, since they throw valuable light on the continuing GOP war against Clinton. If Bob Dole had been running for president in the fifties, sixties, or seventies, he might well have been a dream candidate of the GOP's center-right. With his longtime ties to agriculture, food, and commodities (and advisers like former Agriculture Secretary Clayton Yeutter and Robert Ellsworth, long a key figure in German-American relations), few could doubt that the senator from Kansas, a major grain-exporting state, was at heart a free trader unlikely to rock establishment boats. On the other hand, like Clinton, Dole had long since moved to accommodate the increasing demand within big business for more aggressive pursuit of American commercial interests. Robert Lighthizer, a key campaign adviser and lightning rod for suspicious free traders, was a director of the Economic Strategy Institute and a leading trade lawyer for firms bringing complaints before the International Trade Commission.[76]

A known champion of budgetary balance and fiscal orthodoxy, Dole also had many friends on Wall Street, in houses such as Smith Barney and Merrill Lynch. Until Steve Forbes finally entered the fray, Dole worked dutifully at expanding this network by courting skeptical supply-siders. For example, his insistence on going back to the old dollar/peso rate, as many supply-siders in the investment community urged, helped produce the stalemate among Republicans that led to the GOP leadership's failure to muster enough votes to win congressional approval of the Mexican bailout.[77]

Dole had also staked out some of the high ground in the hottest sector in the American political economy. Deeply involved in the revision of telecommunications law, Dole garnered far more contributions from this sector than any other GOP candidate. Though data sets like mine are not perfectly adapted for analyzing sometimes minute intra-industry differences, it is obvious that the Bells were ringing for Dole, while broadcasters were much chillier. Just before the bill cleared Congress, Dole openly attacked the Clinton administration and the broadcast networks for their plan to lend the networks, and no one else, additional free channels during the transition to high definition TV. Earlier, of course, he had picked the famous fight over rap lyrics and TV content with Time-Warner.[78]

He had also gone out of his way to court the GOP's vast constituency of low-wage employers, in sectors like retailing and fast food, by aggressively battling the Democrats when they finally—after they had lost control of Congress and faced a presidential election—moved to raise the minimum wage. The longtime champion of the insurance industry also had roundly inveighed against the Clinton health care program.[79]

Still, many on the right mistrusted Dole. They suspected that at heart he was a closet "moderate." Supply-siders doubted that the longtime member of the Senate Finance Committee shared their goals of rapidly shrinking taxes and government. Dubious about his penchant for striking deals, many free-market champions of smaller government also looked askance at the legions of "special interests" that were lining up behind the Kansan in search of particular benefits, such as the tobacco industry, casinos, the Gallo family, Carl Lindner, Archer-Daniels-Midland, etc. Some even feared that Dole, who was himself partially disabled from a war wound and who had championed the Americans with Disabilities Act, might be soft on some health care issues. And though Dole was as committed as anyone in the party to spending on weapons and the military, his longtime ties to Armenian national groups in the United States occasionally attracted comment. (Squeezed between Russia, and its ancient enemy, Turkey, the Armenian government generally tries to cooperate with the colossus to its north. In contrast to earlier bids for the White House, this time Dole did not do especially well within the oil industry. It is perhaps of interest that a number of foreign policy strategists have publicly rued what they believe is the excessive influence wielded over U.S. policy toward Transcaucasia by American national groups from the region.)[80]

The result was that within the GOP, Dole's support base strongly resembled the Pecos River: a mile wide, but only inches deep (Table 11.6). The obvious lack of enthusiasm, along with the active hostility from many on the right, tantalized potential GOP challengers. They could see plainly that for many of their colleagues, including many big-ticket investors, the Senate Majority Leader who threatened to block a vote on raising the minimum wage was still not far enough on the *right*.

Because Dole not only raised money like a fifties Republican, but spent like one, his campaign might have faced real trouble if he had had to make it all the way to California under his own power, instead of shifting to the friendly sponsorship of the Republican National Committee after the early primaries. But this is one of the ways in which money talks loudest of all in American politics. Only Steve Forbes among Dole's mostly late-starting opponents had anything like Dole's resources. Lacking any real cushions to fall back on, and having to field their own organizations to oppose the various state and local

TABLE 11.6
The Republican 1996 Presidential Race: Percentage
of Sample Contributing to Individual Candidates

Dole	
Total—1995–96	46%
Primary	35%
1996	30%
Gramm	14%
Alexander	12%
Forbes	6%
Lugar	6%
Buchanan	0.6%
Keyes	0.1%

Source: Compiled from FEC data, as in text; includes both hard and soft money.

Primary = "early money" as in text; includes 1996 money until nomination certain.

machines delivered to Dole on a platter by incumbent governors and members of Congress, the other candidates had to bail out at the first setback. By contrast, Dole's early start and broad, if unenthusiastic, base allowed him to pursue what might be termed the "Russian Army" strategy of capturing the nomination: Just keep spending until nobody else had any money left.

Texas Senator Phil Gramm, for example, initially sounded as though he were interested not in a presidential bid, but in setting up a high-tech version of the best little whorehouse in Texas. Ransacking mailing lists he had accumulated over the years as a party pitchman for campaign funds, Gramm set out to build a massive war chest by loudly standing up for an almost laboratory-pure version of free enterprise.

But such "purity" had limited appeal. By orienting his campaign almost entirely around eliminating the deficit and trading on his general reputation as a strong free trader and exponent of privatizing almost everything except pork-barrel projects destined for the Lone Star State, Gramm did tap a few rich veins. Some supply-siders and advocates of lower capital gains taxes on Wall Street (metaphorically extended to include giant Boston-based Fidelity, whose owner, Ned Johnson, contributed) opened their coffers, as did a fair number of commercial banks and insurance companies. Some support also arrived from American subsidiaries of some foreign multinationals, who probably appreciated Gramm's preaching on behalf of a strong version of free trade. A number of firms in oil, mining, and metals also contributed, including some that stand out in these sectors for their advocacy of open trade.

Railroads and health care concerns also appeared to recognize a friend in need, as did some firms in telecommunications. (Arizona Senator John McCain, a strong supporter of Gramm's, played a prominent role in the debate over telecommunications policy. His truly free-market approach, however, was simply not that popular within the telecommunications sector even though in the long run such a policy would profoundly entrench oligopoly. Virtually alone among Republican senators, McCain ended up voting against the Telecommunications Act Dole finally pressed.)

But Gramm's appeal to most large investors was distinctly limited, even in Texas. Although Gramm was as big a Pentagon booster as anyone, it may be that his concentration on deficit reduction hurt him with defense concerns. They were assuredly poorly represented in his contributor lists. Almost everyone else also seems to have found him resistible. Around the time he exited the campaign, following a disastrous showing in Louisiana caucuses that originally appeared made to order for him, his average level of contributions from firms in my sample was less than half of Dole's.

Pat Buchanan, Steve Forbes, Lamar Alexander, and, earlier, General Colin Powell, all created ripples of excitement. None, however, was prepared to wage the kind of campaign that would have been required to defeat Dole's army.

Back in December 1995, only days before Powell was due to make his long-awaited announcement about his candidacy, the Dole campaign had New Hampshire governor Stephen Merrill make his own eagerly awaited endorsement of Dole. At the time opinion among insiders was that beating the organization of the popular chief executive would be extremely difficult. By appearing to foreclose the relatively cheap option of mounting the first campaign in New Hampshire, Merrill's decision effectively left the center-right Powell with only two options, both very expensive: Run as a Republican and wage his first serious campaign on a broad front in the South, or run as an independent. Both required fund-raising prowess worthy of Ross Perot (who, some fantasized, might actually agree to foot the bill). But neither Bill Gates nor Warren Buffett was running for president, and there is only one Boss—and a reasonable observer might doubt that even Powell's formidable support among multinational elites would have sufficed without an equivalent of the Texas god from a machine.

Forbes, obviously, did not lack for money—his own, that of his (little heralded) backers in the chemical and pharmaceutical industries, and a surprisingly wide swath of Wall Street, where the supply-side gospel has taken a firm, if limited, root. He also had some high-level connections with the defense and foreign policy establishment, not least those of his magazine's publisher, Caspar Weinberger. But Forbes's initial concentration on the flat tax made him vulnerable to well-financed counterattacks. In a Republican primary, these were inevitable, particularly once real estate, defense (which feared that flatter taxes implied flatter Pentagon spending), and more orthodox financiers concerned with budget balance woke up to the challenge.[81]

Forbes's aggressive stance in favor of Taiwan (a position he shared with Gramm and Buchanan) also separated him from most of American multinational business and the foreign policy establishment. Just as in the nineteenth century British Prime Minister Disraeli occasionally fantasized that the mills of Lancashire might run forever if every Chinaman lengthened his pajamas by a few inches, so now AT&T, GM, and Motorola executives dream of running high-tech factories around the clock to keep up with the Celestial Kingdom's future demand for phones and cars. Intent on breaking into what many believe is destined to become the world's largest market (one, moreover, that is not already captured by the Japanese), American business executives—with notable exceptions, such as textiles, entertainment, or software producers—are willing to do almost anything in exchange for permission to set up behind the Great Wall.

As a consequence, the initial reaction of most of the establishment was a faintly patronizing dismissal of "Forbes—Capitalist Fool." The condescension turned to a mix of horror and anger (coupled with a sudden flurry of interest in campaign finance reform by major party politicians) after Forbes trained his guns on Dole and cratered the Kansas senator's standing in polls. The magazine magnate's poor showing in New Hampshire triggered a wave of clucking in the major media about how money couldn't buy votes, which then turned into real alarm after Forbes trounced Dole in Delaware and everyone in Arizona. By then, however, even Forbes appears to have been put off by the per-vote cost of waging a broad nationwide campaign. When the Dole machine rolled over him in New York and the South, he thriftily withdrew.

At first glance, Pat Buchanan's now famous challenge looks like the polar opposite of Forbes's campaign. But there was a very real sense in which it, too, reflected the preoccupations of one superdonor, Roger Milliken. A strong opponent of the North American Free Trade Agreement (NAFTA), trade with China, and unions, the textile magnate reportedly contributed at least $250,000 to The American Cause, a nonprofit controlled by Buchanan and his sister before Buchanan formally entered the race (when such contributions would have had to be reported to the Federal Election Commission). Milliken also reportedly donated almost $2 million to the Coalition for the American Cause, which lobbied on trade policy and appears to have had close ties to The American Cause. He also contributed to Buchanan's campaign, as did a number of other (rather small) textile firms and a couple of sizable chemical companies.[82]

As a candidate Buchanan sent more than one message (the now famous economic appeals that were probably key to the wide interest his campaign aroused came interlarded with an astonishing amount of what can only be described as sheer vitriol). By concentrating his resources in a few early states (notably New Hampshire, where the most influential GOP organ in the state was strongly in his corner) and appealing to the religious right, he managed to reach just enough voters to create a splash. After tiny New Hampshire, however, his inability to resist playing to stereotype, combined with a lack of resources and a hostile media, spelled doom.

The methods the Dole campaign employed to shut down Lamar Alexander's campaign were wonderfully ironic, and illustrate the profound difference between money-driven campaigns and those imagined by many political scientists. Alexander came from roughly the same part of the Republican political spectrum that Dole did. A bit of a stalking horse for political allies of George Bush, who were not easily reconciled to the Dole candidacy, Alexander's case had some eerie resemblances to Clinton's. In the past he had been a mildly reformist governor of a southern state whose financial dealings—along with those of his wife—had repeatedly raised suspicions. (The GOP couple's material progress, however, closely tracked traditional GOP ideals. In sharp contrast to the Clintons, for whom the crumbs of Whitewater and Tyson Foods appear to have fallen like manna from heaven, the Alexanders had become wealthy.) Now he was an insider running as an outsider, whose top campaign operative (Howard Baker, a former U.S. Special Trade Representative) had long enjoyed very close relations with multinational businesses in and out of the United States.[83]

Alexander's problem, unlike Clinton's, however, was that his rivals Dole, Forbes, Gramm, and even Richard Lugar (who rapidly exhausted the small sums he managed to raise from various free-trade bastions, Indianapolis-based Eli Lilly, and a few other large firms in the Midwest and dropped out) all had plausible claims to be considered free traders, with the latter two sporting credentials that were at least as good as his. Not surprisingly, therefore, his campaign raised a respectable amount of money from traditional citadels of free trade: Wall Street, commercial banks, and foreign multinationals, including, notably, Nissan, whose entry into Tennessee Alexander had spearheaded as governor. He also raised money from some of the usual GOP suspects (health, chemicals); from businesses and the corporate rich in his home state; and some money from cable companies, including giant TCI, which had long operated in Tennessee and had something of a running feud with Vice President Al Gore, formerly senator from that state.[84]

But at the crucial moment, as he closed in on Bob Dole and Buchanan in the final weekend of the New Hampshire primary, he simply lacked the resources to blanket the airwaves with his own ads. Bob Dole, however, did. Here is how the *Boston Globe*, a source not to be suspected of any sympathy for my investment theory of party competition, described the last few days of the campaign:

> While the Dole campaign knew that Buchanan could win New Hampshire . . . it calculated that he had a natural ceiling of support that made him beatable elsewhere. The Dole campaign actually played up Buchanan's chances, suggesting to reporters that he was their main opponent. . . . Alexander had jumped from 8 percent to 18 percent . . . if the trend continued, Alexander would win, Dole campaign officials believed. Moreover, the tracking poll showed that among undecided voters, Alexander was viewed positively by a 57–10 margin, more favorably than any other candidate.[85]

"Terrified that Alexander would become the Jimmy Carter or Bill Clinton of 1996," the Dole campaign unrolled its bankroll:

> [A]s the [final] weekend approached, the Dole campaign launched a surprise attack on Alexander, with a barrage of television ads asserting the Tennessean was "a tax-and-spend liberal who's not what he pretends to be." . . . [Dole's] campaign spent hundreds of thousands of dollars for voters to see the anti-Alexander ads 12 times. . . . The attacks were devastating. . . . Before the ads ran, 44 percent of voters thought Alexander was conservative. . . . Five days later, after the airwaves were saturated with the

"Liberal Lamar" ads, only 22 percent thought Alexander was conservative and 54 percent thought he was moderate or liberal.[86]

228

In a New Hampshire Republican primary, this sort of thing can be lethal, even if relatively few voters had more than a hazy idea of what such labels meant. Though traditional election analyses would never catch it, another form of the Golden Rule was determining the outcome. Facing giant, multi-state media buyouts to stay in the race, Alexander briefly staggered on. Then he folded the campaign, handing Dole the nomination virtually by default.

By then far more people than simply the religious right were dismayed by their party's choice. Under fire from supply-siders (who represent a limited, but very affluent constituency), the Kansas senator finally took the plunge and named Jack Kemp as his running mate. He was promptly rewarded with jibes that the wrong person headed the ticket. All through the rest of the campaign, the ex-Majority Leader alternated between frantic attempts to placate and clumsy efforts to repel his party's vast right wing. In the end, all his toil went for naught, as his candidacy succumbed to a surging political business cycle and public confidence that whoever Bill Clinton was, he was not Newt Gingrich.[87]

A Moment in the Sun

The president's triumphant reelection triggered widespread speculation that his critics on the right would now have to pull in their horns. But it quickly became apparent that his big win over Dole was simply another battle in the long trench war. With subsidies continuing to flow into Paula Jones's suit and Kenneth Starr's investigation widening its focus, the armies of the right had no incentive to quit. Indeed, with Dole out of the way, they could plausibly expect to inherit their fractious party. Funds for the struggle were abundant, as Democratic talk of a "Patient's Bill of Rights" in health care, and possible action by the administration on gun control, tobacco, and other issues persuaded numerous interest groups to "get off their backsides, [and] open up their wallets" as Senate Republican Majority Leader Trent Lott famously adjured lobbyists for the medical-industrial complex.[88]

The end of the '96 election campaign thus brought little respite to the White House and the DNC. While the taxi meter on the president's own legal bills never stopped jingling, DNC finances, swollen by borrowings to repay scandal-touched contributors, bore a marked resemblance to those of some Third World country under IMF tutelage. Particularly as the torrent of leaks from Starr's investigation sent Clinton's poll numbers tumbling, the situation frequently looked desperate—so desperate that the White House and the DNC sometimes quarreled in public over strategies for divvying up what funds they did contrive to raise.[89]

Not surprisingly, an administration willing to rent out White House bedrooms and trade coffee for cash readily latched onto new fund-raising schemes. The second Clinton inaugural, for example, tapped many large firms for sizable contributions through a variety of dodges. The White House and the Treasury also appear to have attempted to fine-tune proposed banking legislation to hold up banks for contributions. And whatever the administration was thinking when it decided after the election to bring the suit against Microsoft, it is a fact that executives from firms such as Netscape, who had contributed to the Democrats in the final stages of the '96 campaign, continued to contribute with some regularity.[90]

The incomplete evidence that is available, however, suggests strongly that the administration's main strategy for surviving its Night on Bald Mountain involved yet another pilgrimage to its mother lodes: telecommunications and investment banking.

Glossed in the press as the White House's "Hollywood" connection, the ties between the president and (some of) his allies in the telecommunications sector eventually garnered a certain amount of publicity. The breathless stories about the White House comings and goings of stars and starlets and Hollywood's vast contributions to the president's legal defense funds and the DNC, however, failed to place these in the context of the administration's long campaign for what this chapter earlier termed the "Great Brain Robbery." Denounced by many civil libertarians and public interest groups, this measure— which the administration finally succeeded in pushing through—importantly tightened commercial controls over reproductions and copyrights, while severely limiting traditional public rights to the "fair use" of information. Conventional press accounts also did not delve into the continuing battles over enforcement of the Telecommunications Act of 1996. Nor did the growing importance of groups such as People for the American Way (which has many links with Hollywood) on the side of the president in the impeachment controversy receive adequate attention.[91]

But all the talk about "Hollywood" at least hints at the relation of investor blocs to major policy outcomes. In the case of the other, more fateful post-election link between major investors and policy, only a single piece of the puzzle ever reached the public eye. This was the bourgeoning campaign by Wall Street and the mutual fund industry to privatize Social Security. Led by State Street (which handles funds for many financial houses) and giant Fidelity Investments, but involving a vast array of firms and front organizations, this effort lifted off well before the 1996 election. With its relations to Wall Street so shaky, the White House jumped at an opportunity to build bridges to the Street and its allies. Clinton appointed a commission to study the question and report back soon after the '96 election.[92]

Long before the commission reported, it was an open secret that many members favored some form of privatization. They were fiercely opposed by a minority, including several with ties to organized labor. This latter group argued that privatizing Social Security was reckless since stock markets do not go up forever. They also objected that privatization would hand the financial world a bonanza in unnecessary fees. More ominously, they suggested, even partial privatization would fatally weaken the whole system by siphoning too much money out of the system. It could also lead to grievous equity problems, as workers whose investments lost money faced penury. Because the issue was so controversial, the administration temporized. This undoubtedly frustrated the investment houses, but it also gave them time to mount a massive public relations campaign. Though many observers suggested the opposite, it appears that they won their chief point when Clinton finally unveiled his own proposals as the impeachment furor was winding down.[93]

While the administration nerved itself to act on Social Security, it appears to have embarked on its boldest program of bridge-building to Wall Street as it fashioned its response to the Asian economic crisis. Here, at perhaps the darkest moment in the run-up to the '98 election cycle—the fall of 1997, for most of which Clinton's popularity remained mired near its lows—the White House struck pure gold. Because so many interested parties continue to find it in their interests to muddy the outcome and because of the shattering consequences of what transpired, this last and most dramatic stage of the run-up to impeachment requires careful delineation.

Ever since the United States had called off the auto war with the Japanese in mid-1995, Treasury Secretary Rubin, his deputy Lawrence Summers, and other White House spokespersons had regularly appeared in public to welcome a higher dollar. From a macroeconomic policy standpoint, this incantation furthered several goals at once. While smoothing out relations with Japan, it encouraged strong capital inflows into the United States. These, in turn, pushed up both the dollar and the stock market, since with the U.S. exchange rate appreciating, foreigners could buy almost anything and expect prices in terms of their home currencies to go up.

Even more important, however, with the U.S. economy reviving, exchange rate appreciation afforded American policymakers a chance to square the circle as the election approached. As devout communicants of the widely espoused "natural rate"-of-unemployment hypothesis, the White House and the Treasury believed that the U.S. rate of inflation would begin to rise as the unemployment rate dropped below the approximately 6.5 percent rate that was widely considered to constitute "full employment." Normal policy rules would then require a rise in interest rates to cool off the economy. But a rising exchange rate has effects on import-competing industries and workers that are similar to an interest rate rise. As their prices rise relative to the rest of the world, firms and workers have to moderate price rises and wage demands to avoid being submerged by foreign competitors. The Treasury therefore encouraged the dollar to rise, while discouraging the (mostly) sympathetic Federal Reserve from raising rates.[94]

The new policy was widely popular with financial markets and helped paper over past policy differences with the administration. But amidst all the accolades for Rubin and the Treasury, policymakers and financial markets lost sight of a key point: While the dollar was rising relative to the yen, most currencies in East Asia were tied to a basket of currencies dominated by the dollar, or pegged (within some margin of fluctuation) directly to the dollar. They thus were rising relative to the yen, too.[95]

In the context of other trends in the world economy, this was a recipe for world historical disaster. For more than two decades, the heavily state-directed economies of East Asia had been shattering all records for sustained economic growth. While the growth attracted many American firms, the state direction generally did not, save when that was employed to discourage unions and political dissidence. Neither did East Asia's increasingly close links with Japan, which American policymakers already were trying crack open. As with the new economies of Russia and Eastern Europe, the Americans, along with enough Europeans to carry the Organisation for Economic Co-operation and Development (OECD) with them, were sure they knew exactly what needed to be done: They pressed Asian countries to liberalize, particularly in the financial sector, which many neoliberals regarded as the key to long-run development patterns. Eventually East Asians began listening to this advice, if only because, as in the case of Korea, financial liberalization was made a precondition for admission to the OECD or gaining something else they wanted.[96]

In the controlled economies of East Asia, however, instituting financial liberalization was like pumping laughing gas into kindergartens. Bank supervision and regulatory "systems" barely existed, and many key financial institutions were rankly political in the worst sense, making rises in interest rates peculiarly difficult. Deregulation of land and other "nontradable" sectors, in addition, opened doors to explosive price increases there.[97]

Particularly after the Mexican bailout convinced many financial managers that the Americans and the International Monetary Fund (IMF) would not permit major defaults in emerging markets, capital poured into the Asian economies. In Thailand, Indonesia, Korea, and other countries, many domestic firms rushed to take on huge dollar-denominated debts, convinced that the peg to the dollar rendered them almost risk free.[98]

The huge capital inflows threatened to appreciate the exchange rates of countries like Thailand that were relatively porous to foreign capital. Trying to maintain their dollar pegs, the East Asian countries mostly lowered their interest rates. In economies where labor is politically weak, this "easy money" strategy led naturally to runaway asset inflation and explosive growth in construction and other (often just deregulated) nontradable sectors. In some cases, this produced mild inflationary pressures, though budget deficits were meager, in marked contrast to apparently similar cases in Latin America. Many banks and other financial intermediaries also used their borrowed dollars to support vast new loans in local currencies.[99]

With Rubin and many others hailing the higher dollar, however, East Asia increasingly found itself in a vise. The continuing thrust outward of China, which had devalued its controlled currency in 1994, put all the Asian "Tigers" under pressure. Now, on the demand side, the collapse of Japan's "bubble" economy was slowing down the fabled Chrysanthemum growth machine, at times virtually to a crawl. Thus Japan was importing less and less from the Tigers. With the European economies striving mightily to meet the tight Maastricht Treaty standards of fiscal balance, growth—and thus import demand—in Europe was also weak. The American economy continued to grow, though as many have noted, over much of this period its growth rate looked robust only by comparison with anorexic economies abroad. By comparison with past U.S. business cycles, growth during most of Clinton's first term was feeble, and we now know that since the dangers of inflation were greatly over-estimated, the growth rate could have been considerably higher than it was. Ironically, even this growth had a downside: Figures on foreign lending from the Bank of International Settlements indicate that as lending by Europeans reached prodigious levels (and Japanese lending leveled off at very high levels) American financiers began cutting back on their loans to East Asia in the spring of 1997. The size and speed of this retraction suggest that it probably did not happen because American bankers knew something their European and Japanese colleagues did not: As Edward Nell has suggested, growth in the United States was instead probably pulling money home, reducing American bankers' need to push foreign loans. The Federal Reserve rate increase of March 1997 can only have accelerated this, though suggestions that this development was a unique catalyst for the ensuing disaster are implausible.[100]

On the supply side, East Asians complained that their economies were having trouble making the transition to more sophisticated forms of industrial production. In part, this difficulty surely reflected the unwillingness of generally repressive regimes to invest in education and infrastructure. It also, however, probably stemmed in part from the problems of being a "branch plant" economy for the Japanese and to a much lesser extent, other foreign, including American, multinationals. There is also no doubt that in particular product lines, such as semiconductors, global overcapacity plagued East Asian firms along with everyone else.[101]

Though the IMF, the World Bank, and other institutions continued to cheer on the East Asians, balance of payments deficits began growing in several countries. Alert foreign investors—including not only the now-celebrated "hedge funds" but investment and commercial banks, and in the end, domestic firms nervous about their dollar exposures—began taking positions against the weaker currencies. Speculation about a rise in Japanese interest rates (which did not materialize) fanned anxieties. In July, after several scares, the Thai baht finally broke. A massive flight of capital from the region began.[102]

At this point, the American government made a fateful choice. In the Mexican crisis, most of the debt consisted of securities held by mutual funds, investment houses, pension funds, and similar intermediaries, rather than traditional bank loans. The relatively minor role of commercial banks was the most commonly cited justification for the breathtaking scale of the bailout: The traditional practice of negotiating some form of accord—normally mediated by governments and IMF—between creditor banks and insolvent governments to stretch out and perhaps reduce the debt could not be implemented. Instead, the United States and the IMF simply fronted Mexico the money to repay the institutional investors.[103]

This break with precedent was acutely controversial, not only in the U.S. Congress, which famously refused to approve it (while also declining to interfere), but among other governments who were members of the IMF. The Germans, in particular, criticized the United States for using the IMF as a sort of emergency piggy bank, at the expense of other possible claimants, such as Russia, where German banks were much more heavily engaged. The issue was so contentious that the Group of Ten (G-10) eventually set up a special panel chaired by the head of the Belgian Central Bank to examine the issue. It reported soberly against such massive bailouts and urged a return to the traditional strategy of negotiated agreements between banks and governments.[104]

On its face, the budding Asia crisis looked made to order for the traditionalists. Though mutual funds and other nonbanks were factors, a lot of the debt in fact originated from banks. Not surprisingly, though the full story is likely to remain veiled for decades, a striking series of articles in *Handelsblatt* indicates that both the creditor banks and some foreign government shareholders in the IMF, notably Germany, expected and wanted precisely this sort of negotiation.[105]

In *Handelsblatt*, however, William Rhodes of Citicorp, who chaired a group representing creditor banks, related how he had urged Treasury Secretary Rubin to proceed along these lines. The Treasury Secretary, however, rejected the approach of working through the creditor banks.[106]

Instead, the American government embarked on a different path—one that involved it in an international reform crusade of breathtaking scope and audacity, implying far bigger roles for the IMF and investment banks. As one Asian country after another collapsed and appealed for assistance, the Americans drew a line in the sand. Rebuffing Japanese proposals for a new Asian Development Bank to ease the situation, the Americans and the IMF (which famously related to the Treasury rather like the dog to the Victrola in the old RCA "master's voice" ad) made aid contingent upon sweeping privatization and liberalization. Likened by the former head of one major Japanese bank to a new "MacArthur scenario," the approach of the Treasury and the IMF sought to institutionalize Anglo-Saxon–style financial capitalism in Asia all at once. In place of the usual closed circle of state-encouraged, "national champion" firms borrowing vast amounts of money from government-controlled savings systems at concessionary rates, the Treasury sought the creation, virtually overnight, of American-style "transparent" markets for stocks and bonds. The United States and the IMF also insisted upon sweeping accounting reforms, far-reaching financial deregulation, balanced budgets, higher interest rates, and freely convertible foreign exchange markets overseen by independent central banks. Integral to the program were vast new loans to countries and restructured firms, to be floated in many cases by syndicates led by major American investment banks, such as Goldman, Sachs.[107]

If successful, this new made-in-America "Greater East Asia Co-prosperity Sphere" promised to open up to Wall Street the pension funds and other savings vehicles of what had been the fastest-growing and highest-saving countries in the world, and to create lucrative new markets for services that are the stock in trade of the investment houses: securities placement, privatization, mergers, and acquisitions. Though the prospect of acquiring new Asian subsidiaries at fire-sale prices certainly attracted many American multinationals with no particular stake in Wall Street, it was perfectly clear who the biggest winners would be. As one high German bank executive observed tartly, such a strategy of debt consolidation through the capital markets, "would profit before all else a few big American merchant and investment banks [Geschaefts- und Investmentbanken] through fat issuing fees [fette Provisionseinnahmen im Emissionsgeschaeft]."[108]

As the Clinton administration went into high gear, so did at least some financial houses whose interest in Asia can be independently documented. In October 1997, for example, with Clinton trailing badly in the polls and under fire in the press, Jon Corzine, the chair of the firm with perhaps the biggest stake of all in these developments, Goldman, Sachs, donated $25,000 to a DNC nonfederal (i.e., soft money) account. A month later he gave $75,000. In January 1998, another burst of public spirit seized the Goldman chair and he proffered $30,000 more. In March, he sent another $15,000—and these totals, which reflect party committees clearly under White House control, do not include additional contributions he made to Democratic senatorial and congressional campaign committees where the connection to the White House is perhaps less clear-cut, or the raft of donations he made to individual congressmen and women, as well as Goldman's own PAC.[109]

Because of its timing, amount, and who was giving, this case is significant all by itself. The extent to which a broader coalition became active, however, is harder to assess. Despite much effort, I have not succeeded in obtaining reliable data on precisely who in the American financial community had what stakes in Asia at the time. This makes straightforward statistical tests of the type I prefer impossible. In addition, however, it is clear from subsequent news reports that many American firms moved swiftly to take advantage of the opportunities thrown up by the Asian collapse; thus the relevant database is really not who was in Asia then, but who was planning to be. By default, one must proceed more informally, almost on a case-by-case basis. Still in the months after the Thai collapse, the roster of firms either already in Asia or known (from subsequent acquisitions) to be interested in heading there that donated substantial sums to Democratic Party vehicles closely affiliated with the White House (rather than House or Senate Democrats, who may have had their own agendas) is impressive: It includes American International Group, General Electric (parent of GE Capital, which expanded aggressively after the Thai blowout), AFLAC, Metropolitan Life (which purchased a large Japanese firm), and Travelers (whose purchase of part of Nikko Securities after swallowing Citicorp and various brokerage houses created a sensation).[110]

The Treasury and IMF plans quickly fell victim to the usual hazards that beset the schemes of mice, men, and women. The initial IMF country plans were bitterly attacked in Asia and elsewhere for their far-reaching demands for microeconomic "reform." In Korea, for example, it has been claimed that the United States insisted on closing particular product lines that competed with various multinational interests.[111] The IMF calls for government budget surpluses are now widely agreed to have made little sense in countries where most foreign debts were owed by firms, rather than the government, and where budget deficits, in contrast to other parts of the Third World, were rare. In Indonesia, IMF demands for closure of insolvent banks triggered a general bank panic.

As in all first-class disasters, other policy mistakes compounded the initial reverses. For months the administration beat on the Japanese to open up their markets and restructure, while blocking Japanese initiatives to ease the crisis. This enraged the world's largest creditor but did nothing to alleviate the collapse. With the Japanese providing cover and some temporary financial help, Malaysia adopted capital controls. Despite huffing and puffing in the Western press, its economy did not collapse. In August 1998, the American policy toward Russia did crash, however. Financial meltdown there led to moratoria (really: defaults) on Russian debts to major Western financial houses. Shocked creditors swiftly withdrew from virtually all emerging markets, in effect draining the oxygen out of the world economy aside from a handful of the largest Group of Seven (G-7) countries. In September, the financial crisis arrived in the G-7 itself, when Long Term Capital Management had to be rescued by a multinational consortium of banks organized by the New York Fed. At almost exactly the same moment as the American government was moving to tighten bankruptcy laws for ordinary Americans, the Treasury organized a new form of G-7 "preventive" package through the IMF to back up the next target, Brazil, and the Federal Reserve cut interest rates three times. As the Brazilian package crumpled, the Japanese began to implement at glacial pace a restructuring plan of their own embracing financial support for supplementary budgets in other Asian countries (effectively a form of international Keynesianism), the lowest interest rates in world history, and a substantial fiscal expansion in Japan itself. Together with Oskar Lafontaine, the new (and briefly tenured) German finance minister, though not the Bundesbank or the new European Central Bank, Tokyo also began building support for reregulation of world capital markets. By then, however, all eyes in America were on Larry Flynt and the U.S. Congress.[112]

Conclusion: The Rake's Progress and Ours

We now have more than enough evidence to answer the question posed at the beginning of the chapter, as to how the American political system could have come so close to breaking down in a period of domestic prosperity. The answer is straightforward, and not to be found in a fog of constitutional rhetoric, far-fetched comparisons with the poorly understood Andrew Johnson precedent, or fanciful speculation about television's admittedly baleful influence on American public life. The American political system is not essentially driven by votes. Public opinion has only a weak and inconstant influence on policy. The political system is largely investor-driven, and runs on enormous quantities of money—more than $4 billion since Clinton took office in narrowly construed and (more or less) publicly recorded electoral expenses along with at least something like ten to thirty times that in lobbying and broader public relations costs.[113]

As a consequence, a candidate like Clinton, who runs as the candidate of a party—the Democrats—that still pretends to have a mass base has an insuperable problem. Ever since America's great "Right Turn" in the mid-seventies, most of American business and the super-rich have espoused increasingly radical versions of "laissez-faire" economics—save, of course, when oil fields are in play, trade needs to be subsidized, or a transnational bailouts become imperative. With an intensity moderated only by extremes in the business cycle, demands for tax "relief," freedom from regulation, cuts in social welfare expenditures, labor cost reductions, and tighter control of increasingly decentralized production systems dominate their consciousness and thus public consciousness. Epitomized in the buzz word "globalization," this "neoliberal" political ideology has had essentially no rival in the Anglo-Saxon countries since 1989. Until the Asian crisis, it was spreading like wildfire over the world, even in places like Russia, where it had no native roots.

Bill Clinton's (and British Prime Minister Tony Blair's) chimerical "Third Way" represented a variant on this approach, one willing to venture a slightly more aggressive use of state power. But though just enough firms and investors were open to these appeals to finance successful campaigns around these themes (particularly in recession), the bulk of the business community was not. Affronted by the prospect of even a small rise in taxes, most reacted with fury at a regime that was almost pathetically eager to be their friend. Nor would most of the pharmaceutical-medical-industrial complex tolerate efforts to limit to its ability to confront people with continuing threats of "your money or your life." Like the gun lobby, the tobacco industry, or the broad range of industries nervous about environmental regulation, they detested the "Third Way" and could afford to spend millions to get what they want. Along with myriads of other promoters of a "revolutionary" break with the remnants of the New Deal (including, at times, the defense industry and parts of finance, as discussed above), these sectors helped power Gingrich's 1994 putsch that thrust aside both the Democrats and less committed Republican leaders like Robert Michel. They also helped bankroll the right-thinking candidates of 1996, including most of those who kept the heat on Dole, whose own schizophrenia clearly reflected their massive weight in the party. These interests also provided major financing for virtually all the leaders of the long drive to impeach Clinton. Dennis Hastert, the new Speaker, was, for example, in the last Congress the GOP "point man" in opposing Democratic proposals for a patient's bill of rights and duly rewarded for it. Gingrich, Livingston, DeLay, and even Judiciary Chair Henry Hyde were also lavishly supported by the same sectors.[114]

For these sectors, "compromise" means forgone profits. They are, accordingly, unbending and expect their political mouthpieces to be similarly unyielding. When, for example, the veteran, highly respected editor of the *Journal of the American Medical Association* published a short piece containing material that appeared helpful to the president's lawyers as they began their opening arguments in the Senate trial, he was summarily fired. There is no reason to believe these groups' attitudes toward Republican (or Democratic) politicians who disagree with them would be any different.[115]

So powerful is the growth of laissez-faire ideology within the GOP that the phrase "Republican moderate" is now almost an oxymoron. The few so-called moderates who remain either are, like the judge whom Helm's protégé Sentelle replaced on the oversight panel for special prosecutor, aging lions from another era; or they have multinationals all their own, like Representative "Amo" Houghton (whose family has long controlled Corning Glass); or they have simply contrived to get elected in the east or midwest (like virtually every representative whose status as a "moderate" was certified in the *New York Times* during the House deliberations on impeachment).[116]

But the moderates have few if any differences of principle with the conservatives. Save for a handful of foreign policy and trade issues, their differences are largely rhetorical and prudential. The weight of the "radical" interests in the party—such as the medical, tobacco, or gun lobbies—is such that it pays virtually no one to oppose them openly, since the opportunity costs of forgone contributions now and in the future are so enormous. Rather, as the case of impeachment vividly illustrates, moderates will go to great lengths to avoid antagonizing the right, even if they privately harbor doubts. The national reputation of the Republican Party is a collective good that no single representative can bank on; the tidal wave of funds that backs up even manifestly unpopular demands of the right, by contrast, is money in the bank for representatives who have to raise thousands of dollars every week to secure reelection.

This diagnosis implies that the bitter, confrontational politics that have marked the last decade or so of American politics will not soon pass. The plain fact is that even the very conservative Democratic Party of Bill Clinton—who has been well described as the most conservative Democratic President since Grover Cleveland—is unacceptably liberal to Republicans and most of the American business community. The quite testable view of this chapter is that barring a major depression (not quite unthinkable any longer, unfortunately, for reasons precisely related to the spread of conservative, pre-Keynesian economic viewpoints), whoever finally supplants Clinton as a Democratic leader is likely to be almost equally unpalatable to the right. Though any other Democratic president is likely to conduct himself (or, perhaps, herself) more prudently than Clinton and thus avoid some of the garish extremes of his tenure, the real tension that shapes American today is the enormous and growing gap between elites and the population. In a changing world economy, their aspirations now diverge more dramatically than ever. As a consequence, the United States is facing many more years of conflict, along with endless media claptrap about "value conflicts" and who really deserves what that often appears to have no political implications at all.

Two other lessons also emerge from this sad episode. One concerns the catastrophic nature of the American campaign finance system. Because they had money, the opponents of Bill Clinton were able to rake over again and again the most minute and personal details of his life, in Arkansas and in Washington. As in other recent cases, where public opinion and policy largely moved on different planes—including most of the "Reagan Revolution," NAFTA, or the recent legislation increasing American contributions to the IMF—organized money succeeded in frustrating popular will. Bill Clinton's own search for campaign funds had equally disastrous consequences. As he entered office, his reliance on

Wall Street led him to reject what we now know was a perfectly sensible plan for modest economic stimulus. His original health plan was excessively complicated and rigid and made far too many concessions to gain support from insurers, or, in the end, from almost anyone else. After the entirely unnecessary 1994 debacle, Clinton's frantic efforts to win back the investment houses and garner enough cash to survive the 1996 race played a role in any number of other disasters, including the overconfident reliance on exchange rate pegs with the Asian currencies; the desperate search for money from almost anywhere, including Asia, to fund the campaign; the embrace of rapid NATO expansion (which blocked Russian ratification of Start II and is destined to make far more mischief); the tunnel vision toward what "free enterprise" really meant in Russia; and the gold-plated (and ham-handed) IMF interventions during the Asian crisis.

It has become fashionable to snort that all of this doesn't matter much, because government really doesn't do that much any more or to argue derisively that Alan Greenspan matters, but the president really doesn't. The evidence for such claims is thin indeed. It is true that, historically, some superpowers have almost seemed to run on automatic pilot for relatively long periods. The outstanding example, perhaps, is that of ancient Rome. Once the emperor Augustus established the eternal city as sole superpower, that polity survived all sorts of dubious machinations, including emperors like Nero, Caligula, and even a horse or two in the Senate. In the present case, however, the response is likely too clever by a half. The rise of the euro means that at least in an economic sense, the United States is unlikely to be the sole superpower for much longer. As is now dawning on both the Treasury and the business community, this is likely to constrain American policy, especially monetary policy, in quite novel ways once the dollar stops going up. Waiving all discussion of the yen for now, the world of the dollar and the euro has two financial centers of gravity. But as Walter Adams Brown's study of the interwar international economy long ago established, such bipolar systems of finance are likely to be uniquely unstable (Brown, 1940). The contemporary dismissal of the role of the president is probably quite wrong; within a remarkably short period of time, one may venture that the very same people who now mock the presidency will be calling for a stronger executive.[117]

Finally one should also not forget to note how a conservative judiciary is acting to supplement money's direct role in the political system. It is not simply that the courts have chipped steadily away at restraints on campaign spending to the point where, with some help from Congress and the FEC, campaign finance is now close to being effectively deregulated.[118] No less significant is the way Chief Justice Rehnquist and other conservative jurists appear to be using the courts to pursue political strategies that transcend traditional understandings of nonpartisanship and impartiality. Behind the Starr-Lewinsky-Clinton carousel were the far less-heralded decisions of Chief Justice Rehnquist to advance the very junior David Sentelle to head the panel overseeing special prosecutors and Sentelle's own peculiar notion of what constitutes judicial balance. Both Starr's selection and his subsequent conduct also demonstrated a breathtaking insensitivity to rather obvious conflicts of interest, as well as the rights of citizens. As one contemplates how the same federal judiciary—particularly the Chief Justice—responded to the challenges of the Iran-Contra special prosecutor, or the attorney general dealt with questions of wrongdoing in the Clinton administration, one inevitably is led to wonder about the future of democratic culture in America.[119]

Notes

1. I am grateful to Robert Johnson, James Kurth, Alain Parguez, Walker Todd, and one friend who took an official position as this chapter was finished for many discussions, and to Jeffrey Klein for encouraging me to resume work on the Clinton presidency. Another special debt is owed William Crotty, without whom this chapter would never have been undertaken, several Speakers of the House ago. On the Asia crisis I have profited from exchanges with Marshall Auerback, Chalmers Johnson, Jan Kregel, Edward Nell, Arturo O'Connell, Frank Veneroso, and Robert Wade. I should also like to thank Anthony Wright, formerly of the Center for Media Education, Washington, D.C. Particular thanks also to Ben Page, then of the Center for Advanced Studies in the Behavioral Sciences, for detailed comments on a draft.
   An early version of the sections of this chapter dealing with Special Prosecutor Kenneth Starr appeared in the *Nation*, March 8, 1999, pp. 11–14. I have also drawn from earlier essays published in *Mother Jones* referenced below. To economize on space, this chapter gathers references in notes placed at the end of paragraphs. The first quotation from the *New York Times* is from Dec. 20, 1998, sec. 3, p. 1; that from the *Boston Globe* is from Jan. 16, 1999, p. A13; the last is from Maureen Dowd, "In the D.C. Matrix," *New York Times*, April 28, 1999, p. A27.
   It is impossible here to sort through the protean usages of the term "postmodernism." For a readable critique, see Palmer (1990). Note that serious empirical theories of reading stress the critical role contextual knowledge plays in the activity (Cole 1990); such considerations are not easily integrated into theories of reading that see it as primarily or essentially text-based and virtually self-referential.
2. For Greenspan, see Kathleen Day, "Reining In Speculative Funds; Prospect of Huge Loss Brings Call for Federal Oversight," *Washington Post*, Sept. 25, 1998, p. F1. A particularly good source on the Long-Term Capital Management bailout is Todd (1998). John Ellis, "Lewinsky Interview Confirms It—Cultural War Is Lost," *Boston Globe*, March 25, 1989, p. A23, claims that NBC News had an "explicit strategy of 'all Monica, all the time.'" Note, however, that NBC is now allied with Microsoft, whose very obvious interest in weakening Clinton is discussed below.
3. Past electoral outcomes of president's party are from Walter Dean Burnham, private communication. In regard to the GOP turmoil, see *New York Times*, Nov. 8, 1998, p. 24. Note the seismic implications of the references to the "pointed expressions of concern" voiced by "potential [Republican] Presidential candidates to both Mr. Livingston and Mr. Gingrich," as well as the remarks attributed to a "veteran Republican" who reported that "the Presidential candidates were saying, 'We can't spend the next two years with an atmosphere that's defined by Gingrich and Armey.'" Considering that the national press was hailing newly reelected Texas Governor George Bush as the odds-on favorite for the GOP nomination in 2000, all this has a very clear meaning.
4. The basic events are too well known to require separate citation here. Livingston's claim as a moderate was a staple of journals such as the *New York Times*.

5. For the polls, see, e.g., *New York Times*, Dec. 21, 1998, p. A21. See also *Boston Globe*, Jan. 21, 1999, p. A23.

6. In truth, a Speaker-elect, since Livingston had not yet been formally voted into office.

7. For Flynt, his ad, and the response, see, *New York Times*, Dec. 22, 1998, p. A25. This also reports Livingston's claim to have decided by himself, while noting right-wing congressional opponents. More and better detail appears in *Boston Globe*, Dec. 24, 1998, p. A14; this mentions Schlafly and Sheldon, along with *Roll Call*. For Falwell, see Frank Rich, "Larry and Lucy," *New York Times*, Dec. 23, 1998, p. A27. Flynt's plans subsequently evolved; cf. *Boston Globe*, Feb. 25, 1999, p. E1.

8. For the judge and Starr's threat, see, e.g., Ferguson (1999b). On the decline in the GOP's image, see below, note 11.

9. Among the many accounts of voting, see, e.g., *New York Times*, Nov. 5, 1998, section B; Nov. 6, 1998, p. A22, which quotes an estimate of national turnout at 36 percent, with Minnesota showing the highest in the country at 59.5. Turnout in the primaries generally dropped sharply in both parties; see, e.g., the Associated Press's "Study Shows Primary Voter Turnout at Record Lows," Sept. 28, 1998, Fox News Online. See also "Polls: Dems Gained Among Key Groups," Associated Press, Nov. 7, 1998, Yahoo! News. Also helpful on reactions to the results is *Washington Post*, Nov. 5, 1998, p. A33. On Ventura and Minnesota, see especially, Micah Sifry, "Jesse 'The Gov' Ventura," *Nation*, Jan. 4, 1999. A useful compendium of results broken down by various groups is *New York Times*, Nov. 9, 1998, p. A20.

10. For the exit polls, see the sources in note 9, above. For the widely discussed Commerce Department data, which involved a slight shift in how the data were calculated, see, e.g., Lester Thurow, "US Consumers, The Euro Should Keep Economy on Even Keel. A Happy Fiscal New Year? Perhaps," *Boston Globe*, Dec. 29, 1998, p. C4.

11. For the GOP's standing with the public, see R.W. Stevenson and Michael R. Kagay, "Republicans' Image Eroding Fast, Poll Shows," *New York Times*, Dec. 19, 1998, p. 1; for the subsequent drop to record lows, see *New York Times*, Dec. 21, 1998, p. 1. For the party re-registration reports, which, if true, would indeed be remarkable, see Steven A. Holmes, "Impeachment: The Electorate; Some Voters Are Making the Switch," *New York Times*, Dec. 25, 1998, p. A30.

12. For Simpson and others, see *New York Times*, Dec. 14, 1998, p. A21. This plain-spoken article, which doubtless emerged in a context of arguments by the president's defenders, clearly became something of an embarrassment. Several later articles attempted various forms of damage control. Most of the arguments put forward were jejune, involving appeals to regional cleavages or suburbanization, which allegedly created districts with "effective" majorities in favor of impeachment. But given the huge majority that formed against impeachment, appeals to redistricting and low voter turnout are implausible in the extreme. Two-to-one majorities nationwide are simply too big to wash out like that, though they might narrow the enormous difference. Appeals to peculiar properties of "Sunbelt" Republican districts are equally implausible; most regional differences in an era of national communications are much smaller than that. Many of these arguments appeal in the end to popular intuitions about safe seats—but of course slip past the key point of the money-driven nature of the political system that confers such enormous advantages on incumbents. For how public opinion actually influences policy see Ferguson (1995).

Simpson's remarks about Americans and the stock market were characteristically Republican in their ingenuousness. Census (1998, 532) indicates that as of 1995, only 40.3 percent of American families owned any stock at all directly or indirectly and that ownership was massively concentrated among higher-income groups.

13. William Pfaff, "US Divide Is Cultural, Not Political," *Boston Globe*, Dec. 28, 1998, p. A17.

14. Flynt detailed his coming revelations in "Playing Dirty," *Boston Globe*, Dec. 29, 1998, p. D1; Flynt's "big fish" quote is from *Boston Globe*, Dec. 19, 1998, p. A13; a useful compendium of the various peccadilloes that have come to light of right-wing congressmen and women is Parry (1998a). For Gingrich's book contract, cf. Sherill (1995, 749), who shows how Murdoch used book contracts with other public officials around the world. For Gingrich's celebrated college course, see *inter multa alia*, Robert A. Jordan, "Conflict of Interest Cloud Looms over Gingrich," *Boston Globe*, Oct. 15, 1995, p. 85. For other GOP congressional scandals, cf., e.g., that concerning Tom DeLay, "The President's Trial: The Whip," *New York Times*, Feb. 6, 1999, p. A8. On conflicts of interest among members of the House committee appointed to investigate Gingrich, see "Ethics Panel Head Tied to GOPAC," *Boston Globe*, Dec. 2, 1995, p. 3.

15. For Ahmanson, the Rutherford Institute, the Jones suit, and Ahmanson's ties to the "Christian Reconstructionism" of Rousas J. Rushdoony and the latter's Chalcedon Institute, see, e.g., Association (1998, 52–53.) Robert Parry, who formerly reported for the *Los Angeles Times*, has authored some of the best reporting on the Starr case in his newsletter *The Consortium*. Many of his essays are available on the newsletter's web site, www.consortiumnews.com, though this can be difficult to search efficiently.

    Note that Scaife and many other conservatives joined religious conservatives in helping to advance the Jones suit. See Parry, "Paula Jones Case," *Consortium*, Nov. 10, 1997; this essay raises questions about the roles of Jerry Falwell and the Rev. Sung Myung Moon, on which see below, note 17.

16. For Scaife, see, e.g., Rothmyer (1981); Saloma (1984, 25–32); note that the summary of grants on pp. 27–29 does not include a single one to religious causes; Ferguson and Rogers, (1986, 86–88); and, e.g., *Wall Street Journal*, Oct. 12, 1995, p. 1. For the Bradley Foundation and its role in Whitewater, see, e.g., Robert Parry, "The Other Whitewater Scandal," *Consortium*, April 27, 1996. For David Koch, see *New York Times*, Dec. 20, 1998, sec. 3, p. 2.

17. The literature on Moon is vast; among the better reviews are the essays written by Robert Parry for his *The Consortium*; these are now available on the newletter's web site noted above, note 15. But for the KCIA and the Japanese industrialists, see particularly Parry (1997, 4); for the recent allegations about behavior; the Reagan era tax case, and the "Emperor" quote, see Parry (1998b).

18. *Boston Globe*, Jan. 22, 1999, p. A29; note that this is an indirect quotation, rather than Kristol's own words. It is of interest that the Christian Right's abhorrence of vice did not prevent its leaders from making timely distinctions between sin and sinner: None, to my knowledge, called publicly for Burton or Hyde to step down, even though they led important committees investigating Clinton. Kristol perhaps underestimated Robertson's past efforts. He in fact promoted the cause fairly often.

19. See the discussion in Ferguson (1995, esp. the Appendix). This paragraph should not be misread as suggesting that public opinion plays no role in policy formation, as the Appendix takes some pains to relate.

20. For 1992, see Ferguson (1995); for 1996, see Ferguson (1996a; 1996b); these latter surveys cover only "early" money, as explained below.

21. Ferguson and Rogers (1986); Ferguson (1995, chapter 6; the table comes from p. 300). One useful piece on high tech and Clinton in the '92 campaign is "High-Tech Leaders Pin High Hopes on Clinton," *Boston Globe*, Nov. 15, 1992, p. A29.

An essay in the *American Political Science Review* has recently attacked my industrial-structure approach to political analysis. Webber and Domhoff (1996) argue that Jews and southerners, and not business structure, are the key variables in explaining business support for the Democrats in the New Deal. Though their focus is the 1936 election, their claim inevitably raises a broader question about this chapter's methods, particularly since Domhoff had previously claimed that support for the Democrats within investment banking and real estate in the 1980s stemmed from a heavy representation of Jews within those sectors. I rejected that argument in Ferguson (1995), in part by observing that real estate changed its alignment between 1988 and 1992, though no plausibly large demographic shift occurred in the industry (p. 335, n. 37). (This chapter's demonstration, below, of a major shift within investment banking during the 1995–96 election, of course, is equally devastating to any such claims.) But the *APSR* article is seriously flawed. Their large database omits many actors who are of first-order importance for my argument. See my discussion of their earlier essays in Ferguson (1995). In addition, their argument for the role of Jews rests heavily on subsamples of donors from firms in mass consumption-oriented sectors such as retailing and firms said (by someone else, in an argument I believe to be interestingly incomplete) to be sympathetic to Keynesian policies. The data analysis is conducted in terms of two-by-two tables using chi square tests, even though the problem is to partial out the effects of several variables at once. They do not attempt a multivariate analysis, which is the only way the point they want to make could actually be nailed down. This is not surprising, for, as it happens, Jews in other industries they do not consider were frequently heavily Republican (such as mining, where all in my sample who donated gave to the GOP). I have therefore undertaken a detailed multivariate analysis of my entire sample for 1936 (some 2,000 individuals arrayed in 405 large firms and major investors—an immense data collection effort, including much new material since my last essays). Using logistic regressions, I conclude that the effect of being Jewish on the probability of contributing to the Democrats is minor; being Catholic (which I also tested) is worth even less; while region has small, perhaps unstable, effects. The bulk of the explanatory weight is carried by the economic variables, of which trade was far and away the most important in 1936. Labor intensity also matters, though more detail will have to wait for another paper (though see Ferguson, 1999a).

This sort of analysis requires a mammoth effort, but it convinces me that a full-scale multivariate analysis of campaign contributions leaves intact the industrial-structure approach, though as datasets improve, ever finer distinctions become possible. But that is normal in social science. I conclude that this chapter's emphasis is not misplaced, though it could of course be sharpened at great expense of time and effort. I should note that region is in my dataset for this chapter, but no one now argues that region chiefly determines the political contributions of investors in the world economy of the nineties, and I have tried direct tests without success.

22. See Ferguson (1995, Introduction, chapters 3–4; but esp. chapter 6). This also contains references to the fund-raising and policy statements by various industries and individuals; note that many foundations, such as the Robert Wood Johnson Foundation, were becoming very active in health policy debates. Foundations have historically played a major role in forming U.S. health policy in this century (Brown, 1981). A useful overview of the pro-reform forces appeared in *Investors' Business Daily*, Sept. 9, 1993, pp. 1ff., "Who's on Board with Reform," though the journal was less than enamored of the notion or its supporters. The piece, however, is useful for bringing out many rather obvious economic alignments. Compare Martin (1995). This essay is critical of "industrial structure" accounts of policy such as mine for failing to notice that the best predictor of firms'

behaviors is often membership in a formal or informal policy network. But this is a platitude; the proper question is why firms are in these networks. Martin's essay simply begs the question: it fails to test any reasonable industrial-structure account of the policy network, or to consider what the failure of the whole reform enterprise said about possible weaknesses in the original network.

23. Again, for details, see the discussion in Ferguson (1995, esp. pp. 296–305); for the polls, see the discussion and references on p. 282. On high tech see also *Boston Globe*, Nov. 15, 1992, p. A29.

24. Ibid., pp. 275-76.

25. For the bond market, ibid., p. 275; for the optimism in the polls, see *New York Times*, Jan. 13, 1993, p. A13.

26. See the discussion in Ferguson (1995, chapters 5 and 6).

27. See Alan Ehrenhalt, "Highjacking the Rulebook," *New York Times*, Dec. 20, 1998, sec. 4, p. 13.

28. On the tax plan and related maneuvers, see Ferguson (1995, 278–79), and Meeropol (1998, chapter 10).

29. Here the literature is vast. Cf., *inter alia*, Meeropol (1998, chapters 10, 11); Ferguson (1995, "Postscript"); and Ferguson (1999b).

30. For the statistics, see FEC, "1994 Congressional Fundraising Climbs to New High," April 28, 1995; the quotation comes from p. 1; and FEC, "FEC Reports on Political Party Activity for 1993–94," April 13, 1995. The notion of "total" spending here is quite narrow, leaving out, for example, a variety of issue ads that do not directly come from or mention candidates.

31. Perhaps not entirely unaccountably. Tobacco advertising has long been a mainstay of much of the print press.

32. Most of this section relies on Ferguson (1999b); for Kessler and the FDA, see particularly, Cooper (1994, 43–47; 853ff.).

33. Cf. Ferguson (1999b).

34. Cooper (1994, 843).

35. Ibid., 854–55.

36. *Washington Post*, July 14, 1994, p. A4; this references the *New England Journal of Medicine* article.

37. Ferguson (1999b); see also Robert Parry's articles on Sentelle, Rehnquist, and the oversight panel, available at the time this chapter went to press on the joint web site of his newsletter, *The Media Consortium* and *If Magazine* (www. consortiumnews.com).

38. Ferguson (1999b).

39. Ibid.; this references an article in *Salon Magazine* (an Internet journal) dated Nov. 18, 1998 (but remaining on its web site for months), reporting on Starr's work for the tobacco industry prior to his appointment as special prosecutor and the link with the Paula Jones suit.

40. The estimates for tobacco industry contributions are calculated from data on the web site of the Center for Responsive Politics in Washington, D.C., www. opensecrets.org. The data are in a special section devoted only to tobacco; these numbers are updated from time to time; my calculations were done in early 1999, when data went back only to the summer of 1998. On lobbying and broader forms of political money than campaign contributions, see Ferguson (1992). The demonstrably lopsided character of tobacco's tilt toward the GOP creates creates a misleading impression in my survey of "early money" for Bill Clinton in the 1996 presidential race. As discussed below, note 46, accurate spending totals in elections are hard come by. Thus I usually analyze campaign contributions to presidential candidates as dichotomous variables. Because two tobacco firms (or their executives) gave modest donations to Clinton early in the race, when the Democratic standard bearer was scrounging, tobacco could technically be said to

THE STATE OF DEMOCRACY IN AMERICA

make the grade for inclusion in my Table 11.3, along with the other industries discussed. But this is simply an artifact of the small number of tobacco firms and the generally low level of contributions to Clinton's campaign at that time; thus the table omits it. Tobacco firms did not continue contributing to Clinton even at this low rate. They failed to qualify even in this uniquely artificial statistical sense for Table 11.5, which assesses industrial support for the president over the whole period 1995–96. I mention these results only because they appear to run counter to my main argument.

41. See the discussion in Ferguson (1995, "Postscript," esp. pp. 367ff.).

42. The actual vehicle for the "regime shift" on the yen was a speech by Treasury Secretary Lloyd Bentsen, which plainly stated the new attitude. This immediately impacted foreign exchange markets.

43. See Ferguson (1996a).

44. This phenomenon largely escaped notice until Ferguson (1996a); note, however, the observations in the *Wall Street Journal*, Feb. 9, 1995, which drew a link with the hedge fund investigations and certain large soft-money contributions to the GOP in the late stages of the 1994 campaign. See also the discussion below of fund-raising for the 1996 campaign, which reports statistical tests of the differential rate of contributions by investment houses to Clinton's campaign before and after the change of policy on the yen.

45. See, e.g., *New York Times*, Sept. 24, 1995, sec. 4, p. 1, which certainly reflects the GOP leadership's own propaganda. There is, perhaps, one way to make sense of some of the talk about "small business." There is no doubt that the GOP and its major investors wanted to reach out to smaller business and enroll more of it, rather as it had during the New Deal. But there is still no excuse for confusing hopes with the facts of Table 11.2.

46. This table is constructed on the basis of my final, revised data set for 1996, though it breaks out campaign contributions only for the "early money" time period analyzed in Ferguson (1996b). This makes it quite comparable to the period of the Republican primaries and the period in which Gingrich toyed with the idea of seeking the Republican nomination. The sample and statistical methods employed closely follow my earlier studies of elections, with a few improvements that do not warrant extensive commentary here. See Ferguson (1995, chapter 4 and pp. 269–70, n. 7 and 333–34, n. 27). Put simply, the idea is to slice off the top of the American economic pyramid— the largest firms (not only public, but also privately held firms) and investors on the scale of the Forbes 400 richest Americans—and then trace their political contributions, including PACs and both hard and so-called soft money. For the firms, one tracks the individual contributions of top officers and large owners, as well as soft money from the firm itself. Because all information about totals is suspect—it is, for example, easy to hide money funneled through law firms, consultants, etc.—I typically analyze patterns of contributions arranged as dichotomous variables (i.e., either did or did not contribute), rather than totals. Note that the relevant mean in the table here is that of contributions to Gingrich from the entire sample.

Contributions to Gingrich, incidentally, refers here to his own campaign fund; the famous GOPAC, which he was then backing away from; a newer "Monday" fund he had been patronizing, and the House Republican campaign committee for which he was also prodigiously raising funds. These should not be confused with the campaign funds of any other individual members of Congress. What is striking is the extent of the contributions—roughly comparable to that of Clinton in 1992, a winning presidential candidate, and more than respectable compared with contributions for most declared primary candidates in the GOP. I should note that the discussion of Gingrich certainly tries to go beyond the table, in the sense that I cover contributions from within sectors that do not register in the table but that nonetheless bear discussion. Thus, Gingrich drew rather a lot of money from manufacturing (beyond glass, in the table); this may explain some of his occasional noises about "fair trade," though he was a fairly consistent supporter of the multinationals, NAFTA and the Mexican bailout.

47. Table 11.2 is the sample as a whole.

48. See Ferguson (1996a). "The Annotated List of Major GOPAC Donors," published by *Mother Jones* (and long available on the magazine's web site) confirms the importance of wealthy "big" business donors to Gingrich. The appearance of "Accounting" on Table 11.2, incidentally, probably goes far to explaining why Steve Forbes, rather than Gingrich, emerged as the champion of the flat tax.

49. In the eighties, Reagan was routinely described as the most popular president of all time, or at least in recent decades. This was easily checkable and was not even close to being true. See, e.g., Ferguson and Rogers (1986, chapter 1). Nevertheless, similar statements appeared even in the prestige media for a long time thereafter. A then senior correspondent for the *New York Times* subsequently related to me how, after reading an essay of mine that drew attention to this disparity by presenting a graph comparing Reagan's popularity with that of other recent U.S. presidents (Thomas Ferguson, "F.D.R., Anyone?" *Nation*, May 22, 1989), he was moved to have a set of very similar charts drawn up, which he then set before a key *Times* editor. The paper thereupon dropped such references.

50. For defense and the Clinton announcement, see, e.g., Ferguson (1996a, 63); for the polls on defense, see Ferguson (1995, "Postscript," 364).

51. See, e.g., Khalid Duran, "Superman am Bosporus," *Frankfurter Allgemeine Zeitung*, May 15, 1996, p. 11. For the Russians and Chechnya, see Werner Adam, "Ueber den Kaukasus hinaus," *Frandfurter Allgemeine Zeitung*, Aug. 29, 1996. See also the discussion in Ferguson (1996a); for the Clinton phone call to the president of Azerbaijan, see *Wall Street Journal*, Oct. 9, 1995, p. A8. Many complaints about possible ties between government support for exporters and contributions centered on Commerce Secretary Ron Brown. See, e.g., Ken Silverstein, "Ron Brown's VIP Junkets," *Nation*, June 5, 1995; and the elaborate display available on the web site of Public Integrity (www.publicintegrity.org).

52. See Ferguson (1996a); the *Inquirer* quote comes from *Philadelphia Inquirer*, Aug. 30, 1995, p. A5.

53. See the discussion in Ferguson (1996a).

54. See Ferguson (1996a); some of this paragraph also draws on discussions with Treasury officials and investment managers both at the time and later. Klaus Engelen's review of American-Japanese financial relations, "Die Angst vor dem Rueckzug der Japaner," *Handelsblatt*, June 19/20, 1998, p. 2 is a rare public discussion of aspects of the relations between the Treasury, Fed, and their Japanese counterparts that are fundamental to any assessment of this period's political economy. Note in particular the discussion of arrangements for dollar support in the event of a mass liquidation of Treasury paper by distressed Japanese banks.

55. For the dollar's fortunes against various currencies and the politics of industry, cf. *Frankfurter Allgemeine Zeitung*, March 14, 1995, p. 23.

56. See e.g., Johnson (1998). Arrangements to buy bonds as elections approached were nothing new. See the discussion and references in Ferguson (1995, chapter 6, p. 284). For the Fed-BOJ accord see the discussion in Engelen, "Angst," note 54, above. This latter agreement was integral to the whole package.

57. The terminus point for the first round of data collection depended in part on when I happened to receive a commission to write about the election. That became "early money," though the logic of events in regard to investment banking really dictates a cutoff point in the late spring of 1995. My cutoff was in early 1996, long after the turn in policy. As should be clear from Table 11.4, my figures here confound policy regimes.

58. Ferguson (1995) discusses at length methods for analyzing contributions. See, especially, chapter 4 and pp. 333–36. See also Ferguson (1992).

59. Beginning from late April, press accounts diverged sharply about the possibilities of an accord. The United States loudly threatened sanctions and penalty tariffs, was hammered by both Europeans and the Japanese, and clearly began to move toward an agreement not later than late May. The deal was announced on June 28, though wrangling about its meaning persisted for some time. See the accounts in, e.g., the *New York Times*.

60. Johnson (1998) suggests the summer for the Rubin-Sakakibara accord on bond purchases; the Fed-BOJ agreements got some publicity slightly later, but seem clearly to date from sometime after the spring. Published sources are few; cf. Engelen, "Angst," n. 54, above. The Fed was, of course, moving to reverse its higher rate policy of the previous year.

61. I tried all the cut points for dividing the data into two groups, beginning in May and continuing through September 1995, with each test mentioned (and deleting November and December 1996 as falling after the election), always getting results that were significant (often at remarkable levels—in many cases .02 or .03), though multiplying tests raises the odds of getting a weaker result simply by chance. The nonparametric tests, of course, make fewer assumptions about the data, though Mann-Whitney, for example, makes rather more than usually acknowledged (cf. Sheskind 1997, 181–82). Note, however, Sheskind's evidence that the test is robust to violations of the assumption of the homogeneity of variance, on p. 182). The central point really concerns the large differences that show up, even though the sizes of the groups are not large.

   The tests were run on the percentage of total contributions to the Clinton campaign (including both hard money and soft money) coming from investment bankers. I followed the advice of the Center's director, Larry Makinson, and defined investment bankers by reference to two closely related occupational codes the Center uses.

   The results suggest that the two periods really are quite different in the rate at which the Clinton campaign succeeded in attracting contributions from investment houses; it is also clear that the average rate of contributions was quite different from the varying rates for investment bankers, even though that category is quite large. For comparisons of the role investment houses played in earlier Democratic campaigns, see the statistics compiled in, e.g., Ferguson (1995, passim).

   A daily yen/dollar series (taken from the Federal Reserve) is available on the web for 1995 at the web site of the Jei Corporation (www.jeico.co.kr).

62. See Ferguson (1996a). The estimates of union contributions rely on the fact that donations by individual union members, in contrast to those of individual business figures, are exiguous. Total union soft money contributions come from the Center for Responsive Politics, "The Big Picture"(for the 1996 election), available on its web site. Total soft-money contributions for the Democrats follow the figures given by the Federal Election Commission on its web site. Table 11.5's results for beverages and glass—two industries that both export heavily and do varying amounts of foreign direct investment—probably witness to White House efforts. The Clinton team made a major issue of U.S. exports of flat glass to Japan (see *Nikkei Weekly*, May 10, 1999, p. 2); the beverage industry has been a classic multinational/export-oriented industry for decades. The accountants doubtless appreciated the president's opposition to Steve Forbes's flat tax every bit as much as poorer Americans whom it would heavily hit.

63. As the New York *Times* discreetly editorialized on March 17, 1999:

   Just as the Clinton campaign was eagerly accepting large donations from contributors who were linked to China or eager to do business there, the Administration was rethinking its policy and fumbling the first of several warnings that China might be stealing advanced nuclear weapons designs from the United States. . . . American corporate executives with commercial interests in China were generously donating to the Democratic Party. Shadowy sources possibly linked to the Chinese Government were making large contributions to the Clinton campaign that were later found to be improper.

See also the paper's earlier story of May 15, 1998, p. 1.

64. In forming judgments about the antitrust suit against Microsoft, it is instructive to recall that the suit appears to have relied heavily on events that took place in 1995. See *New York Times*, October 20, 1998, p. C4. For Clinton's later reversal on shareholder suits, see Miles (2001, 28–37).

65. Ken Auletta, "Pay Per Views," *New Yorker*, June 5, 1995, p. 55, predicted that Dole would "emerge as the major beneficiary of the communications industry" in the election campaign. He also quotes a "prominent Clinton Democrat" to this effect. Thus, perhaps, can the White House spin sophisticates.

66. See the estimates compiled by the Center for Responsible Politics of the largest donors in the 1996 race, available on its web site.

67. The literature is too vast to be surveyed here. See, e.g., Maney (1995); "Master of Bits at Home in the Hub," *Financial Times*, May 28, 1996.

68. Davis (1998) has a penetrating discussion of how all the hype was used to advance the fortunes of certain cable companies, notably John Malone's TCI. TCI certainly promoted such talk, though the movement was far wider. See in particular the often facile Maney (1995).

69. Here again the literature is too vast to be inventoried. See, e.g., *Wall Street Journal*, March 29, 1996; "A Threat to Media Diversity," *New York Times*, July 31, 1995, editorial; Consumer Federation of America, Center for Media Education, et al., to President Clinton, Sept. 20, 1995; Jon Healey, "Rejecting Further Regulation, Senate Easily Passes Bill," *Congressional Quarterly*, June 17, 1995, pp. 1727–31; Memorandum from Jeff Chester and Brad Stillman to Columnists, July 11, 1995; "A Flawed Communications Bill," *New York Times*, June 20, 1995, editorial; "Industry Argues for Deregulation," *USA Today*, May 31, 1995; and the discussion of Bell Atlantic and other phone companies in Davis (1998, passim, but esp. p. 185).

70. For most of this and the next paragraph, see Ferguson (1996a); see also the critical editorial in the *New York Times*, July 31, 1995; a coalition of long-distance carriers including Sprint, AT&T, and MCI placed ads reprinting newspaper editorials critical of the Telecom bill. See e.g., *National Journal*, Nov. 18, 1995, p. 2851. Various news organizations suppressed news and even refused to sell ads in cases they deemed inimical to their interests. See, e.g., Kirk Victor, "Media Monsters," *National Journal*, March 2, 1996, p. 483. The broadcasters' lack of interest in exploring Dole's challenge to the administration's gift of the extra free channel has been widely noted.

71. For the promised antitrust scrutiny, see "Justice Dept. Vows Scrutiny of Bell Deals," *New York Times*, April 29, 1996, pp. D1ff. For the lobbying frenzy after passage of the 1996 Act, see, e.g., *Wall Street Journal*, March 29, 1996, p. 1. For work by the Brookings analysts, see, e.g., Crandall and Furchtgott-Roth (1996).

72. For the copyright bill, see, e.g., *Boston Globe*, May 26, 1996, p. 77; Graeme Browning, "Copycats," *National Journal*, Jan. 6, 1996, pp. 23–26.

73. See Ferguson (1996a, 65); for Social Security, see the discussion below.

74. Democratic congressional leaders feared as late as the beginning of December that the White House might sell out its relatively hard-line position against big budget cuts. See, e.g., *Boston Globe*, Dec. 2, 1995, p. 4.

75. On the lack of excitement for Dole, see, e.g., *New York Times*, May 7, 1996, p. D1.

76. For Lighthizer and trade, see *Wall Street Journal*, Feb. 28, 1996, p. A16.

77. Ferguson (1996b, 64); for Dole and the Mexican bailout, see, e.g., *Wall Street Journal*, Jan. 31, 1995, p. A20. Here I also rely on information privately conveyed by scholars who briefed congressional groups organizing on the issue at the time. After the bailout was essentially in place, Dole became more critical. This evolution can be contrasted usefully with his views on the minimum wage, which hardened over time. Initially, he had signaled a willingness to compromise. See *Wall Street Journal*, Feb. 6, 1995, p. C17. In both cases, political calculations appear uppermost, with the desire to appeal to investor blocs driving everything.

78. For Dole and Time-Warner, see, e.g., Richard Cohen, "Another Day, Another Dole," *Washington Post*, Sept. 7, 1995, p. A19.

79. See the discussion in Ferguson (1996b).

80. For Dole and "special interests," see, e.g., *Boston Globe*, Oct. 8, 1995, p. 34–35; *Boston Phoenix*, March 29, 1996, sec. 1, p. 16; Ferguson (1996b).

81. In New York, some analysts have suggested to me privately that real estate executives became quite active in raising money for candidates opposed to Forbes. This was also my impression of the Boston area. But the multiplicity of candidates in the GOP and the Democratic alternative makes this question tough to sort out via a statistical analysis. There is no doubt about the hostility of many real estate interests to the flat tax, however. The National Association of Realtors mounted a major campaign against it. See Center for Responsive Politics, "Money in Politics Alert," vol. 2, no. 3, Jan. 29, 1996 (available at its web site). Note that accountants generally opposed the proposal, and that large accounting firms show up fairly strongly for Clinton in my sample. I suspect that some of the very richest individual real estate magnates were more sympathetic to the flat tax than their less affluent peers.

82. For Buchanan, Milliken, and the various organizations, cf. Ferguson (1996b); *Capital Eye*, May 1, 1996, pp 1ff. This is a newsletter published by the Center for Responsive Politics in Washington, D.C. See also *New York Times*, March 4, 1996, p. B8. For Milliken's fight against NAFTA, see, e.g., *Wall Street Journal*, Nov. 15, 1993, p. A9.

83. For Alexander's personal history, see, e.g., *New York Times*, Feb. 26, 1996, p. B7;

84. Gore famously denounced TCI's John Malone as "Darth Vader." See Davis (1998, 117–18).

85. *Boston Globe*, March 26, 1996, p. 16.

86. Ibid.

87. It is clear that by the end of the campaign public perceptions of Dole as a candidate cannot have been very helpful, though unlike most analysts, I would emphasize the role media accounts (including criticisms voiced by those with access to the media) play in forming these perceptions. The academic work on public responses to, for example, Ronald Reagan's facial displays, needs to recall more clearly that only a few observers suspected that the president suffered from Alzheimer's Disease in his second term. But more of this another time.

88. Lott's exact words have been differently reported. Compare the versions in the *Boston Globe*, July 10, 1998, p. E1 (where the quote is qualified by "reportedly") and the *New York Times*, June 27, 1998, p. A9. The quote appears to date from 1997.

89. Thus a news story of Sept. 30, 1998, p. A18 in the *Boston Globe* referred to a "long-running feud between the White House and congressional Democrats." The story describes a quarrel over plans to raise money for defense of the president in the impeachment proceedings vs. efforts to elect more Democrats to Congress. White House relations with congressional Democrats had been poor for a long time, not least because of the famous "triangulation" strategy Clinton pursued, which was a deliberate effort to position himself differently from them.

90. A list of contributors to the second inaugural is conveniently available at the web site of Public Disclosure (www.publicdisclosure.org). For the bank bill, see the graphic account in, e.g., *New York Times*, May 14, 1998, p. 1.

91. See the discussion, above, of the Telecommunications Act of 1996. For People for the American Way, see, e.g., *New York Times*, Dec. 1998. Another group worth mentioning was Censure and Move On, which organized mainly on the Internet. This was led by, among others, one "Larry Rockefeller" described in a "National News Release" of the group dated Feb. 5, 1999 as a "long time Republican from New York." The name well summarizes the group's purpose. It sought in particular to, as Rockefeller expressed it, "bring the Republican Party back into the mainstream," instead of leaving it in the hands of "Tom DeLay, Trent Lott, and Ken Starr." The release was put out on the Internet in cooperation with www. moveon.org, originally founded by two Silicon Valley figures, Wesley Boyd and his wife, Joan Blade.

92. For State Street's and Fidelity's role, see "State Street Jumps into Social Security Debate," *Boston Globe*, Feb. 29, 1996, p. 30. For the broader campaign, see *inter alia*, Robert Dreyfuss, "The End of Social Security As We Know It? *Mother Jones*, Nov./Dec. (1996), pp. 50ff.

93. For the disputes over Social Security and Clinton's panel, see *Boston Globe*, Nov. 12, 1998, p. A31. Some analysts regarded Clinton's own Social Security proposals as a repudiation of the campaign against it. See, e.g., Robert Kuttner, "Clinton's Winning Card," *Boston Globe*, Jan. 24, 1999, p. F7. There is something to this, since the proposals largely preserve the traditional plan; this happened because of very aggressive counterorganizing by labor and other groups. But Clinton's proposals disguise the extent to which the investment houses have gained their most lucrative point—both parties are converging on individual accounts. The Clinton proposals look on closer inspection to be part of a bargaining game in which the Democrats are trying to stake out their familiar territory of an overlap between the mass population and investment houses. See, especially, the analysis in David Warsh, "The Red Flag," *Boston Globe*, Jan. 24, 1999, p. D1. The whole effort depends crucially on a budget surplus, which could disappear with either a recession or a small war.

94. Expositions of the "natural rate" hypothesis can be found in virtually all economics texts. The view has a deep hold on financial markets, producing the oddity that stock markets sometimes sink with news of a drop in unemployment as investors fear Fed tightening.

95. See, e.g., Jomo (1998a, 6–10) or Wade (1999a). Most serious analysts take account of this factor. There are perhaps two exceptions: some popular accounts in the United States that lay blame mostly on "crony capitalism" or corruption and some accounts by economists close to some East Asian countries, who insist that all the fundamentals were really sound. They weren't; the balance of payments problems, combined with the short-term foreign borrowings, were dangerous in some crucial cases.

96. See the discussion in Johnson (1998); Jomo (1998a); and Singh (1998).

97. See, e.g., Singh (1998) or Jomo (1998b). Compare behavior in the West, where many financiers wax positively enthusiastic about rising interest rates and central bankers constantly trumpet the need for prudence and restraint. But this happens in systems where firms are accustomed to fairly large swings in interest rates. See also Wade (1999a), a paper that reached me as this manuscript was completed.

98. Many American accounts, particularly those from orthodox economists, pass over the moral-hazard problem the Mexican bailout generated. By contrast, it was a principal concern of German policymakers, at least at the central bank, where prominent members of the directorate raised the question. The Engelen articles cited below should be read in this context, but see especially Marietta

Kurm-Engels and Engelen's "Europa hat dem Westfalen viel zu verdanken," in *Handelsblatt*, Aug. 30, 1999, p. 4, which reviews the then outgoing Bundesbank President Tietmayer's battles with the U.S. Treasury. For the flood of capital into Asia, see, *inter multa alia*, Singh (1998) or Jomo (1998a).

99. On the differences between Asia and Latin America, see, e.g., David Hale, "Developing Country Financial Crises During the 1990s: Will Mexico's Recovery from the 1995 Peso Crisis Be a Role Model for Asia?" privately circulated newsletter; or Singh (1998).

100. See Johnson (1998); Edward J. Nell, private communication; the Bank for International Settlements regularly publishes data on financial flows in and out of various regions; this is available on its web site. My calculations are from versions of the BIS data kindly supplied me by Jan Kregel for the end of June 1997, and the end of 1996 and are consistent with subsequent German press accounts and later discussions of who was holding what bags in emerging markets debt. The spring Fed rate rise, mentioned below, surely helped attract back some of this capital, though the quarter-point rate rise was itself a response to the growth in the economy that was bringing back this capital. It is interesting that virtually no American accounts of the crisis take notice of the Fed rate increase, even if it is stretching a good point to make it solely responsible for the capital flight from Asia. Cf. the single sentence on the rate rise in Woodward (2000, 188).

101. For the Asian complaints about lack of investment in human capital, see the muted discussion in Jomo (1998a, p. 21); Jomo's essay in the *Nikkei Weekly*, Sept. 28, 1998, p. 17, is more to the point and also discusses the difficulties in upgrading exports due to lack of public investment in education and infrastructure. For the "branch plant" problems, see Hatch and Yamamura (1996).

102. In view of the controversy that surrounds the role of hedge funds in this episode, it is perhaps worth remarking that two extreme points of view appear indefensible. One is the claim that hedge funds played essentially no role in the crisis. The other is the suggestion that they were uniquely responsible for it. This latter is impossible to accept, given the importance of commercial and investment banks in foreign exchange markets. Many of these are strongly oriented toward trading profits, particularly in recent years. One could well argue, for example, that Goldman, Sachs, or Bankers Trust rank among the world's largest hedge funds. In the Asian crisis, as in many Latin American currency crises, exporters anxious to hedge their exposures created a tidal wave of sales out of the domestic currency in the final stages of the run.

It is therefore of considerable interest to witness the call for "government regulation of hedge funds" by Jon Corzine, then of Goldman, Sachs at a conference in, of all places, Kuala Lampur, at which Vice President Al Gore famously criticized Malaysian Prime Minister Mahathir. See *New York Times*, Nov. 17, 1998, p. A6.

103. See Hale, "Developing." I do not believe that the now common bank practice of securitizing bank loans negates this point.

104. Cf. Group of Ten, "The Resolution of Sovereign Liquidity Crises," May 1996. This can be downloaded from the Bank for International Settlements web site.

105. The best published sources for the German views and how they differed from those of U.S. policymakers are Klaus Engelen's articles for *Handelsblatt*. See, e.g., that on p. 2 for April 17, 1998; Engelen is certainly correct in noting that the Anglo-Saxon literature has taken virtually no account of these policy divergences. For other instances of German-U.S. divergence, see, e.g., Englen, "Europaeer muessen mehr Einfluss nehmen," *Handelsblatt*, Oct. 20, 1998, p. 2. On the differing roles of bank loans in the crises, see again, Hale, "Developing."

106. Engelen, "Banker Schiessen Gegen IWF-Chef," *Handelsblatt*, Feb. 6/7, 1998, p. 27; this articles quotes Rhodes (indirectly, though very explicitly) as having warned both Rubin and Camdessus that the announcement of a massively public

bailout for South Korea without a simultaneous accord with the creditor banks and other suppliers of capital would be strongly counterproductive and that both the IMF and the Treasury spurned his advice. The article also cites other criticisms by Rhodes and other bankers of the other bailouts in the crisis. In subsequent articles in *Handelsblatt* IMF officials retorted that they had in fact brought in the banks early, though it seems plain they did not. See, e.g., "Tietmeyer kritisiert IWF-Vorgehen," Feb. 24, 1998, p. 27 (where the banks' claims were seconded by the head of the Bundesbank) or Engelen's "Banken frueh in IWF-Hilfe einbezogen," May 4, 1998, p. 34. Though the critique is sometimes implicit, the alignment of the Bundesbank with the position of the commercial banks against the initial stance of the U.S. Treasury has been evident in numerous other articles before and after these. See, e.g., Engelen's "Rueckwind," or the interview with Juergen Stark, by then of the Bundesbank, in *Handelsblatt*, Dec. 9, 1998, p. 27.

107. For the general situation, see e.g., Ferguson (1998); the "MacArthur" quote is from Engelen, "Japan Contra USA," *Handelsblatt*, Dec. 2, 1997, p. 25. See also Wade (1999a, 1999b); the various essays in Jomo (1998b); and Johnson (1998); Wade and Veneroso (1998), among others. An important background essay is Halevi and Kriesler (1998). The alleged "insider" account in Woodward (2000) can instructively be compared with the facts recorded here and the references cited in previous notes.

108. Ferguson (1998). The "fat fees" quote comes from Engelen, "Lasten teilen," *Handelsblatt*, Jan. 21, 1998, p. 2. The role of the big American rating agencies in all this did not escape foreign observers, who charged them with applying different standards depending on what the Treasury and its private allies wanted. See Engelen, "Rating-Ohnmacht," *Handelsblatt*, Feb. 16, 1998, p. 23. This briefly discusses the need for a European rating agency of large size.

109. Ferguson (1998). These contributions, of course, were unlikely to advance the cause of getting votes in the state of New Jersey, where Corzine eventually won election to the U.S. Senate.

110. Given the equivocal outcome of the American pressures as discussed below, it may also be that the response was partly aborted, so that one is left to contemplate less a fact than a hope, though the size of the Goldman contributions is remarkable by any standard. Note that an incomplete tabulation by the Center for Responsive Politics of firm contributions to Democrats in the 1997–98 election cycle shows Goldman in a very high rank indeed. This is available on the Center's web site. The activities of some other investment houses with the GOP leaders in this period also merit scrutiny. I cannot examine the question here, but I believe a number of large houses for which retail stocks, rather than other types of securities, bulk larger, in this instance and others pursued different strategies.

111. Some Korean and United Nations sources have advanced this claim, though none will speak for the record; I have seen a copy of a letter of agreement between Korea and the IMF that seems extraordinary in the level of detail it goes into. Note, however, that Japanese insistence on opening Korean markets to its manufacturers appears to have been about as great as the American pressure.

112. Among many sources for these events, see, e.g., Robert J. Samuelson, "Global Wishful Thinking," *Boston Globe*, Jan. 19, 1999, p. D4; Jeffrey Sachs, "Brazil's Economic Crisis Shows Failure of Bailout Policy by US and IMF," *Boston Globe*, Jan. 11, 1999, p. A19; Wade (1999a); Todd (1998).

113. See the discussion of Andrew Johnson in Ferguson (1995, 69–70); the television reference is to Jonathan Schell, "An American Tragedy," *Nation*, Jan. 11/18, 1999, pp. 5–7, which blamed the impeachment crisis in part on television's alleged ability to nurture an historically novel flight to fantasy. Though this thesis is fairly easy to test, his discussion is virtually data free. I am reminded of Noam

Chomsky's old line from the sixties, that the biggest consumers of ideology were the upper-class ideologues: the evidence from polls is conclusive that most Americans, who watch TV, opposed impeachment. They weren't lost in space, inner or outer. Schell briefly mentions this inconvenient fact, without according it the importance it deserves. For the role of lobbying and contributions, see Ferguson (1992).

252

114. For Hastert, see *Boston Globe*, Dec. 24, 1998, p. A3, which estimates that he received at least $171,455 for his 1998 race from the health industry. The *Globe* for Dec. 21, 1998, p. A13, notes his closeness to House GOP leader Tom DeLay, described (in an understatement) as a "divisive figure" in the party. This article also relates Hastert's efforts to sink the "Patient's Bill of Rights" in far more detail than the *New York Times* piece on Hastert of Dec. 24, p. A12, "Health Care Was Catalyst for Donations to Rising Star." The article also observes that the single largest contributor to Hastert for the last three elections was Bell South. Gingrich's financing was discussed above. Figures published on the Center for Responsive Politics web site for the financing of congressional incumbents indicate that the health care lobby's contributions to Hyde during the 1998 election cycle were the fourth largest among the sectors studied by the Center, if one disregards the "catchall" categories of "miscellaneous business" and "lawyers and lobbyists."

115. See *Boston Globe*, Jan. 16, 1999, p. 1, for the AMA case.

116. See e.g., James Dao, "Undecided Members Tilt toward Impeachment," *New York Times*, Dec. 13, 1998, p. 44. See also *New York Times*, Dec. 15, p. 1 and 22ff. There is no reason to view "region" here as an asocial constant; the main difference might well be the weakness of unions outside parts of the east and Midwest. I believe this has indirect effects even on the media.

117. The public position of the U.S. government has been—and could scarcely be other than—the view that whatever was good for Europe would be good for the United States. But as the launch date for the euro neared, signs of American misgivings grew. In fact, most U.S. policymakers are suspicious of the euro's long-run impact on the United States. See, for example, William Pfaff, "The Un-Americanizing of Europe," *Boston Globe*, Jan. 11, 1999, p. A15. See also the discussion of Europe in Singer (1999).

For the record, one must note the success of the broadcast industry in killing proposals to require the industry to make minimum amounts of free air time available to political candidates. Trent Lott, particularly close to broadcasters, was their (handsomely paid) agent. See *Boston Globe*, Dec. 25, 1997, p. A27.

Shortly after the draft of this chapter was handed in to the editor, a crisis Alan Greenspan could not avert burst out in Kosovo. I regret that for reasons of space it is impossible for me to consider this subject further.

118. Tom DeLay and other Republicans have pioneered the use of organizations designed to make it possible for donors to contribute millions but escape all disclosure requirements. As this chapter went to press, they were finally being forced to report contributions to the IRS. There is also increasing use of state-regulated political action committees, to take advantage of lighter state regulations on political contributions and ever-increasing use of "issue" ads allegedly uncoordinated with campaigns and other dodges. The bourgeoning use of such ads is mixing explosively with the "soft money" to create the prospect of campaigns in which both parties can spend unlimited amounts of money as long as they remain apparently independent of particular candidacies. We are back in the Gilded Age, where virtually anything goes.

119. This chapter went to press before the U.S. Supreme Court, by a 5–4 margin, awarded victory in the 2000 presidential election to the candidate who lost the popular vote but won the money race.

References

Brown, E. Richard. 1981. *Rockefeller Medicine Men*. Berkeley: University of California Press.

Brown, Walter Adams. 1940. *The International Gold Standard Reinterpreted*. New York: National Bureau of Economic Research.

Cole, Michael. 1990. Cultural psychology: A once and future discipline? In J. Berman (ed.), *Nebraska Symposium on Motivation—1989: Cross Cultural Perspectives, vol. 37, Current Theory and Research in Motivation*. Lincoln: University of Nebraska Press.

Cooper, Mary H. 1994. Regulating tobacco. *CQ Researcher* 4: 841–64.

Crandall, Robert W., and Harold Furchtgott-Roth. 1996. *Cable TV: Regulation or Competition*. Washington, D.C.: Brookings Institution.

Davis, L. J. 1998. *The Billionaire Shell Game*. New York: Doubleday.

Ferguson, Thomas. 1992. Money and politics. In G. Hodgson (ed.), *Handbooks to the Modern World—The United States*. Vol. 2. New York City: Facts on File, pp. 1060–84.

———. 1995. *Golden Rule: The Investment Theory of Party Competition and the Logic of Money-Driven Political Systems*. Chicago: University of Chicago Press.

———.1996a. Bill's big backers. *Mother Jones*, Nov.–Dec., 60–66.

———. 1996b. Bob's best buddies. *Mother Jones*, Nov.–Dec., 65–66.

———. 1998. Moneymover. *Mother Jones*, Nov.–Dec., 63.

———. 1999a. Big business leadership and discrimination: An alternative econometric test. *Industrial and Corporate Change* 8: 777–98.

———. 1999b. Smoke in Starr's chamber. *Nation*, 8 March, 11–14.

Ferguson, Thomas, and Joel Rogers. 1986. *Right Turn: The Decline of the Democrats and the Future of American Politics*. New York: Hill & Wang.

Halevi, Joseph, and Peter Kriesler. 1998. History, politics, and effective demand in Asia. In J. Halevi and J.-M. Fontaine (eds.), *Restoring Demand in the World Economy*. Cheltenham, UK: Edward Elgar, pp. 77–92.

Hatch, Walter, and Kozo Yamamura. 1996. *Asia in Japan's Embrace*. New York: Cambridge University Press.

Johnson, Chalmers. 1998. Economic crisis in East Asia: The clash of capitalisms. *Cambridge Journal of Economics* 22: 653–61.

Jomo, K.S. 1998a. Introduction: Financial governance, liberalization, and crises in East Asia. In K. S. Jomo (ed.), *Tigers in Trouble*. London: Zed Books, pp. 1–32.

———. 1998b. *Tigers in Trouble*. London: Zed Books.

Maney, Kevin. 1995. *Megamedia Shakeout*. New York: Wiley.

Martin, Cathie Jo. 1995. Nature or nurture: Sources of firm preference for national health reform. *American Political Science Review* 89: 898–913.

Meeropol, Michael. 1998. *Surrender: How the Clinton Administration Completed the Reagan Revolution*. Ann Arbor: University of Michigan Press.

Miles, Sara. 2001. *How to Hack a Party Line: The Democrats and Silicon Valley*. New York: Farrar, Straus, and Giroux.

National Education Association. 1998. *The Real Story Behind 'Paycheck Protection'—The Hidden Link Between Anti-Worker and Anti-Public Education Initiatives*. Washington, D.C.: National Education Association.

Palmer, Bryan. 1990. *Descent into Discourse*. Philadelphia: Temple University.

Parry, Robert. 1997. The dark side of Reverend Moon: Hooking George Bush. *Consortium*, 28 July, 3–8.

———. 1998a. The impeachment conspiracy. *IF Magazine*, Nov.–Dec., 29–34.

———. 1998b. Rev. Moon's dark shadow. *IF Magazine*, Nov.–Dec., 4–7.

Rothmyer, Karen. 1981. Citizen Scaife. *Columbia Journalism Review*, July–August.

Saloma, John S. 1984. *Ominous Politics*. New York: Hill and Wang.

Sherrill, Robert. 1995. Buying his way to a media empire. *Nation*, 29 May, 749–54.

Sheskin, David. 1997. *Handbook of Parametric and Non-Parametric Statistical Procedures*. New York: CRC Press.

Singer, Daniel. 1999. *Whose Millennium? Theirs or Ours?* New York: Monthly Review.

Singh, Ajit. 1998. "Asian capitalism" and the financial crisis. New School for Social Research, New York City.

Todd, Walker. 1998. Financial Problems of a Large Hedge Fund. *FOMC Alert* 2:6–8.

U.S. Bureau of the Census. 1998. *Statistical Abstract of the United States*, vol. 1998. Washington, D.C.: U.S. Government Printing Office.

Wade, Robert. 1999a. Lessons from the Asian crisis. Paper presented at the Annual Meeting of the Asian Development Bank, Manila, Philippines.

———. 1999b. The U.S. role in the Asian crisis. Massachusetts Institute of Technology.

Wade, Robert, and Frank Veneroso. 1998. The gathering world slump and the battle over capital controls. *New Left Review* 231:13–42.

Webber, Michael J., and G. William Domhoff. 1996. Myth and reality in business support for Democrats and Republicans in the 1936 presidential election. *American Political Science Review* 90: 824–33.

Woodward, Bob. 2000. *Maestro: Greenspan's Fed and the American Boom*. New York: Simon and Schuster.

12

The Battle between Issue Expanders and Containers: The Elderly behind the Wheel in the Twenty-First Century

ROGER W. COBB AND JOSEPH F. COUGHLIN

Politics involves a battle over who is going to control the political agenda. The selection of issues for active consideration by decision makers is one of the pivotal questions that all political systems must decide. Which questions will receive serious attention: drugs, immigration, alternative forms of power, education, or smoking? All of the above or none of the above? Issue conflict involves a dynamic process in which participants can come and go; the basis of the conflict can change so dramatically that initial positions can be submerged. All protagonists are constantly looking for ways to enhance their position and devalue the arguments of the opponents.

There are two sets of participants in any political conflict. The issue *initiators* or *expanders* are those who want a hearing for their grievances. They consist of those who have not been previously heard or those who have received past attention but believe the political response was inadequate. Those advocating consideration of new issues are usually political amateurs, and issue involvement is their first excursion into the political world. If initiators are successful, they will weaken, threaten, or restructure some existing set of symbolic or power relationships.

Some persons or groups will be negatively impacted by that result. This group is called the *containers* because they want to narrow the scope of conflict. Their principal desire is to prevent the initiator from gaining the attention of the public and relevant decision makers: to maintain their advantage as reflected by the status quo. Containers can assume one of two forms. The first is the economically impacted group. If the expander is successful in getting on the agenda, laws are passed forbidding certain types of activities. Such regulations are going to cost some groups money. Their opposition can be predicted.

255

Environmentalists vs. developers is an illustration of this battle. A second type of container is the symbolically impacted group. It deals not with economics but with identity. If people feel their "way of life" is threatened, then they fight to maintain their position. Government not only allocates economic benefits, but it confers legitimacy on various groups and identities and endorses or sanctions their practices. The battle over gay rights illustrates that process. All political disputes involve ongoing battles between these two groups to gain the political advantage (Cobb and Ross 1997).

Initiators vs. Containers: Who Has the Advantage?

Over a generation ago, E. E. Schattschneider (1960, 71) first described the playing field for all those conflict combatants. It was not level but tilted. He noted that "organization is the mobilization of bias. Some issues are organized into politics while others are organized out." Bachrach and Baratz (1970, 58) added that the "mobilization of bias strongly favors those currently defending the status quo." Containers usually win disputes over issue conflicts for a variety of reasons:

1. The institutional agendas of all organizations are clogged with old business. Budgetary items involve annual inspections. Contentious issues that have been put off (e.g., abortion, school prayer, immigration) continuously reappear. Indeed, decision makers have more than an ample quantity on their collective plates to digest without the presence of any new items. Such a prospect makes the efforts of any new issue group daunting, to say the least (Cobb and Elder, 1983).
2. Most governmental officials move into the container camp. Given the resource limitations of all governmental units and the clogged agendas, officials are not predisposed to entertain new issue positions. Bureaucrats particularly like to exist in a world without encumbering additional conflicts where all the participants are happy in debating allocation of resources among existing recipients. New players raise concerns of unpredictability and uncertainty and bring in new conflicts. All of these elements represent an uncertain scenario. Officials value regularity, predictability, and known outcomes. The alliance between officials and adversely affected groups is normally not codified or organized. But their basic interests overlap in desiring minimal input from initiators.

   Bureaucrats are further constrained by the "idea climate" that exists at the time. Kingdon (1995) described the organizational agendas of two policy areas between 1976 and 1978, health and transportation. In each, the time period studied was dominated by one specific innovation or idea: health by the creation of a new structural entity, the health maintenance organization; and transportation by deregulation. Any idea that was not linked to the predominant mode of thought was doomed. All innovations had to be seen in terms of those constraints. Thus, issue advocates must be able to link their idea to the dominant idea pervading the policy network or wait until the next rhetorical wave appears.

3. The ramifications of solutions to potential problems also benefit the containers. Most new issue proponents require increased governmental regulation in an issue area, which costs money. All governmental units are cost-conscious and extremely reluctant to invest money in new issue areas. As a result, cash-strapped legislators and bureaucrats are not going to look happily on any claimants who want to spend more money to solve their grievance unless their case is made in a compelling fashion. A favorite container strategy is simply to argue that "it costs too much" and it is much safer and easier to do nothing, entailing no further financial commitments.

4. Initiators are often inept in advancing their cause. This group is often politically inexperienced, naïve, and uniformed about the ways of the political world. Enthusiasm can often lead to tactical errors, foolish mistakes, and inappropriate use of organizational resources. Most political activists refrain from becoming involved in new issue disputes, thereby limiting the types of experiences that initiators can drawn upon in making their case to the public and decision makers.

5. The passage of time is normally not an advantage for the initiator. The initiator needs to strike quickly while there is some public attention and member enthusiasm. As time passes, the interest of many relevant parties (media, initiators themselves, their target audience) wanes and moves on to other issues. Often an initiator is aided by the occurrence of an event that points to the existence of a particular problem (focusing event) such as the Exxon oil spill, but such occurrences must be exploited before the passage of too much time. Schattschneider (1960) argued that the passage of time leads to another factor that impairs the success of initiator groups. Issue displacement involves the intrusion of other events onto the political scene, thereby reducing or minimizing the impact of one particular cause.

6. An absolute requisite for initiator success is issue visibility. The only means by which the public can become acquainted with a private grievance is through the media. Expanders can provide themes that the media favor: conflict, tragedy, deviance, anecdotal severity of an issue, and occasionally celebrity linkage to a grievance (Deering and Rogers 1996). If an issue can attain media spotlight, the possibility of expanding the scope of the issue is great. However, the media can absorb only a limited number of issues at any one time, and their attention span is notoriously short (Baumgartner and Jones 1993).

7. A final restrictive element refers to the arsenal of weapons available to the container. Unlike initiators, all containers have gone through the process of gaining agenda access at one prior point to account for their present privileged position. There is a clear resource inequality between the contending parties. Containers have the bulk of experience, political connection, media access, and organizational resources. Cathie Jo Mar-

tin has shown in chapter 10 how small businesses aggressively defend their hard-fought gains against further governmental regulation. In addition, containers have the power to shift the venue for the conflict, further taxing the resources of the initiator. Bringing suit against the initiator for alleged illegal actions can drain the resources and commitment of a contending group (Prang and Canan 1996).

Of all these advantages, the most frequently mentioned is material resources. In most political conflicts, the resource differentials of the two sides are strikingly uneven and do in part account for why a particular issue does or does not receive serious consideration from the relevant governmental unit. However, the resource argument cannot explain the following types of outcomes: (1) situations in which the party with far greater resources does not win an agenda conflict (e.g., tobacco companies); (2) situations in which the resources of opposing groups may be so different that making a clear decision about who possesses more is far from straightforward (e.g., a conflict in which one of the parties has symbolic resources while the other relies on cash); and (3) simple material-based explanations that avoid the question of spelling out how specific resources are converted into political outcomes in a given agenda conflict.

Then Why Should the Initiator Bother?

Given all these container advantages, why should the initiators even attempt to influence political decisions? Obviously the assumption that one has a grievance, feels intensely, and believes in the rightness of the position will lead many to political activity. However, there is a more basic argument that underlies most agenda disputes. Agenda conflicts are not just about what issues government chooses to act on, but they are also about competing interpretations of political problems and the alternative worldviews that underlie them. These concern how people ought to lead their daily lives, how society ought to be organized, what should or should not be done by government, how we should treat the environment, and so on. The strategic choices open to issue initiators and opponents turn attention to cultural and symbolic forces that are crucial in determining the ability of opponents to prevent the serious consideration of a new issue. Cultural processes, and especially the dynamics of identification, matter when they invoke threats and deep fears and affectively link political grievances to existing worldviews and individuals to political groups. These connections often account for the high commitment and intensity of involvement on matters that often seem trivial to outsiders. Quality-of-life issues mobilize major sectors of the public. For example, environmentalists define events affecting the use of public lands as crucial to their identification as citizens.

What Determines an Issue Victory—Objective Reality or Cultural Framing?

Most issues have an objective basis in fact. There are individuals or groups who are negatively impacted by the actions or words of others. Grievances can be quantified to show the scope and severity of a problem. Stone (1997) notes that numbers give a legitimacy to a problem to justify public discussion of its ramifications. However, in a sense initiators are faced with a daunting task. They must show that their issue can be ranked high on some misery scale that requires action. However, facts and objective studies of problems are not the primary motivations for political actions. If they were, political units would be more active in areas such as the homeless and immigration. Initiators who use only objective indicators to justify societal and governmental attention to their plight will often find few takers.

Edelman (1964) emphasized the role of language and the ability to connect particular policy concerns with deeply held cultural symbols. It has been argued that to be effective, the president must embody a symbolic posture to buttress his program. Political conflict is cultural contestation. Rochefort and Cobb (1994) discussed how the definition of a problem can determine the likelihood that other groups will rally around a particular cause. Both initiators and containers attempt to frame the issue in language that will produce the most positive response from the public and governmental officials.

Felstiner, Abel, and Sarat (1980–81) argue that the process of transforming a private grievance into a public problem requires three separate steps: naming, blaming, and claiming. The first, naming, labels the grievance in such as a way that it will be accepted by the public at large. Edward Carmines shows in chapter 8 that affirmative action is viewed quite differently by white liberals depending on how the problem is stated. They are much more responsive to issues phrased in racially inclusive language, while they resist framing racial issues in racially exclusive terms.

For the greater part of the twentieth century, the loss of mental acuity in the aging process was thought to be normal. Senility was a fact of life. There was no problem. But in the mid-1980s, the problem was redefined as one of Alzheimer's disease, which had been discovered in 1907. This disease was not synonymous with senility and could affect those younger than 65. Suddenly it became a public issue with research paths opening up to alleviate a problem that had had minimal public visibility. As a malady with no cure, it was now viewed as a significant public health concern by the media and the public. Old-age maladies were seen in a completely different light (Butler 1984). Senility was a private issue; Alzheimer's was a public concern.

Blaming is the second phase of issue transformation. When negative events occur, people look for explanations of what caused the unpleasant outcome. Attributions of responsibility are a key mechanism used by people to make sense out of their social world. In the political domain, finger pointing is a common exercise. As Iyengar noted "people think about responsibility instinctively, and attribution of responsibility represents a powerful psychological cue" (1991, 10). In issue conflicts, a particular culprit is blamed for the unfair treatment a target group has received. Outside groups often identify a grievance perpetrated by others as the reason for their plight. In the case of job safety, pollution, and destruction of the environment, people who were made homeless, poor, or sick because of the actions of others can be portrayed as innocent targets. One natural enemy is business and its desire for maximum profits; another is government portrayed as a set of faceless bureaucrats insistent on enforcing unfair regulations that intrude on people's lives.

In recent years, the role of the target has been redefined as one of "victim." Victims are normally portrayed as politically weak or helpless but deserving of support. They deserve sympathy because they are unwilling recipients of negative actions imposed on them by others. They define the situation as being put into an unpleasant situation through no fault of their own. Schneider and Ingram (1993, 334–36) argue that there are two crucial dimensions of target evaluation: positive and negative constructions, and perceptions of strength and weakness. They posit that those most deserving of victim status are those that are seen to be positively but politically weak. Rochefort (1989, 132–35) takes a similar tack by arguing that social welfare populations will tend to receive greater support if they are seen as victims of circumstances beyond their control, people with a high degree of need, and groups with a positive societal image. The eighties and nineties have seen an explosion in this usage. Recent claimants of this status include children, the disabled, the elderly, or any in a dependent status, particularly when seen as objects of abuse: sexual, physical, economic, or psychological. Victim status is now claimed by any individual, ethnic, or gender group responding to a demeaning act or remark, or anyone pursued by the media or government.

In fact, the strategy has been so widely used that it has been copied by containers who now portray themselves as victims of unfair initiator onslaughts or coverage. Though containers cannot claim weakness or helplessness, they can argue they have been unfairly accused by the initiators (with the help of the media) and are deserving of support. This can be seen in a variety of contexts. Timber interests in the Northwest and developers have argued that they are the victims of extreme environmentalists who have interfered with their business, attempting to place harmful grievances on formal agendas without justification (Switzer 1997). Tobacco companies argued they have been unfairly portrayed in the media as benefiting from the health miseries of smokers.

The third step, claiming, involves making specific demands on the government to change its policy. Initiators make arguments to attract support and widen the scope of concern. Advocates stress that their issue involves large numbers of people (scope), with devastating consequences (severity), affecting future generations (spillover), which is unique (no precedent). Containers will make the reverse arguments, attempting to privatize the issue to a few selfish malcontents pushing a grievance that does not now impact others and will not affect others in the future, and claiming that a problem, if it exists, can be dealt with using current resources. Both sides will rely more heavily on ambiguous claims than on objective, factual statements to buttress their plight when appealing for public support. Initiators will couch their arguments in threatening terms using negative language, while containers will dispute their contentions as groundless. The key in claiming is to link the issue position to values that are salient in the culture at that time. Americans have always been responsive to appeals of liberty, freedom, equality, and reduced governmental regulation.

Application to a Twenty-First Century Issue: Elderly Drivers

What is the politics of the next century going to look like? One trend that is already apparent is the existence of more elderly persons. We are an aging nation. Using an arbitrary age of 65, in 1988, 12 percent of the population fit into that group. Today, we approach 14 percent. By 2020, that group will compose approximately 20 percent of the population and continue growing subsequently. The political system is only beginning to deal with some of those ramifications, such as the shrinking size of the Social Security, Medicare, and Medicaid funds. The aged are and will continue to be one of the most rapidly growing demographic groups in the country.

How are they going to get around? Driving appears to be the main answer. The increasing number of the elderly in the population and their corresponding growth in the proportion of drivers who are over 65 years is depicted in Figure 12-1. One of the myths is that older Americans "are largely residents of high-density urban areas, dependent on public transit for their mobility" (Rosenbloom 1988). However most people over 65 live in suburban or rural communities, hold driver's licenses, and own automobiles. Their preferred

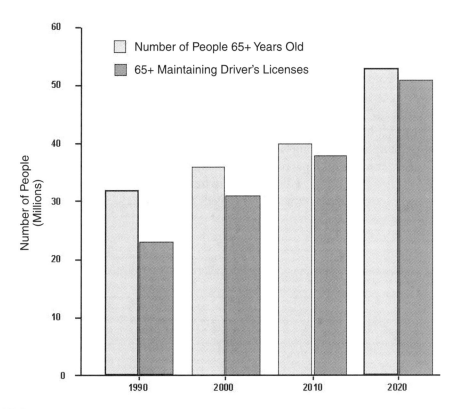

FIGURE 12-1
Projected Growth in the Number of People 65+ Years Old and the Number Maintaining a Driver's License*

*2000–2020 Population estimates reflect US Census middle series projections, driver license projections are based upon authors' extrapolation of FHWA data 1977–1994.

mode of travel is the car. As one other expert notes, "the importance of being able to drive doesn't diminish with age, if anything it becomes even more important (Tull 1995, 1). Between 1965 and 1990 the number of elderly who drive has increased by over 50 percent.

However, studies have shown that aging increases vision and behavioral impairment in skills related to driving. There have been four areas of concern: visual search, recognition of a problem, evaluation (making a decision to act), and response (foot to brake pedal). Each slows with age. However, research has also shown that "older drivers continue to drive as long as possible and resist change to their preferred mode of travel" (Jette and Branch 1992, 25).

Objective Reality and Elderly Drivers: What Do the Facts Show?

Given that there are more and more elderly drivers on the road, are they unsafe? What do the studies show? Are the experts convinced there is a problem? The evidence is not conclusive. There is a division of opinion on the issue even based on the facts. Again it depends on how the problem is measured. If the focus is on total fatalities, the total number of persons killed on U.S. roads reached a high of over 50,000 in the early eighties but has decreased to nearer 40,000 in the past five years. If one looks at age groups by crash involvement rates in pure magnitude, then youth have the highest rate and the elderly the lowest rate, as shown in Figure 12-2. The elderly drive fewer miles than other groups and consequently are involved in fewer crashes (USDOT 1996).

However, if the statistic is not an absolute number but a relative statistic based on a ratio of accidents to the number of miles driven, the pattern changes dramatically. The most reckless remain the youth aged 15–24, but then the second most dangerous driving-age group on the road is the elderly (over 65). This was observed in a Department of Transportation (DOT) report: "[T]here is a well-established U-shaped relationship between driver age and per-mile accident involvement rates, with older drivers having greater rates of accidents,

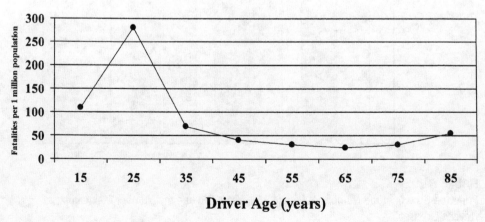

FIGURE 12-2
Fatalities per 1 Million Population

FIGURE 12-3
Fatalities per 100 Million Vehicle Miles of Travel

injuries, and fatalities than middle-age drivers" (USDOT 1996, 1). This relationship is depicted in Figure 12-3. Further, the statistics show a sharp escalation with age. There is a small increase in the late sixties, a substantial increase in the early seventies, and then a dramatic increase through the eighties (USDOT 1996). Given an accident situation involving a driver over 65, the older driver will likely be found at fault (Evans 1991). While driver fatalities fell in the 1980s, there was a 43 percent increase in driver fatalities for those over 65. They are more likely to die or have serious medical problems from their injuries because they are more physically vulnerable (Luchter 1994).

Thus, objective reality and the statistical studies do not resolve the problem or even point clearly to a political solution. There is evidence for both sides of the issue. Each side can counter the empirical studies with those of their own, giving the legislators, bureaucrats, and the public an ambiguous and confusing issue. How has the problem been defined?

Initiators and Containers in the Elderly Drivers Debate

Initiators. Who are the groups concerned with elderly driver safety who want governmental action? The principal group consists of those families who lost a member in an accident caused by an elderly driver. In Massachusetts, psychiatrist Kathy Larned used her medical stature and financial resources to set up an institute to study the problem and lobby the state legislature after the third family member had been killed in a traffic mishap by an elderly driver. Victims' families want additional restrictions placed on elderly drivers, in the form of greater testing procedures, making it more difficult for them to get their licenses renewed. They favor the use of governmental funds to target problematic elderly drivers before they cause a crash. Most of these organizations do not have sizable cash resources but rely on intensity and conviction to pressure political officials into action. Their fury will not soon pass. A second group consists of some transportation and medical officials who believe that special care must be exercised in granting elderly drivers the unrestricted power to operate their cars. A third group is the media themselves. Their attention to the issue is sporadic, but when attention is focused on the problem it is usually dramatic, spotlighting an elderly driver who causes an accident that harms one or more people. The driver is normally not portrayed in a positive fashion. Anecdotal accounts of accidents outnumber the few articles devoted to an analysis of the problem. However, anyone reading one of the accident stories would conclude that something needs to be done (e.g., Grogan 1994).

Containers.   Who is opposed? The elderly as individuals and as a group are prime adversaries to those pushing driving reforms targeting them. As individuals, most elderly still get around through use of automobiles. Any additional governmental restrictions are seen negatively. The group protecting such drivers is the American Association of Retired People (AARP). One of the largest and most powerful pressure groups in the country, it is exceedingly active on all elderly issues at both the federal and state levels. It wants no restrictions placed on elderly drivers and favors leaving the laws as they are.

Defining the Issue of Elderly Drivers

How has this issue been managed in the political arena? In one scenario, the most rapidly growing segment of the population has an unsafe driving record and will kill even more people in the future. Others claim that this same group is the safest segment of society when behind a wheel and no problem exists. Who has been more successful in defining the problem, the initiators or the containers?

Naming.   How has the problem been named? The obvious name is the "elderly driver problem." However, this problem never appears on the top list of problems the public is concerned about. Even the name has not appeared frequently in print. The term "elderly" does not have a negative resonance in our culture. Even the initiators have realized the limitations of naming the problem in this fashion. The former head of the Massachusetts effort, Larned argued that the problem needed to be renamed. She preferred the "impaired driver." This term was originally used to refer to alcohol- or drug-related driving (U.S. House of Representatives, 1995). Now it is used to refer to people with some type of medical condition that limits their driving effectiveness. Using this term avoids the notion of stigmatizing older people and focuses on those who are "impaired," an age-neutral term. As Larned notes:

> There are people in their 80's who are competent drivers but there are a lot of people who have no way of assessing their own skills and how their abilities are changing and how a medical condition could result in a car crash. . . . Research has shown that age is not a critical factor. It is ability and it is impairment. (Johnson, 1995, 6)

However, this tactical maneuver has not changed how the issue is viewed. Though the naming of the problem avoids negatively depicting an age group, its breadth becomes a drawback. The term is used in so many different contexts that its meaning is lost. Waller (1992, 10) notes: "[T]he definition of what represents a reportable impairment to driving is so vague that most persons with medical conditions believe it does not apply to them."

Blaming.   Who or what is responsible for the problem? Who gets blamed? Personally impacted initiators all have anecdotal horror stories that they tell and retell. Larned said that the 82-year-old woman who killed her husband was told by her doctor not to drive, had seizures, was not taking her prescribed medicine, and had been in five previous accidents within the past few years. Here the emphasis is clear. The initiator will place the blame squarely on the person who was at the wheel: the driver. Further, Larned does not even use the term "accident" in her speech and writing, preferring instead to use the term "crash." If one talks about accidents, it does not stress the intentionality of the driving act. It says that something went wrong but does not specify what. But if one uses the term "crash" or "motor vehicle violence," that places greater responsibility on the driver and suggests that the incident could have been avoided (Johnson, 1995, 6). Intentionality is one of the most important parts of a conflict scenario and helps people sort out what happened and whom to blame (Stone 1997).

How do containers handle the problem of injuries caused by older drivers? Whom do they blame? There are a variety of strategies that have been employed. Their general strategy is to claim victim status and that they have been unfairly singled out for attention that is not justified. They look for others to blame. The first is to blame those drivers with an even higher accident rate regardless of the statistics used: the young drivers. Focus the attention on them, not older drivers. Containers have statistical support for this position. Second, they blame the media for incendiary stories about elderly driving accidents. Yes, they happen, but accidents occur for all age groups, so why pick on the elderly? Third, they target the victim families for launching a vendetta against them. Yes, an elderly person caused an accident, but you can't blame a group for the failures of a few.

In addition, they will blame situational factors that were present at the time of the accident. Most accidents occur during bad weather, on poorly lit roads, at night, or as a result of an automobile dysfunction. In other words, blame the situation, not the individual. Anyone facing those conditions could be involved in a crash. It had nothing to do with age.

Claiming.   The third element in the translation of a private grievance into a public problem involves the claims made by both parties. The expanders will rely on a number of claims. The first is the statistical claim cited earlier. Elderly drivers are the second worst age group when measured by miles driven. They are a rapidly growing group and their physical skills decline with advanced age, particularly those that involve split-second decisions requiring depth-perception skills. The problem is unique in that other age groups do not have declining physical skills, and it requires a special response. In contrast to the objective data, the emotional language of human loss and the pain it produces is found in the retelling of each accident story. As one member of a victim's family said: "My trauma was pretty substantial. You can heal sexual abuse and physical abuse but you can't heal this. You can't bring the loved one back. My world was shattered" (Johnson 1995, 6). Expanders will appeal to the values of life, family cohesion, and safety. These are powerful symbols that attract public support. Finally, the expanders argue that there is no dearth of solutions for the problem. The key decision point in controlling drivers is license renewal. What is required is a tougher evaluation of this driving group before relicensing takes place. All of the test vehicles (eye test, driving test, knowledge test) need to be more stringent. Doctors should be required to report to the relevant authorities those older persons with physical ailments that would bring into question their driving performance.

Containers will use a variety of claims to support their position. First, they will claim that elderly drivers are the safest age group behind the wheel. They are the only age cohort to self-regulate its driving. They tend not to drive at night, during rush hour, in bad weather, or in unfamiliar areas, so they generally avoid the most risky driving conditions. In addition, their trips are shorter in length, although they make as many trips as other age groups if commuting to work is not counted (Lerner, Morrison, and Raffe 1990, 5).

Second, they make claims relying on a cultural perception that sees the age group in very positive terms. In an analysis of twenty-five congressional hearings chosen at random between 1946 and 1995 on issues related to the aged, McGonagle (1997) found that 70 percent of all references to the elderly were positive. What was the basis of their perceptions? Witnesses saw the elderly as positive members of the community making contributions in a variety of ways. Policies that encourage the elderly to live at home rather than be institutionalized were generally favored. Ten percent referred to the elderly in negative terms, normally focusing on needs (financial need, security needs, or medical needs). This particular issue reinforces that image of keeping the elderly mobile, active, and contributors to the community.

Now it is true the term "elderly driver" does not connote as positive an image. Many link that image to the time they were on a road in which they were stuck behind an elderly driver going too slowly or driving erratically. But those images are situation-specific. Take the driver out of that context and the intensity is reduced. Containers have fought this image by pointing to the excellent driving records of most older drivers.

Containers also couch their claims in appeals to basic elements of our political culture. One is the belief in fair and equal treatment. Why single out one group of drivers for special restrictions when they are not applied equally to all age groups, particularly younger groups? Cries of "discrimination," "unequal treatment," "due process," and "just cause" frame the elders' response. Why test them when their licenses are up for renewal and let all of the age groups through without scrutiny? Certainly, some of the drivers in all of these age groups are unsafe. Then use the testing procedures to ferret out all unsafe drivers regardless of age. Many lawmakers are loath to tread in such contestable waters.

Another value appeal relates to the notions of independence, freedom, and the avoidance of government intrusion into our daily lives. The elderly are dependent on cars to get around. The driver's license is their passport to the world beyond their homes. To deny them their driving privilege makes them then lonely and dependent on others and causes a loss of self-esteem. As one safety official said, "It takes away their independence and their ability to travel with whom they want and when they want to" (Thomason 1993, A1). Some refer to the issue as one of "automobility."

Containers also appeal to another symbol that has gained prominence in the passage of years. The notion of rights has been expanded by court decisions during the past three decades. Nearly every activity of human behavior has now been linked to a "right" that cannot be denied. Transportation is no expectation. Elderly refer to driving as a "right" in much the same breath as they mention the rights guaranteed by the constitutional founders. Getting behind the wheel of a car is a basic right to support mobility. How can that be denied? That kind of symbolic appeal resonates with the driving majority. Further, opposition to increasing governmental regulation strikes a responsive chord with many Americans. This is a case in which regulators might directly intervene in the daily lives of citizens rather than as some faceless bureaucrats filling out forms.

Governmental Officials as Containers

Governmental officials involved in determining transportation policy have not been advocates of reform in this policy area. Why? Their principal concern on the roads is to maintain safety. Safety is defined as keeping deaths and injuries on the highways as low as possible. In order to achieve that, they must identify the main threats to road safety. But who is that? There are so many targets to choose from that any individual problem often gets lost in the shuffle. In the sixties and seventies the main problem was the speeding driver and the emphasis was on lower speed limits and stricter enforcement of the traffic laws. However, in the early eighties, with the advent of Mothers Against Drunk Driving, the emphasis shifted to the alcoholic-impaired driver, and most states focused on lowering the levels for determining when a driver is drunk. Also in the eighties the emphasis on driver safety focused on the use of safety belts and getting people strapped in prior to turning on the ignition switch. The "belted driver" was the objective for traffic experts. Over the last three decades, there has been a spotlight on younger drivers, who have the worst safety records. In the past year, the emphasis has shifted to the "aggressive driver," with the term "road rage" indicating people who are taking out their anxieties and personal problems behind the wheel (Palmer 1997). Given all these problems, it is difficult for officials to maintain the focus on one set of dangerous problems. In such a situation, given limited governmental funds and a need to prioritize transportation problems, the elderly driver quickly moves away from the spotlight.

Most governmental officials do not want to take elderly drivers off the road and favor extending their driving privileges as long as possible (Mercier and Falb 1997). However, some recognition of the problem is required by bureaucrats to show concern for all age groups. In this case, the emphasis has not been in tightening regulations for licensing renewal but instead focusing on symbolic or cosmetic changes. Most states have produced larger, easier-to-read signs so that the elderly are able to make decisions with greater accuracy on the highways. Some states have moved toward restricted driving licenses limiting the time, place, and conditions of driving. But most states have not seriously reconsidered the relicensing procedure.

What's to Be Done? The Battle Over Solutions

Analysts have noted that most problems are not considered by officials unless a solution is available (Wildavsky 1974). In the elderly driver context, there are really three types of possible responses: restricting licenses, which is the expander's solution; cosmetic action, which has been the bureaucratic response; and inaction, which is favored by the containers. Retesting older drivers when their licenses come up for renewal would require hiring thousands of new road inspectors, larger facilities, and an enlargement of highway bureaucracies throughout the nation. But when attention is focused on the problem, containers can always point to a solution with strong cultural support: the technological fix.

In this case, it is the "smart car." Automobile manufacturers are currently developing such vehicles, which apply advanced electronics, communications, and sensing technologies to enhance the safety of driving. In the ultimate prototype, the technology does all the driving and the passenger is merely a passive participant. This would provide all drivers with obstacle detection systems, improved night vision capability, maps to reach an objective with minimal congestion, and detection devices to warn the driver of inadvertent lane changes (Birch 1995). However, the extent to which the elderly driver can adapt to such technology has yet to be fully realized. Not all researchers believe that the technologically based driving tools will make road management safer for the elderly (Chandler 1997). Despite the research dissensus, the container can argue that the problem is still minor and will be solved by the time the elderly population expands in the next century.

Who Has the Policy Advantage?

What can be learned from the case of regulating elderly activity in driving? Here is an age group rapidly growing in size that is prone to more highway problems than all other age groups except the youth. Yet politicians have shown no inclination to seriously consider remedial action. Despite howls of protest from victims' families, only a handful of states require road retesting of elderly drivers when their licenses expire. Most states require a vision acuity test or a simple knowledge quiz. However, the majority have not even seriously considered the issue much less acted. This has been a clear win for the container. Many point to the material resources of the AARP as the reason. Though the AARP is one of the largest pressure groups in the country with considerable financial resources, such an analysis is too simplistic. Material-based explanations simply do not adequately address the problem of successful issue containment.

Driving by the elderly has remained a nonissue for most states because the problem has not been framed as such. The aged have a positive group image and can rely on a variety of strategies to keep the expanders from enlarging their cause to the general public: (1) confusing the media and the audience with conflicting statistical claims; (2) blaming other age cohorts with a worse safety record; (3) pointing to self-regulating driving habits; (4) linking their cause to deeply held cultural values such as independence and freedom; (5) having support from transportation officials beleaguered with other problematic groups; and (6) pointing out that expander solutions are costly and perhaps discriminatory.

Indeed, an analysis of elderly residential and mobility patterns shows that most live in the suburbs and the rural areas. Existing or expanded urban transit will not meet their mobility requirements. Buses are found in limited numbers outside the urban area. Alternative transportation strategies are required to ease the elderly out of their cars. An array of possible strategies (small buses, vans, cars, etc.) has been investigated and some pilot projects have been undertaken. However, this strategy has not been vigorously pursued by more than a few public agencies at the moment. Without such a viable alternative, the elderly are going to be reluctant to leave the driver's seat.

Conclusion

The American political process provides opportunities for aggrieved individuals and groups to place their demands on the relevant governmental agenda. However, new issues must compete for the attention of overburdened officials with serious time and resource constraints. This disposition to pass over new issues, along with opponents' strategies to actively resist consideration of proposals for new actions, means that many grievances fail to get serious attention.

Agenda conflicts can be understood at two levels. One is about whether government will or will not seriously consider a particular grievance that has been raised by expanders. Second, agenda conflicts are about competing interpretations of public problems, but behind them are alternative worldviews involving how people ought to lead their lives and how society ought to act. Initiators must demonstrate that even if the specific grievance they raise is new, acting on it is consistent with many long-standing values. Opponents emphasize new issues as a threat to core elements of widely held worldviews. If opponents can demonstrate that proposed actions challenge identities in unacceptable ways, then issues will usually not attain agenda access. The thought of governmental regulations forcing people out of their cars, limiting their mobility, and providing no viable options will not strike a responsive chord with most people.

References

Bachrach, Peter, and Morton Baratz. 1970. *Power and Poverty*. New York: Oxford University Press.

Baumgartner, Frank, and Bryan D. Jones. 1993. *Agendas and Instability in American Politics*. Chicago: University of Chicago Press.

Birch, S. May 1995. New technology directions at Ford. *Automotive Engineering*, 69–71.

Butler, Robert N. 1984. How Alzheimer's became a public issue. *Generations* 9 (4): 33–35.

Chandler, David. 1997. Navigation aids lose many drivers, researcher says. *Boston Globe*, 4 April, A12.

Cobb, Roger W., and Charles D. Elder. 1983. *Participation in American Politics: The Dynamics of Agenda Building*. Baltimore: Johns Hopkins University Press.

Cobb, Roger W. and Marc H. Ross, eds. 1997. *Cultural Strategies of Agenda Denial: Avoidance, Attack and Redefinition*. Lawrence: University Press of Kansas.

Deering, James, and Everett Rogers. 1996. *Agenda-Setting*. Beverly Hills, CA: Sage.

Edelman, Murray. 1964. *The Symbolic Uses of Politics*. Urbana: University of Illinois Press.

Evans, L. 1991. *Traffic Safety and the Driver*. New York: Van Nostrand Reinhold.

Felstiner, William L. F., Richard I. Abel, and Austin Sarat. 1980–1981. The emergence and transformation of disputes: Naming, blaming, claiming. *Law and Society Review* 15: 631–53.

Grogan, John. 1994. Older driver turns store into drive-in. *Palm Beach Sun-Sentinel*, 2 December, 1B.

Jette, A. M., and L. G. Branch. 1992. A ten-year follow-up of driving patterns among community-dwelling elderly. *Human Factors* 34: 25–31.

Johnson, Betsy. 1995. The question of the older driver. *Hamilton Wenham Northshore Weekly*, 6 January.

Kingdon, John. 1995. *Agendas, Alternatives and Public Policies*. New York: HarperCollins.

Iyengar, Shanto. 1991. *Is Anyone Responsible? How Television Frames Political Issues*. Chicago: University of Chicago Press.

Lerner, Neil, Melanie Morrison, and Donna Raffe. 1990. *Older Drivers' Perception of Problems in Freeway Use*. Washington, DC: AAA Foundation for Traffic Safety.

Luchter, Stephen. 1994. Health Care Costs and Transportation. *Transportation Quarterly* 48: 427–49.

McGonagle, Doris. 1997. The characterization of a target population: The elderly. Presented at the 1997 Annual Meeting of the American Political Science Association, Washington, DC, August.

Mercier, Cletus R., and Scott R. Falb. 1997. License renewal for older drivers: Analysis of the Iowa experience in reexamination of high-risk drivers. *Policy Studies Journal* 25: 157–74.

Palmer, Thomas C. 1997. Pacifying road warriors. *Boston Globe*, 25 July, A1, B5.

Prang, George, and Penelope Canan. 1996. *SLAPP's: Getting Sued for Speaking Out*. Philadelphia: Temple University Press.

Rochefort, David A. 1989. *American Social Welfare Policy*. Boulder, CO: Westview.

Rochefort, David A., and Roger W. Cobb, eds. 1994. *The Politics of Problem Definition: Shaping the Policy Agenda*. Lawrence: University Press of Kansas.

Rosenbloom, Sandra. 1988. "The Mobility Needs of the Elderly." In *Transportation in an Aging Society*. Vol. 2. Washington, DC. Transportation Research Board of the National Research Council, 21–72.

Schattschneider, E. E. 1960. *The Semi-Sovereign People: A Realist's Guide to Democracy in America*. New York: Holt.

Schneider, Anne, and Helen Ingram. 1993. The social construction of target populations: Implications for politics and policy. *American Political Science Review* 87: 334–47.

Stone, Deborah. 1997. *Policy Paradox and Political Reason*. New York: HarperCollins.

Switzer, Jacqueline. 1997. *Green Backlash: The History and Politics of Environmental Opposition in the U.S.* Boulder, CO: Lynne Rienner.

Thomason, Art. 1993. Road risks increase with age of motorist. *Arizona Republic*, 3 December, A1.

Tull , A. 1995. The older drivers and highway safety. *World Traffic Safety Symposium*. New York City, April 20.

United States Department of Transportation (USDOT). 1996. *National Passenger Transportation Survey*. Washington, DC: U.S. Department of Transportation.

United States House of Representatives. 1995. *Transportation and Related Agencies' Appropriations, 1995*. Hearing, Committee on Appropriations, Subcommittee on Transportation. 104th Congress, 1st Session.

Waller, Julian. 1992. Research and other issues concerning effects of medical conditions on elderly drivers. *Human Factors* 34: 3–15.

Wildavsky, Aaron. 1974. *Speaking Truth to Power*. Boston: Little, Brown.

Contributors

Edward G. Carmines is the Rudy Professor of Political Science at Indiana University—Bloomington. He has done research on the politics of race, the development of political issues in American politics, and political methodology. His work has won several honors, including the Gladys M. Kammerer Award twice from the American Political Science Association for the best political science publication in the field of U.S. national politics and policy, and four outstanding-paper awards at academic conferences. He has also been a fellow at the Center for Advanced Study of the Behavioral Sciences at Stanford University.

Roger W. Cobb is a professor of Political Science at Brown University. He has coedited and coauthored several books in American politics and public policy, including *Participation in American Politics: The Dynamics of Agenda*; *The Politics of Problem Definition: Shaping the Policy Agenda*; and recently the *Cultural Strategies of Agenda Denial: Avoidance, Attack and Redefinition*. He is coauthor with Joseph Coughlin of a book on the politics of older driver licensing, forthcoming with Johns Hopkins University Press. Professor Cobb has also coauthored a number of articles on older driver policy and politics. His Ph.D. is from Northwestern University.

M. Margaret Conway is a distinguished professor emeritus of Political Science at the University of Florida. Her research interests include political participation, political socialization, and women and politics. Her publications include *Political Participation in the United States* and *Women and Political Participation* and a number of other books and seminal articles on political parties, political participation, and American politics.

Joseph F. Coughlin is the director of the Massachusetts Institute of Technology's Age Lab—Technology for Healthy Aging Laboratory. He teaches public policy and strategic management. Dr. Coughlin conducts research addressing older adult consumer behavior and new technologies. He has published extensively in transportation and aging policy journals and advises business and government on the consumer behavior of older adults. He is coauthor with Roger Cobb of a book on the politics of older driver licensing, forthcoming with Johns Hopkins University Press. His Ph.D. is from Boston University.

William Crotty is the Thomas P. O'Neill Jr. Chair in Public Life and director of the Center for the Study of Democracy at Northeastern University. He has written extensively on political parties and elections and is the recipient of the Lifetime Achievement Award of the Political Organizations and Parties Section of the American Political Science Association. He has also served as president of the Midwest Political Science Association and the Policy Studies Organization and is national chair of the Progressive Political Science Caucus.

Jack Dennis is the Hawkins Professor of Political Science at the University of Wisconsin–Madison. His work has focused mainly on political socialization, electoral behavior, political communication, and political psychology. He has had a special interest in the phenomenon of partisanship, in terms of identification with a political party, independence, and orientations toward the party system more generally. His contribution here is part of a series of works of this kind that began with an article he published in the *American Political Science Review* in 1966. He is the author of a number of books and articles in these areas.

Michael S. Dukakis is the former three-term governor of Massachusetts and was the Democratic nominee for president in 1988. He is currently Distinguished Professor of Political Science at Northeastern University in Boston and visiting professor of public policy at UCLA's School of Public Policy and Social Research. He has written and lectured extensively on public policy, including issues of health delivery systems and transportation. He is the coauthor with former United States Senator Paul Simon of *How to Get into Politics—and Why* (Houghton Mifflin, 2000).

Thomas Ferguson is a professor of Political Science and senior assistant provost of the University of Massachusetts, Boston. He received his Ph.D. from Princeton and taught formerly at MIT and the University of Texas, Austin. A contributing editor to the *Nation* and contributing writer to *Mother Jones*, Ferguson is the author of many books and articles, including *Golden Rule: The Investment Theory of Party Competition and the Logic of Money-Driven Political Systems* (University of Chicago Press, 1995).

Betty Glad is the Olin D. Johnston Professor of Political Science at the University of South Carolina. She has also taught at the University of Illinois, Urbana. Her most recent publication is *The Russian Transformation: Political, Sociological, and Psychological Aspects* (coeditor and contributor, St. Martin's Press, 1999). Other works include *Jimmy Carter: In Search of the Great White House*; *The Psychological Dimensions of War*; *Key Pittman: The Tragedy of a Senate Insider*; and *Charles Evans Hughes and the Illusions of Innocence*. She has served as president of the International Society for Political Psychology and vice president of the American Political Science Association. She was a recipient of the American Political Science Association's Frank J. Goodwin Award in 2000 for her contribution to the development of the political science profession. In 1997 she received the Harold Lasswell Award of the International Society for Political Psychology for a lifetime of outstanding contribution to political psychology.

Casey A. Klofstad holds a B.S. in Political Science from the University of Wisconsin–Madison (1999). He is currently pursuing his Ph.D. in Political Science as a National Science Foundation Graduate Research Fellow at Harvard University. His current research has centered on examining the strength of pluralistic institutions in the United States, an effort that culminated in the drafting of a senior thesis titled, "The Relationship between Partisan and Interest Group Support: A Test of Comparative Support Theory." He has presented works at numerous academic conferences, including the 1998 American Political Science Association national meeting as coauthor of the chapter adapted for this volume. He has also worked as a project assistant at the University of Wisconsin Survey Center and as a constituent caseworker for a United States senator.

George E. Marcus is a professor of Political Science at Williams College. He is the former executive director of the International Society of Political Psychology and is cofounder and the former coeditor of the journal *Political Methodology*. He was director of the Public Opinion Program for Journalists, sponsored by the Roper Center and Williams College, and is vice chairman of the Board of Directors of the Roper Center. He is author and coauthor of a number of pathbreaking studies of democratic values and norms. In addition to a number of articles, his major publications include *Political Tolerance and American Democracy* (1982, 1989, 1992), coauthor; *With Malice Toward Some: How People Make Civil Liberties Judgments* (1995), coauthor; and *Reconsidering the Democratic Public* (1993), coeditor. He has received a number of foundation awards and professional recognitions and is currently exploring the role of emotions and reason in political thinking.

Cathie Jo Martin is an associate professor of Political Science at Boston University. She is the author of *Stuck in Neutral: Business and the Politics of Capital Investment Policy* (Princeton University Press, 2001), and *Shifting the Burden: The Struggle over Growth and Corporate Taxation* (University of Chicago Press, 1991). *Stuck in Neutral* was partially funded by the Robert Wood Johnson and the Russell Sage Foundations; *Shifting the Burden* by the National Science Foundation. She is currently working on a study of employers and the welfare state in Denmark and the United Kingdom, funded by the German Marshall Fund and the Danish Social Science Research Council. Professor Martin received her Ph.D. from the Massachusetts Institute of Technology in 1987. She received a postdoctoral fellowship to work with the M.I.T. Commission on Industrial Productivity, which produced *Made in America*, published by M.I.T. Press in 1989.

Donald R. Matthews is a professor emeritus of Political Science at the University of Washington, Seattle. His book *U.S. Senators and Their World*, first published in 1960, is a much-honored, classic analysis of the forces structuring policy outcomes and political behavior in the Senate. His extensive research contributions also include studies of black (and white) politics in the south, the operations of the United States House of Representatives, and the functioning of the presidential nominating systems. He has also written on other aspects of American politics, including the political role of the news media. His most recent research has taken him to Western Europe and resulted in *Parliamentary Representation: The Case of the Norwegian Storting* (1999), a book written with Henry Valen.

Diana Owen (Ph.D. University of Wisconsin–Madison) is an associate professor of Political Science at Georgetown University. Her areas of specialization include political communication, public opinion, political socialization, political culture, and mass behavior. She is coauthor, with Richard Davis, of *New Media and American Politics* (Oxford, 1998) and *Media Messages in American Presidential Elections* (Greenwood, 1991). Her publications include articles on campaign media, talk radio, and the political implications of the Internet. She also has written about pre-adult political learning, civic education, and adult political orientations. She is currently completing *Mass Communication and the Making of Citizens* (Columbia University Press), which focuses on the role played by mass media in the process of political socialization over the past half-century. She is the cofounder of Georgetown University's Communication, Culture, and Technology Program, an interdisciplinary graduate program with an emphasis on the role and application of new technologies in society.

Paul M. Sniderman is a professor of Political Science at Stanford University. He has done work on the psychology of political choice, the politics of race in America, democratic theory, and, most recently, the interplay of prejudice and politics in Europe. His work has won, among other honors, the Woodrow Wilson Foundation Prize, 1992, best book published in political science; the Gustavus Meyers Center Award, 1994, Outstanding Book on the Subject of Human Rights; the Harold D. Lasswell Award, 1998, from the International Society of Political Psychology for distinguished scientific lifetime contribution to the study of political psychology; and the Gladys M. Kammerer Award, 1998, from the American Political Science Association for the best political science publication in the field of U.S. national policy.

INDEX